1937

This book may be kept

vol 1

The Letters of
GERARD MANLEY HOPKINS
to
ROBERT BRIDGES

Gerard Manley Hopkins
1863

The Letters

of

GERARD MANLEY HOPKINS

to

ROBERT BRIDGES

Edited with notes &
an Introduction
by

CLAUDE COLLEER ABBOTT

PROFESSOR OF ENGLISH LANGUAGE AND
LITERATURE IN THE UNIVERSITY OF
DURHAM

LONDON
OXFORD UNIVERSITY PRESS
1935

OXFORD
UNIVERSITY PRESS
AMEN HOUSE, E.C. 4
London Edinburgh Glasgow
New York Toronto Melbourne
Capetown Bombay Calcutta
Madras Shanghai
HUMPHREY MILFORD
PUBLISHER TO THE
UNIVERSITY

PRINTED IN GREAT BRITAIN

PREFACE

WHEN Mrs. Bridges told me, in July 1931, that Robert Bridges had wished me to edit the letters written by Gerard Hopkins to himself and R. W. Dixon, I gladly accepted the privilege she extended to me of making this book. To know Robert Bridges was to love him and wish to serve him, even though the service were small. Here, then, was the opportunity. To come into contact with the friendship of three such men has been, as it could not fail to be, a signal happiness, especially as Mrs. Bridges helped me with the work from the beginning. These volumes have profited throughout from her knowledge and devotion.

The letters written by Gerard Hopkins to Robert Bridges fill almost to bursting two small leather wallets, with the postcards thrust into the inside pockets. Robert Bridges had arranged the letters roughly in chronological order, though there were a few others in MS. book A which had to be restored to their places, and finer points of date or order to be settled. He had evidently contemplated publication—indeed, he may almost be said to have prepared the letters for publication, so far as his own wishes were concerned, by making a few annotations, and by cancelling or cutting out names and occasional passages that he did not wish to be printed. These annotations and gaps are recorded in the footnotes. Two letters, written towards the end, he tells us that he burned, but he gives no reason. It seems probable they were letters of anguish and distress (the prose counterpart of certain of the sonnets) that he knew his friend would not wish to have printed. There are, also, one or two fragments of letters, the other parts of which have evidently been lost by mischance. It is difficult to say whether the series is complete, apart from these qualifications; but the evidence seems to show that little is lost. Robert Bridges evidently intended to keep everything written by Hopkins, and to a remarkable extent he succeeded.

My first thought after reading the letters was that their value

12.807
77

would be much enhanced if the other side of the correspondence could be found and printed too. What had become of the letters written by Robert Bridges? These, unhappily, Mrs. Bridges has been unable to find. She had never seen them, and thought it very unlikely that they still existed. There is, moreover, evidence in a letter from Father Wheeler, S.J. (dated 27 October 1889, from University College, Dublin), that the letters were returned to Robert Bridges on his friend's death. These are the pertinent sentences:

'F. Hopkins had a presentiment that he would not recover—but I am sure he took no measure to arrange his papers, and gave no instructions about preserving or destroying them. Any suggestion to that effect would be made to me—and he never broached the subject at all. . . . So I cannot fancy what he would have wished to be done with them. As for myself I looked in a hurried way through his papers but cannot say that I read any of them. Letters which I recognized by your writing or initials I set apart to forward. Many others I destroyed: and when I learned your wish to sift these writings in view to publication or selection I gathered them together indiscriminately and sent them to be used by you or his parents, at your discretion.'

It seems, therefore, that the letters were returned, and that the writer destroyed them. Mrs. Bridges tells me that it is just what he would be likely to do. (It must be remembered that Robert Bridges wished no biography of himself to be published.) One side of this fruitful friendship, therefore, has to be deduced from what remains. That is a grave misfortune.

The worth of these letters to our understanding of Gerard Hopkins will be at once apparent. They add to his stature. They are (so far as is known) richer in revelation and range of interest, more sustained over a long period of years, than those addressed to any other friend. But though they form a central document of his life and thought, they do not stand alone. The letters to and from Canon Dixon have their place: so have those to and from Patmore, which I hope to print later with other letters to friends less well known. It is probable, indeed, that more of his letters will be available than at one time was likely after this lapse of time. Moreover, he kept diaries. These, Father Lahey tells us, were of two kinds: one set recorded his spiritual experiences and the other his daily observations. Of the first it seems that nothing can now be known, since Father Lahey says, though he gives no authority for his statement, that Hopkins burned them himself. It is desirable that full and definite confirmation of this act should be given. But the ordinary diaries are still in existence; they were 'rediscovered' by Mr. Gerard Hopkins after this book was well begun. It is to be hoped they will be published in full. With the poems and letters they no doubt provide the essential commentary for an understanding of the poet's life and genius. His music, some of which was discovered quite lately, is of importance: a preliminary account of it has been attempted in Appendix III. Surely, also, good fortune will add to his writings some of the papers on classical scholarship or metre mentioned in these letters. There seems to be no reason why they should have been destroyed. To my inquiry about such things Father A. Gwynn, S.J. (from University Hall, Hatch Street, Dublin, on 18 May 1932), wrote:

'. . . Some time ago I was asked—as Librarian of this house—to have a look for any papers that may have survived from Father Hopkins's *Nachlass*. There are, I believe, a few old note-books in the house, which I myself saw when I came here some six years ago; but they seemed to me then to have nothing of any importance, being mainly ordinary lecture-notes from his Oxford Professors—among whom I remember only Jowett's name. But unfortunately these papers seem to have been mislaid, as so often happens. All that was important, however, was sent to London at the time of his death, and is now in the keeping of the English Jesuits.'

To pursue the inquiry further would have been outside my province as editor of these letters.

So much, then, for the place of this correspondence in the body of the poet's writings. Some words about my editing of the text are necessary. With my determination to print all the letters in full no one vitally interested in poetry or in Hopkins will quarrel. It seemed better to establish the text once and for all, since the poet is a classic, and whatever was left out would assuredly one day be wanted. My omissions are soon numbered and will be found recorded in footnotes. I have suppressed one name and, in deference to a family objection, one passage.

The letters have been printed from photostats and reference has been made to the original on any difficult point. Mrs. Bridges corrected her proofs from the originals: mine were done from the photostats. The O.U.P. provided both galley-slips and page-proofs. The margin of possible error in the text is, I believe, small. It was neither possible nor desirable to print all the writer's cancellations, but any that seemed to have value as indicating a first turn of thought are mentioned in the footnotes. The few mistakes due to hasty writing have been corrected in the text and the original reading is recorded below. Very occasionally a word or letter omitted inadvertently has been supplied in square brackets. No use has been made of the objectionable word *sic*. Readers may assume that any spelling or punctuation in the text that seems strange belongs to Gerard Hopkins. It is important that this should be remembered.

The question of where to place annotations was difficult. My first impulse was to banish notes to the end of the book and leave the text free. This plan, which would have meant numbering the lines, was soon seen to be impracticable for several reasons, the chief being that many of the letters are concerned with points of textual criticism needing immediate elucidation. A compromise has therefore been adopted: information deemed important to the reader at the moment is placed in the footnotes; longer notes are gathered at the end of the book. I cannot hope that my annotations will please everyone. For the most part I have tried to give the kind of help that I should myself have been grateful for, and have refrained from comment on the subject-matter of the letters. It would have been possible, of course, to gloss the text more 'curiously'; but notes 'are necessary evils', and, generally, the more interesting the matter the less they are wanted. The poet's remarks and theories on classical metre I am not competent to discuss.

Preface

My gratitude to Mrs. Bridges I have already tried to express. I am also indebted to many other helpers, both friends and strangers: to Miss Grace Hopkins, the poet's sister, and to Mr. Gerard Hopkins, his nephew, for many acts of help and courtesy, and for their sanction of this publication; to Mr. Frederick Page, not only for the index and ready help with some of the notes, but also for his vigilant interest while the work was passing through the press; to Father Keating, S.J., and Father Lahey, S.J., for their published writings on the poet; to Father A. Gwynn, S.J., Father John Ryan, S.J., Father L. Hicks, S.J., Father Philip Watts, S.J. (editor of the *Stonyhurst Magazine*), Mr. Thomas Hayes (Clerk to the Governors of St. Bartholomew's Hospital), Mr. J. G. T. Buckle (Secretary of University College Hospital), and the authorities of Balliol College, Oxford, for their prompt replies to my questions; to my former colleagues in the University of Aberdeen, Mr. John Macdonald and Mr. R. J. Getty, and to my colleague at Durham, Mr. R. P. Wright, for help with classical quotations and allusions; to Mr. Christopher Saintsbury for permission to quote at length from one of his father's *Academy* reviews; to the Librarians at the British Museum and the Universities of Aberdeen and Durham for their courtesy; and to Mr. Kenneth Sisam and the staff of the Clarendon Press for their never-failing patience and care. While this book was passing through the press, Mr. Humphry House kindly tried to solve some of my difficulties, particularly regarding early years and friendships, by reference to the poet's diaries, but unfortunately he could find little that was of help. The undergraduate note-books and the main diary (1868–75) contain, he tells me, very few references to Robert Bridges. Other obligations are, I think, acknowledged in their context; but I should like to apologize now if I have failed to thank any one I ought to have thanked. For all faults in plan and errors in execution I am alone responsible.

The portraits and facsimiles explain themselves. I am particularly grateful to the O.U.P. for allowing me to have far more accurate reproductions of the two photographs of Hopkins than

Preface

have been made hitherto, and also for granting my plea that a characteristic sonnet should be included in facsimile.

A knowledge of the following contractions is necessary to readers of the footnotes:

Memoir: The Poems of Digby Mackworth Dolben, edited with a Memoir by Robert Bridges. 2nd ed. 1915. The Memoir is reprinted in *Three Friends* (O.U.P., 1932).

Life: Gerard Manley Hopkins, by G. F. Lahey, S.J., 1930.

Poems: Poems of Gerard Manley Hopkins, edited with notes by Robert Bridges, 1918, 2nd ed., 1930.

P.W.: The Poetical Works of Robert Bridges. 6 vols. 1898–1905.

G. of L.: The Growth of Love.

The Correspondence of Gerard Manley Hopkins and Richard Watson Dixon is referred to throughout as Volume II. The Appendixes, and also the Index to both volumes (which takes no count of introductory matter), will be found there.

Finally, my Introduction is an essay towards the understanding of a poet for whose work I have a particular reverence and affection.

C. C. A.

THE CASTLE,
UNIVERSITY COLLEGE,
DURHAM.

x

CONTENTS

LIST OF ILLUSTRATIONS

LIST OF LETTERS

TO ROBERT BRIDGES

* Postcard.

xiii

List of Letters

* Postcard.

xiv

INTRODUCTION

'THE generall end therefore of all the booke is to fashion a
gentleman or noble person in vertuous and gentle discipline.'
So writes Spenser in expounding to Raleigh the whole intention
of his *Faerie Queene*; and we at once associate his knightly figures
with the Renaissance ideal of a complete man defined in many
treatises, and made flesh and blood, in our literature, by a Wyatt
or a Sidney. It is, indeed, with some difficulty that we look
before and after the Elizabethans to find other mirrors of chivalry
and courtesy, so enamoured are we of the energy abounding in
that pregnant age, when

> The noble hart, that harbours vertuous thought,
> And is with child of glorious great intent,
> Can neuer rest, vntill it forth haue brought
> Th'eternall brood of glorie excellent.

But though the brood of glory be eternal, neither the noble
heart nor the pattern of the progeny runs to one mould. Every
age has its own examples. From these volumes emerge three
figures worthy to adorn a concourse of chivalry however exalted,
three poets whose endeavours to perform the purpose of God as
they understood it witness to that diversity in excellence which
is the prevailing beauty of the spirit of man.

Robert Bridges had a genius for friendship. His was the art
of discovering eager minds whose interests and endeavours were
akin to his own. Like called to like in the instructed give-and-
take that counts for so much in a poet's life. Yet splendid
though such tributes as those to Dolben and Dixon are, it is
doubtful whether his gift anywhere emerges more clearly than
in the indirect testimony of these letters from Gerard Hopkins,
letters that would be hard to better as the delicate record of a
long and fruitful fellowship.

The quality of this friendship and the degree of reserve it
carried will be evident as the reader advances. But all reserve
disappears when poetry and the writing of poetry is in question.

Introduction

This was the art that mattered most to both of them, though by the one his own gift was sacrificed in part to God's glory, whereas for the other, who sought the principle of beauty in all things, the office of poet was a dedication pursued throughout a long life with an ardour, tenacity, and integrity rare even in English poetry. Hopkins had a seed-bearing mind. Bridges eagerly acknowledged what he owed as a poet to his friend's explorations in prosody. For Hopkins, Bridges was his best, and indeed his only, critic, since Dixon must be counted rather an admirer than a critic. How important these two minds were to each other will become gradually apparent. What will immediately strike the reader is the insight these letters give into the course and pattern of Hopkins's life: his interests, difficulties, work, the very taste of his mind are here. The nobility and fineness of the man shine out. The contribution of Bridges to the correspondence has to be divined, but its importance may to some degree be measured by the response evoked. 'Happy the man these letters were written to: he could have no finer tribute,' is likely to be the reader's thought. It is singularly fitting that the last letter of all should bear with it the deeply moving sonnet to R. B. that was also Gerard's last poem.

In the matter of poetry, certainly, the intimacy is complete. Hopkins was an able, subtle, and honest critic. To him Bridges (after his first book) submitted his poems and plays as they were written, and his judgement, arrived at in no haphazard fashion but from the working of a full mind, is always individual and searching.[1] To Bridges he, in his turn, sent his poems. Bridges, indeed, was his audience: an audience at first disconcerted by the strangeness of his friend's 'barbarous' approach to poetry, but fully alive to the nervous newness of the genius that streaked and dappled the 'plumage of far wonder and heavenward flight', though always critical of what seemed to be needless oddness

---

[1] Books and their writers count for a good deal in this correspondence. Everything that Hopkins says is of interest and value, though his knowledge of English poetry is uneven. Like many other poets, he is an excellent and far-ranging critic. But it is probably true to say that his criticism dates him with more certainty than any other part of his writing. Perhaps that would be true of any writer.

and obscurity. It was Bridges who kept, either in manuscript, or in copy, poems that might otherwise have been lost; and it is extremely doubtful whether we should have so complete a body of Hopkins's poetry had it not been for his friend's devotion. This was exemplary throughout. The 'lov'd legacy' could not have been more carefully treasured, nor the growing reputation more tenderly nurtured. It may safely be said that the work of no poet has ever been treated by a contemporary with greater reverence. The volume of 1918 is a masterpiece of editing.

The manner in which this edition was led up to is interesting as helping us to appreciate Bridges's conception of his duty to his friend, especially as this conception has been to some small extent misunderstood. Criticism has fallen under two heads: annoyance at the exclusion from his edition of certain early or definitely Roman Catholic poems;[1] and rebuke for his delay in publishing the poems in bulk. The first objection is soon answered. Bridges had no wish to handicap the appeal of his edition by printing in it a body of inferior work that might distract attention from what was valuable. He knew that Hopkins would not have wished these verses to be published. Nevertheless, when the edition had made the reputation secure, and a new impression was called for, he made no objection to the inclusion of early and rejected work, since there is a sense in which everything written by a considerable poet is of value. How little is added to the essential work of Hopkins is now as apparent to all who know the difference between pious verse and religious poetry as it was then to Bridges.[2]

The second criticism is more plausible and more ungenerous. It is easy to say 'Why not have published the poems at once?'; a little thought would have shown that Bridges had considered

---

[1] See, e.g., *The Saturday Westminster Gazette*, 8 March 1919, and *The Universe*, 14 March 1919, with a reply on 21 March 1919.

[2] For one piece, *Ad Mariam*, *Poems*, 84, see R. B.'s note in *Poems*, p. 102. It seems incredible that G. M. H. should have written this imitation of Swinburne (on whose poetry see his opinions, *passim*) at any time, and especially as late as 1884. Only the discovery of a manuscript copy in his handwriting will begin to shake my unbelief.

and rejected such a project. A poet of Hopkins's kind must either create his own audience or have it created for him.[1] To create it for him, to win gradual recognition, was the friendly task that Bridges set himself. But before that effort is considered it is worth while to mention that the first guardian of a man's work is himself. Both Bridges and Dixon repeatedly urged Hopkins, without success, to publish his poetry. They were puzzled and grieved at the fetters he fastened on his gift as poet, unhappy at his avowed indifference as to whether his work was printed or not. Yet he writes urging his friends, as a duty, to gain the widest public they can for their own verses,[2] and laments because Dixon's poetry seems to have been published almost in vain. And since he knew the worth of his own poetry it is impossible not to read into this concern for the work of others a repressed desire that his own work should find a fit audience. Yet how was that to be possible when he shrank from asking the consent of his superiors and was dismayed lest even a small poem should be printed without authority given? The 'quarrel' between priest and poet was never fully reconciled in his mind. It is possible to divine a deep fear lest his poetry might be in some way antagonistic to his vocation. One further reason for this shrinking from publication may be that his later poetry would not go the way he wanted it to go. Two attempts at publication were checked: *The Month* rejected both the *Deutschland* and the *Eurydice*. Later friendly efforts, such as those of Dixon, failed. He seems to have banished all thought of printing his poetry. The main onus for delay in publication, even though he was a Jesuit, rests therefore with Hopkins himself. He was content to leave his work for Bridges to make known in his own way and at a fit time.

That fit time was not at once. Bridges as a poet, in 1889, was known only to the elect. No publisher in the 'nineties would

[1] It is not perhaps amiss to recall how long it was before Thomas Hardy gained recognition as a poet.

[2] He writes, e.g.: 'A great work by an Englishman is like a great battle won by England.'

have ventured on a volume of Hopkins's poetry on his recommendation. In tone and temper this work was at a last remove from the characteristic verse and prose of the period. The irresponsible wit of Wilde, the 'evil' line of Beardsley, Dowson's pretty frailty, Davidson's dogged revolt, the aesthetics of Symons, and the preciously distilled mystery of the early Yeats—all these have their place, but their spirit has nothing to do with the spirit of Hopkins. From a definitely Roman Catholic point of view there was a wider appeal in the domestic passion of Patmore, the delicate if bloodless orthodoxy of Alice Meynell, and the flamboyant ritual of Francis Thompson. In these surroundings Hopkins would have been regarded merely as an oddity. Bridges did not wish the book to drop unheeded, nor did he want his friend's name to be environed by the barbarous noise

> Of owls and cuckoos, asses, apes, and dogs.

Rightly he walked warily. In 1893 he persuaded A. H. Miles to give Hopkins a place in the well-known anthology, *Poets and Poetry of the XIXth Century*; he himself wrote the introductory memoir to the eleven poems printed, a selection that gives a fair idea of the poet's range and worth.[1] This attempt at introduction roused a small but gradually increasing interest. In 1895 H. C. Beeching, then rector of Yattendon, made two anthologies for Methuen. For *Lyra Sacra* Bridges gave him four of Hopkins's poems,[2] and one poem[3] for his *Book of Christmas Verse*. These verses, with the letters from Hopkins in Basil Champneys's *Life* of Patmore (1900), and Father Joseph Keating's account of him[4] written in 1909, gave those who were curious—and they were few—some indication of what manner of man and poet Hopkins was. In 1915, in his *Spirit of Man*, Bridges printed seven of his friend's pieces,[5] and it was the wide

---

[1] These are (the numbering is that of *Poems*): part of 50, part of 73, part of 44, selected lines from 77, 3, 8, 9, 26, 31, 33, 51.

[2] 78, 7, 2, 24. [3] 37.

[4] 'Impressions of Father Gerard Hopkins, S.J.', *The Month*, July, Aug., and Sept. 1909.

[5] 26, 31, 51, part of 3, the first stanza of 4, 16, 27.

success and sale of this anthology both in England and America, and the knowledge that the time was now ripe, that led him to agree to Mr. Humphrey Milford's wish for an edition of Hopkins's poems. This very considerable and extremely accurate piece of work was published in 1918, and the affectionate care that went to its making can only be estimated by those who have undertaken similar work. The poems were, generally, well received;[1] that is, they were read with eagerness by the 'little clan' that knows 'great verse'. How small this clan was can be seen from the publisher's figures for the edition, which was not exhausted for ten years.[2] They are figures that effectively kill the legend, invented in our own day, of a public panting to read poetry arbitrarily withheld. The taste of the 'public' in such matters is always negligible.

So much, then, for the progress of Hopkins towards publication and recognition. It is no doubt a pity that the few who might have rejoiced in him at once had to wait nearly thirty years before they knew his full measure; but such misfortunes are not unknown to literature. More striking is the fact that his work waited so long, after 1918, before its more general discovery in universities and places where poetry is studied and, on occasion, cultivated. During the last few years, however (aided by the second edition of the poems in 1930), he has been widely talked of, if not widely read; and this popularity has led to a fashion for his verses and attempts to imitate his style which as matters stand to-day may be taken as a sign of health rather than folly. He is accepted by the young as one of their contemporaries, and—a more doubtful privilege—he has even been affiliated to the Martin Tuppers of our day whose scrannel pipes have infected the field of poetry with mildew and blight.

[1] The reviews of the book that I have read are not in general remarkable for understanding. It was welcomed on the right lines in the *T.L.S.* of 9 Jan. 1919 (perhaps by Professor Phillimore).

[2] 750 copies were printed; 50 were given away; 180 sold in the first year; 240 in the second year; then an average of 30 a year for six years, rising to 90 in 1927. The last four copies were sold in 1928. The price was twelve shillings and sixpence.

Introduction

It is easy to see why Hopkins the spare and astringent should particularly appeal to this generation, but strange to find him regarded as a poet in key with contemporary experiment and disillusion. Two things have helped towards this misconception: his originality (in which may be counted his anticipation of modern experiments in technique) and the retarded publication and realization of his work. Yet the misconception is glaring. Hopkins is an Englishman and a Victorian. How intensely he loved his country, how firmly he was rooted in her loveliness of earth, how strongly a patriot and man of his age, his poems and letters abundantly testify. He may be a strange Victorian, but he belongs to that company. No other moment could have produced him. It is a commonplace that every poet is vitally influenced by his age, either by sympathy or revolt or a combination of both. The measure of his greatness is often the measure of his apartness. This is the case with Hopkins. His modernity means not that he belongs, spiritually, to us, but that by transcending in great measure the dead conventions of his contemporaries he is free of all ages and entombed by none. The main reasons for this distinction are his searching honesty and the peculiarly personal statement that is the core of his best work. A desire to emulate these qualities would be more salutary to those who aspire to follow him than tinkerings with technique.

He has probably engaged most attention as an explorer in prosody and an experimenter in technique. Too much, and little to the purpose, has already been written about him from this point of view. He himself says what need be said in the explanatory Preface printed with his poems, and in these letters, particularly where he describes sprung rhythm to Dixon.[1] For the system of stress which he set out to explore and methodize he had, of course, good warrant in English poetry. Stress as he conceives it is native to the genius of the language and may be taken as the logical development of his metrical studies, almost as alternative to the 'counterpoint' learned chiefly from Milton. Coleridge, among others, had felt the importance of

[1] Vol. ii, Letter XII.

xxi

stress to pattern, tone, and modulation, but such a work as *Christabel* was too lightly woven and capricious to please the exacting demands of this poet who aimed 'at an unattainable perfection of language'.[1] Where Coleridge was content to let the metre follow the tune in his mind, Hopkins demanded from himself an exact system of prosody, rules to be obeyed. Instead, therefore, of what might have been a freeing or loosening of bonds, we have a tightening and concentration, a more rigorous art. Hopkins abhorred facility, and deplored any departure from the canons he had aimed at, as may be seen from his criticism of Bridges's use of sprung rhythm. The fascination of what is difficult and yet more difficult sometimes involved him in a struggle for technical conquest to the detriment of poetry.

Despite, therefore, the fresh and characteristic loveliness of poems so various as *Pied Beauty* and *Spelt from Sibyl's Leaves* there are weaknesses to remark in this system of sprung rhythm as elaborated and used by Hopkins, attractive though it be. To call it a system is not altogether accurate. There may be a system implicit in the poems: he was certainly working towards one, though he never fully formulated it. Often in practice he takes complete freedom and dragoons words to fit his rhythm by a personal or capricious stress which has no more justification than a private symbolism. Beyond that comes a more important qualification: he is too greedy as poet and prosodist, and too anxious to 'load every rift ... with ore'. He feels no bar to the use of stress, alliteration, assonance, internal- and end-rhyme in the same poem. This excess is probably more often a loss than a gain. He is helped towards what is often a magnificent concentration by the elimination of weak words and the determination to say nothing at second hand. At times he loses in clarity, word-music, and spontaneity. Everything he writes is written with intention, but it is often possible to question the justice of

[1] The quotation, from Robert Bridges, continues: 'as if words—each with its twofold value in sense and in sound—could be arranged like so many separate gems to compose a whole expression of thought, in which the force of grammar and the beauty of rhythm absolutely correspond.'

the demands he makes on word-order and grammar by omission and emphasis.[1] Occasionally his work is as much a piece of highly artificial mosaic as a mediocre passage from Pope, or one of Milton's least-inspired verse-paragraphs. He seems to have judged Old English poetry by his reading of *Piers Ploughman*.[2] Had he known the *Beowulf*, the Elegies, some of Cynewulf, and the best of the Riddles he would have seen that for one considerable body of lofty poetry stress and alliteration were sufficient, and rhyme was either an accident or intrusion. As it is, though the rhythm he evolved justifies itself triumphantly in many a short poem, it is difficult to imagine its successful use in a work of length.

His idiom, as might be expected, is very much his own. He aspired to use the language of living speech, and a few 'precious' words apart, he succeeded. His contempt for all archaisms may be seen in his remarks on Doughty's prose, or better still in his uneasy acceptance of Dixon's medievalism. His own idiom emerges as strangely and strongly personal in his best poems as Wordsworth's or Keats's; but there are in his more experimental work weaknesses and violences belonging rather to mannerism than style. What idiom he had arrived at after trial and discipline is best seen, perhaps, in the later sonnets, though these can hardly be looked on as the fulfilment of his explorations in prosody. The discipline in poetry that he had undergone, his rigorous self-honesty and habits of mind are all seen in these most poignant poems, but it is difficult to believe that their pain-swept simplicity makes them his *Samson Agonistes*. The abundant vitality of the poems following on the *Deutschland* warrants the conviction that the crop from the mature tree should have been richer.

[1] At the same time it is well to point out that he never cultivates obscurity for obscurity's sake. Any 'obscurity' that his work may hold comes from an honest concentration that expands to thought and needs no help outside itself. Whether this concentration is always poetically effective is another matter; but certainly neither laziness nor cleverness has part in it.

[2] *Poems*, 8, l. 3, has a flavour of Old English; and *Poems*, 24, l. 18, 'And ripest under rind' recalls medieval lyric.

Introduction

The letters to Bridges start only when the Oxford days are nearing their end, so that the beginnings of Hopkins as a poet must be sought elsewhere: in the early work that has survived, possibly in the Diaries, and in Father Lahey's *Life* where the poet's parents and his schooldays at Highgate begin to grow real. The strange and meditative boy who delighted in painting and music and shrank from ugliness, who wrote verses almost lavishly sensuous yet fulfilled astonishing acts of self-denial, foreshadows the man, and the poet's strife. The main outlines of those decisive years at Oxford—he went up to Balliol in 1863 in his twentieth year—already stand out clearly in their temper, friendships, religious bent, and, above all, in the steps leading to his conversion from the doctrines of Pusey to the Roman Catholic faith. How greatly he was influenced by the spirit of time and place and the religious ferment of the hour is apparent too. His devouring fervour was no isolated phenomenon. It was shared at the time by several of his friends. There is something akin to it in the account Bridges gives of the fevered enthusiasm of Dolben and the preoccupation with questions of religion and ceremony that seized on other of his own friends at Eton. To say that the Oxford of that day turned Hopkins from a rebellious boy-poet into a Jesuit priest would no doubt be to exaggerate her influence; but it seems possible that he might have been content to glorify God through his poetry had he gone up even ten years later. As it was, the Oxford years decided not only the course of his life but the current and temper of his poetry. His conversion in 1866 was followed two years later by his entry into the Jesuit novitiate.[1] He then burnt what verses he had written—probably our loss is not serious—and 'resolved to write no more, as not belonging to my profession, unless it were by the wish of my superiors; so for seven years I wrote nothing but two or three little presentation pieces which occa-

[1] Since the example of Newman counted for much with him it is well to recall that the controversy with Charles Kingsley and the resultant *Apologia pro Vitâ suâ*, which brought Newman so effectively into sympathetic public interest, belong to 1864.

xxiv

sion called for'. The wreck of the *Deutschland*, in December 1875, lifted this self-imposed ban, and he became again a poet.

Not all the verses written before 1868 were destroyed. Enough remain to show the bent of his youthful mind. The most significant of the earliest pieces is *A Vision of the Mermaids*, the prize poem written while he was still at school. This is far more than a boyish exercise in heroic couplets after the manner of Keats. Despite an unpruned luxuriance of taste for richness and colour resulting in a surfeit of epithets, there is a native craftsmanship in the writing and a welling-up of youthful lyricism strong in promise. It is the work of a youth delighted with the evidence of his awakened senses, fed chiefly through the eye,

> Plum-purple was the west; but spikes of light
> Spear'd open lustrous gashes, crimson-white; . . .

but rejoicing also in a poetic energy alive to other gradations than those of colour:

> Soon—as when Summer of his sister Spring
> Crushes and tears the rich enjewelling,
> And boasting, 'I have fairer things than these'
> Plashes amidst the billowing apple-trees
> His lusty hands, in gusts of scented wind
> Swirling out bloom till all the air is blind
> With rosy foam and pelting blossom and mists
> Of driving vermeil rain; . . .

This quality of sensuous apprehension, later to be disciplined and enlarged by concentration, and uniting with poetic vision certain attributes of painter and musician, is to be one of the main characteristics of Hopkins's poetry. Few poets have felt more deeply the beauty of earth.

Of the other early poems not much need be said. There are echoes here and there of Wordsworth and Arnold; verses such as *Barnfloor and Winepress* and *Easter* are of no essential value save to show which way his mind is moving; in *St. Dorothea* he experiments for the first time, rather preciously, with stresses; and *The Habit of Perfection*, ostensibly a rebuke to the power of the senses whose speech he would turn to divine uses, lingers fondly on such phrases as 'palate, the hutch of tasty lust' and 'feel-of-primrose hands' that lean rather to the sensuous than the stern. The poems of his youth, then, are not as a whole remarkable in achievement. Between the ages of 24 and 32 he was silent as a poet, dedicated to the service of Christ. That does not mean that he never thought of poetry, or of what he might write. Evidently he pondered deeply the questions of prosody and rhythm. But the poems of those years were never written, and behind the momentous *Wreck of the Deutschland*, that amazing introduction to his mature poetry, lie the meditation, experience, and priestly training of more than seven years.

The difference of this poem in tone and texture is remarkable. The strain is indeed sterner braced. The *Deutschland* no longer seems grim and forbidding as once it did, yet, a few noble passages and images apart (how certain, for example, the mastery of rhythm in the first stanza), the reader is roused rather to astonishment at the technical strength and resource than delight in the poem as a whole. For this qualified approval the subject of the poem is principally responsible. 'All depends upon the subject,' said Arnold, 'choose a fitting action, penetrate yourself with the feelings of its situations; this done, everything else will follow.' This subject, the drowning of five exiled nuns (and forty-five other people) is unable to bear the stress of an ode so ambitious. The poet is handicapped by the academic religious subject and by his determination to make the poem safe as doctrine. The work is marred by the something of propaganda and 'presentation-piece' that pervades it, and becomes definitely smaller—excited, violent, overpitched—as the main subject[1] is approached and the poet strives to justify his choice. It is curiously built. The two parts can almost be regarded as two separate poems, and the first, loosely linked to the other, is the more important. To read this brings to mind pent-up flood waters at last released by the bursting of a dam. It is as if the turmoil in his own heart, long inarticulate, had at length forced utterance in this agonized surrender of self to the purpose and

[1] Stanza 20.

might of God. The poet in him could no longer be disregarded in confinement, and the passionate personal statement is perhaps the main factor in shaping the new rhythm that had long been haunting his ear.[1] Thence comes too that feeling of strain and stress, of lines mightily hammered out on an anvil or hewn with great strokes. Yet often the result is incommensurate with the effort. The poet pursues the spirit: he is not unobtrusively possessed by it. Hopkins never again finished anything so ambitious as the *Wreck of the Deutschland*. The writing of it made his style, and his confidence in himself as poet, secure.

Then follow his most fruitful years as poet. To the short period 1877-9 or -80 belongs much of his more immediately attractive work,[2] poems that seem to reflect or recall a time of rustling calm and tendrilous poetic apprehension. The torrent of the *Deutschland*, become a stream of smoother and purer flow, issues in a series of sonnets that witness to the poet's sensuous awareness. This intensity of feeling is not allowed to stand altogether alone. The senses are leashed to a purpose, praise of God.

The poems of this group are comparatively simple, and contain little that can lead to the charge of obscurity. They are written in an almost colloquial language that avoids both romantic flourish and Wordsworthian 'simplesse'. Freshness of approach, an individual music, and a temper of mind that may be called lovingkindness, characterize them. They are poems written to the glory of God by a man who is looking on the world as charged with His grandeur and revealing His bounty and presence. But always as I read them I feel that the poet is primarily seized by the beauty of earth, and that though a man of exquisitely tempered and religious mind, his senses, not his religion, are in the ascendant. Let us grant the conviction that God made this loveliness and that it bears living

[1] Is it fanciful to hear behind his rhythm something of Campbell's *Battle of the Baltic* and Cowper's *Loss of the Royal George*?

[2] One of R. B.'s observations is here in place: 'G. M. H. dated his poems from their inception, and however much he revised a poem he would date his recast as his first draft.'

witness to His affection. Hopkins says little more than this on the religious side of these poems, and he says this side with no particular distinction. On the other hand, his visions of earth and her creatures make a bevy of astonishing and new felicities rarely to be matched in English poetry. These are, therefore, only secondarily religious poems. The yeast of the religious spirit has not worked through them. The fusion of earthly beauty and exemplum is often so incomplete that the second is merely the addendum of a poet captive in the first place to the beauty besieging his senses. This loveliness is here for its own sake. Thus *Pied Beauty*, that deeply moving and magical thanksgiving for things 'counter, original, spare, strange', is not a devotional poem save in the way that all poems witnessing to beauty are devotional. It is possible that these poems could not have been written unless Hopkins held the faith he did hold: even the sensuous poetry of the *Faerie Queene* might have been different without Spenser's fighting Protestantism, core of allegory, and nobility of mind. Moreover there is nothing aggressive in the religious statement, no abatement of joy in the poet's recognition of beauty. Yet the dedication of *The Windhover* does not hinder the poem from being first of all a magnificent tribute to a natural thing perfectly done, and even in the *May Magnificat* what matters most is not the praise of Mary, but such stanzas as

> When drop-of-blood-and-foam-dapple
> Bloom lights the orchard-apple
> And thicket and thorp are merry
> With silver-surfèd cherry
>
> And azuring-over greybell makes
> Wood banks and brakes wash wet like lakes
> And magic cuckoocall
> Caps, clears, and clinches all.

Hopkins hated the industrialism of the north, the horror of poverty in cities, the defilement made by man who had seared all with trade and 'lost that cheer and charm of earth's past prime'. He had no sentimental delusions about grime, factories, and mechanical 'progress'. But he knew that

> nature is never spent;
> There lives the dearest freshness deep down things;

and this knowledge, gained from an intensity of loving observation and expressed with the startling newness and delicacy that might surprise the perception of a man who was told he had but a day to live, is one of the first qualities in his poetry. This felicity, often so exquisite in its rightness that shock and recognition come together, goes at once to the heart of a countryman. Sometimes it is a lavish simile—

> How a lush-kept plush-capped sloe
> Will, mouthed to flesh-burst,
> Gush!—flush the man, the being with it, sour or sweet,
> Brim, in a flash, full!;[1]

at others, a season: the juice and joy of spring

> When weeds, in wheels, shoot long and lovely and lush;
> Thrush's eggs look little low heavens, and thrush
> Through the echoing timber does so rinse and wring
> The ear, it strikes like lightnings to hear him sing;
> The glassy peartree leaves and blooms, they brush
> The descending blue . . .

or

> In Summer, in a burst of summertime
> Following falls and falls of rain,
> When the air was sweet-and-sour of the flown fineflower of
> Those goldnails and their gaylinks that hang along a lime.

Bird song, cloud-scapes, and those bright boroughs the stars are his particular delight. His truly inward descriptions have a country savour, and the flush and bloom that means life. They are breathed on and warm. Surely, one thinks, there could be no better witness to the glory of God than work manifesting such

[1] This example (from the *Deutschland*) is, perhaps because of rhyme-greediness, over-wrought. A sloe is not 'lush', nor does it 'burst' on the tongue like a grape. It is a spare fruit, and must be bitten. The rough-sharp astringency of taste experienced is here partly lost.

gift of His spirit. Occasionally there is a note of foreboding, an undertone of fear and sense of personal imperfection.[1]

With this joy in earth and her creatures it is natural that a delight in man and his beauty, both of body and mind, should go hand in hand. The drowned sailor in the *Eurydice*, 'all of a lovely manly mould', shows how deeply he was stirred as a poet by bodily beauty put to right uses and growing naturally to be a part of its surroundings. Harry Ploughman's vivid churlsgrace and strength, and the sight of Felix Randal's 'mould of man, big-boned and hardy-handsome' wrecked by sickness, move him to a like response, a feeling of brotherhood due partly, no doubt, to the admiration of the contemplative man for nature's active life in which the means are adjusted to the end, and the sinew and brain of the craftsman are magnificently equal to his task. Even more deeply is he moved by the loveliness of youth and young manhood 'breathing bloom of a chastity in mansex fine', a bloom doomed to mutability and threatened by spiritual disaster, yet capable of attaining to the 'handsome heart' and hallowing grace. There is something not altogether subdued to the Christian purpose in this side of the poet's work.[2] Here is one point at which he touches, with fastidious difference, Walt Whitman.[3]

The great achievement of the years 1877 and 1879 was not to be repeated. The spring of poetry ran to the last, but less readily and through increasingly difficult country. Only three poems belong definitely to 1880: the remaining eight years muster about twenty pieces between them, including some considerable fragments.

---

[1] *Poems*, 12, ll. 7–8:   My heart in hiding
      Stirred for a bird,—the achieve of, the mastery of the thing!;
Poems, 16, l. 11:   Only the inmate does not correspond.

(A line that anticipates the very accent of Edward Thomas); or 15, ll. 7–8.
[2] See *Poems*, 72, *Epithalamion*, a late work presumably left unfinished because no amount of ingenuity would have achieved a balance.
[3] His remarks on Whitman are of considerable interest, e.g. : 'I always knew in my heart Walt Whitman's mind to be more like my own than any other man's living. As he is a very great scoundrel this is not a pleasant confession.'

Introduction

The causes of this falling-off in output are many. After his ordination to the priesthood in 1877 the duties and responsibilities of his office engaged him more and more. The feeling of personal imperfection grew, and he seems to have felt increasingly the difficulty of reconciling the offices of priest and poet. It is as if he knew there was a strife between what he could do as poet and what he ought to do as priest, that it was wrong to indulge a gift savouring of ambition and that Christ wanted from him not verses but service. There is evidence (besides 'presentation pieces') of a determined effort to coerce his poetry into narrowly Roman Catholic channels, as if here might be found appeasement and equilibrium for both sides of his nature. In November 1879 he is thinking of a tragedy on the martyrdom of St. Winefred and of another on Margaret Clitheroe who was pressed to death in 1586. The first of these he worked at, on and off, the next five or six years, and, though it could never have been finished, considerable fragments exist to show how determined was his attempt.[1] It is noteworthy, though, that the most important of these are the Maiden's Song, that most musical meditation on beauty and mutability, and the astonishing and lengthy speech of Caradoc the murderer, who is to 'die impenitent, struck by the finger of God'. In both these the poet will out. What remains of *Margaret Clitheroe* promises ill.[2] In September 1881 he intends to write a great Ode on Campion's martyrdom, and there is further mention of it in June of next year. No trace of this has been found, though it was begun, and in 1886 had 'got on a little'. The attempt, therefore, to fetter his muse was a failure. The poet in him was not possessed by the spirit of these martyrdoms and was too honest for task-work. The priest in him chose the subjects; the subjects did not choose

[1] Even as late as 2 Oct. 1886 he writes: 'Some scenes of my Winefred have been taking shape here in Wales. . . . I now definitely hope to finish it.'

[2] If Crashaw's poem 'The Flaming Heart upon the Book and Picture of the seraphical saint Teresa' be taken as a guide, and especially the famous passage beginning 'O sweet incendiary! shew here thy art', then neither here nor in his invocation of the nun in the *Deutschland* is G. M. H. working within his province.

the poet. It is possible to imagine what heart-searchings and travail lie behind this endeavour.

From his zeal for his work and the exercise of his priestly functions he gained but rarely, so far as can be judged, the satisfaction and partial peace that comes from work giving rest to the spirit. To say that his was a nature not easily satisfied would be to understate the case. With himself he was searchingly relentless in the standards he imposed. It is, indeed, difficult in English letters to find a parallel to the self-abnegation and flagellation this poet deemed necessary to the purpose of God. A nature so framed would probably not have found happiness in any sphere. His Order knew his qualities and limitations as a priest, and evidently tried to give him opportunities of various kinds that would discover what he was best fitted for. But he was not an easy man to use. Bridges, after numbering his personal qualities, goes on to say: 'Yet he was not considered publicly successful in his profession. When sent to Liverpool to do parish work among the Irish, the vice and horrors nearly killed him: and in the several posts, which he held in turn—he was once select preacher in London, and had for a while some trust at Oxford—he served without distinction.'

The Dublin professorship to which he was appointed in 1884 must have seemed to his superiors a happy solution of the problem how a man of his scholarship and training could best be employed. A reviewer, combating Bridges's summary of this last phase, protests that 'it was absurd of Mr. Bridges to speak of the classical examiner's work as drudgery; it was nothing of the kind: there could hardly have been found for him in all the Irish Province a less exhausting work'. For most men that might be true, but for over-sensitive Hopkins the heavy examination work, with its numberless opportunities for questions of conscience, became worse than drudgery, became torment. As a patriotic Englishman too (though one who understood what the problem was) he found residence in the Dublin of that day extremely distasteful, especially as he was unable to agree with the policy pursued by the leaders of his church in Ireland. He felt he was in exile. The evidence of these letters reinforces the already overwhelming evidence of the poems as to the bitter suffering of those last years.

The forces antagonistic to the writing of poetry were therefore many, and they are not yet numbered. After a time the leisure that he could command became increasingly dissipated. The study and writing of music gradually absorbed him more and more, and even if this interest was to some extent akin to and helped his verse, it is impossible not to deplore the pursuit of another art by a poet of his small leisure, though that pursuit was far from barren. In music he worked under grave disadvantages; but though Bridges was discouraging (obviously grudging the time lost to poetry) he held to the belief in his own inspiration. In a letter of 1 April 1885 he says, of a piece of his music: 'it is a test too: if you do not like it it is because there is something you have not seen and I see. That at least is in my mind, and if the whole world agreed to condemn it or see nothing in it I should only tell them to take a generation and come to me again.' Such words show plainly the seriousness of his interest. One is tempted to think that music instead of poetry became his dominant passion. Did he, perhaps, believe it possible for him to glorify God more completely and wholeheartedly in this sister art? Notes are more impersonal, less earth-bound and dangerous than words. Or had he reached that stage in poetry when music rather than words seemed the natural creative continuation? Some of his earlier poems[1] seem to aspire to the state of music; and the sonnet that is perhaps the most characteristic of all is almost a piece of modern orchestration.[2] Whatever the reason my feeling is that music would have absorbed him had he lived. In December 1887 he writes to Dixon: 'I am at work on a great choral fugue! I can hardly believe it.'

[1] e.g. The Woodlark (64, 1876), Binsey Poplars (19, 1879), The Leaden Echo and the Golden Echo (36, 1882).

[2] *Poems*, 48 (1888). See also 'On a piece of music' (67, undated).

Other interests, besides music, helped to draw him away from poetry: or rather it would be better to say, since they were part of his food as poet, demanded a tithe of his leisure. His office led him naturally to think of such work as a commentary on St. Ignatius's 'Spiritual Exercises', a treatise on the subject of Sacrifice, and a new edition of St. Patrick's 'Confession'. His duties as a professor also encouraged him in what he felt to be necessary projects of scholarship, in particular works on Greek metre and the dramatists. In October 1886 he has made 'a great and solid discovery about Pindar or rather about the Dorian and Aeolian Measures or Rhythms' and hopes to publish something when he has read more. This book is persevered with: it will amount to writing 'almost a philosophy of art', and later a 'good deal' of it is done. Then there is mention of a paper, perhaps book, on the choruses of Aeschylus with emendations, a paper quasi-philosophical on the Greek negatives, and another on readings and renderings of Sophocles. He even contemplates, in 1886, 'a sort of popular account of Light and the Ether'. Such versatility is both amazing and disconcerting, for his letters show that he was no dabbler and could doubtless have written something of worth on all these subjects had time allowed. But to one man one life; and versatility is more common than genius.

As he grew older it may be that his powers as a poet grew naturally less when his senses dulled and the 'visionary gleam' fled. On the evidence of his late work, though, that is difficult to admit. What is certain is that the will to be a poet lessened as the claim of the priesthood became stronger; and the letters to and from Dixon, of 1881-2, central documents to an understanding of both men, show this very clearly. Dixon, not fully understanding what his friend's second Noviceship meant, wrote, on 11 October 1881, 'I suppose you are determined to go on with it: but it must be a severe trial—I will say no more.' Evidently he assumed that Hopkins might still withdraw from the Order if he wished, and seems to have hoped that he would. Hopkins, in his reply, explains this mistake and the purpose of the Noviceship, and ends, 'the man who in the world is as dead to the world as if he were buried in the cloister is already a saint. But this is our ideal.' When Dixon writes again (26 Oct. 1881) he makes no reference to this ideal or his own mistake, but at once urges the claims of poetry:

'But first, I hope that you are going on with poetry yourself. I can understand that your present position, seclusion and exercises would give to your writings a rare charm—they have done so in those that I have seen: something that I cannot describe, but know to myself by the inadequate word *terrible pathos*—something of what you call temper in poetry: a right temper which goes to the point of the terrible; the terrible crystal.'[1]

Towards the end of his long answer (29 Oct.–2 Nov. 1881) Hopkins approaches this searching request and replies that the priesthood must come first:

'I am ashamed at the expressions of high regard which your last letter and others have contained, kind and touching as they are, and do not know whether I ought to reply to them or not. This I say: my vocation puts before me a standard so high that a higher can be found nowhere else. The question then for me is not whether I am willing (if I may guess what is in your mind) to make a sacrifice of hopes of fame (let us suppose),[2] but whether I am not to undergo a severe judgment from God for the lothness I have shewn in making it, for the reserves I may have in my heart made, for the backward glances I have given with my hand upon the plough, for the waste of time the very compositions you admire may have caused and their preoccupation of the mind which belonged to more sacred or more binding duties, for the disquiet and the thoughts of vainglory they have given rise to. A purpose may look smooth and perfect from without but be frayed and faltering from within. I have never wavered in my vocation, but I have not lived up to it.'

Dixon, deeply moved by this bleak asceticism, says beautifully what needed to be said in a letter (4 Nov. 1881) that mingles concern and affection. Only part of his pleading can be quoted here:

'So I will say nothing, but cling to the hope that you will find it

---

[1] The date at which Dixon used this much-quoted phrase is perhaps worth notice.

[2] Dixon had begged him to pursue poetry, not fame.

consistent with all that you have undertaken to pursue poetry still, as occasion may serve: & that in so doing you may be sanctioned & encouraged by the great Society to which you belong, which has given so many ornaments to literature. Surely one vocation cannot destroy another: and such a Society as yours will not remain ignorant that you have such gifts as have seldom been given by God to man.'

But Hopkins, while content to leave his poetry to the special guidance of God, goes on to show from his knowledge of the Order how difficult it is for a Jesuit to be an artist of any kind: 'Our Society values, as you say, and has contributed to literature, to culture; but only as a means to an end. Its history and its experience shew that literature proper, as poetry, has seldom been found to be to that end a very serviceable means' (1 Dec. 1881). Dixon again begs that poetry may have its place: he is, moreover, certain 'that as a means of serving, I will not say your cause, but religion, you cannot have a more powerful instrument than your own verses'.

It is difficult to think that Dixon is wrong in this matter. For him poetry as one of the supreme manifestations of the spirit of God in man was of the utmost value: and that so signal a gift as his friend's should be deliberately sacrificed in God's service instead of being used to that end was to him a monstrous distortion. 'Surely one vocation cannot destroy another.' For Hopkins, however, there was danger to his soul in the exercise of his gift as poet. He feared the temptation as one of the secret solicitations of the world. Poetry, now seen to be a side-issue, must not be allowed to come between himself and God. He endeavoured to build his spiritual life on a rock where he should be alone with God, and on this rock he was willing if need be that the sail of his verse and all else that drew him back to earth should founder. It is a state of mind where the humblest worker for God's kingdom rises superior to the most famous of men. No wonder Dixon was troubled, divided between admiration as a Christian priest for this tremendous idealism and despair as a poet at its ruthlessness. Perhaps even more emphatic in its clarity is a letter to Bridges of 3 February 1883, where Hopkins implies his determination to imitate the abnegation and holiness of Christ in a passage on 'true virtue' that might almost belong to the Milton of *Paradise Regained*:

I quite understand what you mean about gentlemen and 'damfools'; it is a very striking thing and I could say much on the subject. I shall not say that much, but I say this: if a gentleman feels that to be what we call a gentleman is a thing essentially higher than without being a gentleman to be ever so great an artist or thinker or if, to put it another way, an artist or thinker feels that were he to become in those ways ever so great he wd. still essentially be lower than a gentleman that was no artist and no thinker—and yet to be a gentleman is but on the brim of morals and rather a thing of manners than of morals properly—then how much more must art and philosophy and manners and breeding and everything else in the world be below the least degree of true virtue. This is that chastity of mind which seems to lie at the very heart and be the parent of all other good, the seeing at once what is best, the holding to that, and the not allowing anything else whatever to be even heard pleading to the contrary.

To pass, then, to the poems of his middle mature period (roughly 1880–3: 1884 is blank) is to be conscious of a clouding over of that fresh vision in which the dappled beauty of earth proclaimed the grandeur of God. The almost lyric note gives place to a mood more charged with meditation that fathers a weightier utterance and demands for its expression a more intricate music. This tendency is already apparent in the laboured tribute to Duns Scotus, his chief among philosophers, and in his over-subtle praise (blending the parochial with the magnificent) of Purcell's divine genius; and the buffeting of his spirit by life's riddle, 'the blight man was born for', is best expressed in the tremendous and undoctrinal chords of *Spelt from Sibyl's Leaves*, where contemplation of night's mystery conveys to his haunted mind the terror of annihilation and reverses all his former joy.[1] This poem is perhaps the masterpiece of his more elaborate style, for the sonnet *That Nature is a Heraclitean Fire . . .*, where the comfort of the Resurrection jumps out of the pattern, is not 'all to one thing wrought'. With the poet's deepening experience of

---

[1] Cf. *Poems*, 13, and *Poems*, 32, last seven lines.

life's poignancy goes a fuller realization of man's pathos and importance:

> And what is Earth's eye, tongue, or heart else, where
> Else, but in dear and dogged man?[1]

or

> To man, that needs would worship | block or barren stone,
> Our law says: Love what are | love's worthiest, were all known;
> World's loveliest—men's selves.[2]

Such comprehension prepares the way for his last sonnets which belong to the quintessential poetry of man's spirit in travail and explore the darkest places of human suffering. These poems[3] are salt with the taste of his blood and bitter with the sweat of his anguish, the work of a man tried to the utmost limit of his strength and clinging to the last ledge where reason may find a refuge. Their authority and truthfulness cannot be questioned. Here, indeed, is a chart of despair, agony, and frustration, made by one who still believes in the justice of God. That the chart was mapped at all shows how urgent was the need for self-expression to alleviate, even though it could not resolve, his conflict.[4]

Though beaten to his knees, though he has wrestled with God and not prevailed, some strength is left to him still:

> Not, I'll not, carrion comfort, Despair, not feast on thee;
> Not untwist—slack they may be—these last strands of man
> In me ór, most weary, cry *I can no more.* I can;
> Can something, hope, wish day come, not choose not to be.[5]

---

[1] *Poems*, 35, ll. 9–10.

[2] *Poems*, 38, ll. 9–11: see also *Poems*, 34, sestet.

[3] In this final group (1885–9) fall, more particularly, *Poems*, 40, 41, 44, 45, 47, 50, 51. Nos. 42 and 43 turn with compassion and admiration to the 'natural man'. The poet's persistent use of the sonnet form is in itself evidence of the self-limitation of his powers. One feels that he chose it partly because he had some hope of concentrating on, and finishing, a poem of this length that along with discipline of form gave scope for individual pattern.

[4] Petty and superfluous beside it is that clever and rootless verse of our own day which apes the discovery of kindred desolation.

[5] *Poems*, 40, ll. 1–4.

Yet so wild and dizzy is the pitch of torment that, save sleep, there is no comfort:

> O the mind, mind has mountains; cliffs of fall
> Frightful, sheer, no-man-fathomed. Hold them cheap
> May who ne'er hung there. Nor does long our small
> Durance deal with that steep or deep. Here! creep,
> Wretch, under a comfort serves in a whirlwind: all
> Life death does end and each day dies with sleep.[1]

Exile and isolation might be borne:

> Only what word
> Wisest my heart breeds dark heaven's baffling ban
> Bars or hell's spell thwarts. This to hoard unheard,
> Heard unheeded, leaves me a lonely began.[2]

God sends no answer; nor is there peace or joy in Christ:

> I am gall, I am heartburn. God's most deep decree
> Bitter would have me taste: my taste was me;
> Bones built in me, flesh filled, blood brimmed the curse.
> Selfyeast of spirit a dull dough sours. I see
> The lost are like this, and their scourge to be
> As I am mine, their sweating selves; but worse.[3]

In a mood that recalls the Fool in *Lear* he begs a truce to this self-torment;[4] and like a puzzled child after the pain of punishment is past, asks God what purpose has a chastening that continually thwarts:

> birds build—but not I build; no, but strain,
> Time's eunuch, and not breed one work that wakes.
> Mine, O thou lord of life, send my roots rain.[5]

It is a plaint that is echoed in the farewell sonnet to Bridges.

The pity of these poems is hardly to be borne: the depth of it is the measure both of his lofty devotion and his consciousness of failure. Exile, isolation, and defeat are of their essence. There is in them no rapturous one-ness with Christ that has been known to follow such self-surrender; none of the peace of God that passeth all understanding. To his fellow Jesuit and biographer the celebrated "terrible" sonnets are only terrible in the same

[1] *Poems*, 41, ll. 9–14. [2] *Poems*, 44, ll. 11–14. [3] *Poems*, 45, ll. 9–14.
[4] *Poems*, 47. [5] *Poems*, 50, ll. 12–14.

way that the beauty of Jesus Christ is terrible. Only the strong pinions of an eagle can realize the cherished happiness of such suffering. It is the place where Golgotha and Thabor meet. Read in this light his poems cease to be tragic.' The critic who can read these sonnets in any light so that they 'cease to be tragic' is thinking, surely, in terms of pathological Christianity, not of poetry. Their evidence, and the evidence of the letters, is directly contrary. Four of these sonnets 'came like inspirations unbidden and against my will'. How far they must be from the spirit in which he wanted to write no one can doubt. The poet in him was too honest not to face the thought that his sacrifice had brought not peace but a sword. It is perhaps not fanciful to feel that this sacrifice of self aroused a measure of regret and a realization that his persecuted gifts should have been more fully used. Despite his determination to surrender all, the strife between poet and priest remained unsolved.

How can a poet best serve God? Milton's answer to this question in a time of great tribulation ends on a note of resignation to the divine will; but he is sure of what his service will be when opportunity offers. The sonnet *On his Blindness* should be read again in this setting. There is a kinship of spirit between the two poets. But what was possible to the resolved will of Milton the heretic was beyond the powers of Hopkins the priest. He lacked, so it seems to me, just that serene certainty of how to serve God. It is here that the evidence of the 'spiritual' diaries would have been particularly valuable: it may happen that the more mundane records bring light. But without further witness it is difficult to believe in 'the cherished happiness of such suffering'. The emphasis for me, indeed, is on the deep regret following on the knowledge that his poetical gift had been used in part only, and that part not always to his satisfaction as priest:

> And that one talent which is death to hide
> Lodged with me useless.

It is in a dilemma such as this that

> Selfyeast of spirit a dull dough sours.

xl

Patience, resignation is the 'hard thing'. She masks 'Our ruins of wrecked past purpose', but in the mind is a rasping discord:

> We hear our hearts grate on themselves: it kills
> To bruise them dearer.[1]

If the earlier work of Hopkins may be likened to hill-side broom in brilliant blossom then the last poems bring to mind these same bushes on a bleak wintry slope bending their dark strands to the buffeting wind with a steel-like patience and strength. Probably it is best, despite what seem to be notable exceptions, for poetry to be a part-time occupation. But there is a limit to the obstacles that the poet in a man can overcome, and Hopkins the poet was too severely tried by the discipline he thought necessary to Hopkins the priest to flourish freely. The stamina and assuredness of a Milton were not his. What this remarkable gift might have produced in circumstances more propitious it is idle to wonder, since for no different work would we surrender the bitter beauty and taste of his last sonnets. Yet it is difficult to read his poems without lamenting that here is a part only of what he should have written, and without marvelling at the individual imprint he gives even to work admittedly occasional. To a poet endowed with senses so rare, understanding so deep, so fine a sense of rightness, and so masterly a power over words, anything would seem possible. It is not only a question of inner conflict. Most poets have been able to resolve and use that to their purpose. With Hopkins the case is different—save where the barriers of reserve are unexpectedly broken—for what conflict there is tends rather to suppression than release. In part, no doubt, the will to write became gradually less since the mere routine of living was so irksome. That discomfort, however, is a consequence rather than a cause. It results chiefly from the fact that he suffered slow martyrdom as a poet, and that the martyrdom was self-inflicted.

[1] *Poems*, 46, ll. 1, 6–7, 9–10. See also vol. ii, pp. 137–8 (? 3 July 1886), for remarks on life's inadequacy and Christ and failure.

Though Hopkins seems to have undergone a religious discipline comparable in sternness to that suffered by mystics, it is not easy to see how the ill-defined term 'mystical' can be applied to his poetry. His work lacks the inevitable fusion of the divine and temporal, the savour given by the subtle interpenetration of the spirit working through the whole man, that is vouchsafed those who, in subduing all else to His contemplation and service, have felt the warmth of God. Consider for a moment the quiet fire that burns beneath Herbert's homely images and orderly convictions, and present even in his rare attempt at rebellion:

> But as I rav'd and grew more fierce and wilde
> At every word,
> Me thought I heard one calling, *Childe*:
> And I reply'd, *My Lord*.

Or taste the 'virgin apprehensions' of Traherne, the fountain of joy that wells up in his Meditations:

'You never enjoy the world aright, till the Sea itself floweth in your veins, till you are clothed with the heavens, and crowned with the stars: and perceive yourself to be the sole heir of the whole world, and more than so, because men are in it who are every one sole heirs as well as you. Till you can sing and rejoice and delight in God, as misers do in gold, and Kings in sceptres, you never enjoy the world.'

Or experience Vaughan's shaping spirit of imagination, his lightning flash of vision that illuminates Earth's darkness and this 'false life':

> Thou art a toylsom Mole, or less
> A moving mist.
> But life is, what none can express,
> *A quickness, which my God hath kist.*

This sureness that persists in spite of disappointment and temptation, these thoughts that

> transcend our wonted theams,
> And into glory peep

are not the portion of Hopkins. He is, we feel, a more complex nature than these seventeenth-century poets. He is perhaps beyond them in stature. But this rare reward was not for him. He can best reveal to us the loveliness of God's kingdom on earth, the beauty of those made in His image, and the pains of mortality.

If there need be any comparison with another poet, it should be with Donne.[1] Hopkins is the kind of poet Donne might have become had he been born in 1844. Points of dissimilarity between the two are, of course, clamant. In temper they are generally poles apart. Yet if the native sensuousness of Hopkins be equated to the arrogant sensualism of the love poems, is there not kinship in their mental strife, restless curiosity, candour, complexity, and struggle towards asceticism, and resemblance in the startling newness of their work with its individual vigour of utterance and density of texture? They have the same contempt for means that have lost vitality. Donne's rejection of the decadent Petrarchan formula is paralleled by the way in which Hopkins turns his back on the sweets of Tennyson and the blind alley of Pre-Raphaelite medievalism. Both are philosophers and pioneers. Donne would have agreed with Hopkins that 'a kind of touchstone of the highest or most living art is seriousness; not gravity but the being in earnest with your subject—reality'. Donne, perhaps, had the firmer foothold in the dedicated life he had adopted, but nowhere can the agonized tension of Hopkins's last poems be better matched than in Donne's *Hymne to God the Father*, or in such a poem as the sonnet beginning

> Batter my heart, three perfon'd God; for, you
> As yet but knocke, breathe, fhine, and, feeke to mend.[2]

Neither poet is remarkable for humility.

The nobility of Hopkins emerges clearly from the poems, yet the knowledge of being in the presence of a rare spirit is deepened by reading his letters to Bridges. Like all good letters they stand

---

[1] There are certain resemblances between Milton and Hopkins; but any comparison between the work of the two poets, which must depend chiefly on the weight and accent of certain sonnets, seems to me ill advised.

[2] *Holy Sonnets*, No. xiv.

alone: no one else could have written them. And like all good letters they bring the whole man resolutely before us as nothing else could. They give us the background to the poems and provide a most valuable commentary. They show us if not the tragedy of a man the tragedy of a poet.

It is a serious correspondence. There is in it little friendly banter or affectionate small-talk. Evidently it held a place of honour in the lives of both poets. Each gave of his best. The friendship between them was not lightly achieved. Almost at the start the interest of Bridges had to stand the shock of his friend's conversion and the circumstances accompanying it; and something of the delicacy of the situation is reflected in Hopkins's punctilious gravity over the 'affair of the bottle', a small matter in which Bridges had asked his help. For a time the pace is decidedly rallentando. One has the uneasy feeling of two sensitive natures reaching out towards attraction yet waiting to be sure. There is even a danger that communication may cease.[1] Fortunately Hopkins faced the task of stirring the reluctant fire.

The flames fluttered. Presumably Hopkins did not know that his friend was a poet until he saw a review of the 1873 volume. This discovery, strengthened by the gift of *The Growth of Love* and a common interest in Milton's prosody, leads to the letter[2] in which Hopkins praises the great and feeling genius of Bridges's sonnets and first sets the seal on their interest in each other. By August of the same year he is in full glow, expounding sprung rhythm, pungently defending the *Deutschland* from the imputation of 'presumptious jugglery', and ending with an appeal to deeper issues that could hardly go unregarded:

'I cannot think of altering anything. Why shd. I? I do not write for the public. You are my public and I hope to convert you.

'You say you wd. not for any money read my poem again. Nevertheless I beg you will. Besides money, you know, there is love.'

[1] Following on G. M. H.'s 'Communist' letter there is a big gap (Aug. 1871–Jan. 1874), and another later (Feb. 1875–Feb. 1877).
[2] 3 April 1877.

Introduction

Not only did he wish to convert Bridges to his experiments in prosody. Before long he is anxious to attempt a more serious conversion. He writes:[1]

'When we met in London we never but once, and then only for a few minutes before parting, spoke on any important subject, but always on literature.[2] This I regret very much. If it had ended in nothing or consisted in nothing but your letting me know your thoughts, that is some of them, it would have been a great advantage to me. And if now by pen and ink you choose to communicate anything I shall be very glad. I should also like to say one thing. You understand of course that I desire to see you a Catholic or, if not that, a Christian or, if not that, at least a believer in the true God (for you told me something of your views about the deity, which were not as they should be).'

That Hopkins should wish to bring Bridges to his own God is understandable. He took the step with misgiving: 'I feel it is very bold, as it is uncalled for, of me to have written the above. Still, if we care for fine verses how much more for a noble life?' The advice was not well received. Bridges, who was not a potential proselyte, repelled this intrusion into his personal faith and the means to grace proposed (the giving of alms 'up to the point of sensible inconvenience') with some warmth. He cared much both for fine verses and a noble life. The differences disclosed by this incident, and others like it, may be taken as the measure of reserve in the intimacy of the two poets. These differences did not mar the friendship. It was too well founded on personal regard for that. But always there was a line between them which neither could easily cross. This was inevitable. To Bridges the priesthood raised an insuperable barrier: he had, and rightly, a profound distrust of the Society of Jesus. Their ways are therefore widely divergent. Hopkins, anxious for the discipline of a church, found, it would seem, a measure of compensatory freedom (at all events for a time) in making

[1] 19 Jan. 1879.
[2] This presumably means: 'we spoke superficially about the books of others rather than about ourselves'. Otherwise the words are ominous.

xlv

a path of his own in poetry and music.[1] Bridges, who refused dogmas, accepted as a poet the discipline of tradition and found freedom therein. It is revealing, in this regard, to observe what felicitous use Bridges made of sprung rhythm and the qualified approval Hopkins gave to his experiments.

To some extent, therefore, we perceive the attraction and clash of two very different and finely sensitive natures. Of the two Bridges was the more sure of his course: the values of life he had arrived at are the more unified and firmly held. He gave up the practice of medicine, for which he had great gifts, that he might dedicate himself, following his original intention, to what seemed more important, the rigorous pursuit of poetry. Religion meant for him not assent to a particular creed but a manner of life dependent on the discipline of his own mind and body. He was first and always a poet; and his *Testament of Beauty* is but the final statement of a position implicit in his earlier work. For him the poet and the man are one. Poetry is, in itself, a religion. The purposes of Hopkins, less capable of satisfaction or appeasement in life, betray, in his life and poetry, greater mental strife, less certainty and poise. After a time his poetry seems almost to be a concession to the weaker side of him. It is our good fortune that his name belongs to literature and not to hagiography. Yet flowing deep beneath all divergence between these friends is a current of affection fed by many springs. How living this was may be seen in a passage (of 22 Oct. 1879) directed against the despondency that had fallen on Bridges following on Gerard's criticism of his verses:

If I were not your friend I shd. wish to be the friend of the man

[1] Two observations in Peacham's *Compleat Gentleman* (Chap. X: *Of Poetry*) are so apt to Hopkins that they may have place here:

'The poet, as that Laurell *Maia* dreamed of, is made by miracle from his mother's wombe, and like the Diamond onely polished and pointed of himselfe, disdaining the file and midwifery of forraine helpe.'
and

'the true use and end [of poetry] . . . is to compasse the Songs of *Sion*, and addresse the fruit of our invention to his glory who is the author of so goodly a gift, which we abuse to our loves, light fancies, and basest affections.'

that wrote your poems. They shew the eye for pure beauty and they shew, my dearest, besides, the character which is much more rare and precious.

The amend is handsome. More than one road leads to nobility.

There is no need to pursue here the course of this deepening friendship made doubly precious to Hopkins by uncongenial exile, nor is it opportune now to discuss what is perhaps the central problem raised by these letters, though that problem is implicit in this short introduction. If instead of watching the natural growth of a poet's mind we are conscious of checks that lead to a gradual hardening of colours, that is because the poet willed it. His hope was set elsewhere. The general end of his life and endeavour, to return for a moment to Spenser, was 'to fashion a gentleman or noble person in vertuous and gentle discipline' acceptable to God, and to do this he felt constrained to sacrifice children of his thought that might have defied the scourge of mutability. Yet enough remain to give him a place apart among the poets of his time, enough to make him inexpressibly dear to those for whom beauty wears many masks, travail and despair besides joy and delight. Fame, for long avoided, at last found him out. He who feared to be Time's eunuch has defeated Time with many a poem that both breeds and wakes.

I

Elm Cottage, Torquay.

DEAR BRIDGES,—I left Manchester more than a month ago and after a month on the borders of Dartmoor at Chagford am now writing, as you may see, fr. Gurney's[1] house at Torquay wh. place I leave in a few minutes for Hampstead. Else nothing cd. have been so delightful as to meet you and Coles[2] and Dolben.[3] Mr. Geldart[4] is secretary of the Manchester City Mission and his office is in what they have the face to call Piccadilly, if I remember right. It is nearly opposite a big public building and is in the middle of the place. They live at Bowdon, eight miles off. Tell Coles it is safer to address Oak Hill, Hampstead. Give my love to him and Dolben. I have written letters without end to the latter without a whiff of answer.[5]

Believe me yr. sincere friend,

GERARD HOPKINS.

Aug. 28, 1865. I write to you by Coles' direction. I wish you or Coles—but he was not there then, I suppose—wd. have written so that I might have heard while in Manchester, and seen you.

Forgive Mrs. Gurney her blotting paper.

[1] Frederick Gurney, of Balliol, took a 3rd in Greats at Michaelmas 1864; vicar of St. James the Less, Plymouth, 1875–84.

[2] Vincent Stuckey Stratton Coles (1845–1929), friend of R. B. and Dolben at Eton, the leader of their 'Pusey-ite' group, 'pre-eminent for his precocious theological bent and devotion to *the cause*, . . .'. He was at Balliol, and took a 3rd in Greats in 1868. See NOTE A.

[3] Digby Mackworth Dolben (8 Feb. 1848–28 June 1867), the young enthusiast and poet whose life is exquisitely told by R. B. in the *Memoir* prefixed to his friend's *Poems*.

[4] Presumably the father of Edmund Martin Geldart, scholar of Balliol, who in 1867 took a 2nd in Greats: he was sometime in holy orders, but later became a Unitarian. G. M. H. knew him well at Oxford.

[5] G. M. H. met Dolben but once, while the latter was visiting R. B. at Oxford in Feb. 1865; 'but he must have been a great deal with him, for Gerard conceived a high admiration for him, and always spoke of him afterwards with great affection' (*Memoir*, p. lxxiii). Dolben entrusted to G. M. H. some, at least, of his verses (*Memoir*, p. xc).

II

DEAR BRIDGES,—I gave up all idea of going to the north, either the Lakes or Cumbrae, long ago and with it the possibility of seeing you. I am surprised to think that I have let so much time go by without writing and very earnestly beg your pardon for it. I wanted very much to have availed myself of your kind invitation, but it seemed right in going to read to be near a church with a weekly celebration[1] and this prevented my going to the Lakes while Cumbrae was put out of the question by other reasons. I am now at a farm between two and three miles fr. Horsham in Sussex with Garrett[2] of our college and Macfarlane[3] of St. John's, and the place is rather a fool's paradise for the church is not what we expected and we are a long way off. The farm is as ugly as can be but the country very pretty. Addis[4] and I had a week's walk on the Wye etc at term end, but most of the time it rained. Our time here expires next Monday and then I go to Shanklin in the Isle of Wight where my people now are. I have not heard any news except that Challis[5] of Merton, if you remember him, has left the English Church. Thanking you very warmly for your kind offer believe me very sincerely yours.

GERARD M. HOPKINS.

Whiting's Farm, Horsham, Sussex.—July 24, 1866.

[1] The first letter of G. M. H. to Newman, stating that he is anxious to become a Catholic, is dated, from his home at Hampstead, 28 Aug. 1866.

[2] Alfred William Garrett took a 3rd in Greats in 1867, entered the Indian Education Service, Bengal (1868–84), and later became Inspector of Schools, Hobart, Tasmania, where he was born. 'I think I said that my friend, William Garrett, was converted and received shortly after hearing of my conversion, . . .' (G. M. H. to Newman, 15 Oct. 1866).

[3] William Alexander Macfarlane, afterwards Macfarlane-Grieve (1844–1917), took a 2nd Class in Classical Mods. in 1865, and was a master at Radley College 1867–88. He was ordained in 1866.

[4] William Edward Addis (1844–1917), one of G. M. H.'s most intimate friends at Oxford (see *Life* for his reminiscences of G. M. H., and references to him *passim*). He was Snell Exhibitioner at Balliol; and was received into the Roman Catholic Church before G. M. H. (*Life*, p. 37), a fact which H. P. Liddon stresses in his affectionate letters to G. M. H. See NOTE B.

[5] Henry William Challis (2nd Class Math. 1863) became a barrister-at-law.

III

DEAR BRIDGES,—I got your letter the day before we left Horsham. Thank you very much for the kind proposal you make. I should like nothing so much as to stay at Rochdale,[1] more especially (if one can say that) when you hold out the possibility of Dolben[2] being there. You are kind enough to speak of reading: it would be impossible for me now to take any more holidays, my work is in such a state, yet I am afraid it sounds very odd to propose to read on a visit. We shall go home to Hampstead in three weeks fr. this time. After that all my time is my own to the end of the Long. I fear I find no news to tell you in return for yours. Challis did know Dr. Pusey I remember; he did not confess to him I think though. He never had much belief in the Church of England, and his going over in itself wd. prove as little as any conversion could ever do against it since he never used the same strictness in practices (such as fasting) as most of our acquaintance would, but on the other hand if its effect is to make him a strict catholic and to destroy his whimsies, that would say something. I have seen none of the new essays except the autobiography.[3] What egregious fun that is! It is by Mrs. Lea, a cousin of Simcox's[4] and friend of Coles', I understand. With many thanks, believe me, dear Bridges, very sincerely yours,

GERARD HOPKINS.

Aug. 4, 1866.—Cintra, Shanklin, Isle of Wight.

IV

DEAR BRIDGES,—Your letter has been forwarded. I am most happy to come any day in the first week of September which you like to name. We go home to Hampstead tomorrow. I hope

[1] R. B.'s father died on 10 May 1853; his mother afterwards married the Rev. Dr. Molesworth, vicar of Rochdale, where he used to spend his vacations from Eton and Oxford.
[2] Dolben was unable to go (see *Memoir*, p. ci).
[3] This I have not traced.   [4] G. A. Simcox: see p. 181, note 1.

3

you are better than when you wrote. Believe me affectionately yours,

GERARD M. HOPKINS.

Cintra, Shanklin, Isle of Wight. Aug. 26. [1866]

V

DEAR BRIDGES,—Will Saturday suit for me to come? I would come earlier, on Wednesday, but I have some things which I must do first in town, as we only got home yesterday. If Saturday would suit you, I shd. leave home on Friday and sleep at Birmingham[1] where I have some business I must manage to do at some time while I am in the north, most conveniently I think then. If not Saturday, by the same rule I shd. have to come on this day week. Will you be so kind as to let me know if Saturday will do? Do not think about meeting me, thank you, as this going to Birmingham throws out the trains, and as I should come in good time on Saturday I shd. find little difficulty I suppose in getting to Dr. Molesworth's. Believe me yr. affectionate friend,

GERARD HOPKINS.

Oak Hill, Hampstead, N.W.—(put N.W.—it may save a post).— Aug. 28, Tuesday. [1866]

VI

DEAR BRIDGES,—I had not forgotten about Mr. Street.[2] I called there today, but he was out: you shall hear however as soon as possible. At Mayer's too I was unsuccessful, for they had, it seemed to me, not much of the altar service of any kind and no bottles[3] at all, only cruets, which were not to the purpose! I am

---

[1] On this day, 28 Aug. 1866, G. M. H. also wrote to Newman, to whom he says: 'I am anxious to become a Catholic, and I thought that you might possibly be able to see me for a short time when I pass through Birmingham in a few days, I believe on Friday. . . .' (*Life*, pp. 33–5).

[2] George Edmund Street (1824–81), the well-known architect.

[3] A good deal more will be heard about this 'bottle' and 'stopper', and the commission G. M. H. so punctiliously performed, no doubt to his friend's affectionate amusement, especially as to qualms about expense. See NOTE C.

not sure now where to apply but I will try and find out and, unless you want the bottle ordered or got more immediately than I can be sure of doing it, it will give me pleasure to go about it. Am I to design the stopper? if you still wish it and it shd. turn out after all that my design wd. cost too much I cd. always fall back on the Maltese cross, wh. has no objection, I suppose, except that it is so common.

Dr. Newman[1] was most kind, I mean in the very best sense, for his manner is not that of solicitous kindness but genial and almost, so to speak, unserious. And if I may say so, he was so sensible. He asked questions which made it clear for me how to act; I will tell you presently what that is: he made[2] sure I was acting deliberately and wished to hear my arguments; when I had given them and said I cd. see no way out of them, he laughed and said 'Nor can I': and he told me I must come to the church to accept and believe—as I hope I do. He thought there appeared no reason, if it had not been for matters at home of course, why I shd. not be received at once, but in no way did he urge me on, rather the other way. More than once when I offered to go he was good enough to make me stay talking. Amongst other things he said that he always answered those who thought the learned had no excuse in invincible ignorance, that on the contrary they had that excuse the most of all people. It is needless to say he spoke with interest and kindness and appreciation of all that Tractarians reverence. This much pleased me, namely a bird's-eye view of Oxford in his room the frame of which he had had lettered *Fili hominis, putasne vivent ossa ista? Domine Deus, tu nosti.* This speaks for itself. He told me what books to get and then left me at lunch-time to Mr. John Walford[3]—discovered at football. Mr. Walford gave me lunch in the refectory and shewed all the school and the oratory, then

---

[1] Newman's letter to G. M. H., asking him to fix a day for his visit to the Oratory, is dated 14 Sept. 1866. See *Life*, p. 35.

[2] 'heard' cancelled.

[3] John Thomas Walford, formerly 'one of the junior masters at Eton' (where he had made Dolben's acquaintance) and later a Jesuit. See Ward's *Life of Newman* for letters from Newman to him.

walked back and took me to St. Chad's cathedral. He told me to remember him very kindly indeed to you and to say how glad he shd. be to see you on yr. way to Oxford, if you liked it. You have much common interest fr. Eton[1] etc, and of course he wd. avoid all religious subjects, I am sure.

I am to go over fr. Oxford to the Oratory for my reception next term—early in the term I must make it, and since a Retreat is advisable for a convert, Dr. Newman was so very good as to offer me to come there at Xtmas, which wd. be the earliest opportunity for it. He thought it both expedient and likely that I shd. finish my time at Oxford, and next term at all events I shall be there, since I shall announce my conversion to my parents by letter at the time of my reception. And now I have even almost ceased to feel anxiety.—Sept. 22.

You were surprised and sorry, you said, and possibly hurt that I wd. not tell you of my conversion till my going to Birmingham made it impossible any longer to conceal it.[2] I was never sorry for one minute: it wd. have been culpably dishonourable and ungrateful, as I said before, not to have done one's best to conceal it: but I do not mean that, but this—the happiness it has been the means of bringing me I cd. not have conceived: I can never thank you enough for yr. kindness at that time. Notwithstanding my anxiety, which on the day we filled the aquarium was very great indeed, it gives me more delight to think of the time at Rochdale than any other time whatever that I can remember. I did not see Mrs. Molesworth

[1] R. B. was at Eton 1854–63; he played in the Oppidans' Wall and Field football teams. At Corpus Christi, Oxford (1863–7), he stroked the college Eight. The best record of R. B.'s Eton days is to be found in his *Memoir* of Dolben.

[2] Writing to the Rev. E. W. Urquhart (q.v., p. 7) on 24 Sept. 1866 G. M. H. says: 'Fr. Bridges I hid it with difficulty while I stayed at Rochdale, till my going to Birmingham made concealment useless. His kindness at the time when he did not know what was the matter with me I perpetually thank God for.' He mentions that he was staying with Garrett at the time of his conversion, which 'when it came was all in a minute'.

at the last: will you give her for me my very greatest thanks for her kindness? Dr. Molesworth I did say Goodbye to. I am most distressed to think that the news of my conversion, if they hear it, may give them pain and alarm for you, but you must remember that when I came to Rochdale I did not look upon my reception as to be so soon as it really was to be. You see the point of what was on my mind at the vicarage was chiefly this, that my wishes about you cd. not be gained except at your own and their trouble and grief. This will make it plain how I feel that wherever I go I must either do no good or else harm.

Walford believed that Dolben had been mobbed in Birmingham.[1] He went in his habit without sandals, barefoot. I do not know whether it is more funny or affecting to think of.

My father and mother are still abroad and are or will soon be at Dinan in Brittany, where it happens that Urquhart[2] now is, coaching Morris. I hope they will meet. My mother, my brother says, has some prejudice about Urquhart, I conceive because he is looked upon as leading me over to Rome.

I heard first fr. Dr. Newman of Mr. Riddell's death.[3] He was always most kind to me. He was so good that one scarcely can regret his loss, but for our college it is very sad and disastrous.

I did leave something behind, my sponge, wd. you be so kind as to bring it if you can, though I am afraid I cd. not ask for anything more inconvenient.

I am now going to see Mr. Street and I can find out fr. him,

[1] Dolben himself describes this visit in a letter to R. B. hypothetically dated 1 Sept. 1866. See *Memoir*, pp. cii–ciii.

[2] Edward William Urquhart (1839–1916), a Balliol man, took a 2nd in Classical Mods. in 1859, and a 1st in Greats and History in 1861. He was ordained in 1862, and was vicar of King's Sutton, Northamptonshire, 1873–86. At one time he was private tutor for the Honours School of Law and Modern History.

[3] On 24 Sept. 1866 G. M. H. sent to Urquhart a notice from the *Guardian* of the death, on 14 Sept. 1866, of the Rev. James Riddell, Fellow and Tutor of Balliol, a much-loved scholar: 'a man of singular goodness, innocence, and purity; . . .'. He had been G. M. H.'s tutor.

7

you know, any detail about the bottle. You shall hear this evening, if I have seen him.

Believe me, dear Bridges, with the utmost gratitude your very affectionate friend,

GERARD HOPKINS.

Oak Hill, Hampstead, Sept. 24, 1866.

VII

DEAR BRIDGES,—Mr. Street was again not in this morning. He was to be in in the afternoon but I found I cd. not go then, and now he will[1] not be home till Friday or Saturday. On Saturday however I hope to catch him. Hart's, if I remember is the place for all sorts of ecclesiastical furniture and I will go there soon.

Do you know Bradley?[2] Yesterday at St. Alban's I saw him serving in some way in choir, and I saw too another Oxford man, whose name I do not know, with a delightful face (not handsome), altogether aquiline features, a sanguine complexion, rather tall, slight, and eager-looking: I did not know he was one of the faithful before. His face was fascinating me last term: I generally have one fascination or another on. Sometimes I dislike the faces wh. fascinate me but sometimes much the reverse, as is the present case.

G. M. H.

Hampstead. Sept. 24. [1866]

VIII

Oak Hill, Hampstead, N.W.

DEAR BRIDGES,—Many thanks. Another bad cold has kept me fr. going to town of late. I am so sorry for Hames. I forgot to tell you that on my last day coming softly down stairs I overtook him playing the piano. What you wd. find him doing next was with him as impossible to foretell as with Mother Hubbard's dog. At the station he was most attentive and most unintelli-

[1] Here a superfluous 'be' in MS.   [2] Not further identified.

21

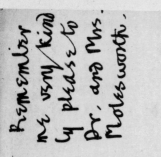

Remember me very kind ly please to Dr. and Mrs. Molesworth.

Oak Hill,
Hampstead,
n.w.

Dear Bridges, — Many thanks. Another bad cold has kept me fr. going
to town of late. I am so sorry for
Hames. I forgot to tell you that on
my last day coming softly down
stairs I overtook him playing the
Piano. What you wd. find him doing next was with him as impossible to foretell as with Mother
Hubbard's dog. At the station he
was most attentive and most unintelligible. Pray do not apologise
for yr. absence: indeed one is
so glad when people put one on
such terms that they allow one
not to incommode them — if you
follow that involution of speech.

It curiously happens that I have
seen two people we were talking

gible. Pray do not apologise for yr. absence: indeed one is so glad when people put one on such terms that they allow one not to incommode them—if you follow that involution of speech.

It curiously happens that I have seen two people we were talking about. The first is the Corpus man whose name I wanted to know. I met him riding in one of our roads a few days ago and I stared at him in order to note his features but not very comfortably, for he plainly recognised my face. As far as I can give it this is the description of him: he has plenty of thick rather curly dark auburn hair parted in the middle and εὐφυέας¹ whiskers of the same; his eyes are deep set and I think rather near together; the fault of his face is that the features are too broad and depressed; his forehead is wide across and narrow upwards to the hair; he looks happy. I drew him when I got home but some touches destroyed the likeness at last. The other is Clarke of Magdalen.² I saw him at St. Joseph's Retreat at Highgate. I was wrong about his madness or exaggerated, at all events he is sane now, but he had *two* mad friends, who raged about Oxford. He is a Passionist, 'Brother George', much paler than of old and all in habit.

You never said anything that gave me any reason to think you were being converted. Many thanks for your promise. You seem so puzzled at my silence: I want you to understand that it was fr. no natural reticence, which is not in me, but fr. the plain conviction of the unkindness and—to use the word which I fancied people wd. give it—treachery of letting you know. And please believe it was meant for a real silence: having decided not to tell you I meant you not to know: hints or constructive conclusions wd. have been both weak and mean. Though you call yourself 'of a plain blurting disposition' I think you wd. however agree that silence is an excellent discipline and especially during the process of conviction (this of course is neither here nor there to my silence at Rochdale)— indeed you have several times said as much. In fact it occurs

¹ 'shapely': Homer, *Il.* xxi, 243.
² Possibly William A. Clarke, who took a 2nd in Classical Mods. in 1868.

to me that you are unusually reticent and certainly have a great respect for reticence. And then you ask what I thought about your taking my disclosure quietly. If I had thought the things which you put, could I have written as I did or meant to? But of course you know I thought nothing of the sort. You will force me to express again what I wanted you to believe before.—

TRUMPERY,

MUMMERY, AND G. M. HOPKINS FLUMMERY

DESIGNER.

☞ REMOVED TO THE OTHER SIDE OF THE WAY ☜

Sept. 28, 1866.

Remember me very kindly please to Dr. and Mrs. Molesworth.

IX

Oak Hill, Hampstead, N.W.

DEAR BRIDGES,—I am sorry to say I cannot as I meant go on yr. commission today, but I will tomorrow. I wish I cd. have been quicker. I wrote to ask if you know whenabouts the Autumn Greats Schools come on, for Ed. Bond[1] is going in then and naturally wishes to have the exact time. I suppose you got my letter about Mr. Street, but I am aiming my letters at a venture at Thorndon. Yrs. affectionately,

GERARD HOPKINS.

Oct. 5. [1866]

X

DEAR BRIDGES,—I am rather puzzled about the bottle and can take no further step till I have heard fr. you. I have been to Keith's (the man Mr. Street recommended) at 41 Westmoreland Place, City Road, N.—an incredible place to live at and hard to find—and seen what they have (I did go before but it was then no good.) They have only three shapes, which are in fact

[1] Edward Bond (1844–1920), of Merchant Taylors' School and St. John's College, Oxford, took a 1st in Classical Mods. in 1864 and a 1st in Greats in 1866, and was made Fellow of Queen's College, Oxford, in 1869.

three sizes, and to my mind only the biggest is at all nice. I am not satisfied with it: I give you a rough recollection of it. It is correct, I suppose, (the original I mean) and unobjectionable but it does not attract one. It had a stopper of yellow metal, like this, anything but nice, with a flimsy band of pattern round it. That at all events I wd. not have. To have a stopper capped

with silver with a silver Maltese cross, disk, or what it might be surmounting it wd. cost a great deal more (in fact the yellow metal is a two penny-halfpenny thing); engraved with the sort of design I showed them it wd. be nearly a pound. I have said they had only three sizes (practically one) and so there was no choice, but to blow a new bottle fr. a new design cd. be done for a little less than two pounds. Certainly if both these things were done I shd. still be under the sum you named but it was plain that one ought to be able to do everything for a good deal less and it wd. be useless to waste money. You see if you wished a new bottle blown I doubt if I cd. design it: a design for a stopper is one thing, for a bottle quite different. The first question then I want you to answer (for I am obliged to ask you to be so kind as to write at once) is this—Will you have the above bottle or will you wait and get one at your leisure?—$\epsilon\check{\iota}\eta$ δ' $\check{\alpha}\nu$ $\pi\hat{\alpha}\nu$ $\dot{\epsilon}\nu$ $\tau\hat{\omega}$ $\mu\epsilon\gamma\acute{\alpha}\lambda\hat{\omega}^1$ $\chi\rho\acute{o}\nu\omega$.[2] Coles wd. give you greater resources for he is always engaged in ordering something or other,

---

[1] Really '$\mu\epsilon\gamma\acute{\alpha}\lambda\omega$'.
[2] Cf. Herodotus v. 9: $\gamma\acute{\epsilon}\nu o\iota\tau o$ δ' $\check{\alpha}\nu$ $\pi\hat{\alpha}\nu$ $\dot{\epsilon}\nu$ $\tau\hat{\omega}$ $\mu\alpha\kappa\rho\hat{\omega}$ $\chi\rho\acute{o}\nu\omega$—'all is possible in the course of time'.

etc. 2nd. If you have the bottle will you have a plain round shield-shape silver stopper (on the top of which there cd. still be a simple design) or that with the surmounting handle (like the Maltese cross ones)? The latter, as I have said, wd. be nearly £1, the former not much more than half that, I believe. To complicate things Mr. Keith was not there today and I had

to deal with an uninventive youth. I am to see him on Wednesday however, when there will also be a design of a Maltese-cross stopper wh. will assist me. I have done all sorts of designs but I cannot send you any as I want this to reach you without delay. Mr. Street spoke of the price of what I shd. want as about 30s. I think it wd. be less for the above one: perhaps he included the stopper. The smallest size I think was 18s., the biggest therefore might be 25s. With the shield-shape stopper in silver the whole wd. be less than £2, so write.

I know you must know who Edward Bond is, I have so often spoken of him. He is a scholar of St. John's whom I have known ever since I have been at Oxford and rather longer, and intimately, for he lives at Hampstead. He is handsome and very tall and his mother is extremely nice.

The sun was eclipsed today. I saw it all up the City Road, to such a pass have natural phenomena come. Always yours,

G. M. H.[1]

Hampstead, Oct. 8, 1866.

XI

DEAR BRIDGES,—I fear you will think I have done your business very unsatisfactorily. When I got to Keith's today Keith was not there and I believe the assistant, who did not appear,

[1] Initials twisted into an ecclesiastical device.

probably because he was afraid to, had told him nothing about the engagement. As I had not heard fr. you either I cd. not have had a more ἀμήχανον[1] condition of things. But I will tell you what is to be done. In the first place I understated the price of the cruet; it wd. be 30s. with the stopper and as that can be worth very little it can be little less without it. But on second thoughts I like the cruet and think you might easily have worse: but this you shall see for yourself, for I have got a life-size tracing of it. And now about the stopper. The boy that I saw today—young Keith, I suppose—said it wd. be 25s. and he seemed to know more about things than the other fellow. But the cruet and stopper together wd. be £2 10s. Now if you wish to have my design I can send it them drawn to life size and let them send the cruet and stopper to Thorndon, but if I were you I wd. not: there are these alternatives—a plain silver-capped stopper such as I spoke about, on which if you liked you cd. have a design of mine rather simpler than the other—this wd. be a great deal less expensive; and secondly what I have drawn below, which you may like. Its price I do not know, but if you like it I will ask: I saw a drawing of one which was gilt. It was a great misfortune that Keith was not at home, in fact it had no business to have happened. You will see that I have left it open with Keith's but I *can* settle everything now by letter, so that all the personal part of this business is done. You  shall see my design if you wish at Oxford: whether you will like it is another thing. I shall leave this open, as a letter fr. you may come tonight.

Your affectionate friend,

GERARD HOPKINS.

Hampstead, Oct. 10, 1866.

I have kept on forgetting to ask you this, to copy out yr. air

[1] 'awkward'.

13

(harmonised I mean of course) for Johnson's verses.[1] Will you please have this for me when we meet?

As my brother explains to me that I cannot hear fr. you now before nine tomorrow—and in fact it is now past ten at night—I shall close this.

I did not close it but no letter still this morning, which is ODD.[2]

XII

Oak Hill, Hampstead, N.W.

DEAR BRIDGES,—I have to begin with a handful of apologies. I have taken the design to Keith's but the things will not be ready by Christmas (as I soon began to fear wd. be the case) but by a week after it. I really am most sorry and also ashamed that I shd. have given you so much annoyance, but I think perhaps the fault was almost more in not seeing how long I might be when I undertook the design than in being so long when it was undertaken. The price of the cruet and stopper will be about £2 10s.—I have before told you about the cruet, the stopper will be a cork capped with silver from which rises a silver disk with a cross and some of the instruments of the Passion etc on the obverse side and a smaller design on the other. I cannot tell whether it will come out well in engraving and I fear at any rate you will think it a very twopenny-half-penny thing to have taken so long doing. And next I must beg yr. pardon for not having seen Mr. Street yet: I will go tomorrow if possible and if not on Wednesday—and also for not answering yr. note before: I cd. not bring myself to do so till the cruet was off my mind.

I have had an invitation fr. Dr. Newman to spend the week

[1] Of this air Mrs. Bridges knows nothing: she thinks R. B. must have destroyed it and all other of his musical compositions. The reference is to William Johnson, later Cory, 1822-92, poet, historian, and master at Eton. See p. 29, n. 4.

[2] Here should be read the letters from H. P. Liddon to G. M. H. entreating him to pause before taking 'the final and fatal step' (*Life*, pp. 38-42). On 21 Oct. 1866, as Newman's diary records, he went to Birmingham from Oxford, and 'was received'.

before term begins at the Oratory,[1] and I am hoping the plan will not cause any pain here which wd. prevent my availing myself of it.

Do you hear fr. Dolben? I cannot make out whether he is really going both to matriculate and reside next term.[2] I have not heard fr. him for some time. Addis is living with his brother on Highgate hill and Wood is staying with him: the latter is going to Rome for the rest of the vacation in a few weeks or for longer and will most likely be at Oxford no more after this except to pack his things away.

I will write perhaps more at length presently. Unless you think they wd. not be pleased, remember me kindly to Dr. and Mrs. Molesworth. Believe me, dear Bridges, with all Xmas wishes always affectionately your friend,

GERARD M. HOPKINS.

Dec. 22, 1866.

P.S. When you are next writing will you send yr. airs? I will copy out the *Summa*[3] for you shortly, but I intend to add a good deal to it some day and your copy will be a very imperfect version in other ways.

If you happen by any chance to have the statutes by you will you kindly look out for me what in the way or stead of Divinity is to be taken in for Greats by those who are not *in gremio Ecclesiae Anglicanae*?

[1] 'Could you not come here for the week before term? I want to see you for the pleasure of seeing you—but, besides that, I think it good that a recent convert should pass some time in a religious house, to get into Catholic ways—though a week is not long enough for that purpose.' (Letter from Newman, 16 Dec. 1866, *Life*, pp. 45-6.) Newman had formerly proposed his coming to the Oratory for Christmas vacations, but agreed that home was the best place for him then, if he could be there with comfort.

[2] Dolben, now more and more absorbed by religious matters, wrote to R. B. from Malvern (the date is tentatively 1 Sept. 1866) to persuade his friend to visit Finedon Hall, his home, at Christmas. He says, also, 'I . . . shall not come up to Oxford till January for matriculation, as I am absolutely unable to work hard, even if I wished to do so.' He attempted to matriculate in May 1867, fainted in the examination, and failed. (*Memoir*, pp. cvi–cvii.)

[3] See R. B.'s note to *Poems*, 52: he prints four only of the sixteen lines.

XIII

DEAR BRIDGES,—Mr. Street has a great press of work on his hands now and till the beginning of the year; he is doing designs for the new National Gallery which must be done, I believe, by that time. He cannot therefore do the design for you for a fortnight or perhaps more, and then he will. I cannot say he said this with any more assurance than the other time.

It is not much more than an hour to Xmas day: I am sitting up for the midnight mass. Believe me always yr. affectionate friend,

GERARD M. HOPKINS.

Christmas Eve, 1866. Oak Hill, Hampstead.

Dec. 26. I neglected to send this off yesterday.[1]

XIV

DEAR BRIDGES,—I heard of Dolben's death[2] the day I returned fr. Paris by a letter fr. Coles[3] wh. had been a week waiting for me. Edgell[4] has since written me a few more particulars. I have kept the beginning of a letter to you a long time by me but to no purpose so far as being more ready to write goes. There is very little I have to say. I looked forward to meeting Dolben and his being a Catholic more than to anything. At the same time from never having met him but once I find it difficult to realise his death or feel as if it were anything to me. You know there can

[1] G. M. H. took his degree, a 1st in Greats, in the spring of 1867: he had taken a 1st in Classical Mods. in 1864. (For R. B.'s remarks on his method of work see *Memoir*, p. ci.) Easter he spent at the Benedictine Priory by Hereford. On 7 July 1867 he writes to Urquhart: '. . . I am hoping to go to Paris with Pontiatine next week but at present I am in the position of writing letters to him which I believe he never gets. After a week or ten days I return. I have no plans till some time in August, when Pater is going to ask me down to Sidmouth.' On 17 Sept. 1867 he became a master at the Oratory, a post offered him by Newman on 22 Feb. 1867, but he did not return there after the Christmas vacation (*Life*, pp. 46–7).

[2] He was drowned when bathing in the river Welland on 28 June 1867 (*Memoir*, pp. cx, cxi, and cxiv).

[3] One of the few men in close touch with Dolben. See *Memoir*, pp. cv–cvii.

[4] This seems to be Alfred Wyatt-Edgell, afterwards Lord Braye.

very seldom have happened the loss of so much beauty (in body and mind and life) and of the promise of still more as there has been in his case—seldom I mean, in the whole world, for the conditions wd. not easily come together. At the same time he had gone on in a way wh. was wholly and unhappily irrational. I want to know whether his family think of gathering and publishing, or at least printing, his poetry. Perhaps you will like to hear what Dr. Newman says.[1] 'Yes, we heard all about Dolben. The account was very pleasant. He had not given up the idea of being a Catholic, but he thought he had lived on excitement, and felt he must give himself time before he could know whether he was in earnest or not. This does not seem to me a wrong frame of mind. He was up to his death careful in his devotional exercises. I never saw him.' Some day I hope to see Finedon and the place where he was drowned too. Can you tell me where he was buried?[2]—at Finedon, was it not? If you have letters from him will you let me see them some day?

Many thanks about Rochdale. It is, as you say, impossible that I shd. see you this vacation. I may be in Oxford next term for a day or less, when of course I shall come to you. I am now staying with Urquhart, who desires to be remembered. On the 10th of next month I shall go to Edgbaston; on the 17th their school begins. I shall address this to Rochdale for you may very well have left Newmarket.

I hope your reading is going on well. So far as time allows will you write again please? I suppose your music is in abeyance but I hope it will on no account be stopped permanently. When you write let me hear everything you have to tell. Believe me always your affectionate friend,

GERARD M. HOPKINS.

Aug. 30, '67—at Urquhart's, Bovey Tracy, Newton Abbot, in Devon.

P.S. Thanks for Miss Dolben's letter, wh. I enclose.

[1] For R. B.'s criticism of these remarks by Newman see the Note on pp. 140–1 of *Memoir*.
[2] He was buried 'under the altar at Finedon' on 6 July 1867.

XV

DEAR BRIDGES,—Many thanks for your letters. Do you know I am so hard at work I have scarcely any leisure at all. I am nearly sure I shall not take my degree this term, certainly not on the 7th or 10th. How long shall you be up after Greats? I mean you will be up next term, will you not? If by any chance I shd. come to want to take my degree this term I shall write, and in any case many thanks for your offer.

The last I heard of you was from Addis who met you in Bridgenorth and from one of his pupils who knew of it.

It is quite true, as you say, that there was a great want of strength in Dolben—more, of sense. Edgell told me he had some mortuary cards done and offered me one and till this minute I had never written for it. Nettleship[1] wrote to me in the vacation: he lives in Northamptonshire and his father had been over to see Mr. Dolben and found him very much cut up.

Is not the thought of Greats like a mill-stone round your neck now? It was to me.

I have written so many accounts of what this place is like that I can not write any more.[2] But I am very fond of my boys and as there is nothing but boys visible that is really saying everything there is to be said about the general pleasantness of the place. I have taken to playing football but got lamed to some degree by a kick on the ancle. I have also begun the violin and if you will write a trio or quartet I will some day take the first or second part in it.—I will write a better letter some other day.

I sincerely hope you have better accounts of Mrs. Molesworth. —Believe yr. ever affectionate friend,

GERARD M. HOPKINS.

The Oratory, Edgbaston. All Saints' [1 November], 1867.

[1] Richard Lewis Nettleship (1846–92), Scholar of Balliol (1864: resident Oct. 1865), and later a distinguished Fellow and tutor of the college. See *D.N.B.* He lived at Kettering.

[2] He describes his work at the Oratory in a letter to Urquhart of 30 Sept. 1867. For this see NOTE D.

You ask about the *Doctor*.[1] I have only read it here and there and never the story part. I used to like it very much. I cannot tell now whether I think it really good or no.

XVI

DEAREST BRIDGES,—Thanks for your photograph. It is like—so most photographs are—but I mean it has an expression of yours, and photographs often miss expression altogether. Though not the best that could be done I must say I like it.

With regard to the invitation very many thanks for your kindness. But I think I will, if you will let me, refuse it. I cannot feel at my ease with regard to Dr. and Mrs. Molesworth, but beyond that too I am very unwilling, I cannot exactly explain why, to come to Rochdale. Instead of the excuses I might have given I have put it in what I am afraid you may call the rudest way. But the very pleasure I had in my stay last year is part of the reason why I do not wish to make another, if you can understand. I do not know what you will think of all this.

After what you tell me about the Doctor are you not beginning to think more particularly about what you are going to be? I want to hear about this.

I had heard nothing at all about O'Hanlon's death[2] but what you told me till yesterday, when Challis spoke of it. In coming here he had spent two hours at Oxford and heard of it fr. Hood of Brasenose. I must tell you that Challis is now staying at the Oratory and I hope will be here permanently.

I own I felt a good deal of satisfaction that you liked the pattern for the cruet. I thought before that it had very likely come out badly in the execution—a natural thing with an amateur's designs—and in any case that the people at Thorndon did not like it, or else you wd. have said they did.

---

[1] *The Doctor* (1834–47), by Robert Southey, whose name was first added to the posthumous sixth volume.

[2] Hugh Francis O'Hanlon (1843–67), Scholar of Brasenose and Fellow of Lincoln, died on 8 Nov.

I wish I knew exactly when you are in the schools. A 2nd is the class I have always imagined you wd. get: mind it is a good one.[1]

Believe me yr. very affectionate friend,

GERARD HOPKINS.

Do not again address me with that alphabet of initials, please.

Nov. 12. [1867]

XVII

DEAR BRIDGES,—I still think I had rather not come to Rochdale in the vacation, if you will allow me to make the refusal. But I thank you very much for the offer. I ought to have written this before, but every leisure time of Sunday was interrupted by people coming in: an oak is a great device, do you know, but I have none and cannot tell how to supply its place.

Greats begin on Thursday, I believe. If you will be properly composed and confident I have no doubt that you will do well.

Believe me yr. ever affectionate friend,—

GERARD M. HOPKINS.

Nov. 19, '67. The Oratory.

Edgell is going to send me a photograph of Dolben which he had done, but I do not understand when that could have been.

XVIII

DEAR BRIDGES,—Would it be possible for you to see me on yr. way home? Certainly it would if the degree day does not fall too late. But when does it fall? You must write and say. The holidays here begin tomorrow fortnight and I do not expect to stay more than one or two days later, since that (the 20th) brings one within five days of Christmas.

As one is never surprised at anything anybody does but only sometimes at what they say I will not be surprised at your

---

[1] R. B. took a 2nd in Greats in the Michaelmas term, 1867.

Robert Bridges
c. 1863–4

going this pilgrimage with Muirhead.[1] Of course you must enjoy it and travelling I quite think is a great means of education. By starting immediately I suppose you mean immediately after Christmas, I shall hear more.

Pontiatine[2] and Redington[3] are coming to see me on the 15th. Remember me kindly to Muirhead the next time he comes in. Believe me always yr. affectionate friend,—

GERARD M. HOPKINS.

The Oratory. Dec. 5, 1867.

XIX

Oak Hill, Hampstead, N.W.

DEAR BRIDGES,—I shall be very glad indeed to have yr. book:[4] it wd. be a great godsend. When exactly and where shall you be in town? for I shall be here—at least as a head-quarters— till about a week—well until you sail at all events, so if you will let me know we can meet, that is you can come here.

I am afraid Pontiatine must be much disappointed. I was much, at least a good deal, dissatisfied[5] at the class list.

Everything else I will talk about when I see you.

Will you bring the book?

Believe me yr. affectionate[6] friend,—

GERARD M. HOPKINS.

You sometimes now address me by my Christian name and I like it but I do not you by yours, for first it wd. not feel natural

---

[1] Lionel Muirhead, of Haseley Court, near Oxford, artist and country gentleman, had been at Eton with R. B. He was a great friend and a constant visitor at Yattendon and Chilswell. The 'pilgrimage' was to Egypt and Syria. After returning R. B. went with Dr. Sanday to study German in Germany.

[2] Basil Pontiatine, a Ch. Ch. man, took a 2nd in Greats in 1867.

[3] Christopher T. T. Redington (1847–99) was also at Ch. Ch. and took a 1st in Greats in 1868. He was later an Irish Privy Councillor.

[4] Not a book of his poems: R. B.'s first volume, of 1873, was written shortly before publication. See p. 23.

[5] Written over 'disappointed'.   [6] MS. 'affectionately'.

to me and secondly it wd. be unnecessary, for your surname is the prettier.

Christmas wishes.

Christmas Eve, 1867.

XX

DEAR BRIDGES,—Your note limited me really to but one time for calling, namely noon yesterday, and then my aunt kept me. I am now at Croydon and shall not be able to see you therefore before you go. I am very sorry indeed for this: it is the great inconvenience of my invitations and that comes of the short holidays.

This note accordingly is to say goodbye. The year you will be away I have no doubt will make a great difference in my position though I cannot know exactly what. But the uncertainty I am in about the future is so very unpleasant and so breaks my power of applying to anything that I am resolved to end it, which I shall do by going into a retreat at Easter[1] at the latest and deciding whether I have a vocation to the priesthood. Do not repeat this.

You will write, I hope, from abroad. Believe me always your affectionate friend,—

GERARD M. HOPKINS.

You asked a little time ago about W——.[2] I believe he is gone to India: he said he was going but I have not heard since. His lapse is a most dreadful thing but I have nothing new to say about it: he suffered terrible pain before he finally gave up his belief.

Blunt House, Croydon, S. Jan. 9, 1868.[3]

[1] Newman had already advised the Retreat at Easter, and on 7 Feb. 1868 wrote: 'You need not make up your mind till Easter comes, as we shall be able to manage matters whether you stay or we have the mishap to lose you.' (*Life*, p. 47.)　　　　　[2] Editor's omission.

[3] The break of nearly six months between this letter and the next is accounted for by R. B.'s absence from England. The Retreat already mentioned determined G. M. H. to enter the priesthood. For Newman's letter

XXI

DEAREST BRIDGES,—I am going to start for Switzerland[1] next week with Edward Bond of St. John's and we shall be there a month or less. I shall not be able to see you when you come up to town therefore. As soon as possible after my return I go, as perhaps Challis told you, into the Jesuit noviciate. My address will then be Manresa House, Roehampton, S.W. and perhaps sometime when you are in town you might come and see me: it is quite near, and easy of access by Putney or Barnes. I cannot promise to correspond, for in that way the novices are restricted, but I have no doubt that now and then I shd. be able to send you a letter.

I have both yr. books[2] safe and thank you very much for the loan. I have had the box in which the big one is a little heightened, because after it had been opened and in my room some little time the book swelled up as I fancied, perhaps from the heat of the room, so that I did not like to press the lid down on it as before. After this had been done it was screwed up: this was at Easter when 1 was leaving Edgbaston and since then it has not been opened. They shall be sent to you wherever you like, if you will say the place.

Perhaps you will say whether I have any chance of seeing you before I go to Roehampton. In case, as I am afraid it will turn out, I have none I will wish you goodbye with the warmest wishes for yr. happiness. I hope Mrs. Plow[3] is now in better health. Believe me very affectionately your friend—

GERARD M. HOPKINS.

Hampstead, June 27, '68.

of pleasure at the announcement (14 May 1868) see *Life*, p. 47: 'Don't call "the Jesuit discipline hard": it will bring you to heaven. The Benedictines would not have suited you.'

[1] For extracts from his diary of this tour, from 19 July to 1 Aug., see *Life*, pp. 149–56.

[2] It is not known what books these were.

[3] R. B.'s sister Harriett Louisa, married to the Rev. Antony John Plow, vicar of Todmorden. A daughter of this marriage became Mrs. H. C. Beeching.

XXII

DEAR BRIDGES,—I have been back since Saturday night. Yr. letter came before I started and yr. books were sent after I had gone. My mother directed of course that they shd. be paid for and I hope they were but we cannot ascertain till the carrier people send in their bill. I shd. be glad to hear also that they came safe.

I shall be here, I am expecting, till some time in September,[1] when I shall enter the 30 days retreat which begins the noviciate. After the retreat I can always be seen by calling at Manresa House, Roehampton, S.W.—it is easily accessible—and can be written to but the letters will of course be read and I doubt whether I shall be able to write in answer. But I hope we shall now meet soon and for that reason I need not write much.

I cannot send my *Summa* for it is burnt with my other verses: I saw they wd. interfere with my state and vocation.[2] I kept however corrected copies of some things which you have and will send them that what you have got you may have in its last edition.

Write and say when and where you will be in town and believe me ever yr. affectionate friend

GERARD M. HOPKINS.

Oak Hill, Hampstead. Aug. 7, '68.

P.S. I hope you will master the peculiar beat I have intro-duced into St. Dorothea.[3] The development is mine but the beat is in Shakspere—e.g.

Whý should thís desert be?[4]—and

---

[1] For his diary from 24 Aug. to 1 Sept. see *Life*, pp. 156–8.

[2] From now till *The Wreck of the Deutschland* (which dates from Dec. 1875) he wrote no poetry 'but two or three little presentation pieces which occa-sion called for'.

[3] See R. B.'s note to *Poems*, 1. The expanded version in A carries certain accents, e.g.

> I bear a basket lined with grass.
> I am só light and fair
> Men must start to see me pass
> And the básket I bear, . . .

It differs considerably from the version printed in *Poems*, Appendix, 82.

[4] *As You Like It*, Act III, sc. 2, l. 133.

Thoú for whóm Jóve would swear[1]—where the rest of the lines are eight-syllabled or seven-syllabled.

XXIII

MY DEAR BRIDGES,—It is nearly a fortnight since my mother gave me the sad news of Mrs. Plow's death but I have not till today had an opportunity of writing to you, as I wished to do. I cannot help thinking that perhaps for her own sake she could not have much wished to live longer with such dreadful grief[2] upon her memory but it is different with you and with your mother: I have wondered with myself how Mrs. Molesworth would bear all these things. I know nothing but the fact of your sister's death, so that I can only speak generally. No doubt her health never really recovered the first shock. What suffering she had! Even during Mr. Plow's life she had troubles, you told me, and it appeared in her face. But sufferings falling on such a person as your sister was are to be looked on as the marks of God's particular love and this is truer the more exceptional they are. I wonder what will become of her child: she had not more than one living, I think.

I am very sorry you had your journey here for nothing, as I afterwards found: at the time the community was unluckily in a three days' retreat. I wd. make this letter longer if I had more to say but as I know no particulars about yourself and I cd. not say anything else that wd. interest you I think it is better to send it off: as it is I have had it some time in my drawer. Let me assure you of my most earnest sympathy, which I can the more easily give as I had the happiness of a little knowing your sister, and believe me always your affectionate friend—

GERARD M. HOPKINS.

Manresa House, Roehampton, S.W. April 29, 1869[3].

[1] *Love's Labour's Lost*, Act IV, sc. 3, l. 117.
[2] For her husband's sudden death.
[3] He records in his diary for 1869: 'A penance which I was doing from Jan. 25 to July 25 prevented my seeing much that half year.'

XXIV

MY DEAR BRIDGES,—I am afraid that if you come on Sunday I shall be able to be but a short time with you, for I am away till a quarter past five. Would Saturday afternoon suit you— say a quarter to four? If you do not care to come on Sunday and cannot on Saturday perhaps you will let me know. I have only time for this line. Believe me yr. affectionate friend—

GERARD M. HOPKINS.

Manresa House, Roehampton. Oct. 14, '69.[1]

XXV

MY DEAR BRIDGES,—I hear nothing whatever of you and the fault is certainly mine. I am going to address this to Rochdale, because you may have changed your lodgings in town. I am now at Stonyhurst reading philosophy and mathematics: at present it is holidays. I shall be here some long time to come, I expect. Perhaps you have seen the place: it is bare and bleak but the rivers are beautiful. I shall not write more now, indeed I have nothing to say. Please tell me all about yourself.[2] I am

---

[1] Father Lahey says (*Life*, p. 128): 'The two years spent at Roehampton were of but slight external importance. Hopkins fulfilled the office of Porter with due credit, and preached a panegyric on St. Stanislaus, the patron of Jesuit novices, which for its brilliancy and beauty was remembered long afterwards by those who heard it.' From 1870 to 1873 he attended the course of Philosophy at St. Mary's Hall, Stonyhurst, the house of studies for Jesuit scholastics. He did not, at this time, teach at Stonyhurst College. St. Mary's Hall is a separate building, situated about three hundred yards from the College, and now the Junior School, since the scholasticate was removed to Heythrop (Oxon.) in 1926.

[2] R. B. entered St. Bartholomew's as a medical student in 1871, at the age of twenty-seven. He remained there for seven years. After qualifying and serving as House Physician to Dr. Patrick Black for one year, he was appointed Casualty Physician in 1877, which post he held for two years: his experience of this time is analysed in his 'Account of the Casualty Department' (published in vol. xiv of the *Hospital Reports* for 1878) which exposes the short-comings of the system in vogue—'it is not unusual for a casualty physician to see 150 patients in less than two hours'. Previous to this he had contributed one paper to the *Reports* on 'A Severe Case of Rheumatic Fever Treated with Splints'. In 1878 he became Assistant

sure I must have behaved unkindly when you came to Roehampton. Believe me always your affectionate friend—

GERARD HOPKINS.

Stonyhurst College, Whalley, Lancashire. April 2, 1871.

XXVI

MY DEAR BRIDGES,—Our holidays have begun, so I will write again. I feel inclined to begin by asking whether you are secretary to the International as you seem to mean me to think nothing too bad for you but then I remember that you never relished 'the intelligent artisan'. I must tell you I am always thinking of the Communist future. The too intelligent artisan is master of the situation I believe. Perhaps it is what everyone believes, I do not see the papers or hear strangers often enough to know. It is what Carlyle has long threatened and foretold. But his writings are, as he might himself say, 'most inefficacious-strenuous heaven-protestations, caterwaul, and Cassandra-wailings'. He preaches obedience but I do not think he has done much except to ridicule instead of strengthening the hands of the powers that be. Some years ago when he published his *Shooting Niagara*[1] he did make some practical suggestions but so vague that they should rather be called '*too* dubious moonstone-grindings and on the whole impracticable-practical unveracities'. However I am afraid some great revolution is not far off. Horrible to say, in a manner I am a Communist. Their ideal bating some things is nobler than that professed by any secular statesman I know of (I must own I live in bat-light and shoot at a venture). Besides it is just.—I do not mean the means of getting to it are. But it is a dreadful thing for the

---

Physician to the Hospital for Sick Children in Great Ormond Street, and subsequently also to the Great Northern (now Royal Northern) Hospital.

During these years he was twice in France for some months, spent a winter in Paris, and made a tour of the Netherlands. In 1874 he was for some months in Italy.

[1] First printed in *Macmillan's Magazine*, vol. xvi, pp. 319–36, 1867, and in the same year separately published with some additions and corrections.

greatest and most necessary part of a very rich nation to live a hard life without dignity, knowledge, comforts, delight, or hopes in the midst of plenty—which plenty they make. They profess that they do not care what they wreck and burn, the old civilisation and order must be destroyed. This is a dreadful look out but what has the old civilisation done for them? As it at present stands in England it is itself in great measure founded on wrecking. But they got none of the spoils, they came in for nothing but harm from it then and thereafter. England has grown hugely wealthy but this wealth has not reached the working classes; I expect it has made their condition worse. Besides this iniquitous order the old civilisation embodies another order mostly old and what is new in direct entail from the old, the old religion, learning, law, art, etc and all the history that is preserved in standing monuments. But as the working classes have not been educated they know next to nothing of all this and cannot be expected to care if they destroy it. The more I look the more black and deservedly black the future looks, so I will write no more.

I can hardly believe that this is August and your letter dated May. True there has been here and I believe elsewhere no summer between. There seems some chance now. In a fortnight we are going, also for a fortnight, to Inellan in Argyleshire on the Clyde. After that I expect to pay my people a short visit down near Southampton, where they have taken a cottage. None of them are turned Catholics: I do not expect it.—Believe me your affectionate friend

GERARD HOPKINS, S.J.

Stonyhurst, Whalley, Lancashire. Aug. 2, 1871.

XXVII

MY DEAR BRIDGES,—My last letter to you was from Stonyhurst.[1] It was not answered, so that perhaps it did not reach

---

[1] In Sept. 1873, as this letter shows, he had returned to Roehampton to teach 'rhetoric'. An extract from his diary for 1874 (*Life*, p. 138) is in place here: 'Our Schools at Roehampton ended with two days of examination

you. If it did I supposed then and do not know what else to suppose now that you were disgusted with the *red* opinions it expressed, being a conservative. I have little reason to be red: it was the red Commune that murdered five of our Fathers lately—whether before or after I wrote I do not remember. So far as I know I said nothing that might not fairly be said. If this was your reason for not answering it seems to shew a greater keenness about politics than is common.

I heard of you lately from an Eton and Oxford man I met— So and so, he told me, breeds fowls and Bridges writes—but nothing distinct. But in last week's *Academy* I came upon an appreciative review of a Mr. Bridges' poems, Robert Bridges the title shewed.[1] And the characteristics the writer found in the poems were true to you. Did I ever before see anything of yours? say in Coles' book? I cannot remember. But given that you write and have changed then I can fancy this yours—

> Next they that bear her, honoured on this night,
> And then the maidens in a double row.[2]

Short extracts from six poems were given. To have seen these gave me an occasion to write again. I think, my dear Bridges, to be so much offended about that red letter was excessive.

One of my sisters,[3] who has become musical beyond the common, urged me to find her the music you wrote for 'O earlier shall the roses blow'[4]: I hunted for it twice without finding it but I cannot have lost it. I never was quite reconciled to the freak of leaving off away from the keynote and have put

before St. Ignatius' feast—the 31st [of July]. I was very tired, seemed deeply cast down, till I had some kind words from the Provincial. . . . The tax on my strength has been greater than I have felt before: at least now at Teignmouth I felt myself weak and can do but little. But in all this Our Lord goes His own way.'

[1] The *Poems* of 1873: a review (two columns) by Andrew Lang in the *Academy* of 17 Jan. 1874. See NOTES E and F.

[2] From V. Elegy. *On a Lady, whom Grief for the Death of her Betrothed killed.* (*P.W.*, vol. ii, book i, 14.)

[3] Grace Hopkins.

[4] A song from *Ionica* (1858), by William Johnson, later Cory: 'roses' should be 'rosebuds'.

imaginary endings to it several times. I myself am learning the piano now, self-taught alas! not for execution's sake but to be independent of others and learn something about music. I have very little time though. I am professor of rhetoric here since last September. Always yr. affectionate friend

GERARD M. HOPKINS, S.J.

Manresa House, Roehampton, S.W. Jan. 22, 1874.

XXVIII

St. Beuno's College,[1] St. Asaph, North Wales. Feb. 20, 1875.

MY DEAREST BRIDGES,—The above address shews how impossible it is for me to execute your kind and welcome wish by calling at Maddox Street. There was never any moral difficulty, I could have got leave to spend more than an hour and a half with you, but a long crow-flight is between us—one over which the crowquill, to follow the lead of my own thoughts, does not carry. But if you had sent me such an invitation last year, when I really was at Roehampton, what a pleasure it would have been and what a break in the routine of rhetoric, which I taught so badly and so painfully!

You will wonder what I do under the sign of those Welsh saints. Study theology—for four years from last September. We live on a hillside of the beautiful valley of the Clwyd, but now the other side of the valley vanishes in mist and the ground is deep in snow.

Feb. 22—It was yesterday waistdeep in the drifts.

I have quite forgotten what I may have said in my last letter. What you write about yourself interests me of course but is beyond me: I have had no time to read even the English books about Hegel, much less the original, indeed I know almost no

---

[1] In Sept. 1874 G. M. H. had come here to study theology for four years. Reminiscences of him at this time are given in the *Life*, pp. 132-3. Probably this was one of the happiest periods of his life: it was certainly one of the most fruitful for his poetry. The Welsh 'scene' had, as his poems show, a peculiar attraction for him. See *Life*, p. 138, for the entry in his diary of 6 Sept. 1874.

German. (However I think my contemporary Wallace[1] of Balliol has been translating him). I do not afflict myself much about my ignorance here, for I could remove it as far as I should much care to do, whenever it became advisable, hereafter, but it was with sorrow I put back Aristotle's Metaphysics in the library some time ago feeling that I could not read them now and so probably should never. After all I can, at all events a little, read Duns Scotus[2] and I care for him more even than Aristotle and more *pace tua* than a dozen Hegels. However this is me, not you. But it explains why I can do nothing more than say how much I like to hear about you and how glad I am you are as you say, nearer the top than the bottom of Hegel's or anybody else's bottomless pit.

I wd. have answered more promptly but I saw that you would not be in London for some little time. The close pressure of my theological studies leaves me time for hardly anything: the course is very hard, it must be said. Nevertheless I have tried to learn a little Welsh, in reality one of the hardest of languages.*

Believe me always your affectionate friend

GERARD M. HOPKINS S.J.

* Hebrew is part of our curriculum.

XXIX

St. Beuno's (and not Bruno's) College, St. Asaph (nor yet Asaph's), North Wales. Feb. 24, 1877.[3]

DEAREST BRIDGES,—You have forgotten or else you never got a letter I wrote *from this place* a year or so ago: it was in answer to one of yours about Henry Heine and other things, and there

---

[1] William Wallace (1st in Greats 1867, Fellow of Merton, Craven Scholar, 1869, Professor of Moral Philosophy at Oxford, 1882) published, in 1874, *The Logic of Hegel, Translated . . . with Prolegomena.*

[2] On his enthusiasm for Duns Scotus see *Life*, pp. 131–2, and his sonnet, *Duns Scotus's Oxford*, dated March 1879 (and in another copy, 1878). Jesuit theologians follow St. Thomas Aquinas.

[3] Part of the reason for the long break between this letter and its predecessor is no doubt to be found in R. B.'s fear (mentioned here by G. M. H.) that his letters were read by others.

too you, with the same kindness and futility as now, proposed to come and see me at Roehampton hundreds of miles away. Instead therefore of coming to see me or, as your present letter proposes, my going to see you which would indeed be the greatest pleasure but cannot however be, write that long and interesting letter. And as for your letters being opened—you made that an objection before, I remember—it is quite unreasonable and superstitious to let it make any difference. To be sure they are torn half open—and so for the most part as that one can see the letter has never been out of the envelope—but how can a superior have the time or the wish to read the flood of correspondence from people he knows nothing of which is brought in by the post? No doubt if you were offering me a wife, a legacy, or a bishopric on condition of leaving my present life, and someone were to get wind of the purpose of the correspondence, *then* our letters would be well read or indeed intercepted. So think no more of that.

And as your letter to which I am to answer has yet to be written and I am on Saturday to undergo a very serious examination I will say no more now. The pamphlets,[1] you know, need not wait for the letter, only I shall not read them through this week: how I wonder what they are about!—Always your affectionate friend

GERARD M. HOPKINS S.J.

Usen't you to call me by my christian name? I believe you did. Well if you did I like it better.

XXX

St. Beuno's College, St. Asaph, North Wales, April 3, 1877.

DEAREST BRIDGES,—You have no call to complain of my delay in writing, I could not help it: I am not a consulting physician

---

[1] These were:

(a) The Growth of Love. / A Poem / in Twenty-four Sonnets. / Ewd. Bumpus, / Holborn Bars, London. / 1876. / Price One Shilling. Pp. (unnumbered) 28. The last sonnet has '1875' at its foot.

(b) *Carmen Elegiacum . . . de Nosocomio Sti Bartolomæi Londinensi* . . . 1877 (first printed in 1876). Pp. 23. For full title see NOTE G.

and have little time and now I am very very tired, yes 'a thousand times and yet a thousand times' and 'scarce can go or creep'.

As for this letter, it is to soothe you and stop your mouth; I will write more elsewhen.

The elegiacs are in my judgment most elegant and Latin, full of happinesses. Nevertheless they are often obscure or crabbed. You cannot say you have reached the consummate smoothness of this sort of thing—

> Donec eris felix multos numerabis amicos,
>   Nubila si fuerint tempora solus eris.[1]

The subject has no interest except in the quaintness of bringing all those folk in.[2] The couplet that amuses me most, so far as I remember now, is the one—

> Quale animal numquam etc.[3]

Foolish sneer at Rome near the beginning:[4] making pilgrimages is *omnibus gentibus insitum.* The italic introductory verses are the smoothest, the last the hardest and worst. I don't know when I remember to have read so much good Latin verse together, still I look upon such a performance as a waste of time and money (a pretty penny it must have cost you printing). That bit about Dr. Gee going shooting with somebody else is beyond

---

[1] Ovid, *Tristia,* i. 9. 5–6. The second verse should be: 'tempora si fuerint nubila solus eris'. G. M. H. had begun to write it correctly, then altered his mind.

[2] After an introduction, the history of the hospital's foundation by Rahere is related, famous names in its school of medicine are recalled, and the staff-physicians, surgeons, junior members, and consultants—all mentioned by name and characterized.

[3] ll. 47–8. Quale animal nunquam peperit bona terra, ut haberet
      Spina duas alas bis totidemque pedes:

[4] Perhaps ll. 35–8 are in question:
      Numina quod melius perhibent neglecta piari
      Imperii tumulo posse, deûmque loco.
      (*Montibus his toto sua culpa remittitur orbi;*
      Quis tantum fati credat habere locum?)

everything obscure:[1] what is it all about? what is the verse of Phaedra?—the *Phèdre*, I suppose, or what? and does he play the flute or is it the stethoscope?

Hoc genus infidum etc.[2]—Now how do you explain that? *This way of study is treacherous and the knowledge drops from the reader's mind before he goes to bed*—is that it? and in the next line *arte* means *practically*? It is . . . d obscure. *Viridi . . Halgo* is laughable to be sure and so are lots of things.[3] How do you parse *ascendi* in 424?[4] (I allow that 'ante cubantes' *sounds* very idiomatic but it cannot mean what you seem to want it to. Or do you mean *is slept off and so dies before the sleeper*?). More hereafter.

The sonnets are truly beautiful, breathing a grave and feeling genius, and make me proud of you (which by the by is not the same as for you to be proud of yourself: I say it because you always were and I see you still are given to conceit; witness your fussing about the 'Romana venustas' epigram and quoting 'Haec tua jam, dixit' etc.).* I have scarcely read them all

* At least, you know, it looks like it.

---

[1] ll. 371–80:

> Sæpe hunc Anderidâ sub cælo Octobris ab urbe
>   Venatum in silva ruris agebat amor.
> Cum quo, mirum adeo! venabula ferre lacerto
>   Visus, postque canes in nemus ire Geus:
> Tantum non Phædræ versum hunc confessus amico,
>   *Si Venerem tollas barbara silva tua est.*
> Nec jam mutarat tantas agrestibus artes,
>   Cesserat haud ferro ligneus ille tubus:
> Quem nisi nunc reducem fecissem, sponte volentem
>   Crederat elapsum lector abesse suâ.

G. M. H.'s main difficulty is resolved by the line italicized by R. B., which is an adaptation of Ovid, *Heroides*, iv (Phaedra Hippolyto), 102.

[2] ll. 447–8:

> Hoc genus infidum studii perit ante cubantes,
>   Hæc doctrina parum sufficit arte suis:

[3] ll. 331–2:

> Pelve cavâ Viridi jus circumscribitur Halgo,
>   Plura tamen prægnans femina jura dabit.

[4] l. 424.   Ultimus ascendi sic pede montis apex:

yet but at present like the 5th best[1] (the thought however is the same as in *Winter's Tale*—'I wish you A wave of the sea that you might ever do Nothing but that' etc or words to that effect)—barring the weak third line:[2] you mean something more like—

Her fall of fold is daylight in my view—

and barring the barbarous rhyme of *prow* and *show*:[3] I can't abide bad rhymes and when they are spelt alike I hate them more. More by token, you hold also the hoary superstition of *love* and *prove*. In general I do not think you have reached finality in point of execution, words might be chosen with more point and propriety, images might be more brilliant etc. I will give some instances. In IV the personification is wrong:[4] in general it is a principle of grammar and language of old and of poetry now that what acts is masculine, what receives action feminine. The tongue cannot be feminine in a language where its gender is not fixed already as such. Rather the heart might as a queen send the tongue as an eloquent ambassador; but your image, I don't know what it means. In VII 9[5] it seems to me you should have said something more like—

Disheartenèd, well I am one of you—

and 13 should be—

Beneath the lamp of truth am found untrue—

---

[1] *The Growth of Love*, v. *Love Strengthened* (*P.W.*, vol. i. 31: final form somewhat altered).

[2] 'Tis joy the foldings of her dress to view.

[3] This rhyme remains.

[4] IV. *Timidity* (*P.W.*, vol. i. 28: some changes). It began:
    A thousand times has, in my heart's behoof,
    My tongue been set his passion to impart:
    A thousand times has my too coward heart
    My mouth reclosed, and fixed her to the roof.
'Her' in l. 4 was later altered to 'it'.

[5] VII. *Uncertainty* (*P.W.*, vol. i. 23):
    Disheartened pilgrims, I am one of you;
(Unaltered later, save for 'dishearten'd'.)

not 'I am found'.[1] VIII 8 is weak;[2] the rhythm is not expressive, it only halts. 'Scheming new tactics' 13 is pleonastic. IX 3 'of cost' I cannot understand at all.[3] XII 14 is not satisfactory: it seems it should be 'and she was lost'.[4] No more is XIV 5. It ought to be—

And three who all the rest had all outdone—

'far' seems to add no force.[5] And 7 is not strong either.[6] Let this suffice.

But the turns and recoils of your thought (which generally take place in the sestet) are admirable—e.g. I sestet;[7] II 11;[8] III 13, 14 (a really magical stroke);[9] IV throughout;[10] V throughout, best 9;[11] VIII sestet;[12] IX 12;[13] XII 4.[14]

[1] Beneath the lamp of truth I am found untrue, : reading kept.
[2] VIII. *Love Advanced* (*P.W.*, vol. i. 56)   Why
      Dost thou not at one stroke this rebel slay?
(Unaltered, as is the whole sonnet, save for minor changes in punctuation.)
[3] IX. *Fear*. A discarded sonnet, beginning:
      In that dark time, when joys that now delight
      This pampered sense shall vanish and be lost;
      And without rival shall appear of cost
      The subtler powers our mortal passions slight:
[4] XII. *Music*. A discarded sonnet, dealing with Orpheus and Eurydice. It ends:
          his desire
      Mastered his will, he turned, and all was lost.
[5] XIV. *Self-Awakened* (*P.W.*, vol. i, 18: considerable changes).
      And three who all the rest had far outdone, : unaltered.
[6] I saw, and godlike Buonarroti's powers, : unaltered, save for a hyphen.
[7] I. *Introduction*. Afterwards discarded; the sestet runs:
      I pray you, ye that read me, when ye con
      The terms of fancy, question not, nor say
      Who was perchance the lady he looked on?

      I tell you she is not of mortal clay:
      Once she was truly, but she died unwon,
      By death transfigured to the light of day.
[8] II. *Retrospect* (*P.W.*, vol. i, 58: practically re-written).
      But all that seemed divine, all that was new,
became: To life's desire the same, and nothing new:
[9] III. *First Love* (*P.W.*, vol. i. 59: several changes).
Only two changes in punctuation in the last two lines.
[10] IV. *Timidity*. See p. 35, note 4.   [[11, 12, 13, 14] See notes opp.]

About the rhythm. You certainly have the gift and vein of it, but have not quite reached your perfection. Most of your Miltonic rhythms (which by the by are not so very marked as your letter led me to suppose they would be, and I think many modern poets employ them, don't they?) are fine, e.g. I 5, 11;[1] II 11;[2] IV 11;[3] IX 11;[4] XII 4, 13;[5] XIII 12, 13.[6] But III 1[7] has scarcely enough justification (you will allow there must always be a reason and a call for the reversed rhythm); XIII 11[8] on the other hand might well be reinforced—

The happier gift to me cánnot belong—

(You mean *cánnot* of course, not *can nót*).

I have paid much attention to Milton's rhythm. By the by, calling Milton rough reminds me of what Garrett (do you remember him?) overheard at the King's Head—that inn at

[11] v. *Love Strengthened.*
        Ah! but her launchèd passion when she sings.
[12] VIII. See p. 36, note 2.
[13] IX. See p. 36, note 3.
        But then resistless, unmistakeably,
[14] XII. See p. 36, note 4.
        Alas, their sweetest strains left mine eyes wet.

---

[1]   So the perfected soul, now her own mate,
and: Who was perchance the lady he looked on?
[2] See p. 36, note 8.
[3] But fear lest with my fears my hopes should end:
[4] See p. 36, note 3.
        Ill-feeding flies, coward, of puny stings:
[5] See above, note 14, for l. 4.
l. 13:   His hand fell, his voice faltered, his desire
[6] XIII. *Poetry.* Later discarded, beginning:
        The lower animals have this defence,
        Be they ill-hurt or venomously stung,
        Their instinct guides them to that plant among
        The herbs whose virtues salve the wounded sense.
ll. 12, 13: 'Tis in the poet's skill, whose science pure
        Is stored in that eternal city of song,
[7] See p. 36, note 9.
        'Twas on the very day Winter took leave.
[8] See note 6, above.
        The happier gift cannot to me belong?

37

all events at the corner of Holywell Street. An undergraduate
was entertaining some friends and had ordered port. 'Waiter,
I think there is something dirty floating in this wine.' 'I see
nothing but a piece of beeswing, sir.' Collapse. These are the
lines, I suppose, which these folk think will not scan—

> By the waters of life, where'er they sat—[1]
> Light from above, from the fountain of light—[2]
> But to vanquish by wisdom hellish wiles—[3]
> Home to his mother's house private returned—[4]

etc. The choruses of Samson Agonistes are still more remarkable: I think I have mastered them and may some day write on
the subject. However J. A. Symonds has written a paper on
Milton's verse somewhere[5] and it has, I see, received attention
of late. His achievements are quite beyond any other English
poet's, perhaps any modern poet's. It happened that the other
day, before you had written to me on the matter, I composed
two sonnets[6] with rhythmical experiments of the sort, which I
think I will presently enclose. How our wits jump! Not but
what I have long been on metrical experiments more advanced
than these. You will see that my rhythms go further than
yours do in the way of irregularity. The chiming of consonants
I got in part from the Welsh, which is very rich in sound and
imagery.

General remarks—In spite of the Miltonic rhythms and some
other points your sonnets remind one more of Shakspere's.
Milton's sonnets are not tender as Shakspere's are. Yours are
not at all like Wordsworth's, and a good thing too, for beautiful
as those are they have an odious goodiness and neckcloth about
them which half throttles their beauty. The ones I like least are

---

[1] *Paradise Lost*, Book XI, l. 79.
[2] *Paradise Regained*, Book IV, l. 289.
[3] Ibid., Book I, l. 175.   [4] Ibid., Book IV, l. 639.
[5] *The Blank Verse of Milton*, *The Fortnightly Review*, December 1874: best
read in *Blank Verse*, 1895, pp. 73–113: also part of Appendix (pp. 411–28) to
Sketches and Studies in Italy, 1879.
[6] No sonnet in R. B.'s edition bears the exact date of this letter; but *God's
Grandeur* and *The Starlight Night* are probably in question.

those that have a Tennysonian touch about them, as vi[1] and vii,[2] not for want of admiring Tennyson to be sure but because it gives them a degree of neckcloth too. I have not yet *studied* them: at a first and second reading the drift and connection is very hard to find; you seem to mean it to be so. The Our Father sonnet is very beautiful,[3] so is the one on your mother's picture,[4] so is xxii,[5] so are they all and full of manly tenderness and a flowing and never-failing music. The more I read them the more I am delighted with them. Don't like what you say of Milton,[6] I think he was a very bad man: those who contrary to our Lord's command both break themselves and, as St. Paul says, consent to those who break the sacred bond of marriage, like Luther and Milton, fall with eyes open into the terrible judgment of God. Crying up great names, as for instance the reviews do now Swinburne and Hugo, those plagues of mankind, is often wicked and in general is a great vanity and full of impious brag and a blackguard and unspiritual mind.

I think I see what ix 3, 4[7] mean now. It is/And the subtler powers which now our mortal passions make light of, being then without anything to neutralise them will appear of importance.

About Benson etc[8]—That was a lamentable business. I am glad to know it, it throws light to me on what the Epistles say of the avarice of the Gnostic heresiarchs. For what concerns myself I am surprised that those words should have made much impression on you, for I have no doubt that every sect and party employs them of its renegades: they seem made to hand. Nevertheless it is particularly stupid of the Puseyites to do so,

[1] vi. *Art* (*P.W.*, vol. i, 16: practically re-written).
[2] vii. *Uncertainty* (*P.W.*, vol. i. 23: somewhat altered in the sestet). The 'Tennysonian touch' is not apparent: probably it was the spirit of doubt that G. M. H. criticized.
[3] xxiii. *Prayer* (*P.W.*, vol. i. 69: with alterations).
[4] xvii. *Tenderness* (*P.W.*, vol. i, 40: minor changes only).
[5] xxii. *Hope* (*P.W.*, vol. i. 54: minor changes of spelling and punctuation).
[6] xviii. *Praise.* Not reprinted in *P.W.* See NOTE H.
[7] See p. 36, note 3.   [8] To this I have no clue.

since according to them 'verts', as they sillily call them, do no more than if a bird built her nest first in one, then in another bough of the same bush. Benson must have spoken *a priori* of me, for we were not acquainted: I think I may have once met and had a few words with him but that is all.

The examination of which I spoke is called *ad audiendas confessiones*.

You say you don't like Jesuits. Did you ever see one?

Who was St. Beuno? Is he dead? Yes, he did that much 1200 years ago, if I mistake not. He was St. Winefred's uncle[1] and raised her to life when she died in defence of her chastity and at the same time he called out her famous spring, which fills me with devotion every time I see it and wd. fill anyone that has eyes with admiration, the flow of ἀγλαὸν ὕδωρ is so lavish and so beautiful: if you have not read her story (in Butler's *Lives* or elsewhere) you should, though you should treat it as fable, as no doubt you do the Gospels. As for St. Beuno he is a mythological centre to the Welsh and crystallises superstitions or till lately did, as for instance odd marks on cattle were called Beuno's marks.

I hear this morning April 8 that poor A— W—[2] of Trinity is stark mad. He always had insanity in him.

Your affectionate friend

GERARD M. HOPKINS S.J.

And don't *you* say *my* lines don't scan. Observe that I treat *ng* as elisionable, like a Latin *m*.

XXXI (Postcard)

[Postmark imperfect] 6 April [1877].

A junk of a letter is under weigh laden to her gunwales with judicious remarks.

G. M. H.

---

[1] The story of St. Wenefride, or Winefride, V.M., will be found in the Rev. Alban Butler's *The Lives of the Primitive Fathers, Martyrs, and other Principal Saints* . . ., vol. xi (3rd ed., 1799), pp. 71–80.   [2] Editor's omission.

XXXII

St. Beuno's, St. Asaph. June 13 1877.

MY DEAREST BRIDGES,—I see I must send a line to 'put you out of your agony'. Want of convenience of writing was the only cause of my delay. Having both work here to do and serious letters to write I shrank from the 'distressing subject' of rhythm, on which I knew I must enter. I could not even promise to write often or answer promptly, our correspondence lying upon unprofessional matter. However you shall hear me soon.

Yesterday's news was my first knowledge of Dr. Molesworth's death.[1] You do not say how he disposed of his wealth. I am very glad your mother is coming to live with you[2] and shall have all the more reason to visit you—if ever that day should come. What will become of Westwood, Holyoak, Thistlethwaite, the painter in short?[3]

His Virgil[4] is very likely a failure but it cannot be said that Wm. Morris is an ass, no.

I cannot write more now. Your affectionate friend

GERARD M. HOPKINS S.J.

XXXIII (Postcard)

I hope to be in town for a fortnight or so from the 25th. Shall I be able to see you? I was writing, but am not sure whether the letter will go before me and certainly it will be shorter than it was to have been.

G. M. H.

St. Beuno's, St. Asaph. July 18 [1877]. [Postmark doubtful.]

XXXIV

St. Beuno's, St. Asaph. July 23 1877.

DEAREST BRIDGES,—'All would not do', I could not get that letter finished and have made up my mind not to go on with it.

---

[1] He died on 21 April 1877.   [2] At 52 Bedford Square, London.
[3] This seems to mean: 'What will become of Wooldridge if your mother comes to live with you?' See p. 99, note 3.   [4] Published in 1876 [1875].

I was not so brazen as to give myself a tacit invitation to stay with you, as your note seems to imply. Parentage of course will 'put me up', up at Hampstead. But since you say I am to come for dinner, and that at 7, and I am unwilling to be out late, it will be necessary, I think, for me to avail myself of your offer and sleep that night. I look forward, I need not say, to seeing and hearing your treasures (poetical and musical) and yourself. Believe me your affectionate friend

GERARD M. HOPKINS S.J.

I forgot to post this yesterday. July 24.

XXXV

Oak Hill, Hampstead, N.W. Aug. 8 1877.

MY DEAREST BRIDGES,—My bag turned up last night, I therefore send the *Deutschland* herewith:[1] please return it as soon as you conveniently can. I am not sure what day I shall leave Hampstead, as I depend on our Provincial.

To complete the set I enclose the sonnet you have already got, a little corrected.[2] Also correct the skylark one thus—[3]

Man's spirit will be flesh-bound when found at best,
And un·cumberèd: meadow-down is not distressed

For a rainbow foot ing it nor he for his bones· risen.

An article by E. W. G(osse) in July's *Cornhill*, 'a Plea for Certain Exotic Forms of Verse', speaks of and quotes you—a

[1] Part of R. B.'s note to this poem (*Poems*, p. 104) should be recalled here: 'The labour spent on this great metrical experiment must have served to establish the poet's prosody and perhaps his diction: therefore the poem stands logically as well as chronologically in the front of his book, like a great dragon folded in the gate to forbid all entrance, and confident in his strength from past success. This editor advises the reader to circumvent him and attack him later in the rear; for he was himself shamefully worsted in a brave frontal assault, the more easily perhaps because both subject and treatment were distasteful to him. . . .'

[2] This might be one of several written at St. Beuno's.

[3] *Poems*, 15: the last three lines. The printed version has, in l. 2, 'But' for 'And'.

Triolet from your early book.[1] It seems that triolets and rondels and rondeaus and chants royal and what not and anything but serving God are all the fashion.

I heard my sister murmur that she hoped you had not forgotten your promise about the music.*

By the by I should have told you that I would long ago have asked you to dine and sleep here (the latter now impossible) but I thought, and think, that you would not care.

I cannot write more now. Believe me your affectionate friend

GERARD M. HOPKINS S.J.

P.S. The *Deutschland*, though in sprung rhythm, is marked with accents, not great colons, which I had not then thought of. Please remark the difference between ∞, which means a counterpoint, and ⌣, a circumflex, over words like *hēre*, *hēar*, *thēre*, *bēar*, to express that they are to be made to approach two syllables—*he-ar* etc. No, it should be ∼, not ⌣.

* It was the slow movement from a sonata of Corelli's.

XXXVI

Oak Hill, Hampstead, N.W. Aug. 10 1877.

DEAREST BRIDGES,—I shall have no opportunity of seeing you again either at your house or here, for I mean to go to St. Beuno's on Monday. What mystery is there about the Provincial? He is head of our province and as he wants to see me on Sunday there is no longer any reason for my not going away on Monday, as I meant at first.

Much against my inclination I shall have to leave Wales. ✔

My sister was quite in earnest about Corelli and really admires

[1] *The Cornhill Magazine*, July 1877, pp. 53–71. 'In England the triolet is a new comer, but it has already begun to be cultivated. The first specimens printed here, as far as I have been able to discover, were two by Mr. Bridges, in 1873. They were not quite so airy as one might wish, but still, in honour of their precedence, let one ["When first we met we did not guess," *P.W.*, vol. ii, book i. 16] be quoted here.'

him. We don't remember your saying anything about *Quis habitabit*.

Thanking you for your kind entertainments I remain your affectionate friend

GERARD M. HOPKINS S.J.

At my uncle's last night I found your first volume, which he had come to know at Rome and lent about to his friends, but I had not time to read much.

XXXVII

St. Beuno's, St. Asaph. Aug. 21 1877.

DEAREST BRIDGES,—Your letter cannot amuse Father Provincial, for he is on the unfathering deeps outward bound to Jamaica: I shd. not think of telling you anything about his reverence's goings and comings if it were it[1] not that I know this fact has been chronicled in the Catholic papers.

Enough that it amuses me, especially the story about Wooldridge and the Wagnerite, wh. is very good.

Your parody reassures me about your understanding the metre. Only remark, as you say that there is no conceivable licence I shd. not be able to justify, that with all my licences, or rather laws, I am stricter than you and I might say than anybody I know. With the exception of the *Bremen* stanza,[2] which was, I think, the first written after 10 years' interval of silence, and before I had fixed my principles, my rhymes are rigidly good—to the ear—and such rhymes as *love* and *prove* I scout utterly. And my quantity is not like 'Fĭftўtwō Bĕdfŏrd Squāre', where *fĭftў* might pass but *Bĕdfŏrd* I should never admit. Not only so but Swinburne's dactyls and anapaests are halting to my ear: I never allow e.g. *I* or *my* (that is diphthongs, for $I = a + i$ and $my = ma + i$) in the short or weak syllables of those feet, excepting before vowels, semi-vowels, or *r*, and rarely then, or when the measure becomes (what is the word?) molossic[3]—thus: ∪–∪|∪–∪|∪–∪, for then the first short is almost long. If you

---

[1] Thus in MS.   [2] *The Wreck of the Deutschland*, stanza 12.
[3] No: amphibrachic.

44

look again you will see. So that I may say my apparent licences are counterbalanced, and more, by my strictness. In fact all English verse, except Milton's, almost, offends me as 'licentious'. Remember this.

I do not of course claim to have invented *sprung rhythms* but only *sprung rhythm*; I mean that single lines and single instances of it are not uncommon in English and I have pointed them out in lecturing—e.g. 'why should this ∶ desert be?'—which the editors have variously amended; 'There to meet∶ with Macbeth' or 'There to meet with Mac ∶ beth'; Campbell has some throughout the *Battle of the Baltic*—'and their fleet along the deep∶ proudly shone'—and *Ye Mariners*—'as ye sweep∶ through the deep' etc; Moore has some which I cannot recall; there is one in *Grongar Hill*;[1] and, not to speak of *Pom pom*, in Nursery Rhymes, Weather Saws, and Refrains they are very common— but what I do in the *Deutschland* etc is to enfranchise them as a regular and permanent principle of scansion.

There are no outriding feet in the *Deutschland*. An outriding foot is, by a sort of contradiction, a recognized extra-metrical effect; it is and it is not part of the metre; not part of it, not being counted, but part of it by producing a calculated effect which tells in the general success. But the long, e.g. seven-syllabled, feet of the *Deutschland*, are strictly metrical. Outriding feet belong to counterpointed verse, which supposes a well-known and unmistakeable or unforgetable standard rhythm: the *Deutschland* is not counterpointed; counterpoint is excluded by sprung rhythm. But in some of my sonnets[2] I have mingled the two systems: this is the most delicate and difficult business of all.

The choruses in *Samson Agonistes* are intermediate between counterpointed and sprung rhythm. In reality they are sprung, but Milton keeps up a fiction of counterpointing the heard rhythm (which is the same as the mounted rhythm) upon a

[1] Perhaps: Sometimes swift, sometimes slow,
  or: Along with Peace close ally'd,
[2] e.g. *Walking by the Sea* and *In the Valley of the Elwy*.

45

standard rhythm which is never heard but only counted and therefore really does not exist. The want of a metrical notation and the fear of being thought to write mere rhythmic or (who knows what the critics might not have said?) even unrhythmic prose drove him to this. Such rhythm as French and Welsh poetry has is sprung, counterpointed upon a counted rhythm, but it differs from Milton's in being little calculated, not more perhaps than prose consciously written rhythmically, like orations for instance; it is in fact the *native rhythm* of the words used bodily imported into verse; whereas Milton's mounted rhythm is a real poetical rhythm, having its own laws and recurrence, but further embarassed by having to count.

Why do I employ sprung rhythm at all? Because it is the nearest to the rhythm of prose, that is the native and natural rhythm of speech, the least forced, the most rhetorical and emphatic of all possible rhythms, combining, as it seems to me, opposite and, one wd. have thought, incompatible excellences, markedness of rhythm—that is rhythm's self—and naturalness of expression—for why, if it is forcible in prose to say 'lashed: rod',[1] am I obliged to weaken this in verse, which ought to be stronger, not weaker, into 'láshed birch-ród' or something?

My verse is less to be read than heard, as I have told you before; it is oratorical, that is the rhythm is so. I think if you will study what I have here said you will be much more pleased with it and may I say? converted to it.

You ask may you call it 'presumptious jugglery'. No, but only for this reason, that *presumptious* is not English.

I cannot think of altering anything. Why shd. I? I do not write for the public. You are my public and I hope to convert you.

You say you wd. not for any money read my poem again. Nevertheless I beg you will. Besides money, you know, there is love. If it is obscure do not bother yourself with the meaning but pay attention to the best and most intelligible stanzas, as the two last of each part and the narrative of the wreck. If you

---

[1] *The Wreck of the Deutschland*, st. 2, l. 2.

46

had done this you wd. have liked it better and sent me some serviceable criticisms, but now your criticism is of no use, being only a protest memorialising me against my whole policy and proceedings.

I may add for your greater interest and edification that what refers to myself in the poem is all strictly and literally true and did all occur; nothing is added for poetical padding.

Believe me your affectionate friend

GERARD M. HOPKINS S.J.

XXXVIII

Mount St. Mary's College, Chesterfield.[1]

DEAREST BRIDGES,—The above has been my address since October and you may send the Deutschland to it or she will in course of time be lost.

I was pleased and flattered to hear of your calling at Oak Hill and Mrs. Molesworth with you, which was very kind, and that twice: nothing pleasanter could have happened. Remember me very kindly to her and say how glad I was.

Write me an interesting letter. I cannot do so. Life here is as dank as ditch-water and has some of the other qualities of ditch-water: at least I know that I am reduced to great weakness by diarrhoea, which lasts too, as if I were poisoned.

Today Feb. 25 [1878] is a holiday in honour of Pope Leo XIII, or else this note would have lain still longer no doubt.

Believe me your affectionate friend

GERARD M. HOPKINS.

XXXIX

Mount St. Mary's College, Chesterfield. April 2 1878.

MY DEAREST BRIDGES,—Your last letter was very kind indeed, but I should have lost all shame if under any circumstances I

[1] G. M. H. was 'sub-minister' here. After completing his theological studies he was ordained to the priesthood, and went to Farm Street Church, London, as select preacher.

47

had allowed such a thing to be as for you to come hundreds of miles to cure me.

I am overjoyed to hear of your and Mrs. Molesworth's intercourse with Oak Hill.

It was pleasing and flattering to hear that Mr. Pater remembers and takes an interest in me.

My muse turned utterly sullen in the Sheffield smoke-ridden air and I had not written a line till the foundering of the Eurydice the other day[1] and that worked on me and I am making a poem—in my own rhythm but in a measure something like Tennyson's *Violet* (bound with *Maud*);[2] e.g.—

> They say who saw one sea-corpse cold
> How hé was of lovely manly mould,
>   Every inch a tar,
> Of the bést we bóast séamen áre.
>
> Look, from forelock down to foot he,
> Strung by duty is strained to beauty
>   And russet-of-morning-skinned
> With the sún, sált, and whírling wínd.
>
> Oh! his nímble fínger, his gnárled gríp!
> Léagues, léagues of séamanshíp
>   Slumber in his forsaken
> Bones and will not, will not waken.[3]

I have consistently carried out my rhyming system, using the first letter of the next line to complete the rhyme in the line before it.

---

[1] 24 March 1878.

[2] Evidently *The Daisy* is in question, one typical stanza from which is quoted, as the kinship in metre would hardly have been suspected.

> How faintly-flush'd, how phantom-fair,
> Was Monte Rosa, hanging there
>   A thousand shadowy-pencill'd valleys
> And snowy dells in a golden air.

[3] This passage, the most beautiful in the poem (ll. 73–84), was thus probably the nucleus round which it was built. R. B. printed a later version, which illustrates the poet's care in correction.

Well, write those things that 'will tickle me'.

The Deutschland would be more generally interesting if there were more wreck and less discourse, I know, but still it is an ode and not primarily a narrative. There is some narrative in Pindar but the principal business is lyrical. This poem on the Eurydice is hitherto almost all narrative however.

And what are you doing?

From notices in the *Athenaeum* it would appear that Gosse, Dobson, and Co. are still fumbling with triolets, villanelles, and what not.[1]

Believe me your affectionate friend

GERARD M. HOPKINS S.J.

April 3.

XL

Stonyhurst College, Blackburn (or Whalley). May 13 1878.[2]

DEAREST BRIDGES,—Remark the above address. After July I expect to be stationed in town—111 Mount Street, Grosvenor Square.

I hope your bad cold is gone.

I am very glad to hear the Rondeliers have come to see the beauty of your poetry. I have little acquaintance with their own. I have read a rondeau or rondel by Marzials in the *Athenaeum*[3] beginning and ending 'When I see you': it was very graceful and shewing an art and finish rare in English verse. This makes me the more astonished about *Flop flop*.[4] Is his name Spanish, Provençal, or what? Barring breach of

---

[1] There is, for example, in the issue of 23 March 1878, a letter from Austin Dobson on 'The Rondeaux of Wyatt the Elder' and a review of 'Latter-Day Lyrics; being Poems of Sentiment and Reflection by Living Writers. Selected . . . by W. Davenport Adams. With a Note on some Foreign Forms of Verse by Austin Dobson.' The third section contains twenty-two examples of 'exotic' forms of verse in English poetry; and these the reviewer, Edmund Gosse, holds to be the distinguishing feature of the book.

[2] MS. has, by mistake, '1877'.

[3] A Rondel in the issue of 21 April 1877. See NOTE I.

[4] Theophilus Julius Henry Marzials: he was of French extraction.

confidence I wish I could have seen his letter and that of the habitually joyous.[1] I think that school is too artificial and exotic to take root and last, is it not?

I enclose you my Eurydice, which the *Month* refused.[2] It is my only copy.[3] Write no bilgewater about it: I will presently tell you what that is and till then excuse the term. I must tell you I am sorry you never read the Deutschland again.

Granted that it needs study and is obscure, for indeed I was not over-desirous that the meaning of all should be quite clear, at least unmistakeable, you might, without the effort that to make it all out would seem to have required, have nevertheless read it so that lines and stanzas should be left in the memory and superficial impressions deepened, and have liked some without exhausting all. I am sure I have read and enjoyed pages of poetry that way. Why, sometimes one enjoys and admires the very lines one cannot understand, as for instance 'If it were done when 'tis done' sqq.,[4] which is all obscure and disputed, though how fine it is everybody sees and nobody disputes. And so of many more passages in Shakspere and others. Besides you would have got more weathered to the style and its features— not really odd. Now they say that vessels sailing from the port of London will take (perhaps it should be / used once to take) Thames water for the voyage: it was foul and stunk at first as the ship worked but by degrees casting its filth was in a few days very pure and sweet and wholesomer and better than any water in the world. However that maybe, it is true to my purpose. When a new thing, such as my ventures in the Deutschland are, is presented us our first criticisms are not our truest, best, most homefelt, or most lasting but what come easiest on the instant. They are barbarous and like what the ignorant and the ruck say. This was so with you. The Deutschland on her first run worked very much and unsettled you, thickening and

---

[1] Edmund Gosse.

[2] The Jesuit magazine which 'dared not print' the *Deutschland* either.

[3] The poem was eventually printed from a copy of April 1878, corrected some years later.   [4] *Macbeth*, Act I, sc. 7, ll. 1 sqq.

clouding your mind with vulgar mudbottom and common sewage (I see that I am going it with the image) and just then unhappily you *drew off* your criticisms all stinking (a necessity now of the image) and bilgy, whereas if you had let your thoughts cast themselves they would have been clearer in themselves and more to my taste too. I did not heed them therefore, perceiving they were a first drawing-off. Same of the Eurydice—which being short and easy please read more than once.

Can you tell me who that critic in the *Athenaeum*[1] is that writes very long reviews on English and French poets, essayists, and so forth in a style like De Quincey's, very acute in his remarks, provoking, jaunty, and (I am sorry to say) would-be humorous? He always quotes Persian stories (unless he makes them up) and talks about Rabelæsian humour.

My brother's pictures, as you say, are careless and do not aim high, but I don't think it would be much different if he were a batchelor. But, strange to say—and I shd. never even have suspected it if he had not quite simply told me—he has somehow in painting his pictures, though nothing that the pictures express, a high and quite religious aim; however I cannot be more explanatory.

Your bodysnatch story is ghastly, but so are all bodysnatch stories. My grandfather was a surgeon, a fellow-student of Keats', and once conveyed a body through Plymouth at the risk of his own.

Believe me your affectionate friend

GERARD M. HOPKINS S.J.

May 21 1878.

Please remember me very kindly to your mother.

To do the Eurydice any kind of justice you must not slovenly read it with the eyes but with your ears, as if the paper were

---

[1] The marked file of the *Athenaeum* gives Watts (better known as Theodore Watts-Dunton) as the writer of these very readable reviews on Shelley, Hugo, Swinburne, and others.

declaiming it at you.[1] For instance the line 'she had come from a cruise training seamen' read without stress and declaim is mere Lloyd's Shipping Intelligence; properly read it is quite a different thing. Stress is the life of it.

XLI

Stonyhurst, Blackburn. May 30 1878.

DEAREST BRIDGES,—It gave me of course great comfort to read your words of praise. But however, praise or blame, never mingle with your criticisms monstrous and indecent spiritual compliments like something you have said there.

I want to remark on one or two things.

How are hearts of oak furled?[2] Well, in sand and sea water. The image comes out true under the circumstances, otherwise it could not hold together. You are to suppose a stroke or blast in a forest of 'hearts of oak' (=, ad propositum, sound oak-timber) which at one blow both lays them low and buries them in broken earth. *Furling* (*ferrule* is a blunder for *furl*, I think) is *proper* when said of sticks and staves.

So too of *bole*, I don't see your objection here at all.[3] It is not only used by poets but seems technical and *proper* and in the mouth of timber merchants and so forth.

'This was that fell capsize'[4] is read according to the above stresses—two cretics, so to say.

I don't see the difficulty about the 'lurch forward'?[5] Is it in the scanning? which is imitative as usual—an anapaest, fol-

[1] Part of G. M. H.'s note may be added: 'The scanning runs on without break to the end of the stanza, so that each stanza is rather one long line rhymed in passage than four lines with rhymes at the ends.'

[2] *The Loss of the Eurydice*, ll. 5–6.
One stroke
Felled and furled them, the hearts of oak!

[3] Ibid., ll. 15–16:
Must it, worst weather,
Blast bole and bloom together?

[4] Ibid., l. 37.

[5] Ibid., l. 41:   Then a lurch forward, frigate and men;

lowed by a trochee, a dactyl, and a syllable, so that the rhythm is anacrustic or, as I should call it, 'encountering'.

'Cheer's death'[1] = the death of cheer = the dying out of all comfort = despair.

'It is even seen'[2]—You mistake the sense of this as I feared it would be mistaken. I believe I have to be a brave and conscientious man: what I say is that 'even' those who seem unconscientious will act the right part at a great push.

About 'mortholes'[3] I do wince a little but can not now change it. What I dislike much more however is the rhyme 'foot he' to *duty* and *beauty*. In fact I cannot stand it and I want the stanza corrected thus—

> Look, foot to forelock, how all things suit! he
> Is strung by duty, is strained to beauty,
>   And brown-as-dawning-skinned
> With brine and shine and whirling wind.[4]

The difficulty about the Milky Way is perhaps because you do not know the allusion: it is that in Catholic times Walsingham Way was a name for the Milky Way, as being supposed a fingerpost to our Lady's shrine at Walsingham.[5]

'O well wept' should be written asunder, not 'wellwept'. It means 'you do well to weep' and is framed like 'well caught' or 'well run' at a cricketmatch.[6]

---

[1] Ibid., ll. 46–7:
> ... care-drowned and wrapped in
> Cheer's death, ...

[2] Ibid., ll. 53–6:
> It is even seen, time's something server,
> In mankind's medley a duty-swerver,
>   At downright 'No or yes?'
> Doffs all, drives full for righteousness.

[3] This word is not in the printed text: it was probably used as the end word of l. 40, to rhyme with 'portholes', or instead of this last.

[4] This is the printed version.

[5] ll. 101–2:
> That a starlight-wender of ours would say
> The marvellous Milk was Walsingham Way

[6] l. 105:   O well wept, mother have lost son;

Obscurity I do and will try to avoid so far as is consistent with excellences higher than clearness at a first reading. This question of obscurity we will some time speak of but not now. As for affectation I do not believe I am guilty of it: you should point out instances, but as long as mere novelty and boldness strikes you as affectation your criticism strikes me as—as water of the Lower Isis.

I see I have omitted one or two things. If the first stanza is too sudden it can be changed back to what it was at first—

> The Eurydice—it concerned thee, O Lord:
>
> O alas! three hundred hearts on board—

But then it will be necessary to change the third stanza as follows, which you will hardly approve—

> Did she pride her, freighted fully, on[1]
> Bounden bales or a hoard of bullion?—

About 'grimstones'[2] you are mistaken. It is not the remains of a rhyme to *brimstone*. I *could* run you some rhymes on it. You must know, we have a Father Grimstone in our province.

I shall never have leisure or desire to write much. There is one thing I should like to get done, an ode on the Vale of Clwyd begun therein.[3] It would be a curious work if done. It contains metrical attempts other than any you have seen, something like Greek choruses, a peculiar eleven-footed line for instance.

What you have got of mine you may do as you like with about shewing to friends.

Is your own ode on the Eurydice done?[4] Will you send it, as well as other things; which shall be returned.

Believe me your affectionate friend

GERARD M. HOPKINS S.J.

[1] For did she pride her, freighted fully, on: in the printed version.

[2] This word is not in the text printed; but in the MS. of the poem (copied out by R. B.) it is cancelled in st. 7, where 'Heavengravel' is printed.

[3] Probably unfinished, or made use of elsewhere: not among the fragments in *Poems*.

[4] Never completed, if begun: unknown to Mrs. Bridges.

You are kind enough to want me to dine with you on coming up to town. I should have to go to our house at once. I shall have, no doubt, little time when in London but still we shall manage to meet.

May 31.

XLII (Postcard)

I forgot to answer about my metres (rhythms rather, I suppose). Do by all means and you will honour them and me.

G. M. H.[1]

June 9 1878.

XLIII

111 Mount Street. July 13. [1878]

DEAREST BRIDGES,—This ought to have been written before, but let us dissemble it.

I will call on you if nothing hinders (there something easily may) on Monday about two: you say Monday is free, but if you were engaged it wd. not inconvenience me. Dine out we seldom do. I am at present writing 3 sermons to be preached in August; I have little else to do (of duty) and so employ myself in making up my theology, but my work will soon thicken. I am, so far as I know, permanently here, but permanence with us is ginger-bread permanence; cobweb, soapsud, and frost-feather permanence.

I earnestly hope my delay will not have kept you off the Surrey hills. Yours

GERARD HOPKINS.

XLIV

111 Mount Street. Monday evening. [15 July 1878.]

MY DEAR BRIDGES,—In your last but one you said Monday was a free day, that was why I proposed coming this afternoon. Walking to Bedford Square is no great thing and it is mostly more convenient to me to chance finding you than to write. I

---

[1] The importance of this message will be evident later.

will call on Wednesday afternoon however if nothing comes between, but do not inconvenience yourself to stay at home. Dining is out of the question, neither is the hour convenient.

Yours

GERARD HOPKINS.

XLV

111 Mount Street, W. Tuesday afternoon. [16 July 1878.]

DEAREST BRIDGES,—You will learn that I have just called at Bedford Sq. I brought with me a basket of clean linen but did not deliver it. It comes now between these sheets. The Hurrah-ing Sonnet was the outcome of half an hour of extreme enthusi-asm as I walked home alone one day from fishing in the Elwy. I am going to send you a slightly amended copy of the Falcon sonnet.[1] The Curtal Sonnet[2] explains itself, for an experiment in metre (that is, in point of form it is an experiment). I have several things unfinished and one finished, if I could find it. I enclose a poem my father would like you to see. It appears to me that it echoes and expands the thought and in part the wording of 'The summer's rose is to the summer sweet' etc and Gray's 'Full many a flower' stanza; which is a great drawback.

I wanted to make some oral remarks on your Faded Flower song,[3] which is very charming, though not fully filed. Could you not end something like—

Sweet hues have marriage made
With as sweet scents—

or   With sweeter scents—[4]

and   Thy death be that flower's death
And sky thy tomb—?[5]

---

[1] *The Windhover.*

[2] *Pied Beauty.* The note G. M. H. wrote to this poem (preserved in A) is given here: 'when the last syllable of a word has an *l* or *n* preceded in punctuation by a dull pass-vowel (as *dappled, bitten*) this last syllable is not so much a syllable by itself as strengthens the one before it, so that the true scansion is—"dappled: things" &c. But when a vowel begins the next word the syllable counts.'   [3,4,5 See notes opp.]

Also I wish the rhyme *exquisite* could be amended, especially as the next stanza contains a real rhyme to that word.[1]

Believe me your affectionate friend

GERARD M. HOPKINS S.J.

Send my father's poem back, please.

XLVI (Postcard)

[Postmark, London, W., 8 August 1878.]

I will come tomorrow as near after one as Bedford Square is near here, I mean I shall start at one and wish I had said so at once. I cannot come today, because 4.45 is within a quarter of an hour of our dinner time. After two tomorrow do not wait: something will have kept me at home. It must only be a call, as next Sunday's sermon must be learnt better than last's.[2]

I was very little nervous at the beginning and not at all after. It was pure forgetting and flurry. The delivery was not good, but I hope to get a good one in time. I shall welcome any criticisms which are not controversy. I am glad you did not like the music and sorry you did not like the mass.

G. M. H.

Edgell lives in the street and comes to church here regularly.

[3] The reference is to a draft of 'I have loved flowers that fade' (*P.W.*, vol. ii, book ii, 13: which makes three minor corrections in the first printed version—that of 1879).

[4] The measure is:

> I have loved flowers that fade,
> Within whose magic tents
> Rich hues have marriage made
> With sweet unmemoried scents:

G. M. H. proposed another rhythm altogether.

[5] R. B. had written:

> Fear not a flowery death,
> Dread not an airy tomb!

---

[1] This word does not occur in the earliest printed version: possibly it rhymed with 'delight' in the first stanza.

[2] For some remarks on G. M. H. as preacher, with part of one of his sermons, see *Life*, pp. 133–5.

XLVII (Postcard)

[Postmark, London, W., 22 August 1878.]

I sent no notice because I did not know beforehand that I was going. I will come at lunch time on Friday if nothing hinders.

G. M. H.

XLVIII (Postcard)

Beaumont Lodge, Old Windsor. Nov. 3 1878.

I am here for my yearly retreat of eight days and shall be back in town on Tuesday week. But I am to leave London. I meant today to have brought you back your *Academy's*. I will do so on my return. I daresay we may not meet again for years.

G. M. H.

XLIX (Postcard)

St. Aloysius' Church (or Presbytery or 'something churchy'), St. Giles's, Oxford. Dec. 9 1878.

Here I am stationed.

The reason why I could not see you was that after returning from Windsor I cd. not well get to Bedford Sq. except on Thursday afternoon.

More of my acquaintances are up than I thought would be. I have seen Pater. The Paravicinis[1] (Mrs. P. is a convert) very kind. The Puseyites are up to some very dirty jesuitical tricks. Our house very comfortable. Will write.

G. M. H.

L (Postcard)

St. Giles's, Oxford. Dec. 16 1878.

I am very glad of your news. As the French say, j'aurais beau chercher. I had made some searches and was going to undertake more. I suppose your explanation is the true one, for I too

---

[1] Francis de Paravicini (1843-1920), a contemporary of G. M. H. at Balliol, was Fellow of Balliol 1878-1908. See *Life*, p. 133, note.

thought I had got the thing.¹ As it is, please address it to the Rev. Cyprian Splaine, Beaumont Lodge, Old Windsor, who when I was there expressed a curiosity to see my two almost famous Rejected Addresses.² By the by you do spell badly, which once you faintly denied: this time it is 'draw' for 'drawer'. I can shew you.

LI

Catholic Church, St. Giles's, Oxford. Jan. 19 1879.

DEAREST BRIDGES,—In introducing yours and Mr. Dixon's³ Muses to each other I find myself crossed. I have just heard from him. He says his publishers are Smith, Elder, and Co. and as he says nothing about being out of print (indeed that would imply a run and a demand) no doubt you can still get his books, now you know where.⁴ He says *he* cannot get *yours*. Perhaps you told me the impression was sold—of the pamphlet, the G. of L. I mean. But if so you must have some copies. Could you not forward one 'with the author's compliments' to the Rev. R. W. Dixon, Hayton Vicarage, Carlisle? or else through me? I wish you would, and it is your own interest, for a poet is a public in himself.

Now Mr. Dixon having asked me whether I did not myself write, bearing in mind my prize poem⁵ at Highgate (where, I dare say I told you, I first knew him) I told him yes and what, and thereon he asks to see them, and so he shall when I have

---

¹ *The Wreck of the Deutschland.*
² The above, and *The Loss of the Eurydice.*
³ The letter from G. M. H. that began his friendship with R. W. Dixon is of 4 June 1878.
⁴ Dixon had at this time published two books of poems: *Christ's Company and other Poems* (1861) and *Historical Odes and other Poems* (1864). The original sheets are even yet (27 June 1934) not exhausted.
⁵ G. M. H. wrote two school prize poems, *The Escorial* (Easter 1860), and *A Vision of the Mermaids* (Christmas 1862). Both are printed in *Poems,* Second Edition; and the O.U.P. also publishes a facsimile of the second. It is interesting to remark that *The Escorial* was the subject set for the Newdigate in 1860, and the prize poem was by John Addington Symonds.

them to send. Which reminds me that I hope you forwarded the *Deutschland* as directed.

When we met in London we never but once, and then only for a few minutes before parting, spoke on any important subject, but always on literature. This I regret very much. If it had ended in nothing or consisted in nothing but your letting me know your thoughts, that is some of them, it would have been a great advantage to me. And if now by pen and ink you choose to communicate anything I shall be very glad. I should also like to say one thing. You understand of course that I desire to see you a Catholic or, if not that, a Christian or, if not that, at least a believer in the true God (for you told me something of your views about the deity, which were not as they should be). Now you no doubt take for granted that your already being or your ever coming to be[1] any of these things turns on the working of your own mind, influenced or un-influenced by the minds and reasonings of others as the case may be, and on that only. You might on reflection expect me to suggest that it also might and ought to turn on something further, in fact on prayer, and that suggestion I believe I did once make. Still under the circumstances it is one which it is not altogether consistent to make or adopt. But I have another counsel open to no objection and yet I think it will be un-expected. I lay great stress on it. It is to give alms. It may be either in money or in other shapes, the objects for which, with your knowledge of several hospitals, can never be wanting. I daresay indeed you do give alms, still I should say give more: I should be bold to say / give, up to the point of sensible incon-venience. *Fieri non potest ut idem sentiant qui aquam et qui vinum bibant*: the difference of mind and being between the man who finds comfort all round him unbroken unless by constraints which are none of his own seeking and the man who is pinched by his own charity is too great for forecasting, it must be felt: I do not say the difference between being pinched and being at one's ease, that one may easily conceive and most people

[1] MS. 'me'.

know, willynilly, by experience, but the difference between paying heavily for a virtue and not paying at all. It changes the whole man, if anything can; not his mind only but the will and everything. For here something¹ applies like the French bishop's question to his clergy whenever one of them came to tell him that he had intellectual difficulties and must withdraw from the exercise of his priestly functions—*What is her name?* in some such way a man may be far from belief in Christ or God or all he should believe, really and truly so; still the question to be asked would be (not *who is she?*, for that to him is neither here nor there) but *what good have you done?* I am now talking pure christianity, as you may remember, but also I am talking pure sense, as you must see. Now you may have done much good, but yet it may not be enough: I will say, it is not enough. I say this, you understand, on general grounds; I am not judging from particular knowledge, which I have no means to do and it would be very wrong and indiscreet.

Jan. 23—I feel it is very bold, as it is uncalled for, of me to have written the above. Still, if we care for fine verses how much more for a noble life!

I enclose some lines by my father, called forth by the proposal to fell the trees in Well Walk (where Keats and other interesting people lived) and printed in some local paper. See what you think of them. And return them, please.

Believe me your affectionate friend

GERARD M. HOPKINS S.J.

I forget if I ever told you that Addis had left the Oratory and become mission priest at Sydenham.

Our position here is quiet but we make a certain number of converts both from Town and Gown. Mrs. Paravicini, whose husband is Fellow of Balliol (he was my contemporary and is very kind) and her brother is Robert Williams, may be considered as belonging to both; she is a very sweet good creature. Small as Oxford compared to London is, it is far harder to set the Isis on fire than the Thames.

If you have any poetry to send I shall be very glad. If rough copy, I can mentally allow for the last touches.

It has occurred to me that your Pompeian bell may have been intended for a dog, cat, or other domestic animal and $\tau o\hat{i}\varsigma$ $\check{o}\mu\mu\alpha\sigma\iota\nu$ $\dot{v}\pi o\tau\acute{\epsilon}\tau\alpha\gamma\mu\alpha\iota$[1] might mean that the sound was to guide you where to look for the bearer. We have a belled cat in this house. And sheep bells and cattle bells serve this purpose among others, indeed I suppose it is their first end. I do not see that it can have anything to do with the evil eye: the words wd. rather mean / I help the evil eye / than / I help against it.

I have been holding back this letter as if it wd. mellow with keeping, but it is no good. Jan. 24.

LII

St. Giles's, Oxford. Jan. 29 1879.

DEAREST BRIDGES,—Morals and scansion not being in one keeping, we will treat them in separate letters and this one shall be given to the first named subject: the Preface will wait.[2]

You so misunderstand my words (it seems they ought never to have been written: if they meant what you take them to mean I should never have written them) that I am surprised, and not only surprised but put out. For amongst other things I am made to appear a downright fool.

Can you suppose I should send Pater a discipline wrapped up in a sonnet 'with my best love'? Would it not be mad? And it is much the same to burst upon you with an exhortation to mortification (under the name of 'sensible inconvenience')— which mortification too would be in your case aimless. So that I should have the two marks of the foolish counsellor—to advise what is bad to follow and what will not be followed.

But I said that my recommendation was not open to objection. I did not mean as the doctrine of the Real Presence, which

---

[1] Perhaps: 'I am subordinate to the eyes.'
[2] Presumably the discarded preface eventually prefixed to R. B.'s *Poems*, third series, 1880. See NOTE K.

is true and yet may be objected against; I meant what could not be and was not objected against. Unless you object to doing good and call it 'miserable' to be generous. All the world, so to speak, approves of charity and of the corporal works of mercy, though all the world does not practise what it approves of. Even Walt Whitman nurses the sick.

I spoke, then, of alms—alms whether in money or in medical or other aid, such as you from the cases you come across at the hospital might know to be called for. And I said 'sensible inconvenience'; that is, for instance, you might know of someone needing and deserving an alms to give which would require you in prudence to buy no books till next quarter day or to make some equivalent sacrifice of time. These are sensible inconveniences. And to submit to them you cannot, nevertheless, call the reverse of sensible. But to 'derweesh' yourself (please see the Cairo letter in the last *Athenaeum*—or possibly *Academy*),[1] that would *not* be sensible and that is what you took me to mean and that is what it would have been supremely senseless of me to mean.

I added something about it needing the experience to know what it feels like to have put oneself out for charity's sake (or one might say for truth's sake, for honour's sake, for chastity's sake, for any virtue's sake). I meant: everybody knows, or if not can guess, how it feels to be short of money, but everybody may not know, and if not cannot well guess, how it feels to be short of money for charity's sake, etc as above.

All the above appears to me to be put plainly. It reads to me in the blustering bread-and-cheese style. You will ask why I was not as plain at first. Because the blustering bread-and-cheese style is not suited for giving advice, though it may be for defending it. Besides I did not foresee the misunderstanding. What I did fear, and it made me keep the letter back, was that

[1] *The Academy*, 25 Jan. 1879, p. 76: Letter from Cairo, Egypt, dated 4 Jan. 1879, signed Greville J. Chester, and describing the ceremonies connected with the so-called 'Martyrdom' of Hussein, including the fanatic behaviour of two groups of Darweeshes.

you would be offended at my freedom, indeed that you would not answer at all. Whereas, for which I heartily thank you, you have answered three times.

It is true I also asked you to give me, if you liked, an account of your mind—which wd. call for, you say, self examination, and at all events one cannot say what one thinks without thinking. But this and the almsgiving are two independent things mentioned in one letter. No doubt I see a connection, but I do not need you to.

However if I must not only explain what I said but discover what I thought, my thoughts were these—Bridges is all wrong, and it will do no good to reason with him nor even to ask him to pray. Yet there is one thing remains—if he can be got to give alms, of which the Scripture says (I was talking to myself, not you) that they resist sins and that they redeem sins and that they will not let the soul go out into darkness, to give which Daniel advised Nabuchodonosor and Christ the Pharisees, the one a heathen, the other antichristians, and the whole scripture in short so much recommends; of which moreover I have heard so-and-so, whose judgment I would take against any man's on such a point, say that the promise is absolute and that there is for every one a fixed sum at which he will ensure his salvation, though for those who have sinned greatly it may be a very high sum[1] and very distressing to them to give—or keep giving: and not to have the faith is worse than to have sinned deeply, for it is like not being even in the running. Yet I will advise something and it must improve matters and will lead to good. So with hesitation and fear I wrote. And now I hope you see clearly, and when you reply will make your objections, if any, to the practice of almsgiving, not to the use of hairshirts. And I take leave to repeat and you cannot but see, that it is a noble thing and not a miserable something or other to give alms and help the needy and stint ourselves for the sake of the unhappy and deserving. Which I hope will take the bad taste away. And at any rate it is good of you only to misunderstand and be vexed

---

1 These two words written above 'great one', cancelled.

and not to bridle and drop correspondence. Still I do[1] enclose some lines I wrote some years ago in honour of the Bp. of Shrewsbury's 25th year of episcopate,[2] which I say (but wrongly) to have been the 25th of the reestablishment of the hierarchy: it was the 26th. And though the subject may not interest you the lines may and may take tastes out. I have nothing newer. Yes, I will send also a May piece meant for the 'Month of Mary' at Stonyhurst, in which I see little good but the freedom of the rhythm.[3]

And now no more at present: I assure you I have little time for writing. Believe me your affectionate friend

GERARD M. HOPKINS S.J.

Jan. 30—Remember me very kindly to your mother.

LIII

St. Giles's, Oxford. Feb. 15 '79.

DEAREST BRIDGES,—I should have added in my last that the *Silver Jubilee* had been published. It was printed at the end of a sermon, bearing the same title and due to the same occasion, of Fr. John Morris's of our Society. I have found it since I wrote and the copy I sent you from memory is not quite right. The third stanza should stand fourth and run—

> Not today we need lament
> Your lot of life is some way spent:
>   Toil has shed round your head
> Silver, but for Jubilee.[4]

The thought is more pointed. Please correct it if you put it into your album.

No, do not ask Gosse anything of the sort. (1) If I were going to publish, and that soon, such a mention would be 'the puff

---

[1] This word was originally underlined, but the underlining is cancelled.
[2] *Poems*, 6. Written at St. Beuno's College, 1876.
[3] *The May Magnificat, Poems*, 18.
[4] The printed version has *wealth* for *lot* in l. 2, and no comma in the last line.

premilinary',[1] which it wd. be dishonourable of me to allow of. (2) If I did, a mention in one article of one review would do very little indeed, especially as publishing now is out of the question. (3) When I say that I do not mean to publish I speak the truth. I have taken and mean to take no step to do so beyond the attempt I made to print my two wrecks in the *Month*. If some one in authority knew of my having some poems printable and suggested my doing it I shd. not refuse, I should be partly, though not altogether, glad. But that is very unlikely. All therefore that I think of doing is to keep my verses together in one place—at present I have not even correct copies—, that, if anyone shd. like, they might be published after my death. And that again is unlikely, as well as remote. I could add other considerations, as that if I meant to publish at all it ought to be more or ought at least to be followed up, and how can that be? I cannot in conscience spend time on poetry, neither have I the inducements and inspirations that make others compose. Feeling, love in particular, is the great moving power and spring of verse and the only person that I am in love with seldom, especially now, stirs my heart sensibly and when he does I cannot always 'make capital' of it, it would be a sacrilege to do so. Then again I have of myself made verse so laborious.

No doubt my poetry errs on the side of oddness. I hope in time to have a more balanced and Miltonic style. But as air, melody, is what strikes me most of all in music and design in painting, so design, pattern or what I am in the habit of calling 'inscape' is what I above all aim at in poetry. Now it is the virtue of design, pattern, or inscape to be distinctive and it is the vice of distinctiveness to become queer. This vice I cannot have escaped. However 'winding the eyes' is queer only if looked at from the wrong point of view:[2] looked at as a motion in and of the eyeballs it is what you say, but I mean that the eye

---

[1] Thus in MS.
[2] The first three lines of the sestet of *The Lantern out of Doors*:
> Death or distance soon consumes them: wind
> What most I may eye after, be in at the end
> I cannot, and out of sight is out of mind.

winds / only in the sense that its focus or point of sight winds and that coincides with a point of the object and winds with that. For the object, a lantern passing further and further away and bearing now east, now west of one right line, is truly and properly described as winding. That is how it should be taken then.[1]

LIV

St. Giles's, Oxford. Feb. 22 1879.

DEAREST BRIDGES,—Your precious little volume is to hand[2]— also to head and heart, breathing genius everywhere, like sweetherbs. I shd. like to criticise it in detail throughout, but that may not be. Something however I must say.

The jewel of all, judice me, is no. 2. That is a lovely poem.[3] But nevertheless I must tell you that the first verse appears to me to be faulty. It wd. seem to be divided between the two speakers, as the rest of the piece. If so the first two lines shd. be in italics. And if so, then *lay* should be *lies*. Also *Silence!* shd. be *Hush, hush* or *O hush!* If however it is really the inmate who speaks, then the question will be an ironical, not an earnest one, and mean: How can love awake that has lain asleep so long? and if so this shd. be brought out, as by: Should love again awake . . ? But the other sense is smoother, besides that otherwise the question

[1] The letter may not have ended here.

[2] Poems. / By the Author of / 'The Growth of Love.' / [Printer's Device] / Published by Edward Bumpus, / Holborn Bars, London. / 1879.

[3] The lyric beginning:

> Will Love again awake,
> That lay asleep so long?
> Silence! ye tongues that shake
> The drowsy night with song.

In the first printed version the even stanzas are in italics, but the dialogue form is made more apparent when the poem reappears in *P.W.*, vol. ii, book ii (To the Memory of G. M. H.), 1; and the first stanza is divided thus

> Muse.
> Will Love again awake,
> That lies asleep so long?
> Poet.
> O hush! ye tongues that shake
> The drowsy night with song.

seems absurd, for the longer the sleep has been the nearer must the waking be; if it *is* sleep and not death. And in the last verse I should prefer 'And love will wake'.[1] Now as for the meaning, of that you keep the key. Is it the lady of the Growth or another? In verse 2[2] you seem to say it is the same. On the other hand I thought she had gone to heaven. And indeed she seems to have been actually at the telephone, so to speak, when there was the ring of the night bell. (This is profane). As at present advised, I think it is another (and 'whom once he deigned to praise' is said by way of fresh information), but so that all the women a man falls in love with are one woman, being sort of incarnations, or successive avatars of Beauty, Wisdom, and so on, personified in the feminine. Is this so?

The hymn to Nature[3] is fine and has much impressed the mind of my chief, Fr. Parkinson, the Parkinsonian mind, I shd. prefer to say; who read it murmuringly out over tea, with comments and butter. But as he read it I was struck with a certain failure in the blank verse.[4] The verse-paragraphs drag; they are not perfectly achieved. And there are lines that distinctly echo Milton, I mean distinct passages; and Tennyson too. For instance the line about the elephant is almost word for word from *Paradise Lost*[5] if I am not mistaken, but I cannot look it up.

[1] The original reading, 'Love will awake again', was retained.

[2]   *It is a lady fair*
        Whom once he deigned to praise,
        That at the door doth dare
        Her sad complaint to raise.

[3] *Hymn to Nature*, the opening poem, beginning:
        O wonderful Nature, how I do love thee!
        And yet not for thy wonders do I love thee.
It consists in all of 204 blank-verse lines, and is divided into four parts. R. B. did not reprint it.

[4] The blank verse is not markedly individual, but the 'echoings' complained of are, it will be seen, far from 'distinct'.

[5] l. 35: With wieldy trunk the cumbrous elephant.
Paradise Lost, iv. 345-7.
        th' unwieldy Elephant
        To make them mirth us'd all his might, and wreath'd
        His Lithe Proboscis:

And two lines lower I am reminded of *two* passages of Tennyson, one in *In Memoriam* about the Satyr,[1] the other in the *Golden Supper.*[2] The meaning is very bad.

Elegy[3]—unequal, because, as I told you and I now maintain my past judgment, there are two lines in it echoing Gray's:[4] *they do it, they will do it to every ear, it is a great fault to do it, and they do it.* They are not at all the best lines and they can be easily changed and yet they echo lines which are held to be of faultless and canonical beauty. The subject and measure shd. of themselves have put you on your guard. Gray's poem may be outdone but, if you understand, it cannot be equalled. Otherwise the piece is beautiful and full of music. The meaning is bad.[5]

Dejection[6]—reminds me of a poem of Surrey's addressed to London.[7] I do not like the caoutchouc spring-to of the

[1] ll. 37–9:
> When beasts of like rude skin and mighty bone
> Wallowed in tropic ooze, or broke and browsed
> The tangled trees of rank malarious woods, . . .

In Memoriam, xxxv, stanzas 5, 6.
> . . . If Death were seen
> At first as Death, Love had not been,
> Or been in narrowest working shut,
>
> Mere fellowship of sluggish moods,
> Or in his coarsest Satyr-shape
> Had bruised the herb and crush'd the grape,
> And bask'd and batten'd in the woods.

[2] *The Golden Supper:*
> A dismal hostel in a dismal land,
> A flat malarian world of reed and rush!

[3] *Elegy. Among the Tombs.* This poem was reprinted, with no change but the addition of a comma, in *P.W.*, vol. ii, book ii, 10.

[4] These lines do not choose themselves. Perhaps they are:
> Read the worn names of the forgotten dead,
> Their pompous legends will no smile awake.

G. M. H. might, with more justice, have urged that the poem calls back to the mind Arnold's *Stanzas from the Grande Chartreuse.*

[5] The thought in the last four stanzas must necessarily displease G. M. H., especially such lines as
> Nay, were my last hope quenched, I here would sit
> And praise the annihilation of the pit.

[6] Reprinted without change in *P.W.*, vol. ii, book ii, 11.

[7] *A Satire against the Citizens of London.*

inverted rhythms in the first stanza:[1] it is very unsuitable to the feeling of the subject. But the 4th stanza and thereafter is very beautiful.

Covetousness[2]—beautiful in thought and expression, but the beauty gathers to the end, is least in the first quatrain, and the first two lines are commonplace. Also *he may hear* is not good. It is ambiguous: if it means *It is granted him to hear*, then it is has[3] no fault except the being easily mistaken for the other meaning, but if it means *He perhaps hears* it is feeble and downright padding. I shd. like something such as (it is d—d impertinence of me to say this)—

> All drawn with thirst, all lost on sultry sand,
> The traveller fainting finds into his ear
> Fantastic music steal that lets him hear
> Some liquid fountain of his native land.
>
> . . . .
>
> O cruel jest! he cries, as someone flings
> The sparkling drops in sport or shew of ire.
> O shameless! O contempt of holy things!
> They of their wanton pastime never tire
> That, not athirst, are sitting by the springs,
> While he must quench in death his last desire—

(or 'And he must' etc). For though the sequence of thought of 'But of their wanton play' is beautiful, yet the dropping the connection is more austere and pathetic.[4]

Ode to H etc[5]—very good down to 'sit and write', where it

---

[1] Wherefore to-night so full of care,
My soul, revolving hopeless strife,
Pointing at hindrance, and the bare
Painful escapes of fitful life?

[2] Reprinted as No. 43 of *The Growth of Love* (*P.W.*, vol. i). The sonnet is given in its original form in NOTE J.   [3] Thus in MS.

[4] In its final form the punctuation is amended, and two of G. M. H.'s suggestions are adopted: ll. 10–11 now read:
The sparkling drops in sport or shew of ire—
O shameless, O contempt of holy things.

[5] *Ode Written to H—. From —.* This humorous piece has not been re-

70

shd. have ended. The Horatian humour of the fish is real humour. The vulgar verses about Anne leave a bad taste.

The pieces in sprung rhythm[1]—do not quite satisfy me. They do read tentative, experimental; I cannot well say where the thought is distorted by the measure, but that it is distorted I feel by turning from these to the other pieces, where the mastery is so complete. *The Downs* is the best.[2] But while the line 'Where sweeping'[3] is admirable, you would never in another piece have accumulated epithets as you do in 'By delicate'.[4] The Bird-sonnet[5] shews the clearest distortion, though the thought of the last tercet is truly insighted. The *Early Autumn* very beautiful and tender, but in the octet at all events not perfectly achieved.[6] The *Passer By* in particular reads not so much like sprung rhythm as that logaoedic dignified-doggrel one Tennyson has employed in *Maud* and since.[7]

printed. The poet, recovering his health in solitude, tells of a landslide through which the sea has rolled in upon the town:

> And fish have peered at pan and grate
> That cooked their fathers, free from fright:
> While salty tides did estuate
> Upstairs and downstairs, day and night,
> Even where I used to sit and write.

The snug seaward cottage is wrecked, and untenanted:

> Since that old salt, no more my host,
> Weighing the damage that was done,
> Seeing the 'Anne', his boat, was lost,
> And Anne his wife was saved alone,
> Slipped from his moorings, and has gone. . . .

Two further stanzas, and the best, complete the poem. The lines about Anne savour of Hood rather than vulgarity. It is curious that G. M. H., whose taste in his own comic verses is uncertain, should make this objection.

[1] *A Passer By, The Downs, Sonnet* (I would be a bird,—and straight on wings I arise), *Early Autumn. Sonnet* (So hot the noon was, with lilies the bank so gay).

[2] Reprinted, with a few minor alterations, in *P.W.*, vol. ii, book ii, 7.

[3] Where sweeping in phantom silence the cloudland flies.

[4] By delicate miniature dainty flowers adorned!

[5] Reprinted, with amended punctuation only, as No. 22 in *The Growth of Love* (*P.W.*, vol. i).

[6] Not reprinted in *P.W.*, which is a pity, for the sestet is finely wrought.

[7] Reprinted, without alteration, in *P.W.*, vol. ii, book ii, 2. This judgement is harsh and hypercritical.

71

These are all the faults I find. But by the by you should write *crabbed*, not *crabbèd*,[1] which is as wrong as *blessèd, learnèd, crookèd, wickèd* would be. And there shd. be no commas after *smile* and *lip* on page 15.[2] I daresay there are other mispointings. Now let us stop for a time.

Feb. 24.

Second thoughts—I suppose *he may hear* really is nothing but *he can hear*, as in 'From Hampstead Heath you may hear the Great Bell of Westminster', or 'you may see Windsor Castle', which is somewhat oldfashioned. But the meaning shd. be felt at once.[3] The following is perhaps a better suggestion than the above—

> The traveller, fainting, steal upon (*or* into) his ear
> Finds a fantastic music that lets hear

etc and nearer yours.

Feb. 25—The 'I have loved flowers' song is a gem that shd. be eternal. But to me the workmanship does not seem perfect, and it is not as in 'Will Love again awake?' a slight change in two places I want but a reshaping of each stanza. And this I did to my own satisfaction in and out of bed last night, but to tell you how wd. make you mad. I confine myself to pointing out that lines 5 and 6. ought to be transposed of course: a honey-moon delight, by that mark, ages in a month.[4]

Feb. 26—And finally I must say how pleased and proud I am. Besides the feeling richness of phrase in so many places, the sequence in it, and the constant music, it does me good, the freshness and buoyancy and independence I find in your poems, marked with character throughout and human nature and not 'arrangements in vowel sounds', as Mallock says,[5] very

---

[1] *P.W.*, vol. ii, book ii, 8, *Spring, Ode I*, st. 8, l. 2. The accent is retained.

[2] The commas are retained: *The smile, that rests to play*
                Upon her lip, foretells . . .

[3] Not a rule that G. M. H. wished to be judged by.

[4] This change was made.

[5] William Hurrell Mallock (1849–1923), a Balliol man who won the Newdigate in 1871 (*The Isthmus of Suez*), and took a 2nd in Greats in 1874. He published *Every Man his own Poet* (1872), a series of articles in the *Nine-*

thinly costuming a strain of conventional passion, kept up by stimulants, and crying always in a high head voice about flesh and flowers and democracy and damnation.[1] But no matter what you are *not* like. Neither can I now longer descant on what you are, for I must get this off. I shd. like to hear what critics say; advertise me of particular notices: I can go to the Union and see. Your imagery seems more vivid now than formerly and the stamp of character, as in the Invitation and answer,[2] Waterparty,[3] Friedfish piece,[4] and elsewhere is the finest foundation for all the more imitable graces, itself not imitable. As I am criticising you, so does Christ, only more correctly and more affectionately, both as a poet and as a man; and he is a judge qui potest et animam et corpus perdere in gehennam.

You have not shewn me Mr. Dixon's letter.[5] If you do not like say so; if you do not say so send.

Believe me your loving friend

GERARD M. HOPKINS S.J.

I have two sonnets soaking,[6] which if they shd. come to anything you shall have, and something, if I cd. only seize it, on the decline of wild nature, beginning somehow like this—

> O where is it, the wilderness,
> The wildness of the wilderness?
> Where is it, the wilderness?

teenth Century (1877–8) on *Is Life Worth Living?* (book-form 1879), his best-known work *The New Republic* in 1877, and *The New Paul and Virginia, or Positivism on an Island* in 1878.

[1] The reference is to Swinburne. The second series of *Poems and Ballads* appeared in 1878.

[2] *Spring, Ode I. Invitation to the Country* (reprinted *P.W.*, vol. ii, book ii, 8, with six lines altered), and *Spring, Ode II, Reply* (reprinted *P.W.*, vol. ii, book ii, 9, with four lines altered).

[3] *A Water-Party* (reprinted without alteration, *P.W.*, vol. ii, book ii, 6).

[4] *Ode. Written to H—. From—*. See p. 70.

[5] R. B.'s relations with R. W. Dixon are beautifully recorded in the *Memoir* prefixed to a selection of Dixon's poems (Murray, 1909), and reprinted in *Three Friends* (O.U.P. 1932).

[6] Probably *Duns Scotus's Oxford* and *Henry Purcell*.

and ending—

> And wander in the wilderness;
> In the weedy wilderness,
> Wander in the wilderness.[1]

LV (Postcard)

St. Giles's, Oxford. March 3 1879.

I could not write what you wanted, I was pressed to extremities. Yes, the Historic Odes[2] are dull; 'powerful dullness' G. A. Simcox called that volume. But read in it the Tale of Dauphiny and 'It is the time to tell of fatal love'; in the other volume[3] 'Love's Consolation', in 'St. John' the flight of the Medusa, the archangelic march-past, and the mystical woman whose beauty was like such an assortment of things; also 'Mother and Daughter', the 'Ode to Shadow', 'La Faerie', and, by the by, 'St. Paul' throughout. The obscurity is a great fault: from remarkably clear speaking he will lapse into a gibberish. But the imagery, colouring especially, is rich in the extreme, as like Keats as anyone that has been since has succeeded in being. Pathos very real and touching. Curious wierdness,[4] rather morbid. Very fine metaphysical touches here and there, but lost in wildernesses. The last line of 'Love's Consolation' is a wonderful touch of genius.[5] I do not know that there is anything in his 'periods' I particularly admire.

G. M. H.

Will write soon. Jowett has been preaching curiously.[6]

---

[1] Probably abandoned: it is not in the published poems and fragments: but cf. *Poems*, 33, *Inversnaid*, st. 4.

[2] R. W. Dixon's *Historical Odes and other Poems*.

[3] R. W. Dixon's *Christ's Company and other Poems*.

[4] Thus in MS.

[5] The line, torn from its context, is:

> Wind and much wintry blue then swept the earth.

[6] Benjamin Jowett, Regius Professor of Greek at Oxford, had been Master of Balliol since 1870.

LVI (Postcard)

St. Giles's, Oxford. April 8 1879.

The reason you have not heard from me sooner is that my chief Rev. T. B. P. has thought well to break his collarbone and be laid up in a charming country house commanding the White Horse Vale, throwing the whole of the work at the hardest time of the year on his underling. In fact I am very hard put to it. Yes, I happened to see the *Academy*.[1] But I liked it and meant to tell you. What do you object to in digesting your powers? The physiological difficulty? You must feel that. Otherwise it is no hardship to anyone to say he will do better yet and be more master of himself than even now. Let me mention that the passage of Milton I referred to is P. L. IV 345. if I mistake not. Please look: you will see that you shd. be careful. And I repeat that those stanzas are vulgar; but not because you made a friend of an old fisherman (how little you know to think that!), but because of the 'Anne' and 'Anne' joke suggestive of horn-jokes, Benedicks, and all that kind of thing, tedious when not odious. I do not say yours goes so far as to be tedious or odious, still it may be vulgar. What does Sanday[2] write? Genial admiration? I hope so. Not read my writing? Alas, how far from the path of salvation must that man be that endeavours to persuade his conscience he cannot read my writing! Will he not make his generation messes to gorge his appetite?[3] I have

---

[1] *The Academy* of 5 April 1879 has a short, unsigned, very appreciative review of *Poems*, by the Author of the *Growth of Love*. All interested in poetry are advised to read this pamphlet, which 'contains some very remarkable work. We do not think that the author has as yet fully digested his own powers, and his work is apt to contain blemishes by the side of its beauties. But the beauties are undeniable, and, what is perhaps of more importance, they are not in the least copied or reflected from the beauties of anybody else.' 'I have loved flowers that fade' is quoted as one of the clearest and least blemished poems in the collection, and 'A Passer-by' is remarked on as ' an attempt at a choric rhythm which we take to be choriambic in base'.

[2] The Rev. W. Sanday, the well-known biblical scholar (Corpus Christi College, Oxford, 1st class in Greats, 1865). He was a friend from Oxford days, for whom R. B. had a great affection.   [3] *Lear*, Act I, sc. 1, ll. 119–20.

seen Gosse's book reviewed;[1] what shd. I do reading about Dutch poets that cannot find time for my necessary duties? By the by I think nothing in the book is better than the Town and Country pieces (though the countryman has the best of it): such steady music, like tunes from Storace,[2] Linley,[3] *Midas*,[4] and old English masters; and such a shaping out of two men of character. May you use my suggestions? But why else do I make them? If you will do me the honour. Rather look upon them as shoelasts on which to shape your final handiwork. (This wd. be cobbling; but take the image the easy way of the fur.) Am still more puzzled abt. the person at the door. Had clung to 'Once she was truly' as a literal or historical straw in a sea of allegory. Must withdraw the criticism abt. Gray so far as to say now 'every *right*-minded person'.[5] Will answer questions and conclude in a letter.

GERARD HOPKINS.

LVII (Postcard)

Oxford, April 8 1879.

To continue. That about 'disjunctive' was rubbish, founded upon nothing, and shd. not have been said.

The kind people of the sonnet were the Watsons of Shooter's Hill, nothing to do with the Elwy.[6] The facts were as stated. You misunderstand the thought, which is very far fetched. The frame of the sonnet is a rule of three sum *wrong*, thus: As the sweet smell to those kind people so the Welsh landscape is NOT to the Welsh; and then the author and principle of all four terms

---

[1] *Studies in the Literature of Northern Europe*, 1879.

[2] Stephen Storace (1763–96), writer and producer of operas.

[3] Thomas Linley (1733–95), father-in-law of Sheridan and an English composer of note.

[4] The English Ballad opera, a parody of Italian opera, played in Ireland before it was produced at Covent Garden in 1764. The music was selected from popular melodies, and includes the song, 'Pray goody please to moderate the rancour of your Tongue,' the air of which (see *Grove's Dictionary*), has been variously ascribed to Rousseau, Oswald, and Burney. G. M. H. particularly admired this song.

[5] See p. 69.   [6] *In the Valley of the Elwy, Poems*, 16.

is asked to bring the sum right. The One of the Eurydice is Duns Scotus, on whom I have a sonnet lately done which I will send you. The thought is: the island was so Marian that the very Milky Way we made a roadmark to that person's shrine and from one of our seats of learning (to wit the above) went forth the first great champion of her Immaculate Conception, now in our days made an article of faith.

The Passer By may be spontaneous without being smooth. Our first thoughts in this kind are not our smoothest, e.g. that about 'Grandest feathery' etc reminds one of Tennyson's experiments in Alcaics and so on.[1]

I shall study the Hymn better. What makes the periods drag to me is the suspended grammar: it is like tunes ending on the dominant and what not. I do not remember praising Canon D's. periods. His sequence of phrase and feeling, yes, but in short passages. I wonder, by the by, what you can have said that fell short of expectation. Must be a covetous old canon; shd. think abt. his soul.

G. M. H.

LVIII

April 9 1879. Oxford.

Since my last postcard the good Canon has sent me a 'note of admiration' and makes the characteristic proposal to introduce me to the public by 'an abrupt footnote' under the year 1540 on the same grounds as you were for suborning Gosse.

I return you now his letters, which it gave me the greatest pleasure to read.

I am not surprised at your not liking the May Magnificat, which has about it something displeasing to myself.[2] But the Silver Jubilee I do not regret: it seems to me to hit the mark it

[1] Nor is aught from the foaming reef to the snowcapped, grandest
   Peak, that is over the feathery palms more fair
 Than thou so upright, so stately, and still thou standest.
This, the end of st. 2, remains unchanged.
[2] The lush, yet fresh, beauty of the descriptive writing, which conveys the very 'feel' of May-time, clashes inevitably with praise of the Virgin Mary. Perhaps that is the reason.

77

aims at without any wrying. Both of course are 'popular' pieces, in which I feel myself to come short. As soon as I have time to write them out you shall have 'Duns Scotus's Oxford' (sonnet) and a little lyric 'Binsey Poplars'. Your affectionate

GERARD M. HOPKINS S.J.

I hope the sea will do you good.

LIX

Catholic Church, St. Giles's, Oxford. April 22 1879.

DEAREST BRIDGES,—I fully answered your question about the 'one' in the Eurydice. You seem to have meant to ask two questions about it, but you did ask only one. (You asked also about one of the sonnets.) What you now say shews me that you must have fallen into some unaccountable misunderstanding about the 'hero' stanza.[1] The words are put into the mouth of a mother, wife, or sweetheart who has lost a son, husband, or lover respectively by the disaster and who prays Christ, whom she addresses 'Hero savest', that is, 'Hero that savest', that is, Hero of a Saviour, to save (that is, have saved) her hero, that is, her son, husband, or lover: 'Hero of a Saviour' (the line means) 'be the saviour of my hero'. There is no connection with the 'one' before the aposiopesis; I cannot think how you came to suppose any.

The Anne joke is all that I object to. But beyond that I do not think those stanzas after the fried fish very pointed or equal to the rest.

I do think the Spring Odes excellent. But I will make two objections. The first is on 'astride'.[2] The stanza is very good,

---

[1]   But to Christ lord of thunder
        Crouch; lay knee by earth low under!
          'Holiest, loveliest, bravest,
       Save my hero, O Hero savest.'
R. B. calls this liberty, 'Omission of relative pronoun at its worst.'

[2]   Or sit and sing outright
        Their patient teams astride.
The emendations suggested by G. M. H. were adopted.

but I think that ploughmen never, that is, speaking typically never, bestride their teams, that is, their horses, but always sit side-saddle. Could it not be something like 'Or jaunt and sing outright As by their teams they stride'? Secondly the first two stanzas of the Townsman's answer seem poorer than the rest.[1] The rhymes have a great charm, I envy you the metre; though perhaps the following frame, which is harder, wd. be better still—A B B A A C C A.[2]

Willert[3] said he had been seeing you.

I think I have seen nothing of Lang's but in some magazine; also a sonnet prefixed to his translation of the Odyssey. I liked what I read, but not so that it left a deep impression. It is in the Swinburnian kind, is it not? (I do not think that kind goes far: it expresses passion but not feeling, much less character. This I say in general or of Swinburne in particular. Swinburne's genius is astonishing, but it will, I think, only do one thing.) Everybody cannot be expected to like my pieces. Moreover the oddness may make them repulsive at first and yet Lang might have liked them on a second reading. Indeed when, on somebody returning me the *Eurydice*, I opened and read some lines, reading, as one commonly reads whether prose or verse, with the eyes, so to say, only, it struck me aghast with a kind of raw nakedness and unmitigated violence I was unprepared for: but take breath and read it with the ears, as I always wish to be read, and my verse becomes all right. I do warm to that good Mr. Gosse for liking and, you say, 'taking' my pieces: I may then have contributed fuel to his Habitual Joy.

---

[1] The first stanza is unaltered, but the first four lines of the second:

> For men in street and square
> Her tardy trees relent,
> As some far-travell'd scent
> Kindles the morning air;—

were refashioned, but not, I think, for the better.

[2] The form is A B B A C D C D.

[3] Most probably Paul F. Willert of Corpus Christi College, Oxford (Taylorian Scholar 1863, 1st in Greats, 1866), Fellow of Exeter College, a lifelong friend of R. B.

No, I was not thinking of myself when I warned you of your danger and there was no need. Your only obligations to me you expressed in the discarded preface.[1] 'Hail is hurling'[2] did remind me of myself but I do not well know why: I have something about hail and elsewhere several things about hurling, but that does not amount to hail hurling. 'Father fond' wd. never have occurred to me, at all events it never had.[3] Beyond this I do not think it desirable that I shd. be wholly uninfluenced by you or you by me; one ought to be independent but not unimpressionable: that wd. be to refuse education.

I now enclose two sonnets and 'Binsey Poplars' (in which, more by token, you might say that 'wind-wandering' came from your 'wind-wavering'—which latter is found in Burns and, I suppose, elsewhere). What do you think of the effect of the Alexandrines? That metre unless much broken, as I do by outrides, is very tedious.[4]

I do not much expect to be long at Oxford. I shd. like however to see the Spring out: hitherto there is none.

I do not want those stanzas in the Seaford letter struck out, only I think they might have been better.[5]

I shd. tell you I have the same feeling about the two water-pieces as about the Spring odes. For instance I take a delight

---

[1] The reference is to the pieces in sprung rhythm. There is no preface to *Poems*, 1879, but to *Poems*, third series, 1880, is prefixed an important note about those poems written by the rules of a new prosody, for which the author thanks a friend, 'whose poems remain, he regrets to say, in manuscript.' For this see NOTE K.

[2] *A Passer By*, st. 1, l. 6. When skies are cold and misty, and hail is hurling. *The Wreck of the Deutschland*, st. 3, l. 2, has 'the hurtle of hell', and st. 13, l. 2, 'Hurling the haven behind.'

[3] *Morning Hymn* (reprinted in *P.W.*, vol. ii, book ii, 12), st. 3:
> . . . and near
> As father fond art found.

The Wreck of the Deutschland, st. 9, l. 7:
> Father and fondler of heart thou hast wrung.

and the last line of *In the Valley of the Elwy*:
> Being mighty a master, being a father and fond.

[4] A reference to the sonnet, *Henry Purcell*.

[5] *Ode written to H—. From —.*

in 'Guard, Hamadryades' sqq.[1] A touch less and the humour wd. die out; a touch more (as 'shirts' for 'clothes') and it wd. be buffoonery. The feeling of 'business' (in the dramatic sense) given by scattering in touches of landscape between the stages of landing, stripping, and so on is in the highest degree bright and refreshing. Your affectionate friend

GERARD M. HOPKINS S.J.

LX

St. Giles's, Oxford. May 26 1879.

DEAREST BRIDGES,—Your answerable letterage is three deep at least, but nevertheless work is work and of late Fr. Parkinson has sprung a leak (exema) in his leg and been laid up and I in consequence laid on all the harder: indeed he will never, I believe, be very active more, though now he does go about a little.

I shall be very glad to have your brother's book when it appears,[2] and to trace the prototype of you in it will be very interesting.

I have seen no more reviews of you.

The poem you send[3] is fine in thought, but I am not satisfied with the execution altogether: the pictures, except in the first stanza, are somewhat wanting in distinction (I do not of course mean distinctness), and I do not think the rhythm perfect, e.g. 'woodbine with'[4] is a heavy dactyl. Since the syllables in sprung rhythm are not counted, time or equality in strength is of more importance than in common counted rhythm, and your times

[1] *A Water-Party*, st. 3 (*P.W.*, vol. ii, book ii, 6):
       Guard, Hamadryades,
       Our clothes laid by your trees!

[2] John Affleck Bridges, R. B.'s eldest brother: of the book, *Wet Days*, more will be heard. He also published other verses, two novels, and his reminiscences.

[3] *The Voice of Nature*, printed in *Poems*, Third Series, 1880 (*P.W.*, vol. ii, book ii, 3: unaltered, save for the introduction of one capital letter).

[4] My hedges of rose and woodbine, with walks between. (st. 4, l. 6.)

or strengths do not seem to me equal enough. The line you mark does resemble something in the Deutschland, now that you point it out, but there is no resemblance in the thought and it does not matter.[1] I do not think the line very good; it is besides ambiguous. I understand, I believe everybody would understand, 'O if it were only for thee'[2] to mean/If I had no guide (to nature's true meaning) but thee: the leading thought is that nature has two different, two opposite aspects, teaching opposite lessons of life—that one is between two stools with the two of them. Is it not? The whole mood and vein is remote; unknown to many temperaments; ineffective, I should think, with any; belonging to the world of imagination, but genuinely so. I believe you might have expressed it more pointedly though.

Of course I am very much pleased that you like my period-building (or whatever we are to call it) but do not see what is the matter with Patmore's. It is his Unknown Eros you refer to, I suppose.[3] The faults I see in him are bad rhymes; continued obscurity; and, the most serious, a certain frigidity when, as often, the feeling does not flush and fuse the language. But for insight he beats all our living poets, his insight is really profound, and he has an exquisiteness, farfetchedness, of imagery worthy of the best things of the Caroline age. However I cannot spend more time on his praises.

I agree with you that English terza rima[4] is (so far as I have

---

   1   Ah! if it were only for thee, thou restless ocean
           Of waves that follow and roar, the sweep of the tides;
           Wer't only for thee, impetuous wind, whose motion
               Precipitate all o'errides, and turns, nor abides.   (st. 2, ll. 1–4.)

The last line perhaps owes something to a line in st. 32 of *The Wreck of the Deutschland*:

                             throned behind
    Death with a sovereignty that heeds but hides, bodes but abides.

   2 See note above.

   3 Patmore's *Odes* [not published] have a Preface dated 17 April 1868. *The Unknown Eros and other Odes*, I–XXXI, appeared in 1877; *The Unknown Eros*, I–XLVI, in 1878. G. M. H. first met Patmore in the summer of 1883.

   4 Probably the reference was to the use of this measure by R. W. Dixon for his narrative poem, *Mano*, of which more will be heard later.

seen it) badly made and tedious and for the reason you give, but you are mistak[en] in thinking the triplet structure is unknown: Shelley's West Wind ode[1] (if I mistake not) and some other ones are *printed* in detached 3-line stanzas. I wrote a little piece so printed when at school and published it in *Once a Week*.[2]

The sestet of the Purcell sonnet is not so clearly worked out as I could wish. The thought is that as the seabird opening his wings with a whiff of wind in your face means the whirr of the motion, but also unaware gives you a whiff of knowledge about his plumage, the marking of which stamps his species, that he does not mean, so Purcell, seemingly intent only on the thought or feeling he is to express or call out, incidentally lets you remark the individualising marks of his own genius.

Sake is a word I find it convenient to use: I did not know when I did so first that it is common in German, in the form *sach*.[3] It is the *sake* of 'for the sake of', *forsake, namesake, keepsake*. I mean by it the being a thing has outside itself, as a voice by its echo, a face by its reflection, a body by its shadow, a man by his name, fame, or memory, *and also* that in the thing by virtue of which especially it has this being abroad, and that is something distinctive, marked, specifically or individually speaking, as for a voice and echo clearness; for a reflected image light, brightness; for a shadow-casting body bulk; for a man genius, great achievements, amiability, and so on. In this case it is, as the sonnet says, distinctive quality in genius.

Wuthering is a Northcountry word for the noise and rush of wind: hence Emily Brontë's 'Wuthering Heights'.

By *moonmarks* I mean crescent shaped markings on the quill-feathers, either in the colouring of the feather or made by the overlapping of one on another.

---

[1] Each section, of course, ends with a rhyming couplet. Shelley's *Triumph of Life*, Browning's *The Statue and the Bust*, and Morris's *Defence of Guenevere* might have been added, as considerable modern poems; and the pioneer work of Wyatt and Surrey deserved mention.

[2] *Winter with the Gulf Stream* (*Poems*: second edition, Appendix, 83).

[3] See p. 85.

My sister Kate is staying here with my aunt Mrs. Marsland Hopkins (who has now a house in Holywell).

Believe me your affectionate friend

GERARD M. HOPKINS S.J.

May 31 1879.

LXI

St. Giles's, Oxford. June 22 1879.

DEAREST BRIDGES,—I went to see Dr. Tuckwell the very next morning. I found him, besides the service he did me, a kind and gentlemanly man. He thought it was not so much dysentery I had as an irritation due to the remains left by the operation for piles, though that was some years ago. He gave me á comforting prescription, which did the required work and rather more, so I gave up taking the bottle half through, but keep it by me. I am now well, barring fatigue, which easily comes over me.

I enclose you two sonnets, capable of further finish.[1] I am afraid they are not very good all through. One is a companion to the Lantern, not at first meant to be though, but it fell in. The other is historical, autobiographical, as you would say, or biographical. Remark what strikes you.

By the by your remark on Purcell's music does not conflict with what my sonnet says, rather it supports it. My sonnet means 'Purcell's music is none of your d—d subjective rot' (so to speak). Read it again. Edmund Gurney appears to write very well on music in the *Nineteenth Century*.[2]

I am also writing a piece in the metre of your no. 2, quatrains of sixes, I mean;[3] also a curious little piece something like

[1] *The Candle Indoors* ('Oxford '79') and *The Handsome Heart* ('Oxford '79').

[2] Edmund Gurney contributed two articles to the *Nineteenth Century* (July 1878, June 1879), *On Music and Musical Criticism*. He published *The Power of Sound* in 1880, and was interested in psychical research.

[3] He had already expressed his admiration for this metre. Possibly the fragment entitled *On a Piece of Music* is in question (*Poems*, 67): it begins:

> How all's to one thing wrought!
> The members, how they sit!
> O what a tune the thought
> Most be that fancied it.

84

Binsey Poplars but shorter, in a sort of measure like 'With a hey and a ho, and a nonny nonny no'.[1] I shall shortly send you an amended copy of the *Windhover*: the amendment only touches a single line, I think, but as that is the best thing I ever wrote I shd. like you to have it in its best form.

Believe me your affectionate friend

GERARD M. HOPKINS S.J.

LXII

St. Giles's, Oxford. Aug. 14 1879.

MY DEAREST BRIDGES,—I must try and tersely scribble you something.

That German word is *sache*, not *sach*, except in compounds: you should have set me right.

Your Picnic verses are very good, the rhymes capital, beyond the ingenuity I credited you with. Some lines however are faulty, as 'Anything more delicious'.[2]

Muirhead, who called here on Sunday, was on that party. I mean Muirhead, who was on that party, called etc.

I wish you would send me all the music you have, to try. I wd. return it.[3] I do not yet the present piece nor comment on it, as I have not had an opportunity of hearing it. I feel sure you have a genius in music—on the strength of the only piece I know 'O earlier': it is an inspiration of melody, but somewhat 'sicklied o'er', as indeed the words are.

To rejoin on some points of your criticisms. Though the analogy in the Candle sonnet may seem forced, yet it is an 'autobiographical' fact that I was influenced and acted on the way there said.

I send a recast[4] of the Handsome Heart. Nevertheless the

[1] Perhaps *Morning Midday and Evening Sacrifice* ('Oxford, Aug. '79').

[2] Mrs. Bridges writes: 'R. B. used occasionally to write comic verses with ingenious rhymes to amuse his friends. I know there was one on a river picnic. I have no copy of it, but seem to remember hearing this line quoted, among others.'   [3] See p. 14, note 1, and p. 29, note 4.

[4] 'improved copy' cancelled in MS.

offence of the rhymes is repeated.[1] I felt myself the objection
you make and should only employ the device very sparingly,
but you are to know that it has a particular effect, an effect of
climax, and shd. so be read, with a rising inflection, after which
the next line, beginning with the enclitic, gracefully falls away.
And in like manner with proclitics and so on: if a strong word
and its epithet or other appendage are divided so that the
appendage shall end one line and the supporting word begin
the next, the last becomes emphasised by position and heads a
fall-away or diminuendo. These little graces help the 'overreaving' of the verse at which I so much aim, make it flow in
one long strain to the end of the stanza and so forth.

I am somewhat surprised at your liking this sonnet so much.
I thought it not very good. The story was that last Lent, when
Fr. Parkinson was laid up in the country, two boys of our congregation gave me much help in the sacristy in Holy Week.
I offered them money for their services, which the elder refused,
but being pressed consented to take it laid out in a book. The
younger followed suit; then when some days after I asked him
what I shd. buy answered as in the sonnet. His father is Italian
and therefore sells ices. I find within my professional experience
now a good deal of matter to write on. I hope to enclose a little
scene that touched me at Mount St. Mary's.[2] It is something
in Wordsworth's manner; which is, I know, inimitable and un-
approachable, still I shall be glad to know if you think it a
success, for pathos has a point as precise as jest has and its
happiness 'lies ever in the ear of him that hears, not in the
mouth of him that makes'. I hope also soon to shew you a finer
thing, in a metre something like the Eurydice,[3] not quite

[1] See R. B.'s note on the poem. The first five lines, as the poem is printed,
are:

> 'But tell me, child, your choice; what shall I buy
> You?'—'Father, what you buy me I like best.'
> With the sweetest air that said, still plied and pressed,
> He swung to his first poised purport of reply.
>
> What the heart is! which, like carriers let fly—

[2] *The Brothers* (*Poems*, 30).
[3] *The Bugler's First Communion* (*Poems*, 23).

finished yet; also a little song[1] not unlike 'I have loved flowers that fade'. I have added some strokes to the Vale of Clwyd[2] and have hopes of some day finishing it: it is more like your Hymn to Nature than anything else I can think of, the rhythm however widely unlike. Lastly I enclose a sonnet on which I invite minute criticism.[3] I endeavoured in it at a more Miltonic plainness and severity than I have anywhere else. I cannot say it has turned out severe, still less plain, but it seems almost free from quaintness and in aiming at one excellence I may have hit another.

I had quite forgotten the sonnet you have found, but can now recall almost all of it; not so the other piece, birthday lines to me sister, I fancy.

Baliol is the old spelling and the one I prefer, but they have adopted Balliol and one must conform.

I was almost a great admirer of Barnes' Dorset (not Devon) poems.[4] I agree with Gosse, not with you. A proof of their excellence is that you may translate them and they are nearly as good—I say nearly, because if the dialect plays any lawful part in the effect they ought to lose something in losing that. Now Burns loses prodigiously by translation. I have never however read them since my undergraduate days except the one quoted in Gosse's paper,[5] the beauty of which you must allow. I think the use of dialect a sort of unfair play, giving, as you say, 'a peculiar but shortlived charm', setting off for instance a Scotch or Lancashire joke which in standard English comes to nothing. But its lawful charm and use I take to be this, that it sort of guarantees the spontaneousness of the thought and puts you in the position to appraise it on its merits as coming

---

[1] Presumably *Morning Midday and Evening Sacrifice* (*Poems*, 24).

[2] See p. 54.

[3] *Andromeda*, 'Oxford, Aug. 12, '79.' (*Poems*, 24.)

[4] The first volume of Barnes's poems was published in 1844. A second collection appeared in 1859, a third in 1862; and *Poems of Rural Life in the Dorset dialect*, a collected edition of the above, in 1879.

[5] *The Academy*, 26 July 1879, pp. 60-1: a review in two columns of the collected edition. Gosse makes a comparison with Burns.

from nature and not books and education. It heightens one's admiration for a phrase just as in architecture it heightens one's admiration of a design to know that it is old work, not new: in itself the design is the same but as taken together with the designer and his merit this circumstance makes a world of difference. Now the use of dialect to a man like Barnes is to tie him down to the things that he or another Dorset man has said or might say, which though it narrows his field heightens his effects. His poems use to charm me also by their Westcountry 'instress', a most peculiar product of England, which I associate with airs like Weeping Winefred, Polly Oliver, or Poor Mary Ann, with Herrick and Herbert, with the Worcestershire, Herefordshire, and Welsh landscape, and above all with the smell of oxeyes and applelofts: this instress is helped by particular rhythms and these Barnes employs; as, I remember, in 'Linden Ore'[1] and a thing with a refrain like 'Alive in the Spring'.[2]

By the by I have seen a Westcountryman—V.

S.

S.

Coles—

for the first time since I went down. I am truly fond of him and wish . . . except these bonds.

I should be very glad to see your prose of Michelangelo's sonnets and also your verse,[3] for though I do not like verse–

---

[1] *Lindenore* (Collected ed. of 1887, pp. 377–8):

> At Lindenore upon the steep,
> Bezide the trees a-reachèn high,
> The while their lower limbs do zweep
> The river-stream a-flowèn by; . . .

[2] Perhaps *In the Spring* (ed. cit. pp. 349–50):

> My love is the maïd of all maïdens
>   Though all mid be comely,
> Her skin's lik' the jessamy blossom
> A-spread in the Spring.

[3] Mrs. Bridges knows nothing of these translations; but it may be remarked that two sonnets (XXXV and LXIV) in the final version of the *Growth of Love* are partly based on Madrigals by Michaelangelo. See R. B.'s note.

renderings of verse (according to the saying *Traduttore traditore*), yet I think you could do them if anyone can. I have seen something of them, in particular a most striking one beginning—

Non ha l'ottimo artista alcun concetto.[1]

By the by, inversions—As you say, I do avoid them, because they weaken and because they destroy the earnestness or in-earnestness of the utterance. Nevertheless in prose I use them more than other people, because there they have great advantages of another sort. Now these advantages they should have in verse too, but they must not seem to be due to the verse: that is what is so enfeebling (for instance the finest of your sonnets[2] to my mind has a line enfeebled by inversion plainly due to the verse, as I said once before ''Tis joy the falling of her fold to view'—but how it should be mended I do not see). As it is, I feel my way to their use. However in a nearly finished piece I have a very bold one indeed. So also I cut myself off from the use of *ere, o'er, wellnigh, what time, say not* (for *do not say*), because, though dignified, they neither belong to nor ever cd. arise from, or be the elevation of, ordinary modern speech. For it seems to me that the poetical language of an age shd. be the current language heightened, to any degree heightened and unlike itself, but not (I mean normally: passing freaks and graces are another thing) an obsolete one. This is Shakespeare's and Milton's practice and the want of it will be fatal to Tennyson's Idylls and plays, to Swinburne, and perhaps to Morris.

21 Trenchard Street, Bristol. Aug. 21. I am spending a few days here. I have roughly finished the little song and enclose it.

Remember me very kindly to Mrs. Molesworth and believe me your loving friend

GERARD M. HOPKINS S.J.

---

[1] Sonetto 1 in Biagioli's ed. of 1821. No. v in J. A. Symonds's translation, and called by him *The Lover and the Sculptor.*

[2] Final form (*P.W.*, vol. i, *G. of L.*, 31):
'Tis joy to watch the folds fall as they do.

LXIII

St. Joseph's, Bedford Leigh, Lancashire. Oct. 8 1879.

DEAREST BRIDGES,—I have left Oxford. I am appointed to Liverpool,[1] I do not know for what work, but am in the meantime supplying at the above address. Leigh is a town smaller and with less dignity than Rochdale and in a flat; the houses red, mean, and two storied; there are a dozen mills or so, and coalpits also; the air is charged with smoke as well as damp; but the people are hearty. Now at Oxford every prospect pleases and only man is vile, I mean unsatisfactory to a Catholic missioner. I was yesterday at St. Helen's, probably the most repulsive place in Lancashire or out of the Black Country. The stench of sulphuretted hydrogen rolls in the air and films of the same gas form on railing and pavement.

I had put the letter containing your two sonnets, as I thought, in my pocket, but it is another, older one, and the sonnets are somewhere packed up. Oct. 9. I have found them. No. 39[2] is a beautiful work and breathes that earnestness and tenderness which you have at command. But I make the following remarks. Line 3 is commonplace in cadence; I shd. prefer something like

The leaves and careless ecstasy of May.

The next quatrain is dark. One of two kinds of clearness one shd. have—either the meaning to be felt without effort as fast as one reads or else, if dark at first reading, when once made out *to explode*. Now this quatrain is not plain at first reading nor, if I am right in my taking of it, did that meaning explode. I suppose it to mean / If I could only get rid of the fear, which comes every morning, that that day would put a final end to my lover's hopes. And 'promise of hope' is a pleonasm.

---

[1] Preacher at St. Francis Xavier's Church, Liverpool.

[2] This sonnet was first printed in *Poems*, Third Series, 1880, as XIV, *Regret*. There is now no means of knowing what original was sent to G. M. H., but since the sonnet is almost re-written in its final form (*P.W.*, vol. i, *G. of L.*, 41) the first printed version is given in NOTE L. It will be seen that two of G. M. H.'s suggestions were temporarily adopted. 'The flowers and leafy ecstasy of May' of the final form is perhaps a return to the first reading.

I shd. prefer 'O then were hideous duty'
And then

    'But that 'twas I who once, 'tis this that stings',
(or

    'But that 'twas I who once did, this, this stings')

    ^{2} ^{1}
    'Once dwell within the gate that angels guard
    And should be yet there, had I heavenly wings'/
(or

    'And yet should dwell there').

No. 32^1 seems imperfect in execution, the octet. I want
something like

    'I heard great Hector hurling war's alarms
    Loud in the ears of listless ghosts: he strode
    As though etc
    He still the trust of all, Troy's king at arms.*
    But over those mild meads etc
    Etc
    Like night's poor creeping candle in the road,
    Whose cold flame cannot comfort, only charms—'

Something like that.

Something short of a commentary indeed but more of a clue
than the bare titles wd. be a gain in my opinion to the Growth
of Love, for instance some words added to the titles.

   * or

      'He still Troy's hope, still trusted king at arms.'

---

^{1} First printed in the 1880 volume as XVII. *Failure* (*P.W.*, vol. i, *G. of L.*,
53). The final form is considerably corrected, especially ll. 5–8, but none
of G. M. H.'s suggestions is adopted. The octave first stood:

    I heard great Hector sounding war's alarms,
    Where through the listless ghosts chiding he strode,
    As though the Greeks besieged his last abode,
    And he his Troy's hope still, her king at arms.

     But on those gentle meads where nothing harms
    And purpose perishes, his passion glowed
    Like the cold night-worm's candle, nor scarce showed
    The heart death kills not quite nor Lethe harms.

I cannot well bestow such minute criticism on the others you promise, for time will not allow, but still let me see them.

What, more definitely, is that change that you say has taken place in you?

What part of the country do you reckon the Bridges to have come from?[1]

The little hero of the Handsome Heart has gone to school at Boulogne to be bred for a priest and he is bent on being a Jesuit.

I enclose a poem, the Bugler. I am half inclined to hope the Hero of it may be killed in Afghanistan.[2]

Did you like the song 'The dappled dieaway Cheek'?[3]

I have a greater undertaking on hand than any yet, a tragedy on St. Winefred's Martyrdom and then one on Margaret Clitheroe's.[4] The first has made some way and, since it will no doubt be long before it is finished, if ever, I can only send you some sample scenes. But I hope to be able to send you the murder scene and some more not very long hence.[5] I mean them to be short, say in 3 or even 2 acts; the characters few. I have been writing St. Winefred in alexandrines, and am, I hope, getting a certain control of them, and in sprung rhythm, which lends itself to expressing passion. I seem to find myself, after some experiment, equal to the more stirring and critical parts of the action, which are in themselves the more important, but about the filling in and minor parts I am not sure how far my powers will go. I have for one thing so little varied experience. In reading Shakespeare one feels with despair the scope and

---

[1] They came from Kent, Mrs. Bridges tells me.

[2] In A the following note is written at the end of the sonnet by G. M. H.— 'ordered to Mootlan [Mooltan] in the Punjaub; was to sail Sept. 30.'

[3] Music for *Morning Midday and Evening Sacrifice*, as a pencil note by R. B. shows.

[4] Neither was finished. Of the first there is further mention, and the fragments are considerable. What remains of the second (first published in *Poems*, Second Edition, 1930) is not dramatic in form, and doubtless the poet changed his design. Two consecutive tragedies on the subject of martyrdom may well have seemed excessive.

[5] *Poems*, 58. Caradoc's soliloquy following on his murder of Winefred is the most important fragment.

richness of his gifts, equal to everything; he had besides sufficient experience of life and, of course, practical knowledge of the theatre.

I have not been able to make out much in the hymn music. You shall have it presently.

Remember me very kindly to Mrs. Molesworth and believe me your affectionate friend

GERARD M. HOPKINS S.J.

Oct. 16 1879.

By the by how can you speak of Patmore as you do? I read his *Unknown Eros* well before leaving Oxford. He shews a mastery of phrase, of the rhetoric of verse, which belongs to the tradition of Shakespeare and Milton and in which you could not find him a living equal nor perhaps a dead one either after them.

LXIV

St. Joseph's, Bedford Leigh, near Manchester.
Oct 22 1879

(you will be surprised at this hand: I employ it sometimes with steel pens).

DEAREST BRIDGES,—One thing you say in your last is enough to make me quite sad and I see that I shall have to write at some length in order to deal with it. You ask whether I really think there is any good in your going on writing poetry. The reason of this question I suppose to be that I seemed little satisfied with what you then sent and suggested many amendments in the sonnet on Hector. I do still think 'nor he the charms' and its context obscure and cumbersome.[1] The other[2] I thought very beautiful (I said so), full of feeling and felicities, as 'The breathing Summer's sloth, the scented Fall' and 'sweet jeopardy'; only I called one part obscure. I find it so after your explanation:

---

[1] This phrase was altered before the sonnet was first printed, in 1880.

[2] See NOTE L for the first printed version of this sonnet; the 8th line was altered before publication towards G. M. H.'s criticism.

it is the 8th line that is most in fault, for the rest would bear your meaning if that did. To my mind you cannot be understood unless you write something like 'Last' did something-or-other 'and last had hope in thrall'. The present line is so vague, it might conceivably mean so many things, it stamps the mind with nothing determinate. But you are to know, indeed very likely you experience the same thing, I see your work to its very least advantage when it comes to me on purpose to be criticised. It is at once an unfinished thing, in my eyes, and any shortcoming or blemish that in print I should either not notice or else easily digest with the excellence of the context becomes a rawness and a blot, to be removed before my mind can even sit down to receive an impression of the whole or form a final judgment about it. It is just as if I had written it myself and were dissatisfied, as you know that in the process of composition one almost always is, before things reach their final form. And things you shewed me at Bedford Square in MS and I did not so much care for then, when I came to see them in print I read in a new light and felt very differently about them. Before that they are too near the eye; then they fall into focus. Oct. 23— Therefore in your book almost everything seems perfect and final and exercises its due effect and the exceptions prove the rule, such as the pieces in sprung rhythm, or some of them, and that is just because they *are* experimental and seem submitted to revision, and also the song, truly beautiful as it is, 'I have loved flowers'; but I was not satisfied with the music and mentally altered it: now it comes to me like a thing put by for repairs. And while on repairs and before going further I will say that I think it wd. be better to write 'one irrevocable day'.[1] 'That . . . day' is ambiguous: you mean *ille dies*, the particular day which in fact did etc; I took it for *is dies*, a day such that, whenever it shall come, it is doomed to etc. You see, perfects in dependent sentences, like *held* there, need not be historical pasts; they may also be subjunctives of present or any date, and so I took it.

[1] This correction was made. See NOTE L, l. 6.

94

But now in general. And first to visit the workhouse. Oct. 25—You seem to want to be told over again that you have genius and are a poet and your verses beautiful. You have been told so, not only by me but very spontaneously by Gosse, Marzials, and others; I was going to say Canon Dixon, only, as he was acknowledging your book, it was not so spontaneous as Gosse's case. You want perhaps to be told more in particular. I am not the best to tell you, being biassed by love, and yet I am too. I think then no one can admire beauty of the body more than I do, and it is of course a comfort to find beauty in a friend or a friend in beauty. But this kind of beauty is dangerous. Then comes the beauty of the mind, such as genius, and this is greater than the beauty of the body and not to call dangerous. And more beautiful than the beauty of the mind is beauty of character, the 'handsome heart'. Now every beauty is not a wit or genius nor has every wit or genius character. For though even bodily beauty, even the beauty of blooming health, is from the soul, in the sense, as we Aristotelian Catholics say, that the soul is the form of the body, yet the soul may have no other beauty, so to speak, than that which it expresses in the symmetry of the body—barring those blurs in the cast which wd. not be found in the die or the mould. This needs no illustration, as all know it. But what is more to be remarked is that in like manner the soul may have no further beauty than that which is seen in the mind, that there may be genius uninformed by character. I sometimes wonder at this in a man like Tennyson: his gift of utterance is truly golden, but go further home and you come to thoughts commonplace and wanting in nobility (it seems hard to say it but I think you know what I mean). In Burns there is generally recognized on the other hand a richness and beauty of manly character which lends worth to some of his smallest fragments, but there is a great want in his utterance; it is never really beautiful, he had no eye for pure beauty, he gets no nearer than the fresh picturesque expressed in fervent and flowing language (the most strictly beautiful lines of his that I remember are those in Tam o' Shanter: 'But pleasures are like poppies spread' sqq.[1] and those are not). Between a fineness of nature which wd. put him in the first rank of writers and a poverty of language which puts him in the lowest rank of poets, he takes to my mind, when all is balanced and cast up, about a middle place. Now after all this introduction I come to what I want to say. (If I were not your friend I shd. wish to be the friend of the man that wrote your poems.) They shew the eye for pure beauty and they shew, my dearest, besides, the character which is much more rare and precious. Did time allow I shd. find a pleasure in dwelling on the instances, but I cannot now. Since I must not flatter or exaggerate I do not claim that you have such a volume of imagery as Tennyson, Swinburne, or Morris, though the feeling for beauty you have seems to me pure and exquisite; but in point of character, of sincerity or earnestness, of manliness, of tenderness, of humour, melancholy, human feeling, you have what they have not and seem scarcely to think worth having (about Morris I am not sure: his early poems had a deep feeling). I may then well say, like St. Paul, *aemulor te Dei aemulatione.* To have a turn for sincerity has not made you sincere nor a turn for earnest / in earnest; Sterne had a turn for compassion, but he was not compassionate; a man may have natural courage, a turn for courage, and yet play the coward.

I must now answer the rest of your letter. The Ship is very striking and beautiful in your manner.[2] Only who is to take the advice? parents? I shd. like something more like 'And let him deep in memory's hold have stored'. However I am not to make amendments of this sort. The other is beautiful too, but

---

[1]   But pleasures are like poppies spread:
        You seize the flow'r, its bloom is shed;
        Or like the snow falls in the river,
        A moment white—then melts for ever;
        Or like the borealis race,
        That flit ere you can point their place;
        Or like the rainbow's lovely form
        Evanishing amid the storm.

[2] First printed in the 1880 volume as VI. *The Ship*, with the amendment suggested here, which is retained in the final form (*P.W.*, vol. i, *G. of L.*, 15).

not quite satisfactory in point of finish. The image of the saplings is perhaps not so pointed as some other might have been. (By the by I see nothing to object to in the *rhythm* of 'The careless ecstasy of leafy May'; so far as run goes it runs well enough. I should not alter the line 'Ride o'er the seas' etc.).[1]

I hardly know what you allude to at Oxford, it is better that I should not. I used indeed to fear when I went up about this time last year that people wd. repeat against me what they remembered to my disadvantage. But if they did I never heard of it. I saw little of University men: when you were up it was an exceptional occasion, which brought me into contact with them. My work lay in St. Clement's, at the Barracks, and so on. However it is perhaps well I am gone; I did not quite hit it off with Fr. Parkinson and was not happy. I was fond of my people, but they had not as a body the charming and cheering heartiness of these Lancashire Catholics, which is so deeply comforting; they were far from having it. And I believe they criticised what went on in our church a great deal too freely, which is d—d impertinence of the sheep towards the shepherd, and if it had come markedly before me I shd. have given them my mind.

I doubt whether I shall ever get to Liverpool, but if I settle there I will avail myself of your kind offer. Tomorrow I am going to Wigan (St. John's) for eight days. Today is Nov. 18.

I cannot stop to defend the rhymes in the Bugler.[2] The words 'came down to us after a boon he on My late being there begged of me' mean 'came into Oxford to our Church in quest of (or to get) a blessing which, on a late occasion of my being up at Cowley Barracks, he had requested of me': there is no difficulty here, I think. But the line 'Silk-ashed' etc in the Sacrifice is too hard and must be changed to 'In silk-ash kept from cooling.[3]

---

[1]   And at the prow make figured Maidenhead
        Ride o'er the seas and answer to the wheel. (vi, *The Ship*, 1880.)
The final form has: 'O'erride the seas . . .'

[2] Stanzas 1, 2, 7, 9, 12 of *The Bugler's First Communion* contains rhymes that are ingenious rather than 'spontaneous'.

[3] Originally: Silk-ashed but core not cooling. (See note by R. B.)

I meant to compare grey hairs to the flakes of silky ash which may be seen round wood embers burnt in a clear fire and covering a 'core of heat', as Tennyson calls it. But *core* there is very ambiguous, as your remark shews. 'Your offer, with despatch, of' is said like 'Your ticket', 'Your reasons', 'Your money or your life', 'Your name and college': it is 'Come, your offer of all this (the matured mind), and without delay either!' (This should now explode.) Read the last tercet 'What Death dare lift the latch of, What Hell hopes soon the snatch of, Your offer, with despatch, of!'[1]

It was embarassment made Grace odd that night, I have no doubt: you think she only cares for learned music and she thinks so of you. No question she admires Handel. She stands in dread of your judgment probably.

I sent her your hymn. I mentioned it and she begged to see it. She said it was not original-sounding but it was very sweet: she wd. not be pleased if she knew I repeated her criticism. If I could have found her the music to 'O earlier shall the rose buds blow' she would have thought it original-sounding as well as sweet. Yet it was youthful too. I return the hymn.

Do you like Weber? For personal preference and fellow feeling I like him of all musicians best after Purcell. I feel as if I cd. have composed his music in another sphere.[2] I do not feel that of Handel or Mozart or Beethoven. Moreover I do not

---

[1] The last three lines became:
> What life half lifts the latch of,
> What hell stalks towards the snatch of,
> Your offering, with despatch, of!

[2] Carl Maria Weber (1786–1826). The kinship suggested by G. M. H. is interesting. Weber, though his life was not impeccable, was a conscientious Roman Catholic, serious and devout in disposition: hence the 'virgin sweetness and unearthly beauty' of Agatha in *Der Freischütz*. The religious sentiment of his day, romantic in kind, has been described as made up 'partly of a sort of medieval fanatical Catholicism, partly of an almost pantheistical nature-worship'. Critics remark on his originality ('complete simplicity, combined with perfect novelty'), on his subtle skill in orchestration, but above all on the unrivalled freshness and variety of his interpretations of Nature in dramatic music. In this sphere his work has been compared to that of Beethoven in symphony. His masses are individual.

think his great genius is appreciated. I shd. like to read his life. He was a good man, I believe, with no hateful affectation of playing the fool and behaving like a blackguard.

I cannot undertake to find a motto for the ring.

Remember me very kindly to Mrs. Molesworth   And when is your brother's book coming? Believe me your loving friend

GERARD HOPKINS S.J. Nov 18 1879.

LXV (Postcard)

St. Francis Xavier's, Salisbury St., Liverpool.[1]
Jan. 2 1880.

I never went to Wigan and your letter and the book,[2] for which I thank you, were forwarded here and would seem to have been lying long. I have been here a day or two and am settled. I cannot write more and shall have less time than ever.

G. M. H.

Yes, I did make that mistake about Lethe. What a light!

LXVI (Postcard)

8 Salisbury Street, Liverpool. Feb. 15 1880.

I quite forgot to say and shall be sorry if it is now too late to say that I hope Mr. Woolrych[3] will call as he proposed. I will do

---

[1] R. B. wrote of this sojourn in Liverpool (*The Poets and Poetry of the Nineteenth Century*, ed. A. H. Miles, the vol. *Robert Bridges and Contemporary Poets*, short memoir of G. M. H.): 'When sent to Liverpool to do parish work among the Irish, the vice and horrors nearly killed him: and in the several posts, which he held in turn—he was once select preacher in London, and had for a while some trust at Oxford,—he served without distinction.'

[2] See p. 100, note 2.

[3] For Harry Ellis Wooldridge (1845–1917) see R. B.'s article in the *D.N.B.* There will be found details of his work as painter, musician, critic, and a short character study. He is perhaps best known for his contributions to the history of Music. R. B. adds: 'Among his musical remains are *The Yattendon Hymnal*, 1895–99, edited with the present poet laureate, his lifelong friend, with whom he lived for years in London, and afterwards constantly visited at Yattendon, where he sang in the choir and set music for it.'

99

all that Jenkinson Street and Gomer Street and Back Queen Ann Street and Torbock Street and Bidder Street and Birchfield Street and Bickerstaffe Street and the rest of my purlieus will spare of me to entertain him.

G. M. H.

LXVII

8 Salisbury Street, Liverpool. March 23 1880.

DEAREST BRIDGES,—No, Philip Rathbone never wrote.[1]

The teapot of inclination has been tilted several times till the spout of intention very nearly teemed out the liquor of execution (I am speaking of myself now, not of Mr. Rathbone, and must point out the extraordinary merit of the figure I am employing: I shall work it up), but till now it has not filled the cup and saucer of communication. Time indeed is scanty.

There is in a late letter of yours something very ill written which may be either 'Why *nothing* about my brother's book?'— only you leave out the note of interrogation—or else 'Write *nothing* about my brother's book'. But whether question or prohibition I now stultify it.

I read the book leisurely and have come to be very fond of it.[2] Time however does not allow of more than a few jotted remarks. It is a genuine book every way, the feeling very tender and endearing, the satire and fun is capital. The execution does not satisfy and the pieces are unequal. *Harris*[3] is very good indeed, but more finish and makebelieve pathos, such as we find in 'for

---

[1] Philip Rathbone was a friend of most of the Pre-Raphaelites and well known as a collector of pictures: he did a great deal for the Walker Art Gallery. Probably R. B. had offered to introduce him to G. M. H. See p. 97.

[2] *Wet Days*. By a Farmer. London: Kegan Paul, 1879, pp. xii, 218: it is the book of a man who understands country things, and has a keen eye for beauty and foibles. It is rather the rough material of poetry than poetry itself: there is little economy or concentration. But it has savour.

[3] *On a Nose*: a humorous epitaph on Harris, who has taken his monstrous nose elsewhere; now

Angels its range capacious blame,
'There's nothing sweet since Harris came.'

ever crowned with flowers' and other touches in the *Rape of the Lock*, would carry the last line deeper home. But *Proculus*[1] is broad and vulgar. I see little point in the *Miller*.[2] In the Scarecrow piece[3] I do, but I can't see what the keeper's daughter has to do with it. *Self-Assertion* and *Pretence* are very good.[4] Hitherto *Our Lane*[5] and *'Tis Thirty Years*[6] are my favourites. Everywhere there is a delightful fresh country feeling. It reminds me much of you. Some pieces are Caroline like yours. But your brother appears to admire Browning most of modern poets and to be most influenced by him: the *Elder Brother*[7] is quite Browningesque, so is the *John Bull Club*[8] (who is 'Keep silence, you there' and who are the 'emasculate rhymers'?). *Shebna*[9] is capital, but who *was* Shebna? The allegory-pieces

---

[1] *Proculus, a Tale of Pompeii*, telling how a candidate for office was interrupted in his meal of roast pig by Death, who also surprised his thieving slave girl. The moral is:

> Our meaner acts may outlive us
> As does his supper Proculus.

These verses are certainly clumsy and diffuse: but *On a Nose*, which is praised, broader.

[2] A scene remembered from boyhood of an accident that befell an old miller. It is written in easy, unrhetorical blank verse, and has an authentic tang that admirers of Edward Thomas and Mr. Robert Frost would appreciate.

[3] *The Keeper's Lodge*: another boyhood memory—far less successful than the *Miller*—that might be called, *Meditations on a Scarecrow*. The keeper's 'larder' and his daughter are not essential to it, but the latter's 'full-moon face' is probably there for contrast.

[4] Common-sense advice neatly turned into octosyllabic couplets.

[5] A charming picture of the changes brought by the seasons. See NOTE M for st. 3.

[6] Death first touched his friends thirty years ago: now all are gone, and he is alone.

[7] *The Elder Son*, a modern version of the Prodigal Son, a farmer's commentary, pointed, vigorous, dramatic, on the return of his wastrel brother. It owes its form to Browning, but is not an imitation, either in matter or manner.

[8] *At the John Bull Club; Chairman Loq.* A rollicking onslaught on contemporary poets who will not sing. Obviously indebted to Browning.

[9] *Shebna. On his Unexpected Appearance in our Parish Church*—in a long and unintelligible sermon preached by a young clergyman, a stranger, to farmers worried about their crops. For Shebna see 2 Kings xviii. 18–37, xix. 2; Isaiah xxii. 15, xxxvi. 3, xxxvii. 2.

are dark; I can make nothing of the *Week*—I cannot understand it: it seems to me 'But what can one' should be 'For what can one'.[1] I dislike in regular allegory the mixing the parable and the interpretation: it seems to me a great fault in art. This is done in *Destiny*:[2] surely a farmer cd. ride to the top of a hill, much more look over a fence. And no farmer ('unless he is a bird') could soar. If more strikes me I will write again. Who designed the pretty cover?[3]

Do read a witty paper by James Payn in the *Nineteenth Century* for March on Sham Admiration in Literature.[4] His own books must be well worth reading if they are as lively as that about the gentleman who said 'Give *me Paradise Lost*' and was driven 'to that extremity that'—you will see for yourself what in loco.

Believe me your affectionate friend

GERARD M. HOPKINS S.J.

LXVIII

8 Salisbury Street, Liverpool. June 18 1880.

DEAREST BRIDGES,—I hear you are going to be married. Is this so? who is she?[5]

The *Academy* had a notice of *Wet Days*.[6] It blamed its cynical

---

[1] A short allegory on Hope, in seven couplets. The criticism seems to be justified.

> Comes a chill doubt; 'the battle's lost'.
> But what can one against a host?

[2] The objection is weak: the fence and the hill stand for adventure and ambition, made impossible to the farmer by tasks always to hand.

[3] Clouds and rain: white outlines on dark green.

[4] 'On that same evening, while some folks were talking about Mr. Morris's *Earthly Paradise*, I heard a scornful voice exclaim "Oh! give ME *Paradise Lost*," and with that gentleman I *did* have it out. I promptly subjected him to cross-examination, and drove him to that extremity that he was compelled to admit he had never read a word of Milton for forty years, and even then only in extracts from *Enfield's Speaker*.'

[5] R. B. was not married till September 1884.

[6] In the issue of 3 April 1880: half a column amid reviews of 'Recent Verse'. 'The author seems to be . . . in a perennial rage. . . . We should feel rather inclined to re-christen the book—"The Blues", by A Grumbler.' And a little praise.

spirit but praised the nobility of the thought and quoted *Courcy* in instance. You are surprised that I found no fault with this same cynicism. It is over sour, I think; but your brother's dislikes seem to be much the same as mine and I do not mind hearing someone else say what I feel more strongly than I mean myself to say it.

When you shall next call at Oak Hill I want you to hear my music to the Spring Odes,[1] to which Grace has set accompaniments, which accompaniments I have not myself seen yet. I sorely wish I knew some harmony. And say whether you like them and they suit your meaning in the words. I have also a feeling air for 'I have loved flowers that fade', but that is not quite fixed yet, still less written out. I wish I could pursue music; for I have invented a new style, something standing to ordinary music as sprung rhythm to common rhythm: it employs quarter tones. I am trying to set an air in it to the sonnet 'Summer ends now'.[2]

Some unlucky miscarriage seems to have taken place about Mr. Rae's pictures and Mr. Bowes' Japanese ware and I am afraid I shall not see them.[3]

I have never seen that portrait of me but once.[4] I believe that I am in some ways like my brother Arthur.

When you see Mr. Gosse ask him what were those works on Keats which he speaks of as having lately appeared, in a notice by him of a book by some lady on the same subject.

I will enclose a sonnet and a little lyric,[5] the only things I have written in nine months.

Believe me your affectionate friend

GERARD M. HOPKINS S.J.

---

[1] Mrs. Bridges has never seen any music by G. M. H. to R. B.'s poems, except that she has found the *air* to *I love my lady's eyes*: it has no date or setting.

[2] His own sonnet, *Hurrahing in Harvest*.

[3] See p. 130.

[4] Of this portrait Mrs. Bridges knows nothing.

[5] Presumably *Felix Randal*, 'Liverpool, Apr. 28, '80' and *At a Wedding*, 'Bedford, Lancashire, Oct. 21. '79'.

Remember me very kindly to your mother. It is a great comfort to me when I think of your and her coming to know my people so well. I know my sisters and all of them are much attached to Mrs. Molesworth. I hope your marriage will not lessen this intimacy.

June 21—Wyatt-Edgell[1] that was, Lord Braye that is, is staying with us. So I spoke of you and I found he did not know (that is/does not remember, for I fancy I spoke to him on the subject in London) that you wrote. And now I am considering whether—however I have done it, namely lent him yr. last book. He is going to make a selection from the 3 volumes of poetry he has published and so reduce them to one.

June 23. The line 'most men dislike slops, particularly gruel' does not scan. For we say $pǎ'ticyulǎ'ly$, shortening the 1st and 4th syllables, and the i is long by position. False quantities of this kind abound also in the 'O you chorus of indolent reviewers'. He might have said 'Most men dislike slops and gruel especially'. At all events I answer—

Try the common means used to manage the slop-difficulty—
     You take half a glass of gin: it adds a relish.

And this does scan.

LXIX

8 Salisbury Street, Liverpool. Sept. 5 1880.

DEAREST BRIDGES,—I take up a languid pen to write to you, being down with diarrhoea and vomiting, brought on by yesterday's heat and the long hours in the confessional. Yesterday was in Liverpool the hottest day of the year. Today there is rain.

Your poems have lain long on my table almost unopened, so much has my work set in. Today however I have read all the early volume, which to be sure is only 31 short pages. But of both volumes I will write hereafter,[2] only saying now what a

---

[1] Alfred Wyatt-Edgell, author of *Amadeus and other poems* (1873), *Stormsworth, with other poems* . . . (1877). *Amadeus* is an elegy in memory of Dolben.

[2] The later volume is obviously: Poems / By the Author of / The Growth of Love / [Publisher's Device] / Third Series / Ewd. Bumpus, Holborn

delight I take in them. The present is meant as an answer to your last.

I am very happy that you (and that Woolrych, and by the by I think that is how the name is spelt and not as you write it, Wooldridge) like my music and, as Pepys might say, do pray that the same may continue and increase—upon your further trying of it. But the 'I have loved flowers' is in a rude state, wanting improvements and a third verse, which will considerably differ from the two others, and unluckily Grace has not returned me the rough copy, which was left lying about. I therefore cannot tell whether there was an oversight, as Woolrych thought, in the phrase 'Proclaim the spirit's desire'; but that phrase, though I and Grace too had a great deal of trouble to get it down, is in itself, if you could hear it played or sung, very marked and unmistakeable. The rhythm, to imitate it in verse, is 'Betráying the héart's desíre, betráying the héart's desíre, desíre O'.*

I have now an air for 'Thou didst delight my eyes',[1] which some day you shall see. Your poetry is highly songful and flies into tunes.

Grace made on the first version of the first of the Spring Odes the same criticism as Woolrych, that a greater compass, a higher note was wanted; accordingly I supplied it. I do not feel that now it is too narrow in compass, but perhaps the other one, the Reply, is.

In the setting I should have been glad if Grace had been bolder. The accompaniment should have a shower of semi-

* I believe it shd. be written thus, in monotone—

Bars, London / 1880. pp. 27: blue-green paper covers: price two shillings. The early volume is presumably the second edition (1880) of *Poems*, First Series, in which the nineteen poems, from the volume of 1873, fill thirty-one pages.

[1] First printed in *Poems*, Third Series, ii.

quavers or demisemis, with great chords at certain places. On the words 'And where the bare trunks', where a note is four times repeated, the chord should have been varied four times, rising or descending, an obvious and beautiful effect of counterpoint, and not been repeated, as she has done. If I could make my own harmonies much of the expression of the piece could be conveyed in the accompaniments of course.

The Brothers was rather suggested by Wordsworth than Patmore. It was first written in stanzas in Wordsworth's manner, but when I compared it with his inimitable simplicity and gravity I was disgusted and meant to destroy it, till the thought struck me of changing the metre, which made it do. I do not myself recognise anything Patmorial in it: what do you find? I shall enclose a corrected version. The incident took place at Mount St. Mary's in Derbyshire.

You shall also see the *Leaden Echo* when finished.[1] The reason, I suppose, why you feel it carry the reader along with it is that it is dramatic and meant to be popular. It is a song for St. Winefred's maidens to sing. I hope some time soon to send you some speeches from the play, but I should be sorry for you to have judged what it would be like from the fragments Kate sent me on a blue paper. They were the roughest first thoughts, which in me are of a too lyrical and not enough dramatic cast.

Do you not feel Patmore's pathos? To me it is harrowing. Read for instance the *Azalea* in the *Unknown Eros* and some others there.

I have not studied Wyatt, but Surrey I used to read: he, I think, is a greater man. He was an accomplished rhythmist, not that the experiments in couplets of long twelves and thirteens[2] are pleasing, though this is better than couplets both

---

[1] *The Leaden Echo and the Golden Echo, Poems*, 36. The final version belongs to October 1882.

[2] In MS. 'sixes' and 'sevens' here cancelled. He meant to write 'twelves' and 'fourteens', and makes that correction later, having in mind such a poem as the *Complaint of a Lover that defied Love.*

When Summer took in hand the winter to assail,
With force of might, and virtue great, his stormy blasts to quail . . .

twelves or both thirteens. He has a very fine style free from Euphuism. However, to speak of the sample you send, I must say that I think you have missed the clue. You take the rhythm for free triple time, iambs and anapaests say, and four feet to a line (except the refrain). But to get this you have to skip, in two lines out of these few, a whole foot as marked and stressy as any other foot. This is a licence unpardonable by the reader and incredible in the writer.[1]

Before offering my own thoughts I must premise something. So far as I know triple time is in English verse a shy and late thing. I have not studied *Piers Ploughman* and so cannot pronounce how far triple time is boldly employed in it; at least it must have been suggested. But on the Romance side of our versification triple time appeared, I think, late. It may have been suggested by *Piers Ploughman's* rhythm, as I have said, but partly I conjecture it arose from a simple misunderstanding or misreading of Chaucer and the verse of that date and

---

[1] It is particularly unfortunate that R. B.'s side of the correspondence is here missing. Nothing is easier than to differ on a question of scansion. G. M. H.'s theories in this letter, summary in tone and 'amateur' in scope, may be read as the suggestions of a mind adventuring in this instance beyond the limits of its special knowledge. It seems possible that Wyatt's poem, *The Lover seeking for his Lost Heart* . . ., is in question; it is therefore printed here, in the form in which G. M. H. probably read it, without further comment.

> Help me to seek! for I lost it there;
> And if that ye have found it, ye that be here,
> And seek to convey it secretly,
> Handle it soft, and treat it tenderly,
> Or else it will plain, and then appair.
> But pray restore it mannerly,
> Since that I do ask it thus honestly,
> For to lese it, it sitteth me near;
>   Help me to seek!
>
> Alas! and is there no remedy:
> But have I thus lost it wilfully.
> I wis it was a thing all too dear
> To be bestowed, and wist not where.
> It was mine heart! I pray you heartily
>   Help me to seek!

thereabouts. Chaucer and his contemporaries wrote for a pronunciation fast changing (everybody knows that final *e* for instance
has often to be sounded in Chaucer, but everybody does not know
that mostly it is *not* to be sounded and that the line which scans
by its aid is really to be scanned another way). Their versification was popular and hit the mark in its time, but soon, as far as
I can see, became obsolete, and they being much read and not
rightly scanned thus came to suggest rhythms which they never
thought of. The same sort of thing has, I think, happened often
in the history of verse. And so far, Wyatt's piece might be
scanned as you scan it—but for the two lines with a foot too
much.

Now in particular I suppose that the verse called doggrel (in
which the play of *Royster Doyster* is written and parts of *Love's
Labour*, the *Shrew* etc) arose in this way: I do not know how
else such a shapeless thing can have arisen. If it were a spontaneous popular growth it wd. [be] simpler and stronger. It
must be the corruption or degeneration of something literary
misunderstood or disfigured. Its rule is: couplets, with a pause
dividing each line and on either side of this either two or three
(perhaps sometimes even more) stresses, so that the line may
range from four to six feet, and the rhythm variable too, iambic
or anapaestic.

This wretched doggrel I think Surrey was systematising and
raising in that couplet of his of which I spoke above and, to come
to the point, I conjecture that Wyatt is dealing with the same
thing here. The main point is the pause or caesura; on that the
line turns. The notion of pause or caesura had come to English
versification from two different quarters—from *Piers Ploughman*
and the older native poetry on the one hand, where it is marked
by a sort of Greek colon or by a stroke, and from France on the
other, where it is essential both to the Alexandrine and to the
old ten-syllable or five-foot line of the Chansons and is marked
after the fourth syllable, I find.

The midpause then being essential and the rhyme double, not
triple, which to Wyatt would have been a barbarism perhaps,

he thinks himself at liberty to give each wing of the line two or three stresses at pleasure, as in doggrel, but not, as I have said, more than two syllables, a stress and a slack, to each foot. His rhythm, I have noticed myself in the little I have read of his, is very French and lightsome, lighter than Surrey's and weaker, and that appears here; for instance I think he wd. scan—'ít sittéth me néar',[1] that is, really, 'ít sitteth me néar' or, as I like to write it, 'it sitteth me near', the black ball marking the real

●   ○   ●

or heard stress, the white the dumb or conventional one.

However I write under correction and you may be in a position to bowl me over. But see whether what I suggest will not apply to other of his pieces. I should add that as both parts of his line may begin with the stress or slack at option he gets an effect of sprung rhythm, which however from the weakness of his stresses is slight.[2]

I enclose a little piece composed since I began this letter, not founded on any real incident.[3] I am not well satisfied with it and do not copy it on paper of the size you like.

I hope your Elegy[4] will be immortal, as it deserves to be—for everything and most for the line 'As scarce she dared to be delighted'.[5] But I think the Lethe mythology of the last stanza is a fall-off and unrealises the whole.

Believe me your loving friend

GERARD HOPKINS S.J.

Sept. 10 1880.

I find I have not time just now to copy out the *Brothers*, but will send it shortly. However I have copied the shorter piece out again, improved and on paper of the size you like. Sept 11.

---

[1] This line, as printed in *The Poems of Sir Thomas Wiat*, ed. A. K. Foxwell (1913), vol. i, p. 6, runs: For to lese it, it sitteth me to neere.

[2] This is evidently the important point.

[3] *Spring and Fall.* 'Lydiate, Lancashire, Sept. 7, 1880'.

[4] *Elegy on a Lady, whom Grief for the Death of her Betrothed Killed.* First printed in *Poems*, 1873 (*P.W.*, vol. ii, book i. 14).

[5] St. 6, l. 6.

I forgot to say that the first phrase of the second Spring Ode should be, not—

Be - hold! the ra - diant spring

but—

Be - hold! the ra - diant spring

and so on throughout except for 'Then what charm company'—

G. M. H.

Sept. 13 1880. 8 Salisbury Street, Liverpool.

LXX

Rose Hall, Lydiate, Lancashire (I am often here for a night).
The paper will do as well as other, perhaps better.

Oct. 26 1880.

DEAREST BRIDGES,—I daresay you have long expected as you have long deserved an answer to your last kind and cheering— let us say, number or issue. But I never could write; time and spirits were wanting; one is so fagged, so harried and gallied up and down. And the drunkards go on drinking, the filthy, as the scripture says, are filthy still: human nature is so inveterate. Would that I had seen the last of it.

I must first speak of your book, the last one.[1] I have not got it here, but can make some remarks without reference. What is the place described in *Indolence*?[2] Is it Abingdon? There are two lines I am not satisfied with in it. One is 'And charmèd Indolence in languor lay'. This is open, I think, to the objection made to 'Let observation with extensive view Survey mankind from China to Peru', which meant: Let observation with extensive observation observe all that is observable. For one might as well have said 'And charmèd Languor indolently lay';

[1] *Poems*, Third Series, 1880.
[2] The first poem in the book: save for one change in punctuation, unaltered in *P.W.*, vol. ii, book ii. 7.

the two abstractions are not distinct enough, it seems they ought
not to come together and one be personified and the other not,
when you are on personifying you might turn out a lot, as
Milton does in *L'Allegro* and *Il Penseroso*. And 'pleasurable'[1] is
a prosaic word, I think: can you not find something better? It
is not a bad word, but it falls flatly. (This reminds me that
'test' is to my ear prosaic in 'Thou didst delight', but could
scarcely be changed.) Otherwise the poem is very beautiful,
very fine in execution and style. Style seems your great excellence, it is really classical. What fun if you were a classic! So
few people have style, except individual style or manner—not
Tennyson nor Swinburne nor Morris, not to name the scarecrow
misbegotten Browning crew. Just think the blank verse these
people have exuded, such as *Paracelsus*, *Aurora Leigh*, Baillie's
or Bayley's *Festus*, and so on. The Brownings are very fine too
in their ghastly way.

This reminds me. First you misquote, then you insult me.
I wrote[2] 'Dog, he did give tongue!', not, what you call like
Browning, 'Dog, did he give tongue?' It means, so to say, 'And
by George, sir, when the young dog opened his mouth at last
he did make a noise and no mistake'.

London Snow[3] is a most beautiful and successful piece. It is
charmingly fresh, I do not know what is like it. The rhythm,
as I told you, is not quite perfect. That of the child-piece is
worse[4] and that piece is worse, indeed *it is* Browningese, if you
like; as for instance 'To a world, do we think, that heals the
disaster of this?' or something like that. You are certainly less
at your ease in sprung rhythm. In the snow-piece this has not
been a hindrance however, but perhaps has helped it, by making
it more original in diction. Truth compels, and modesty does

---

[1]   We lingered out the pleasurable hours.
[2] *Brothers*, *Poems*, 30, l. 34. The printed version has:
          Young dog, he did give tongue!
[3] *Poems*, Third Series, 1880, iii (unaltered in *P.W.*, vol. ii, book iii. 2).
One of the poems 'written by the rules of a new prosody': the others are
The Voice of Nature and *On a Dead Child*.
[4] *On a Dead Child*, v (unaltered in *P.W.*, vol. ii, book iii. 4).

not forbid, me here to say that this volume has at least three real echos (or echoes) of me: I do not wish them away, but they are there. The 'snow-mossed wonder' line recalls 'For though he is under' in the Deutschland,[1] 'O look at the trees' the first line of the Starlight sonnet,[2] and 'throned behind' again comes from the Deutschland.[3] I fancy there is another I cannot now recall. O yes, it is in the Voice of Nature—'Precipitate all o'er-rides and swerves nor abides' (is it?): this is in the Deutschland too, I cannot quote it but it ends with 'abides'.[4] It is easy to see why this is: that is the longest piece extant in sprung rhythm and could not help haunting your memory. I do not want them altered, and 'throned behind' having found its way into the midst of a lovely image would not like to be parted from its company. The Voice of Nature is very fine, but the touch in rhythm as well as diction is not quite sure.

Oct. 28. 8 Salisbury Street, Liverpool—The lyric 'Thou didst delight' is, like others before it, a gem.[5] I have music to this which I hope you will like, a little however resembling the quaint old air of 'As once through Cupid's Garden'. I shall send it when I can snatch time and when a difficult minor passage for the third stanza is satisfactory. But more by token, I have got me Stainer's Primer of Harmony and shall perhaps be able to do my own accompaniments by and by.

[1]   Or peering up from under the white-mossed wonder,
       'O look at the trees!' they cried, 'O look at the trees!'
The Wreck of the Deutschland, st. 6, l. 6:
       Since, tho' he is under the world's splendour and wonder.
[2]   Look at the stars! look, look up at the skies!
[3] viii. *Disillusion:*
       For lack of thee, who once wert throned behind
       All beauty, . . .
The Wreck of the Deutschland, st. 32:
       . . . past all
       Grasp God, throned behind
   Death with a sovereignty that heeds but hides, bodes but abides.
[4] The line from *The Voice of Nature* is:
       Precipitate all o'errides, and turns, nor abides;
[5] *Poems*, 1880, ii (*P.W.*, vol. ii, book iii. 12, with first stanza much changed).

You make in this volume great, I think excessive, use of the syncopated rhythm upon words in *ing*, especially in the fourth foot; also of a dissolved rhythm in end lines, like 'living and loving long ago',[1] which I do not very much care for. It is somewhat mechanical and I see that the poetasters have got hold of it.

Disillusion[2] is a bad word; you mean Disenchantment. It is, as bad as Or-de-al and Preventative and Standpoint and the other barbarisms.

Of the sonnets the Nightingale[3] is the largest in style to my mind, the most Miltonic. But I like VI,[4] VIII, X[5] (except the poor ending 'is this disproved'), XIV,[6] and XVI[7] about as much; the others less, they have a certain stiffness of motion and want of mastery in places and are sometimes obscure, especially XIX,[8] which I cannot make out do what I will, who is that conqueror? It might be Love, it might be Death, it might be Time, but there are reasons against each. 'Yet has no secret with the soul pourtrayed' means, I suppose, 'Yet has no secret in common with the there pourtrayed soul', but is a very ambiguous phrase. It reads as if it meant something it cannot mean. But still you understand that every one of them is very beautiful and comparisons apart I should express my admiration more warmly.

If I had to choose three samples from the book I should take

---

[1] *Poems*, 1880, xix:

> Forespent their living and loving long ago.

[2] The title to viii (*P.W.*, vol. i, *G. of L.*, where there is no title).

[3] *Poems*, 1880, ix. Not reprinted in *P.W.*, vol. i, *G. of L.*

[4] *The Ship* (*P.W.*, vol. i, *G. of L.*, 15: minor changes only).

[5] *P.W.*, vol. i, *G. of L.*, 30: end unaltered, two changes in punctuation only.

[6] *Regret* (*P.W.*, vol. i, *G. of L.*, 41: almost re-written).

[7] *The House* (*P.W.*, vol. i, *G. of L.*, 14: almost re-written).

[8] A mistake for xiii. *Identity* (*P.W.*, vol. i, *G. of L.*, 39: reprinted with a major emendation and a few slight changes). The sonnet opened:

> A man that sees by chance his picture, made
> As once a child he was, handling some toy,
> Will gaze to find his spirit within the boy,
> Yet has no secret with the soul pourtrayed.

The line singled out by G. M. H. is unaltered, save for 'hath' in place of 'has'.

'Thou didst delight', *London Snow*, and the *Nightingale* or *Disenchantment* (for that other word cannot stand).

The review in the *St. James's* is pleasing and appreciative, though it might have been stronger.[1]

I have also some answers to make to your last, but will reserve them and send off the present at once. By the by I have broken out into humorous or comic verse: it sounds shocking, but you shall see. Believe me your loving friend

GERARD M. HOPKINS S.J.

You once asked for a piece in my father's handwriting. I enclose one. It was meant for music—not mine, but I nevertheless have some inklings of an air to it.

LXXI A[2]

not sure.

So much for the art. But the things said call for remark too. I take the piece to be truthful,[3] to be the record of something you really find in yourself. You have well to consider what can be the meaning of any such yearning in the mind as your poem speaks of; which if it can be felt now even when the thoughts are drawn off and engrossed by a thousand things, is likely to be some other time its whole life and being. (You yourself say something like this in one of your sonnets.[4]) You express your

---

[1] *St. James's Gazette*, 8 Sept. 1880: a sympathetic unsigned review of one and a half columns, with copious quotations. The critic remarks on the singular charm of the poet's 'grave and old-fashioned music, his philosophic content, his happy acquiescence in the world and in human destiny'; compares his music with Marvell's; and finds his essential charm in his 'reasoned acceptance of life'. But the review ends: 'Oddly enough, the series of sonnets named *The Growth of Love* are the poet's most intimately personal, and least generally attractive, composition.'

[2] This fragment, marked by R. B., 'Never sent found among papers', is obviously part of the first and discarded attempt to write the next letter. The back of the leaf was used for a draft of the opening of *Brothers*, which opening is therefore printed here. Five drafts of this poem exist. See R. B.'s note.

[3] The MS. of *O my vague desires!* (*P.W.*, vol. ii, book iii. 1). See p. 117.

[4] Perhaps *Poems*, 1880, xiv. *Regret* (*P.W.*, vol. i, *G. of L.*, 41). See NOTE L. Mrs. Bridges thinks ix, *G. of L.*, 1876, is the more likely.

belief in the mind's immortality. Any man who is sure or who thinks it likely his mind will have a being after death should remember that there must be besides his own mind other spiritual powers, which may as much affect him then as here the bodily world surrounds and affects his body. Then he should think that the sovereign spirit is God, to whom he should now at once make his approach with the humblest and the most earnest prayers.

Jan. 23—The little lyric 'I love my lady's eyes'[1] is very grace-ful and dainty, though, as you say, unfinished (how do you express incomplete in execution as opposed to incomplete in magnitude or extension?); but the last stanza I cannot make out. Is 'who likes' a mistake for 'who's like'? Who is speaking? All I can see is that the lady seems to be recognized by her listless eye 'when Lubin is away'. The couplets of the first and second stanza might be bettered: 'dainty-warm' is like the *Miller's Daughter*. I am going to enclose the music for it: it is trifling . . . but not more so than the words. By rights it should have a quarter-tone in it.

I am, by this niggling pen, at Gill Moss, having just walked out of town by frost and starlight; I saw deep drifts frozen as hard as ice, and yet I think this part of the country has felt as little of the storm as any. I lost my way, but two children fetching milk led me, said 'you must follow oŏz'. Nothing strikes me [. . . .]

How lóvely the élder bróther's
Life all laced in the other's!
Love-laced; as once I well   Love-laced. This once I well
Witnessed, so fortune fell.   Witnessed, as fortune fell.
When Shrovetide, two years gone,
Bróught our bóys' plays ón,
Why, a part was picked for John,

---

[1] Evidently sent to him in MS. (*P.W.*, vol. ii, book iii. 16). The song was much changed, and the difficulty G. M. H. found in the last stanza cir-cumvented.

Young Jóhn; then féar, jóy
Ran a rével in the élder bóy.
Their night was come now; all
Our company thronged the hall etc

LXXI

Jan. 26 1881. 8 Salisbury Street, Liverpool.

DEAREST BRIDGES,—This is that promised letter, begun on
St. Agnes' Eve,[1] an Eve as bitter as in Keats, but found fault
with and begun again. The weather we are undergoing in
Liverpool is not remarkable except for its severity, or so at least
I wrote at first, but since then I have been into the country a
little way and seen deep frozen snowdrifts—yet these parts have
felt the storm as little, I think, as any—and I am shortly going
down to see the ice in the Mersey and the infinite flocks of sea-
gulls of which I hear. But however I want you, as you are
χιονουργός or χιονότεχνος, a snowwright or snowsmith or whatever one should say, to write me a graphic account of what
London and its neighbourhood have been and looked like at
this time.

Jan. 27—Well, I went. The river was coated with dirty yellow
ice from shore to shore; where the edges could be seen it seemed
very thick; it was not smooth but many broken pieces framed
or pasted together again; it was floating down stream with the
ebb tide; it everywhere covered the water, but was not of a
piece, being continually broken, ploughed up, by the plying of
the steam ferryboats, which I believe sometimes can scarcely
make their way across. The gulls were pampered; throngs of
people were chucking them bread; they were not at all quick
to sight it and when they did they dipped towards it with
infinite lightness, touched the ice, and rose again, *but generally
missed the bread*: they seem to fancy they cannot or ought not to
rest on ground.—However I hear the Thames is frozen and an
ox roasted whole. Today there is a thaw, and the frostings,

[1] 20 January.

116

which have been a lovely fairyland on the publicans' windows, are vanished from the panes.

This morning I got one of his hearty letters from the Canon *and* a great batch of MS poems, most of which I believe you have seen.[1]

But now to business. I have a very great deal of you to answer. To take the last first, the poem 'O my vague desires' is a very noble piece, as fine, I think, as anything you have yet done.[2] It is 'all road' very remarkable. The rhythm too is correct and strong. I make a few suggestions. (1) The rhythm of line 4 wd. be a little improved by something like 'arising' instead of 'rising'. (2) Would it not be a better stroke to have instead of 'For ever soaring . . . dying? O he joy of flight!' something like 'You ever soaring aloft, soaring and dying Flames of joyous flight'? (3) I would have 'Ah! they burn my soul, *My* fires, devour my soul [or "spirit"?] that once was whole'. (4) The word you were in search of instead of 'phantoms' must be 'gledes'—and then you would continue 'day *after* day'. (5) Why should not the last short line have three feet like the others, as 'Could I but control'? 'Could I control' has only two. (6) The next line is the only rhythmically bad one: both rhythm and feeling are bettered by 'My vague desires, my leaping flames of soul'. So too in the next line I would have 'my fires'. (7) The last line might perhaps, but I am not sure, be improved by 'still flying alas!'

The poem is autobiographical, as you would say; it tells of what you really feel in yourself. What then is the meaning of those yearnings or aspirations in the mind? You bear witness against yourself that you have them. And, as you suggest in one of your sonnets, if they are powerfully felt even now, when the mind is drawn off them and engrossed by so many things, it is likely they will be at some other time its whole life and being,

[1] See vol. ii, XII A.
[2] Since the whole poem is essential to an understanding of the text of this letter and of G. M. H.'s proposed emendations (only one of which was adopted), it is reprinted in its final form as NOTE N.

whether they are gratified or not gratified. This poem as well as that sonnet express your belief that the mind is immortal. But there are other minds that act on you now, as for instance you now follow my meaning, acting through sensible channels; hereafter there will be other spiritual powers, it is natural to suspect, which may act on the mind more directly and not by sensible channels; they may surround it and affect it as much as the body is surrounded and affected by other bodies. You cannot wisely neglect this world of being to which you imply that you will come. In it or above it is the sovereign spirit God, to whom you should now at once make your approach with the humblest and most earnest prayers.[1]

The little lyric 'I love my lady's eyes'[2] is very graceful and dainty, though, as you say, unfinished in execution: 'shaded hair' I do not care for and the couplets of stanzas 1. and 2. might be bettered. The last stanza I do not understand at all. Is 'who likes' a mistake for 'who's like'? All I can make out is that the lady is recognized by her listlessness of eye in her lover's absence. I am sure it is unintelligible as it stands. I shall enclose the music to it: it is rather trifling but not more so perhaps than the words. 'Dainty-warm' is too like the *Miller's Daughter*.

I want also to enclose a recast of my *Brothers*. I sent it to Canon Dixon and he objected to the first four lines. Your objection begins *after* them. I have changed it to suit both. Do you think it improved?[3] I know there was and fear there still is a flat where you say, but in narrative poems it needs the highest mastery to get rid of these. Only I do not see the objection to 'lost in Jack' being near the 'diver's dip':[4] the one is a

---

[1] Had G. M. H. lived, he would have read R. B.'s considered philosophy and answer to this and other kindred questions in *The Testament of Beauty*.

[2] See p. 115 and note. 'Shaded hair' became 'sunny hair', and 'dainty-warm' disappeared.

[3] See R. B.'s note in *Poems*.

[4]　　　For, wrung all on love's rack,
　　　My lad, and lost in Jack,
　　　Smiled, blushed, and bit his lip;
　　　Or drove, with a diver's dip,
　　　Clutched hands down through clasped knees. . . .

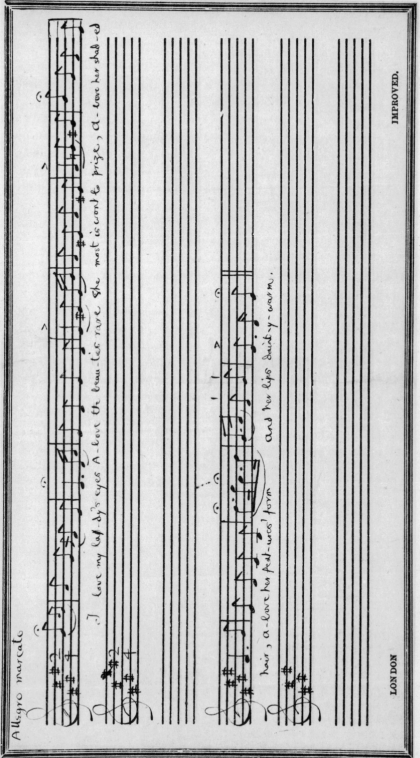

IMPROVED.

LONDON

common metaphor which has almost become 'proper', I mean no longer figurative, in moral matter; the other is descriptive of a physical trick of restless impatience. The couplet you do not like in *Margaret* may be changed back to what it stood before if you like (but in the music I keep it)—

> Leaves you with your fresh thoughts can
> Feel for like the things of man.

I am setting plainchant music to it.

I do not see that the music to the Spring Odes is monotonous, rather it seems to me cheerful.

You should never say 'standpoint': 'Point of view'. ✓

I agree that the *Eurydice* shews more mastery in art, still I think the best lines in the *Deutschland* are better than the best in the other. One may be biassed in favour of one's firstborn though. There are some immaturities in it I should never be guilty of now.

I think I remember that Patmore pushes the likeness of musical and metrical time too far—or, what comes to the same thing, not far enough: if he had gone quite to the bottom of the matter his views would have been juster. He might remember that for more than half the years music has been in the world it had perhaps *less* time than verse has, as we see in plainchant now. Sir Oozy Gore[1] (so to say) says, and I believe him, that strict musical time, modern time, arose from dance music. Now probably verse-time arose from the dance too. The principle, whether necessary or not, which is at the bottom of both musical and metrical time is that everything shd. go by twos and, where you want to be very strict and effective, even by fours. But whereas this is insisted on and recognised in modern music it is neither in verse. It exists though and the instance Pat[2] gives is good and bears him out.[3] For it is very noticeable and cannot be denied that to three foot lines you can add one syllable or two syllables, which makes four feet, with pleasure, and then no more; but that to four foot lines you can comfortably add

---

[1] See p. 199. [2] Written over 'he' cancelled.
[3] 'Prefatory Study on English Metrical Law,' *Amelia*, etc., 1878, p. 66.

nothing. Why, but because we carry mentally a frame of fours, which being filled allows of no more? Thus—

> 'Twas when the seas did roar
> With hollow blasts of wind:
> A damsel did deplore
> All on a rock reclined—

This is in threes. Add a syllable—

> 'Twas when the seas were roaring
> With hollow blasts of wind:
> A damsel lay deploring
> All on a rock reclined—

This is three and a half and still runs smooth. Add one more—

> 'Twas when the seas were roaring, sir—

and so on with 'deploring, sir'. It flows smoothly still and is now four feet. But add one more—

> 'Twas when the seas were roaring, madam,
> With hollow blasts of wind—

And so on. *Now* it overlaps, limps, and is spoilt. And so in practice I find; for whereas in my lyrics in sprung rhythm I am strict in overreaving the lines when the measure has four feet, so that if one line has a heavy ending the next must have a sprung head (*or begin with a falling cadence*) as—

> Márgarét, áre you *grieving*
> Óver Góldengróve

[*and not e.g.* Concérning Góldengróve] unléaving?—

when it has only three I take no notice of it, for the heavy ending or falling cadence of one line does not interfere with the rising cadence of the next, as you may see in the *Brothers*. Now this principle of symmetry and quadrature has, as I think, been carried in music to stifling lengths and in verse not far enough and both need reforming; at least there is room, I mean, for a freer musical time and a stricter verse-prosody.

But about Patmore you are in the gall of bitterness.

Italics do look very bad in verse. But people will *not* understand where the right emphasis is. However they shall not be.

About Wyatt you are very unsatisfactory. On the fragment 'it sitteth me near' you may be right, and as likely as not it is 'sitth', for both will scan, and in Chaucer certainly *all* inflexions are open or contracted at choice. But for the whole you suggested a scanning which I believed, and believe, (no doubt without your materials for judging) to be untenable, and I think I gave reasons why I suggested another, of which you say nothing; but now, does it not meet the case? *does it not do?* Well to be sure if this one piece were all it does; but look at Wyatt, which you have before you, and see whether the principle I employed does not explain others too.

By Surrey's 'couplets of long twelves and thirteens'—a mistake for 'fourteens'—I meant the same as your '6+6 and 8+6'. It is difficult to say what makes a stanza, but I think the writer's own intention shd. decide it, which is signified by his writing or not writing in stanza-form. One certainly has a different feeling towards two lines and the same words treated as one line.

And so much for your letter of alas! Sept. 15, a very flattering and endearing one indeed. Jan. 29 1881.

Feb. 5—I find that after this letter of yours I wrote, not in answer but to comment on your printed poems. I have something now to add about these and to answer your next, which is dated Oct. 30.

'Disillusion' does exist, as typhus exists and the Protestant religion. The same 'brutes' say 'disillusion' as say 'standpoint' and 'preventative' and 'equally as well' and 'to whomsoever shall ask'. You say you always use 'enchantment' in a good sense. Very well, then you use 'disenchantment' in a bad, as its contrary. And that is what is wanted for the sonnet: the sweet enchantment (and not the foolish illusion) is over, there remains a cruel disenchantment (and not a desirable disillusion). Do you see? Where then are you? *Ubi nunc sunt omnes illi Domini et Doctores etc?* as A Kempis says. Besides *desengaño* comes, I presume, from *disincantare* and corresponds to *disenchant*, not *disillusion*—which indeed shd. be *disillude*.

About the echos I believe I have already replied. Some of

them I ought not to have thought echos at all perhaps and one, which you grant to be, I said and say does not matter. I say the same of 'the white-mossed wonder' line, that it does not matter; I cannot help fancying nevertheless that you did have in your memory the line 'For though he is under the world's splendour and wonder', the rhymes being identical and the rhythm almost so. But it is a trifle.

The Dead Child[1] is a fine poem, I am aware, but I am not bound to like it best; I do not in fact like it best nor think it the best you have written, as you say it is. I do not think either the rhythm or the thought flowing enough. The diction is not exquisite, as yours can be when you are at ease. No, but you say it is severe: perhaps it is bald. But indeed 'wise, sad head' and 'firm, pale hands' do not strike me as severe at all, nor yet exquisite. Rather they belong to a familiar commonplace about 'Reader, have you never hung over the pillow of . . . . pallid cheek, clammy brow . . . . long, long night-watches . . . surely, Sir Josiah Bickerstaff, there is *some* hope! O say not all is over. It cannot be'—You know.

I have a few suggestions to make about the rhythm of *London Snow*, which would make it perfect.[2] In 2. for 'the city' read 'London'. Then for 'Hushing' 'It hushed'. Then 'Difference hiding, making uneven even', since 'unevenness', in which the *n* is really doubled, is an awkward word. Then 'To crevices and angles' or 'To crevice and angle'. I suppose you scan 'The éye márvelled—márvelled at the dázzling whíteness; the éar héarkened to the stíllness of the sólemn áir': this is well enough when seen, but the following is easier to catch and somewhat better in itself—'Eye márvelled—márvelled át the dázzling whíteness; ear heárkened to the stíllness ín the sólemn áir'. Then for 'nor of foot' read 'or foot'. For 'awhile no thoughts' better 'no thoughts awhile'. 'Is unspoken': 'is' perhaps is better

---

[1] *Poems*, 1880, v, *On a Dead Child* (*P.W.*, vol. ii, book iii. 4).

[2] These suggestions seem, from two slips, to have been made away from the text; they were not adopted. They are characteristic, and the tendency to concentration is sufficiently clear as they stand.

omitted. In the last line omit 'for'. I know that some of the words thus omitted might on my principles as well be in, with underloopings; but there it is: I put the loops, you do not. Now it makes all the difference with a wheelbarrow whether you do or do not cry 'By leave, Sir!'

Your next letter appears to be that of Nov. 11 and I find there is nothing to answer in it. The next is answered. The next is about the Agamemnon.[1] It was the Balliol company, was it not? What interests me most is about the music. I think I shall write to Paravicini to enquire about the composer and other particulars. I have sometimes set music to a little Greek verse— to a bit of a chorus in the Prometheus Bound and to the words ἀναξιφόρμιγγες ὕμνοι in Pindar[2]—

'A - να - ξι - φόρ - μιγ - γες   ὕ - μνοι

Feb. 6—Since writing the above a Balliol man has happened to call on me and tells me the music was by Parrett of Magdalen.[3] I should very much like to have heard it.

The above strain is not in *Church* plainsong, which, as you are aware, allows no interval longer than the fifth.

Feb. 7—What you say about the run of people not liking nor knowing what to make of your writing and this giving you satisfaction opens out a wide vein of to me saddening thoughts which I shall not now enter on.

My father and mother are now recovered. My mother *was* dangerously ill: it was said to be gastric fever. I have just witnessed a case of remarkable and remarkably rapid recovery

---

[1] The *Agamemnon* of Aeschylus was acted in the hall of Balliol in June 1880, with music by Parratt. It is said to have been the first performance in England of a Greek play in the original, and led, incidentally, to the foundation of the O.U.D.S. The actors were not all Balliol men.

[2] The opening of Pindar, *Olympians*, 2: 'Ye hymns that are masters of the lyre.'

[3] Afterwards Sir Walter Parratt, Hon. Fellow of Magdalen College, and Professor of Music at Oxford, 1908–18.

from typhus in a little lad whom I anointed. It was no doubt due to the sacrament. His doctor, who gave him up, brought another one today or yesterday to see the phenomenon.

Nothing now remains, as I have answered all your letters, but to copy out the humorous pieces you wish to see. But this I had better do later and send this at once. However I must, I think, enclose the amended version of the *Brothers* and the little piece of music. Believe me your loving friend

GERARD M. HOPKINS S.J.

With heigh ho, the wind and the rain. And I must go out to Lydiate. Feb. 8 1881.

Done.

LXXII[1]

write more would weary you.

You asked me not long ago about my dramatic poem. It is a play:[2] I do not hold with dramatic poems. That is it will be if ever it gets done. But since I have been here it has made no way. At Hampstead I did some dozen lines or less. Every impulse and spring of art seems to have died in me, except for music, and that I pursue under almost an impossibility of getting on.[3] Nevertheless I still put down my pieces, for the airs seem worth it; they seem to me to have something in them which other modern music has not got. I have now also one little piece harmonised: it is only two part counterpoint at present, but it sounds impressive and is a vast improvement on the naked air. If I could only finish the harmony to 'Thou didst delight mine eyes' I hope you would like it.

I could say plenty more, but this has been kept far too long already. Believe me your affectionate friend

GERARD M. HOPKINS S.J.

I expect not long hence to leave Liverpool. April 3 1881. Hall Caine has written a review of a poem in the *Academy*.[4]

---

[1] The rest of this letter cannot be found.
[2] *St. Winefred's Well, Poems*, 36, 58.
[3] G. M. H. became, as will be seen, more and more interested in music.
[4] This seems to be a mistake; there is no signed review by him for some months before the date of this letter.

LXXIII

8 Salisbury Street, Liverpool. April 27 1881.

DEAREST BRIDGES,—The magic nib has to my surprise minuetted and gavotted into the syllables of your name. The first movement shall be something of a stately saraband.

Your strange poem 'When from the book' I could not come to like.[1] I found it *very* hard to understand and totally unexplosive: even now I cannot understand all, especially about 'the best who build'. The difficulty is caused in great part by the want of connecting particles, and when one has got over that as far as meaning goes one has again to face it for the sake of the beauty. It takes away ease and flow and charm. The thought no doubt is fine, but the impression the whole gives is what you yourself express: it is like an experiment. I cannot see much in the metre: you *mean* the lines to be so-and-so and can append the scheme of scanning, but in practice they are merely common ten-syllable lines with some Miltonic cadences and counter-pointing. The last line is a sort of hexameter bewitched. (I am afraid this is too lively for saraband). The diction too, though it is distinguished—it has "$\tau\grave{o}$ κομψὸν καὶ τὸ περιττὸν καὶ τὸ καινοτόμον", as Aristotle says of Plato—has no lyric ease.[2]

I am gropingly making my way into harmony and may come to harmonise some of my airs. 'I love my lady's eyes' is perhaps not worth it (my air I mean). But how is it you cannot judge of a melody without hearing a bass? (this is the standard spelling: *you* write 'base'). I do not understand it: a tune is a tune.

I have a good setting for 'Past like morning beam away' by your brother and am trying to harmonise it in four parts. But as it is partly in the Gregorian minor (which has no leading note) I expect I shall find it no easy task.

I hope you will be able to judge of 'Thou didst delight mine eyes' without accompaniment, for I do not see my way to one.

---

[1] Mrs. Bridges knows nothing of this: she suspects that it never matured.
[2] Aristotle, *Polit.*, 2. 6. 6.: 'the decorated and the florid and the novel'.

The air is very marked and curious: Dr. Stainer would say it is 'of a tonality' differing from the ordinary, but what exactly is up with it I do not at present know.

And in general I have become very musical of late, but graviter invita Minerva; rather I am afraid it may be Almighty God who is unwilling: for if I could conscientiously spend even a little time every day on it I could make great progress—not in execution: that is past praying for—but in composition and understanding. Who is the Muse of music by itself? Well, she is the only Muse that does not stifle in this horrible place.

By the by, do you visit University College Hospital? Because if you do I wish you would find out something for me. A young man, Patrick Gahan Byrne, died there on March 26. I want to know what he died of.[1]

My brother Lionel is home from China.[2]

I think nevertheless that even after your explanation the last stanza of 'I love my lady's eyes' is very dark. *Without* explanation I feel sure no one will understand it.

And what is the 1000-line poem about?[3] Nescio quid majus nascetur Iliade.

You give me a long jobation about eccentricities. Alas, I have heard so much about and suffered so much for and in fact been so completely ruined for life by my alleged singularities that they are a sore subject.

Your alluring proposal that I shd. come up to town and see you and Canon Dixon *has nothing but its goodnature to lift it above imbecility.*

I feel much jaded. Lent and Easter Week are a bad time for

---

[1] The hospital record gives his name as Graham Byrne, aged 26, of 1 Newton Street, Holborn. He was admitted on 24 Feb. 1881, and died on 26 March of 'heart failure following rheumatic fever at the age of 12'.

[2] Lionel Charles Hopkins, born in 1854 and educated at Winchester, became a Student interpreter in China in 1874, and was Consul-General at Tientsin when he retired from the service in 1908. He is an authority on early Chinese written characters, and has one of the finest collections in private hands of very early incised bones.

[3] *Prometheus the Firegiver.*

us. Writing was out of the question. Now I am trying to make up arrears.

I got a sudden note from the Canon saying that a Mr. Hall Caine (he lives here) is bringing out a body of modern sonnets,[1] to which he, the Canon, was to contribute two (I hope you contribute many); and that he had sent Mr. H. C. two samples of mine, and would I contribute? So I sent three to choose from; Mr. Hall Caine acknowledged them in a somewhat effusive postcard and promised to write more fully in 2 or 3 days, but did not.

I have at last applied to Mr. Rae to see his Rossettis and received a card of admission, of which I hope to avail myself next week: indeed the admission expires after May 7.

And now about the humorous poems: if I could possibly have written them out before I would; now they shall be done and sent.[2]

Today in lieu of tomorrow, May day, is fixed for the Liverpool yearly procession of horses, which I am in a few minutes going out to see something of. But the procession should begin properly at 2, at which hour I must be in my own loose box; I mean my confessional.

Believe me your affectionate friend

GERARD M. HOPKINS S.J.

April 30 1881.

May 1—The procession was not so very good: some people had thought it shd. be on Monday and so everybody and every horse did not come. A busman or cabman consoled me by declaiming in a voice hoarse with professional passion that he cd. not get on for this damned show. While I admired the handsome horses I remarked for the thousandth time with sorrow and loathing the base and bespotted figures and features of the Liverpool crowd. When I see the fine and manly

---

[1] Sonnets / of / Three Centuries: / A Selection / Including / Many Examples Hitherto Unpublished. / Edited by T. Hall Caine. / London: / Elliot Stock, 62 Paternoster Row. / 1882. With a preface of xxiv pages, dated from Vale of St. John, Cumberland, 1881.

[2] See R. B.'s note to *Poems*, 68. There is mention of certain triolets later.

127

Norwegians that flock hither to embark for America walk our streets and look about them it fills me with shame and wretchedness. I am told Sheffield is worse though. We have been shamefully beaten by the Boers (at Majuba it was simply that our troops funked and ran), but this is not the worst that is to be.

Mr. Hall Caine has written. He is not going to print me, because the purpose of his book (or introduction or prefatory essay to it) is to 'demonstrate the impossibility of improving upon the acknowledged structure whether as to rhyme-scheme or measure'.[1] Poor soul, he writes to me as to a she bear robbed of her cubs. I am replying now and reassuring him and smoothing down. To support himself he shewed some of my sonnets he had (I sent him three and the Canon two) to 'a critic of utmost eminence'; who thought with him. Who will that be, I wonder?[2] However he had *Andromeda* and one cannot say there is any novelty in rhythm there.

I hope *you* are to[3] appear, and numerously, in his volume.

Dreadful to say, he is going to refute me in a special paragraph.* And G. Saintsbury appears to have been refuting me in an article in the *Academy*.[4] This is to be a Nihilist, an influence at once baneful and unknown.

* 'Unless I object.' I think I must, for otherwise some reply seems called for, and it will be equally vexatious to reply and not to reply.

LXXIV

8 Salisbury Street, Liverpool. May 14 1881.

DEAREST BRIDGES,—Saintsbury (I think it is Saintsbury) has in one of the omnium-gatherum columns of Saturday's *Academy* a

---

[1] The preface 'constitutes an argument going to show the legitimacy and purity of the English sonnet, as against the allegation that our sonnet literature is a bastard outcome of the Italian'.

[2] Probably D. G. Rossetti.   [3] MS. 'be appear'.

[4] A lukewarm review (30 April 1881) of *The Death of Themistocles, and other Poems*, by John Nichol, contains the words (with an elaboration of them): 'We have only one charge to bring against him as to the technical part of his work—that he is too apt to break his rhythms without sufficient cause.'

notice of your last issue.[1] It is not an unfriendly notice and expresses real admiration: to be sure it is impertinent, in G. S.'s way. I think he is a good critic, do you know. He is clever and free from crotchets (the bane of acute criticism), and with that to be well read, as I think he is, should make him competent. He writes a bad style, a vulgar style: I grant that.

But alas! you will have been sickened by the vulgarity of my comic poems, I am afraid; especially of 'the Church of England'[2]—which last by the by I sent in an unfinished state. But I have in me a great vein of blackguardry and have long known I am no gentleman; though I had rather say this than have it said.

To return to Saintsbury, criticism, and so on, you are too severe a critic. Morally I mean. Though my worst, my malignant nature is pleased by hearing you or others call people rogues and damfools and egregious asses, yet it is not right. But at any rate why should you insult people and quarrel? Why should you make enemies? It is never good to have enemies and one should never quarrel. You must have insulted Mr. Hall Caine by what you say. And you do not consider that he may perhaps now injure me in revenge for you. People can always injure, they have always their tongues, they can always *say* something that either hurts or harms. Before your note of warning I had written a longish letter to him, gently poking fun. His manner was that I was a 'young aspirant' and he a judge by whose nod I stood or fell—a thing not to be thought. He has not replied and the sonnet business is no doubt at an

[1] An unsigned review of less than a column in the issue of 14 May 1881. It begins with reproving the poet for printing his work in 'furtive pamphlets' and anonymously, yet adds: 'for any appearance of irritation in these remarks we can best account by professing our very high admiration for this mysterious and yet well-known author's work.' Nevertheless 'for the author's experiments in a new prosody we do not care much, though they contain at least the elements of some fine poetry. When the new prosody is worth much, it seems to us to be reducible with advantage to the old.'

[2] R. B. kept, in A, only two of G. M. H.'s comic or humorous poems. This is not one of them. Of the two, one is printed (*Poems*, 68), and R. B.'s note on that mentions the other, which is negligible, but not 'vulgar'.

end. But why should *you* not have contributed?[1]—Now *why* did you refuse? It was rude, for anything I see. Your sonnets would have graced the book, I believe there would have been nothing in it so good; or if it was to be only one, why what harm could one do? One sonnet was not worth quarrelling about.

I have been to see Mr. Rae's pictures: I wrote to Mr. Rae himself. He has built himself a handsome house and it is full of beautiful objects wherever your eye can rest. Mrs. Rae was at home and spent hours in taking me about and shewing me everything, then gave me lunch, and asked me to come again. She was simple and homely and at the same time lively, with a real enthusiasm for art and understanding of it and had nothing whatever of the 'cultshah' manner: I suppose she dates from before it came in. She was very kind, I liked her very much. The pictures were beautiful of course. They still buy: there was that queer landscape of the Beloved in the Canticles by Spencer Stanhope which I saw at the Grosvenor last year. She said by the by that he too had nothing of the modern nonsense, was a gentleman and nothing else. I might run on all about these pictures.

Tell me about Canon Dixon's visit. (Did your mother like him?)[2]

What will befall me I do not know, but I hardly think I shall be much longer in Liverpool.

Believe me your affectionate friend

GERARD M. HOPKINS S.J.

May 15.

LXXV

8 Salisbury Street, Liverpool. June 16 1881.

DEAREST BRIDGES,—There was a Devonshire clergyman who sent Garrick a play, which play Garrick either refused or wanted

---

[1] There is nothing by R. B. in the book. R. W. Dixon contributed three sonnets: *Perished Ideals*, 'Give me the darkest corner of a cloud', and *Humanity*; and there is a note of tempered praise on him.

[2] R. B. had 'never heard of Dixon' until 1878, when G. M. H. told him of his poetry. For this visit perhaps, see *Memoir (Selected Poems)*, pp. xxiv–v.

much altered. Correspondence followed and the clergyman wrote 'Sir, this is growing to be a very serious and terrible affair: I will publish my play as it stands and then where will your judgment appear? Garrick replied that 'in spite of all the seriousness and all the terrors' he held to his opinion, but that as he was on the spot and acquainted with the men he wd. use his good offices with the publishers on behalf of the play. On this the clergyman saw that he had been foolish and gave in. Now in the present case all the seriousness and all the terrors are on your side and especially in your stern lines of this morning and the good offices are on mine, which are that no more shall be sent (there is none now) and that you shall be 'solicited for no further orders'.[1] I do not feel ashamed of the pieces, unless for a certain blackguardry, but will not defend them.

The slip from the *Irish World* was really put in, but was so small that no doubt it fluttered out on opening and was lost. It was the following lines of quotation:

> A spell is laid on sod and stone;
> Day and night 've tampered with;
> Every quality and pith
> Surcharged and sultry with a power
> That works its will on age and hour.

Perhaps the quoter was quoting himself.

Boivin comes from a little French religious print, where I saw it years ago and carried it in my head.[2] It had no name and is perhaps by one of our people.

I do not know whether Edward Bond has yet been to dine with you. I do not believe he wd. like my poems, certainly not at first. Upon my word the comic ones wd. please him best.

The state of the country is indeed sad, I might say it is heartbreaking, for I am a very great patriot. Lamentable as the condition of Ireland is there is hope of things mending, but the Transvaal is an unredeemed disgrace. And people do not seem

---

[1] This phrase is explained by the comic verses that remain unpublished.
[2] This remains a puzzle to Mrs. Bridges and myself.

to mind. You know that our troops ('our gallant fellows', as the reporter had it) ran.

I am sure you are very unjust to Millais (which just at present is a reflection that affords me comfort). He has, I have always seen, no feeling for beauty in abstract design and he never designs; but he has a deep feeling, it is plain, for concrete beauty, wild or natural beauty, much as Keats had. The element of ugliness in him is like the element of ugliness in nature and there is that plainly enough. In Millais I allow there is too much of it, too little of the contrary. But still, as above. And how much ugliness there is in Velasquez! Do you mean to say the Order for Release is not a noble work? and the Proscribed Royalist?[1] The Huguenot has some splendid 'concrete beauty' in the vegetation and so on.[2] But the Brunswicker I do think bad and ugly.[3]

Persuade Hall Caine to put in my 'Andromeda'! Absit. No more is said between us about putting my sonnets in, but as I always have some crotchet in hand my present aim is to get Crawley's[4] sonnets in. And it is my fixed principle never to quarrel.

Believe me your affectionate friend

GERARD M. HOPKINS S.J.

LXXVI

8 Salisbury Street, Liverpool. June 28 1881.

DEAREST BRIDGES,—Let us talk sense. (A) There is no need to 'beg my pardon' for giving me the best advice you have to give, but (B) if you must beg my pardon it takes all the sweet out of it to say 'consistent with' etc—which nevertheless you

---

[1] These two pictures are of 1853.   [2] Of 1852.

[3] *The Black Brunswicker*, a parting scene between an officer and his lover before the battle of Waterloo, was exhibited in 1860: it is generally held to end a period of transition in style.

[4] Richard Crawley, University College, Oxford, took a 1st in Greats in 1865, and was the author of certain books of verse, among them *Venus and Psyche; with other Poems* (1871). None of his sonnets is in Hall Caine's book.

had to say: the upshot is that you should not beg pardon. Now about these blessed verses—In the first place there is not the least hurry nor the least importance in the matter; for what chance is there of anything of mine on any subject in any style at any time appearing? You do not realise how remote and how slight the chance is. July 2—Since writing the above I have this morning received, with much concern, your pencil note saying you are sick of pneumonia.[1] I am afraid you must be very sick. I have attended people in pneumonia and anointed them; they recovered. I shall visit you, I cannot anoint you, but I hope nevertheless that by the time I come you will [be] on the highroad of recovery. This may perhaps be on Tuesday next. And if in the meantime I do not weary you I shall finish off what is begun above. About the verses I have to say this: my brother Lionel once wrote that somebody's joke was 'strictly funny'. Now as in serious poetry the standard and aim is strict beauty and if the writer misses that his verse, whatever its incidental merits, is not strict or proper poetry / so in comedy or comic writing, which Horace says is perhaps not to be called poetry at all, the standard is the 'strictly funny': what falls short of that, however good in other respects, is a failure; what hits that, whatever other faults it may have, is a success. Now staggered as I am and ought to be by your judgment, still the feeling of innocence, the sense of integrity, the consciousness of rectitude have returned and I cannot help thinking, though with hesitation and diffidence, that those verses or some of them are strictly funny.

As for your being able to ruffle me if you chose, no doubt if you touched me on certain sensitive places you would not only ruffle but deeply wound: it does not however follow that everything ruffles me.

[1] This illness, which attacked R. B. in London, was serious, and his recovery slow. In November he went to Italy and Sicily; returned in 1882, having resigned his medical appointments (which he always intended to do when he was forty); and took the Manor House at Yattendon, whither his mother accompanied him. She had been living with him at 52 Bedford Square, London.

About Hall Caine there is some misunderstanding in your mind. I did not express, I do not feel, admiration for him. He may be a competent critic, but the essay on the Supernatural he sent me I think but poorly of.[1] His style is bad. He imitates Matthew Arnold and appears to be his friend: I suppose Arnold was that 'critic of utmost eminence', who agreed with him about my sonnets.[2] But, as I said, I did not wish to quarrel: I have daily experience of the folly of doing it.

I see that Oscar Wild, the 'utterly utter'[3], is bringing out 10s. 6d. worth of poems.[4]

And now, my dear heart, I shall say no more till we meet, when I hope you will be better, the better to see me and even the better for seeing me. I have a little medical anecdote that should amuse you. But I am afraid we are not in agreement about the strictly funny.

Believe me yours affectionately

GERARD HOPKINS S.J.

July 3 1881.

I find I cannot go to town before Tuesday at earliest, so you must not expect me before Wednesday at earliest.[5]

LXXVII

St. Joseph's, North Woodside Road, Glasgow.
Sept. 16 1881.

DEAREST BRIDGES,—How is it you do not know I am here? On Oct. 10 I am to be at Roehampton (Manresa House, as of old) to begin, my 'tertianship', the third year (really ten months) of

---

[1] This essay, *The Supernatural Element in Poetry*, printed 'in the magazine that had once been sub-edited by George Eliot', was part of Hall Caine's introduction to Rossetti. See vol. ii, p. 46, n. 2.

[2] These conjectures seem very wide of the mark.

[3] Bunthorne, *Patience*, 1881.

[4] *Poems*. D. Bogue: London, 1881. Wilde had won the Newdigate with *Ravenna* in 1878.

[5] Mrs. Bridges tells me that other contemporary letters make it plain that R. B. was very seriously ill at this time. She finds no record of this visit, and thinks it most unlikely that G. M. H.'s plan was carried out.

noviceship which we undergo before taking our last vows. Till then I expect to be here mostly, but must go to Liverpool to pack; for I came for a fortnight or so only and left my things: indeed I am going to pieces as I stand.

I began a letter to you a short while ago, but tore it up. Meant to write I have every day for long.

I am very glad you do improve. Still your recovery is very slow and I cannot understand it. You did run well, like the Galatians:[1] how has your good constitution been so unhappily bewitched? I hope nevertheless that all your strength will return.

And the good Canon too lies like a load on my heart. To him I am every day meaning to write and last night it was I began, but it would not do; however today I shall. Besides I have his poems—some here, some left behind at Liverpool. I have some hopes of managing an interview on my way south.

Things are pleasanter here than at Liverpool. Wretched place too Glasgow is, like all our great towns; still I get on better here, though bad is the best of my getting on. But now I feel that I need the noviceship very much and shall be every way better off when I have been made more spiritual minded.

There, I mean at Roehampton, I am pretty well resolved, I will altogether give over composition for the ten months, that I may *vacare Deo* as in my noviceship proper. I therefore want to get some things done first, but fear I never shall. One is a great ode on Edmund Campion S.J.[2] For the 1st of December next is the 300th anniversary of his, Sherwin's and Bryant's martyrdom, from which I expect of heaven some, I cannot guess

[1] Galatians, v. 7 (Authorized Version): Ye did run well; who did hinder you that ye should not obey the truth?

[2] Of this poem, unfortunately, no fragment seems to have survived. In many ways Edmund Campion (1540–81), the brilliant and ill-starred Jesuit, was an attractive and strangely appropriate subject for G. M. H., and much more promising in breadth and pity than the other poems dealing with martyrdom he had contemplated. There is kinship between the two men.

Campion, after torture and a pretence at trial, was executed at Tyburn with Sherwin and Briant on 1 Dec. 1581, and was beatified by Leo XIII in 1886.

what, great conversion or other blessing to the Church in England. Thinking over this matter my vein began to flow and I have by me a few scattered stanzas, something between the *Deutschland* and *Alexander's Feast*, in sprung rhythm of irregular metre. But the vein urged by any country sight or feeling of freedom or leisure (you cannot tell what a slavery of mind or heart it is to live my life in a great town) soon dried and I do not know if I can coax it to run again. One night, as I lay awake in a fevered state, I had some glowing thoughts and lines, but I did not put them down and I fear they may fade to little or nothing. I am sometimes surprised at myself how slow and laborious a thing verse is to me when musical composition comes so easily, for I can make tunes almost at all times and places and could harmonise them as easily if only I could play or could read music at sight. Indeed if I could play the piano with ease I believe I could improvise on it. I have of late been finishing the air, but only the air, of *I have loved flowers that fade.* I find now I can put a second part satisfactorily to myself, but about fuller chords I am timid and incapable as yet. It is besides very difficult to get at a piano. I have now also a certain power of counterpointing (I will not say harmonising) without an instrument: I do not, in my mind's ear, as a musician would do, hear the chords, but I have an instinct of what will do and verify by rule and reckoning the air which I do hear: this suggests itself and springs from the leading air which is to be accompanied.— I got a young lady this evening to play me over some of my pieces, but was not well pleased with them. What had sounded rich seemed thin. I had been trying several of them as canons, but this I found was unsatisfactory and unmeaning and the counterpoint drowns the air. If I could only get good harmonies to *I have loved flowers* it would be very sweet, I think; I shd. then send it you and should like Woolrych to see it too.

I am now writing to Canon Dixon.

I am promised before I leave Scotland two days to see something of the Highlands.

I can well understand that 'what there is unusual in expression in my verse is less pleasant when you are in that sort of weak state', for I find myself that when I am tired things of mine sound strange, forced, and without idiom which had pleased me well enough in the fresh heat of composition. But then the weaker state is the less competent and really critical. I always think however that your mind towards my verse is like mine towards Browning's: I greatly admire the touches and the details, but the general effect, the whole, offends me, I think it repulsive.

Your letters addressed to Liverpool were forwarded very leisurely.

Believe me your affectionate friend

GERARD M. HOPKINS S.J.

Sept. 17 1881.

LXXVIII

Manresa House, Roehampton S.W. Oct. 22 1881.

DEAREST BRIDGES,—I hear on two hands that you are mending, but, as before, very slowly. I earnestly hope that the sickness is not as you feared to leave incurable remains behind it.

This must go by Bedford Square. I shd. have written before, but it is no easy task meeting one's out of door liabilities (any how writing letters is what I mean) with a day so sliced up into the duties of a noviceship as this life is. I see no newspapers, read none but spiritual books. However I have Canon Dixon's MS poems still by me and am trying to get my last criticisms on them done before our Long Retreat (of a month) begins, which indeed will not be yet a while.

I had to leave three volumes, if you can call pamphlets volumes, of your poems behind me at Liverpool; for to carry them longer about with me would have been to claim them as property. And I am afraid they are but lost in that library: who will read them? Now I regret that I did not spend my pocket-money, in the days when pocketmoney was, in binding them together: they wd. better have weathered time so. However you will in time gather all these and more into one volume.

It is raining very heavily, thro' a white fog. But we have been having bright and frosty weather, and the look of nature (whose face I had almost forgotten) was very sonsy, as the Glasgow people say. The great gale, which you must have felt at Torquay, was here terrible, nearly killed two of us, left a scene of havoc, and knocked all round our neighbourhood tall trees down like ninepins. This spot, though it has suffered much from decay of nature and more from the hand of man, is still beautiful. It is besides a great rest to be here and I am in a very contented frame of mind.

You remember my consulting you about a fall in which I broke a ligament of my right arm: you told me it might not heal for eighteen months. I felt it at all events for twelve and even now I am not sure that if I were to throw my arm far enough and hard enough back I might not feel it still; only, as Abernethy said, 'why the devil should I do *so*?' Now the other day I did what I had no business to do; I tried my strength with another man by clasping my hands, cross-fingered, with his and each thrusting forward. Now I had the best of him if only he had played fair, but he brought my left arm down, which is not allowed, and twisted it so hard that something is wrong at the wrist and within these three days, weeks after the event, it has become more painful. This is when I bend it forward, hunch, or $\kappa\upsilon\rho\tau\hat{\omega}$ (is the Greek for it) the wrist. Now is this too, do you think, a broken ligament? and will it take a year and more to mend? and will it at last be as strong as before? But I should say that at the time, unlike my fall down stairs, there was no pain but that of straining, no feeling of a snap.

A letter from my father yesterday said that Mrs. Molesworth now writes cheerfully of your progress. And so I begin to hope that with returning health your mind will recover its vigour soon, your vein glow, and your muse sing. I have never heard yet what was that long and important poem that you were at work upon. As far as our chances of meeting go your being from town just now makes no difference, for if you had been at Bedford Square you would have been laid up more than at Torquay, yet I could not have visited you, and if you had been well I should not have wished just yet to see visitors.

I suppose that I have all Canon Dixon's MS pieces by me that you have seen excepting the two epic works.[1] The best of all, I am inclined to think, is the Ode on Conflicting Claims;[2] at least the execution is nearly perfect and on a level with the thought and feeling, in which he is always a master and never makes a false note. This poem is one of extreme excellence. But he is unequal and the unequality lies in execution, chiefly in his diction, which varies from rich to meagre. He has not a sure hand like Tennyson and will let fall a weak stanza: this is against his success. His command of pathos is exquisite and he excels in all tragic feeling, and that with an extreme purity, a directness of human nature, and absence of affectation which is most rare. I feel in reading him what a gentleman he is and it brings on that feeling that I am a blackguard. His other great excellence is pure imagination, either arising from images in nature (as in the Rainbow poem) or expressing itself in them: I think it would not be possible in literature to find a lovelier example than that Rainbow piece.[3] I hope he will push on with the epic or romance you saw, for he will be more telling in a long than in short pieces, as is natural in one who is rich in matter and imperfect in form. I see no reason why he should not write the finest narrative poem of this age:[4] he will never acquire Tennyson's workmanship and infallibly telling freedom of stroke, which is indeed half of art, but he much excels him in other gifts.

[1] Of R. W. Dixon's Epics, only *Mano* survives. R. B. remembered to have seen 'reams of *Northern Saga*'.

[2] Included in *Odes and Eclogues* (1884) and reprinted in *Selected Poems* (1909).

[3] R. B. says (*Selected Poems of R. W. Dixon*, p. 193) that this poem cannot be found. But evidently G. M. H. refers to the poem he afterwards called *Fallen Rain* (*Selected Poems*, pp. 148-9), which at that time had no title.

[4] This would be no extravagant claim to make for *Mano*.

This letter was meant by way of charity to wile away your time, for I ought to be at other things than letterwriting: it certainly has wiled away mine. Remember me very kindly to your mother and believe me your affectionate friend

GERARD M. HOPKINS S.J.

Oct. 25 1881.

Did my father read his poem?

LXXIX

Manresa House, Roehampton, London, S.W. Dec. 18 1881.

BRIDGES, my dear heart, why have you not written? why did you not reply to my last addressed to you at Torquay and ricochetting off Bedford Square? as this too must do. What plea, what[1] flimsiest pretext have you got? You are well and strong or fast getting so, so Mrs. Molesworth says (more by token I must write to her and find where you are), and having nothing to do. I have, neither shall I waste time on you now. I do not expect to be much longer here. The Canon and I have been corresponding heavily. Yours as you shall use him

GERARD HOPKINS S.J.

LXXX

Manresa House, Roehampton, S.W. Feb. 1 1882.

DEAREST BRIDGES,—I was of course delighted to get your letter and think you must now surely soon be going to be quite strong and well.

I have no time for more than business-like letter writing. At the beginning of Lent I am to take duty at Preston (St. Ignatius's will do for the address) and from the Fourth Sunday in Lent (March 19) to Palm Sunday (April 2) I am to help in mission-services to be given at Maryport on the coast of Cumberland (not so far from Carlisle), I am now therefore closely

[1] MS. 'have'.

employed preparing discourses and instructions. After that I ought to return here, but it may easily happen that some need fixes me elsewhere. I am, as you must remember, like a novice, have been to town only to see the dentist, and could not hope to visit you. You might come and see me and the place is worth seeing, but it could be very seldom. In no case does my probation last beyond August.

The winter has been very mild. Our primroses have been more than a fortnight in bloom and laurels are beginning to flower. It is unnatural and I want to see it colder.

I find the life trying—weakening, I mean. But the calm of mind is delightful: I am afraid I shall leave it behind.

I should hardly wish you to send me your poem here.[1] Either send it to me at Preston or keep it awhile. I am sorry to put off the pleasure, but the time does not suit. I may add that the right to secrecy in correspondence which, as you know, we Jesuits surrender . . . the sentence would be tedious to finish: what I mean is that the right to read our letters claimed by the Society of its subjects but mostly not exercised is here a realised fact; so consult your own taste about what you will say and leave unsaid.

I shall never rest till you change the third line in the sonnet 'In all things beautiful': it weakens and disfigures an otherwise perfect work. Can you not say something like:

> As but to watch her folds fall how they do,
>
> And all $\left.{{\text{her ways are}}\atop{\text{that comes is}}}\right\}$ past expectancy—?[2]

And I hold to the metrical objections I made to some lines in the poem about Flying Flames.[3]

---

[1] *Prometheus the Firegiver.*

[2] In their final form (*P.W.*, vol. i, *G. of L.*, 31) these lines are:

> 'Tis joy to watch the folds fall as they do,
> And all that comes is past expectancy.

[3] The lyric 'O my vague desires' (*P.W.*, vol. ii, book iii. 1). It is worth mention that R. B. also used it towards the end of his *Prometheus*.

I believe I told you that you must be mistaken about the stanza-nature of *terza rima* being *quite* unknown to English poets. Shelley certainly has one or more pieces in that measure printed in stanzas and as a boy I published in *Once a Week* a piece called *Winter with the Gulf Stream* (it was such another winter as this) in the same (but in eights) and so printed. I borrowed also the contrivance of ending with a couplet, which has the convenience of ravelling up the rhymes. Treated in this stanza form the *terza rima* is one of the simplest of measures as it is one of the most beautiful: at each stanza's end you can either rest or go on with equally charming effect. Indeed I think I must try it again.

Yesterday Feb. 2 it froze. We had a holiday and I took two Frenchmen[1] to the South Kensington museums. The frost fog red with smoke made it so dark that we cd. scarcely be said to see. Amidst the bewildering wealth of beautiful things my attention was fixed by the casts from Michael Angelo, the David, two figures of slaves for Julius II's tomb, a Madonna, and others. I thought of the advantage, for which nothing can completely make up, you have of seeing these things on the spot. In the arts of painting and sculpture I am, even when most I admire, always convinced of a great shortcoming: nothing has been done yet at all equal to what one can easily conceive being done. For instance for work to be perfect there ought to be the sense of beauty in the highest degree both in the artist and in the age, the style and keepings of which the artist employs. Now the keepings of the age in which for instance Raphael and Angelo lived were rich, but unsatisfactory in the extreme. And they were both far from having a pure sense of beauty. Besides which they have several other great short-comings. But in poetry and perhaps in music *unbetterable* works have been produced. No room to go on nor time either. But talking of perfection, could you not get rid of *test* in 'Thou didst delight'? Look here: rhyme on *first* and *durst* and you will get something very good. I dare not tell you my thought, for it wd.

---

[1] MS. 'Frenchman'.

be to defeat my own purpose, but do it yourself, simple, suitable, and sweet.[1] Write about things in Italy. Your ever affectionate friend

GERARD M. HOPKINS S.J.

LXXXI

St. Wilfrid's, Preston. April 3 1882.

I HOPE, my dear heart, you are now really better; not better, well; strong, vigorous, lusty, beefish, as apt to pull an oar as to turn a sonnet with the best in either kind. And we may now shortly hope to meet. For I suppose I shall be at Roehampton tomorrow. The address is Manresa (not Manresca) House—it is called after the place where St. Ignatius lived for a year doing penance in a cave—, Roehampton, S.W.

At the beginning of Lent I came from Roehampton here to stop a gap and do some parish work; I then went to Maryport on the coast of Cumberland, to take part in a Mission, which is something like a Revival without the hysteria and the heresy, and it had the effect of bringing me out and making me speak very plainly and strongly (I enjoyed that, for I dearly like calling a spade a spade): it was the first thing of the sort I had been employed in; but no more of this now   On my way back I was detained here to hear Lenten confessions again.

I came by Carlisle and made an appointment with Canon Dixon, so that we spent some hours together, and he gave me dinner and shewed me the Cathedral. Partly through this

---

[1] The first reading was (*Poems*, 1880):
> Thou didst delight my eyes:
> Yet who am I? nor best
> Nor first nor last to test
> Thy charm, thy bloom to prize; . . .

The final form (*P.W.*, vol. ii, book iii. 12) is:
> Thou didst delight my eyes:
> Yet who am I? nor first
> Nor last nor best, that durst
> Once dream of thee for prize;.

sightseeing and more through shyness on his part (not on mine) we did not get much intimate or even interesting talk. I was amused when his hat twice blew off in English Street to watch his behaviour. I wish I could have been with him longer.

I have been reading Purcell's Life in the Great Musicians series:[1] you should.

I forget if I told you that Grace set music to 'Sometimes when my Lady'. It is characteristic, with an old fashioned and suitable flavour about it.

Believe me your loving friend

GERARD.

If the best comes to the best you are already home and free to see me, but do not come this week of course. Let me have a line first.

April 4—I forgot to tell you that Canon Dixon was married in February.

It is a pity you did not write to me while I was here. I must go back tomorrow.

LXXXII

Manresa House, Roehampton, S.W. May 15 1882.

DEAREST BRIDGES,—Will Thursday, which is Ascension Day, do? Come in the afternoon, the earlier the better. But if it rains I should say put it off.

The weather is most bleak and I should like you to see our grounds to advantage, which on a day like this can never be; but besides, the great gale of the 30th felled three of our trees and blighted the foliage in a way I never saw before. The lime tops are almost bare: the young leaves being withered have been falling in the East winds of late and on the ground look like tealeaves after boiling dried.

But we have a remarkable show of buttercups. I suppose you would not see the like in Italy.

---

[1] By William Hayman Cummings (one of the original committee of the Purcell Society, founded 21 Feb. 1876), 1881.

We have also three remarkable pictures of great size by a lady, a sort of 'new departure'.

Perhaps what I took for Manresca was Manrexa, but that is wrong too: x and s are not the same in Spanish, though x and j are.

I would say Wednesday, our usual weekly holiday, but this week I do not feel quite sure about it.

I suppose Mrs. Molesworth did not forward my last letter. On second thoughts I suppose she did. Anyhow you got it.

Strictly, any day would do. But I am chary of my time for study, which now thickens as the time thins.

Believe me yours

GERARD M HOPKINS S.J.

By the by, your note is dated the 12th: it bears today's postmark.

LXXXIII

Manresa House, Roehampton, S.W. June 5 '82.

DEAREST BRIDGES,—My heart warmed towards that little Bertie Molesworth[1] (I do not mean by this that he is so very small), so that if you were to bring him again I shd. be glad to see him. (But I am afraid he felt dull. He is shy I dare say.) However I expect he is no longer with you. It cannot be denied nevertheless that the presence of a third person is a restraint upon confidential talk.

Davis the gardener was discontented that I would not let you buy his peaches: he wd. have let you have them on reasonable terms, he said.[2]

I have been studying the cuckoo's song.[3] I find it to vary much. In the first place cuckoos do not always sing (or the same cuckoo does not always sing) at the same pitch or in the

---

[1] Son of R. B.'s eldest sister Maria.

[2] For the underlying importance of this incident, which R. B. vividly remembered, see *The Testament of Beauty*, Book IV, *Ethick*, ll. 406–58. See also p. 152.   [3] See *Poems*, 66.

same key: there are, so to say, alto cuckoos and tenor cuckoos. In particular they sing lower in flying and the interval is then also least, it being an effort to them to strike the higher note, which is therefore more variable than the other. When they perch they sing wrong at first, I mean they correct their first try, raising the upper note. The interval varies as much as from less than a minor third to nearly as much as a common fourth and this last is the tune when the bird is in loud and good song.

About the book I will not write.[1]

Your affectionate friend

GERARD M. HOPKINS S.J.

LXXXIV

Manresa House, Roehampton, S.W. June 7 1882.

DEAREST BRIDGES,—You might surely have guessed that I had some reason for my silence. It was not want of admiration.

(1) I hope Mrs. Molesworth will not long be laid up. But if she were to be so she would not wish to keep you every afternoon at home. (2) Your niece can do the very thing she has come to do when you give her the opportunity by your absence. (3) There are houses at Roehampton, Barnes, Richmond, Twickenham, Ham, Petersham, Kew, Isleworth, Mortlake, Wimbledon, all near us. (5) Canon Dixon: you have answered this admirably. (6) Your brother: and this. (7) The club: 'this is past and present'; then not future, such as the rest of this week or next.

I have revised nearly twice through. The worst is that one seasons over a thing and one's first verjuice flattens into slobber[2] and sweet syllabub. Or one ripens; yet there is something in 'the first sprightly runnings'.[3]

Your affectionate friend

GERARD M. HOPKINS S.J.

[1] The MS. of *Prometheus the Firegiver*.
[2] Written above 'flattery', cancelled.
[3] Dryden, *Aureng-Zebe*, Act IV, sc. 1, l. 42.

146

Tomorrow, Corpus Christi, you must not come: I shd. be engaged.

I see I have overlooked 4. the Turkish baths. Instead of answering—but by the by too many Turkish baths are not good. An old gentleman (commercial) that I gave a retreat to here nearly died in one.

You were asking me about my own writing. You perhaps forget my mentioning my beginning an ode in honour of Fr. Edmund Campion's martyrdom. Little is done, but I hope to be able to go on with it and that it will not be inferior to the two other odes. It is dithyrambic or what they used to call Pindaric (which as we have Pindar now is unPindaric), I mean in variable stanzas and not antistrophic; like *Alexander's Feast* or *Lycidas*. It has some new rhythmical effects.

But if I must write about Prometheus, then I will shortly say, what it seems scarcely necessary to say, how beautiful and masterly it is, what a sense of style, unknown in our age, in the phrasing and the verse, how vigorous the thought, and how Greek, whether you wished it or not, the choruses, and yet so fresh.

LXXXV

Manresa House, Roehampton, S.W. June 10 1882.

DEAREST BRIDGES,—It was a needless and tedious frenzy (no, the phrase is *not* like Flatman's 'serene and rapturous joys' to which poor Purcell had to drudge the music):[1] another train came up on that train's tail, and indeed it was a dull duncery that overhung us both not to see that its being Ascot day ensured countless more trains and not fewer. There was a lovely and passionate scene (for about the space of the last trump) between me and a tallish gentleman (I daresay he was a cardsharper) in your carriage who was by way of being you; I smiled, I murmured with my lips at him, I waved farewells, but he would not give in, till with burning shame (though the

[1] See NOTE O.

147

whole thing was, as I say, like the duels of archangels) I saw suddenly what I was doing.

I wish our procession, since you were to see it, had been better: I find it is agreed it was heavy and dead. Now a Corpus Christi procession shd. be stately indeed, but it shd. be brisk and joyous. But I grieve more, I am vexed, that you had not a book to follow the words sung: the office is by St. Thomas and contains all his hymns, I think. These hymns, though they have the imperfect rhetoric and weakness in idiom of all medieval Latin verse (except, say, the Dies Irae: I do not mean weakness in classical idiom—that does not matter—but want of feeling for or command of *any* idiom), are nevertheless remarkable works of genius and would have given meaning to the whole, even to the music, much more to the rite.

It is long since such things had any significance for you. But what is strange and unpleasant is that you sometimes speak as if they had in reality none for me and you were only waiting with a certain disgust till I too should be disgusted with myself enough to throw off the mask. You said something of the sort walking on the Cowley Road when we were last at Oxford together—in '79 it must have been. Yet I can hardly think you do not think I am in earnest. And let me say, to take no higher ground, that without earnestness there is nothing sound or beautiful in character and that a cynical vein much indulged coarsens everything in us. Not that you do overindulge this vein in other matters: why then does it bulk out in that diseased and varicose way in this?

Believe me your affectionate friend

GERARD HOPKINS S.J.

June 11—Since writing the above I have luckily come across the enclosed, which contains some of the hymns.

Remember me very kindly to Mrs. Molesworth, who is, I hope, better. Also to Mr. Woolrych. Must meet him next time I am at—but I shall never be there by the by now.

I am just starting for Brentford.

LXXXVI

Manresa House, Roehampton, S.W. June 16 1882.

DEAREST BRIDGES,—But at any rate do not come on Sunday, for I shall be away taking duty at Westminster.

Put S.W. after Roehampton: your last note had five postmarks, one of them very sinister, as if there had been some struggling or straying.

Corpus Xti differs from all other feasts in this, that its reason and occasion is present. The first Christmas Day, the first Palm Sunday, Holy Thursday 'in Caena Domini', Easter, Whitsunday, and so on were to those who took part in them festivities *de praesenti*, but now, to us, they are anniversaries and commemorations only. But Corpus Christi is the feast of the Real Presence; therefore it is the most purely joyous of solemnities. Naturally the Blessed Sacrament is carried in procession at it, as you saw. But the procession has more meaning and mystery than this: it represents the process of the Incarnation and the world's redemption. As Christ went forth from the bosom of the Father as the Lamb of God and eucharistic victim to die upon the altar of the cross for the world's ransom; then rising returned leading the procession of the flock redeemed / so in this ceremony his body *in statu victimali* is carried to the Altar of Repose as it is called and back to the tabernacle at the high altar, which will represent the bosom of the godhead. The procession out may represent the cooperation of the angels, or of the patriarchs and prophets, the return the Church Catholic from Christ's death to the end of time. If these things are mismanaged, as they mostly are, it is not for want of significance in the ceremony.

Prometheus has been twice revised. Whether I shall want to keep it longer I cannot say yet. We want alas! a touch of his trade this bitter June. This morning not only the air is most nipping; the very look is of a winter frostfog.

My best love to Canon Dixon, whom I hope soon to see.

Your affectionate friend

GERARD HOPKINS S.J

149

LXXXVII

Stonyhurst College, Blackburn. Sept. 26 1882.

MY DEAREST BRIDGES,—I *must* break this mournful silence. I began a letter yesterday, but am not pleased with it and now shall be brief.

I have been here[1] since this month came in. My appointment is to teach our 'philosophers' (like undergraduate students) Latin, Greek, and perhaps hereafter English (when I know more about it) for the London B.A. degree. My pupils will be here with the next month. The Provincial further added that what time was left over I might employ in writing one or other of the books I had named to him. But very little time will be left over and I cd. never make time. Indeed now, with nothing to do but prepare, I cannot get forward with my ode. But one must hope against hope.

I did in my last week at Roehampton write 16 pages of a rough draft of a commentary on St. Ignatius' Spiritual Exercises. This work would interest none but a Jesuit, but to me it is interesting enough and, as you see, it is very professional.

I shall try and read the Greek tragic poets, but it is sad how slow I am. I am now in the *Agamemnon* and *Supplices* (Aeschylus's, I mean). How noble is the style! I have made some emendations which seem to be great improvements. But what I pay most attention to is the art of the choric parts, for this was one of the subjects on which I had proposed to write, the art of the Greek lyric poets, including of course the lyric parts of dramatic poets. I have not time at present to tell you what the leading idea or my leading discovery is. In part of course my work here may serve me for the books I should like to write.

The Provincial gave me leave to go to any one of our houses I liked till my term began. I did go for a week to Worcester, where there was, by the by, a very well worth seeing exhibition,

---

[1] He remained on the staff there till August 1884. He taught Greek and Latin to candidates for the external Intermediate and Degree examinations of the University of London.

but then I thought it better to come here at once. He said moreover that if I wanted to go elsewhere I was to apply to him. He would no doubt readily have given me leave to visit you and, had there been the possibility of saying mass, I might therefore have seen Yattenden. But it was not to be.

I wish I could show you this place. It is upon my word worth seeing. The new college, though there is no real beauty in the design, is nevertheless imposing and the furniture and fittings are a joy to see. There is always a stirring scene, contractors, builders, masons, bricklayers, carpenters, stonecutters and carvers, all on the spot; a traction engine twice a day fetches stone from a quarry on the fells; engines of all sorts send their gross and foulsmelling smoke all over us; cranes keep swinging; and so on. There are acres of flat roof which, when the air is not thick, as unhappily it mostly is, commands a noble view of this Lancashire landscape, Pendle Hill, Ribblesdale, the fells, and all round, bleakish but solemn and beautiful. There is a garden with a bowling green, walled in by massive yew hedges, a bowered yew-walk, two real Queen Ann summerhouses, observatories under government, orchards, vineries, greenhouses, workshops, a plungebath, fivescourts, a mill, a farm, a fine cricketfield besides a huge playground; then the old mansion, ponds, towers, quadrangles, fine cielings,[1] chapels, a church, a fine library, museums, MSS illuminated and otherwise, coins, works of art; then two other dependent establishment[s], one a furlong, the other $\frac{3}{4}$ a mile off; the river Hodder with lovely fairyland views, especially at the bathingplace, the Ribble too, the Calder, Whalley with an abbey, Clitheroe with a castle, Ribchester with a strange old chapel and Roman remains; schoolboys and animation, philosophers and foppery (not to be taken too seriously) a jackdaw, a rookery, goldfish, a clough with waterfalls, fishing, grouse, an anemometer, a sunshine guage,[1] a sundial, an icosihedron, statuary, magnetic instruments, a laboratory, gymnasium, ambulacrum, studio, fine engravings, Arundel chromos, Lancashire talked with *naïveté* on the

[1] Thus in MS.

151

premises (Hoo said this and hoo did that)—and, what caps all, if I were shewing it you, as I hope to do (I have to shew it too often: it takes from an hour and a half to three hours: I do it with more pride than pleasure) you could not make me wretched now by either stealing or buying fruit.

I want to hear about Yattenden (or Yattendon?).[1] And when will *Prometheus* be out?

I should be sorry to think you did nothing down there but literary work: could you not be a magistrate? This would be honourable and valuable public duty. Consider it.

I am your affectionate friend

GERARD M. HOPKINS S.J.

Sept. 27 1882.

LXXXVIII

Stonyhurst College, Blackburn. [Early October, 1882.]

DEAREST BRIDGES,—You are in the infinite leisure of Yattenden and you do not write.[2]

I send with this the air to *I have loved flowers that fade*.[3] A young Mr. Fitzpatrick is going to put me an accompaniment to it, but in the meantime I want you to see the tune. Playing it is of little use, unless it were on the violin; the snapping of a piano cannot give the extreme smoothness I mean: it must be sung. If you do not like it I think it must be a misunderstanding, for properly rendered I believe it could not fail to please you.

---

[1] Mrs. Bridges writes: 'My father, Alfred Waterhouse the architect, bought Yattendon estate in 1876. He built himself a house on the hill above the village, and there we went to live in April 1881. The eighteenth-century Manor House was then to let—and this was just when R. B. was looking about for a country house to settle in with his mother. One thing that made him think it would suit her was its close proximity to the church. They settled there in 1882, about September. I don't know how to fix the exact date, but I know R. B. was living there by 29 October 1882, when my brother, Paul Waterhouse, came of age. R. B. later became a member of the local (Bradfield) Board of Guardians.'

[2] R. B. was particularly busy at this time, 'settling in' at Yattendon.

[3] This has disappeared.

152

I want to go on with the study of harmony, but now my scholastic work is beginning and at first at all events I fear I shall not have time even for necessities, let alone luxuries or rather bywork.

I have finished the Leaden and Golden Echoes (meant for a maidens' song in *St. Winefred*) and am pleased with it: I shall send it you when I have put the last touches; it would be rash to send it today.

I want to see *Prometheus* out and when published for people here to see it. Remember me very kindly to Mrs. Molesworth and believe me your affectionate friend

GERARD M. HOPKINS S.J.

Better let me have it soon back, and then if you like it you cd. afterwards have an accompanied copy.

LXXXIX

Look at this: *Saturday Review* Oct. 14 1882: *The Sorrows of Prince Bismarck*:[1] 'On some luckless day the bookseller sends out his catalogue, with such items as "*Love Lies Bleeding*. By G. Hopkins. Pages unopened [this is wrong: it should be *uncut*].[2] Autograph poem and inscription by the author. Published at Five Shillings. Fourpence." Then these catalogues fall into the hands of Hopkins and his friends, and there is wailing and shrieking on Parnassus.' It seems to be meant for me. Andrew Lang perhaps or somebody who knows of me through you. It shews by the by what a shocking bad name mine would be to publish under. For in itself *Love Lies Bleeding* is a good title, for instance for a Shaksperian comedy. Be careful not to betray me to suspects and dangerous people.

'G. HOPKINS.' Oct. 16 1882.

---

[1] An unsigned would-be-witty article. The three sorrows are: the infliction on him by authors of presentation copies (and herein comes the extract made by G. M. H.); the printing of books in 'unpatriotic legible Roman characters'; and attempts at phonetic spelling.

[2] 'Unopened' is right.

¹ I suppose then you are more confirmed at Yattendon than before and so I am more likely to see you there.

Were there two sheets in your letter or three? For the last begins with a small letter as though it were a continuation, though nothing is wanting to the sense, it is true, and the first sheet ends with a stop and a blank after it.

XC

Stonyhurst College, Blackburn. Oct. 18 1882.

DEAREST BRIDGES,—I have read of Whitman's (1) 'Pete'² in the library at Bedford Square (and perhaps something else; if so I forget), which you pointed out; (2) two pieces in the *Athenaeum* or *Academy*, one on the Man-of-War Bird, the other beginning 'Spirit that formed this scene';³ (3) short extracts in a review by Saintsbury in the *Academy*:⁴ this is all I remember. I cannot have read more than half a dozen pieces at most.

This, though very little, is quite enough to give a strong impression of his marked and original manner and way of thought and in particular of his rhythm. It might be even enough, I shall not deny, to originate or, much more, influence another's style: they say the French trace their whole modern school of landscape to a single piece of Constable's exhibited at the Salon early this century.⁵

¹ This separate leaf was misplaced by R. B.: it seems to belong here, or near here, and may perhaps have accompanied the MS. of *The Leaden Echo and the Golden Echo.*

² *Come up From the Fields Father* (*Leaves of Grass, Drum-Taps*, 1909 ed., pp. 236-7).

³ *To the Man-of-War-Bird* (Ibid., *Sea-Drift*, 1909 ed., pp. 204-5) and *Spirit that Form'd this Scene* (Ibid., *From Noon to Starry Night*, 1909 ed., p. 368). This last was printed in *The Academy* of 24 Sept. 1881, from the New York *Critic* of 10 Sept., and headed 'Original Verse'.

⁴ A review of *Leaves of Grass* in the issue of 10 Oct. 1874, pp. 398-400. For this see NOTE P. (On 24 June 1876 there is, in the same paper, a less important review of *Two Rivulets* by Edmund W. Gosse.)

⁵ Three pictures by John Constable were exhibited at the Paris Salon of 1824—*The Hay Wain, A View near London* (*Hampstead Heath*), and *The Lock on the Stour.* They were not sent by the artist, but by a French speculator who had bought them at the Royal Academy.

The question then is only about the fact. But first I may as well say what I should not otherwise have said, that I always knew in my heart Walt Whitman's mind to be more like my own than any other man's living. As he is a very great scoundrel this is not a pleasant confession. And this also makes me the more desirous to read him and the more determined that I will not.

Nevertheless I believe that you are quite mistaken about this piece and that on second thoughts you will find the fancied resemblance diminish and the imitation disappear.[1]

And first of the rhythm. Of course I saw that there was to the eye something in my long lines like his, that the one would remind people of the other. And both are in irregular rhythms. There the likeness ends. The pieces of his I read were mostly in an irregular rhythmic prose: that is what they are thought to be meant for and what they seemed to me to be. Here is a fragment of a line I remember: 'or a handkerchief designedly dropped'.[2] This is in a dactylic rhythm—or let us say anapaestic; for it is a great convenience in English to assume that the stress is always at the end of the foot; the consequence of which assumption is that in ordinary verse there are only two English feet possible, the iamb and the anapaest, and even in my regular sprung rhythm only one additional, the fourth paeon: for convenience' sake assuming this, then the above fragment is anapaestic—'or a hánd | kerchief ... |. desígn | edly drópped'— and there is a break down, a designed break of rhythm, after 'handkerchief', done no doubt that the line may not become[3] downright verse, as it would be if he had said 'or a handkerchief

---

[1] *The Leaden Echo and the Golden Echo, Poems,* 36. Dated: Stonyhurst, 13 Oct. 1882. See R. B.'s note.

[2] Saintsbury had quoted Whitman's description of the grass:
   It is the handkerchief of the Lord;
   A scented gift and remembrance designedly dropt,
   Bearing the owner's name someway in the corners, that we
   May see and remark, and say Whose?

[3] MS. 'becoming'.

purposely dropped'. Now you can of course say that he meant
pure verse and that the foot is a paeon—'or a hánd|kerchief
desígn|edly drópped'; or that he means, without fuss, what I
should achieve by looping the syllable *de* and calling that foot
an outriding foot—for the result might be attained either way.
Here then I must make the answer which will apply here and
to all like cases and to the examples which may be found up
and down the poets of the use of sprung rhythm—*if they could
have done it they would*: sprung rhythm, once you hear it, is so
eminently natural a thing and so effective a thing that if they
had known of it they would have used it. Many people, as we
say, have been 'burning', but they all missed it; they took it up
and mislaid it again. So far as I know—I am enquiring and
presently I shall be able to speak more decidedly—it existed in
full force in Anglo saxon verse and in great beauty; in a degraded
and doggrel shape in *Piers Ploughman* (I am reading that famous
poem and am coming to the conclusion that it is not worth
reading); Greene was the last who employed it at all consciously
and he never continuously; then it disappeared—for one cadence
in it here and there is not sprung rhythm and one swallow does
not make a spring. (I put aside Milton's case, for it is altogether
singular.) In a matter like this a thing does not exist, is not
done unless it is wittingly and willingly done; to recognise the
form you are employing and to mean it is everything. To apply
this: there is (I suppose, but you will know) no sign that Whitman means to use paeons or outriding feet where these breaks
in rhythm occur; it seems to me a mere extravagance to think
he means people to understand of themselves what they are
slow to understand even when marked or pointed out. If he
does not mean it then he does not do it; or in short what he
means to write—and writes—is rhythmic prose and that only.
And after all, you probably grant this.

Good. Now prose rhythm in English is always one of two
things (allowing my convention about scanning upwards or
from slack to stress and not from stress to slack)—either iambic

or anapaestic. You may make a third measure (let us call it) by intermixing them. One of these three simple measures then, all iambic or all anapaestic or mingled iambic and anapaestic, is what he in every case means to write. He dreams of no other and he *means* a rugged or, as he calls it in that very piece 'Spirit that formed this scene' (which is very instructive and should be read on this very subject), a 'savage' art and rhythm.

Extremes meet, and (I must for truth's sake say what sounds pride) this savagery of his art, this rhythm in its last ruggedness and decomposition into common prose, comes near the last elaboration of mine. For that piece of mine is very highly wrought. The long lines are not rhythm run to seed: everything is weighed and timed in them. Wait till they have taken hold of your ear and you will find it so. No, but what it *is* like is the rhythm of Greek tragic choruses or of Pindar: which is pure sprung rhythm. And that has the same changes of cadence from point to point as this piece. If you want to try it, read one till you have settled the true places of the stress, mark these, then read it aloud, and you will see. Without this these choruses are prose bewitched; with it they are sprung rhythm like that piece of mine.

Besides, why did you not say *Binsey Poplars*[1] was like Whitman? The present piece is in the same kind and vein, but developed, an advance. The lines and the stanzas (of which there are two in each poem and having much the same relation to one another) are both longer, but the two pieces are greatly alike: just look. If so how is this a being untrue to myself? I am sure it is no such thing.

The above remarks are not meant to run down Whitman. His 'savage' style has advantages, and he has chosen it; he says so. But you cannot eat your cake and keep it: he eats his offhand, I keep mine. It makes a very great difference. Neither do I deny all resemblance. In particular I noticed in 'Spirit that formed this scene' a preference for the alexandrine. I have the same preference: I came to it by degrees, I did not take it from him.

[1] *Poems*, 19.

157

About diction the matter does not allow me so clearly to point out my independence as about rhythm. I cannot think that the present piece owes anything to him. I hope not, here especially, for it is not even spoken in my own person but in that of St. Winefred's maidens. It ought to sound like the thoughts of a good but lively girl and not at all like—not at all like Walt Whitman. But perhaps your mind may have changed by this.

I wish I had not spent so much time in defending the piece. Believe me your affectionate friend

GERARD.

Oct. 19 1882. I am not sure I shall not ask C. D. to let me see at least one packet of Mano. He should, every one should now, use one of these reproductive processes: it is next to printing and at least it secures one against irretrievable loss by the post. All our masters here use the gelatine process for flying sheets etc.

XCI

Stonyhurst College, Blackburn. Oct. 21 1882.

MY DEAREST BRIDGES,—All you say shall be attended to, but in some of your criticisms you are, I think, not quite at the vein or in the 'humour' of the piece. The question of what they call run-on lines and the rhymes or other final words belonging is difficult. I find it a hardship to alter 'sighs soaring, soaring sighs':[1] I quite believed it to be a hit; like 'mobled queen' good.[2]

Spite—no, bless me, I never said spite. A sally I should call that; though if the G. was intentional no doubt he was wrong and ought not to have done it.[3]

My de-Whitmaniser crossed you on the road. I believe it was stern and a bit of a mouther.

If I should ever be mentioned between you, propitiate Lang, set me right with him; not in the literary way but personally;

---

[1] This line from the *Golden Echo* was not altered:
　　　And with sighs soaring, soaring sighs deliver
　　　Them; . . .
[2] *Hamlet*, Act II, sc. 2, l. 522.　　[3] See the beginning of LXXXIX.

158

make him understand that those snags that are in my style are not in my heart and temper.

'Nay, what we lighthanded' etc[1] means 'Nay more: the seed that we so carelessly and freely flung into the dull furrow, and then forgot it, will have come to ear meantime' etc. No more at present. Your affectionate friend

GERARD M. HOPKINS S.J.

XCII

Stonyhurst College, Blackburn. Nov. 4 1882.

DEAREST BRIDGES,—I return $\Pi. \Pi.$, for my mind is dull and museless and I shd. do no good by keeping it longer and delaying you.

The opening is now richer than before.[2] But the four first lines seem to me perhaps the worst in the play, whereas the frontispiece, Pindar says, $\chi\rho\dot{\eta}$ $\theta\dot{\epsilon}\mu\epsilon\nu$ $\tau\eta\lambda\alpha\upsilon\gamma\dot{\epsilon}s$.[3] The second line I except: it is Miltonic and fine.

The piece about Greek art does not much please me. It strikes me as written in what I call Castalian or Parnassian, that is the language of poetry draping prose thought, a fine rhetoric, such as there is a good deal of in Wordsworth's blank verse (against his principles, by the by). I objected in the same way

---

[1] From the *Golden Echo*:

> Nay, what we had lighthanded left in surly the mere mould
> Will have waked and have waxed and have walked with the wind
>   what while we slept, . . .

[2] No MS. of *Prometheus the Firegiver* is in existence, to Mrs. Bridges's knowledge. The opening lines in the first edition of 1883 are:

> From high Olympus and the domeleſs courts,
> Where mighty Zeus our angry king confirms
> The Fates' decrees and bends the will of the gods,
> I come: and on the earth ſtep with glad foot.

In the final form (*P.W.*, vol. i) 'ætherial' takes the place of 'domeleſs'.

[3] Pindar, *Olympians*, vi, 3–4. The opening is (trans. Sandys): 'On golden pillars raising the fair-walled porch of our abode, we shall build, as it were, a splendid hall; even so, o'er our work's beginning we needs must set a front that shines afar.'

to the account of Rome in C.D.'s *Too much Friendship*[1] and he called it 'that *grind*' and struck it out.

The blotching of the copy with countless corrections is a heavy toll on its charm in reading. I want to see it in plain print.

Although on the one hand the action is so good and its unity so well kept and on the other hand the style so beautiful I have doubts about the play's acting.[2] Experience only can decide; but I do not think it has in a high degree a nameless quality which is of the first importance both in oratory and drama: I sometimes call it *bidding*. I mean the art or virtue of saying everything right *to* or *at* the hearer, interesting him, holding him in the attitude of correspondent or addressed or at least concerned, making it everywhere an act of intercourse—and of discarding everything that does not bid, does not tell. I think one may gain much of this by practice. I do not know if I make myself plain. It is most difficult to combine this bidding, such a fugitive thing, with a monumental style. Your style is monumental. But it can be done: witness Greek plays—and Shakspere's, but those are more monumental and less in bidding, his more bidding and less monumental. I fancy the French drama eminently succeeds in this combination, but the success is not what we should be content with, the rank of the result not being very high. This will be of more importance in your Nero.

The 'O my vague desires' is a unique and wonderful creation, which would never, I should think, be forgotten.[3]

Believe me your affectionate friend

GERARD M. HOPKINS S.J.

P.S. In printing I hope you are not going to give in to that piece of German unlogic of writing 'red white and blue', 'fish

---

[1] *Too Much Friendship, The Story of Septimius and Alcander.* (*The Last Poems of Richard Watson Dixon, D.D.*, . . . 1905).

[2] Mrs. Bridges tells me that the *Prometheus* was acted at a boys' grammar school near Newbury, and she thinks that is the only time it has ever been staged. R. B. saw this performance.

[3] Mentioned here because part of the *Prometheus*.

flesh fowl or good red herring' without stops. The German printers are the worst masters in punctuation that you could take. They ditch their sentences with commas where they break the sense's neck and they leave them out where it is wailing for them. It is worse than writing Virgil Vergil.

XCIII

Stonyhurst College, Blackburn.

Nov. 26 1882. And 'in spite of the boasted civilisation of this so-called nineteenth century' this letter cannot even start from here for more than 24 hours nor reach you before Tuesday morning; nor could it indeed if you lived at Blackburn.

DEAREST BRIDGES,—This is to be a mere jottery. And first if you like to send *Prometheus* I will review and reply as fast as I can.

I wrote to Lang and he is going presently to write to me on the subject of Dragons. I return his letter to you. We are on terms of mother's milk.

Yes, I do wish I could have seen Yattendon.

I have written to Canon Dixon. I hardly dare to undertake anything about *Mano*, because I have somewhat rashly promised to revise for style's sake a historical work by one of ours, which cannot but take a great deal of time, I am afraid.

Of course I do and must pay attention to your criticisms on the Echos and everything else. I am however somewhat dismayed about that piece and have laid it aside for a while. I cannot satisfy myself about the first line.[1] You must know that words like *charm* and *enchantment* will not do: the thought is of beauty as of something that can be physically kept and lost and by physical things only, like keys; then the things must come from the *mundus muliebris*; and thirdly they must not be markedly oldfashioned. You will see that this limits the choice

[1] The first line, in A, is:

How to keep—O is there any any, is there nowhere known any any brooch or clasp, catch, key to keep
Back . . .

of words very much indeed. However I shall make some changes. *Back*[1] is not pretty, but it gives that feeling of physical constraint which I want. More of this perhaps hereafter.

I never saw Hall Caine's sonnet book. I saw some review of it. He has written a memoir of Rossetti.[2]

I always said Gosse was a good fellow and I am glad you speak of him so. I should like to meet him. So I should a little Marzials. Did you tell me or is it my fancy that Marzials looks like a Jew?

Can you really mean that $\Pi.\Pi.$ is to appear this month?—and not this year? There are now only four more days of the month. If you mean that, revision must be done by return—no, by calculation on my fingers the thing is chronologically impossible.

Talking of chronologically impossible and long words the Rev. Wm. Barnes, good soul, of Dorset-dialect poems (in which there is more true poetry than in Burns; I do not say of course vigour or passion or humour or a lot of things, but the soul of poetry, which I believe few Scotchmen have got) has published a 'Speech craft of English Speech'[3] = English Grammar, written in an unknown tongue, a sort of modern Anglosaxon, beyond all that Furnival in his wildest Forewords ever dreamed. He does not see the utter hopelessness of the thing. It makes one weep to think what English might have been; for in spite of

---

[1] *The Leaden Echo*:
    . . . or key to keep
Back beauty, keep it, beauty, beauty, beauty, . . . from vanishing away?
In *The Golden Echo* this theme is answered:
    . . . beauty-in-the-ghost, deliver it, early now, long before death
Give beauty back, beauty, beauty, beauty, back to God, beauty's self and
    beauty's giver.

[2] *Recollections of Dante Gabriel Rossetti*, 1882.

[3] *An Outline of English Speech-craft*, 1878. Barnes was always a student and lover of robust words. In 1854 he published a Philological Grammar, 'grounded upon English, and formed from a comparison of more than sixty languages. Being an introduction to the science of grammar and a help to grammars of all languages, especially English, Latin, and Greek.' His *Grammar and Glossary of the Dorset Dialect*, with 'the history, outspreading, and bearings of South-western English', was published by the Philological Society in 1863.

all that Shakspere and Milton have done with the compound I cannot doubt that no beauty in a language can make up for want of purity. In fact I am learning Anglosaxon and it is a vastly superior thing to what we have now. But the madness of an almost unknown man trying to do what the three estates of the realm together could never accomplish! He calls degrees of comparison pitches of suchness: we *ought* to call them so, but alas!

My sisters met Wooldridge at dinner at Hampstead.

I daresay you made a capital speech. Everyone shd. at least be able to speak on an occasion.

When I reproached you for treating me as if I were not in earnest I meant, and I mean now, to open up no further question; it was only of the injustice to myself I was thinking then. But 'pain' is not the word: it was a mild rebuke to you for being so unreasonable towards me. However a man who is deeply in earnest is not very eager to assert his earnestness, as they say when a man is really certain he no longer disputes but is indifferent. And that is all I say now, that to think a man in my position is not in earnest is unreasonable and is to make difficulties. But if you have made them and can solve them, by a solution which must be wrong, no matter.

The sonnet you ask about is the greatest offender in its way that you could have found. It was written in my Welsh days, in my salad days, when I was fascinated with *cynghanedd* or consonant-chime, and, as in Welsh *englyns*, 'the sense', as one of themselves said, 'gets the worst of it'; in this case it exists but is far from glaring. To answer in detail:[1]

---

[1] The sonnet is *The Sea and the Skylark* (Rhyl, May 1877: *Poems*, 11). The original version, in A, ll. 3–8, ran as follows:

By flood, by fall, low-lull-off or all: roar
Frequenting there while moon shall wear and wend;

Left hand, off land, I hear the lark ascend
With rash-fresh more, repair of skein and score,
Race wild reel round, crisp coil deal down to floor,
And spill music till there's none left to spend.

These lines were much altered: not, perhaps, for the better.

163

The word is *more* and is a midline rhyme to *score*, as in the next line *round* is meant in some way to rhyme to *down*. 'Rash-fresh more' (it is dreadful to explain these things in cold blood) means a headlong and exciting new snatch of singing, resumption by the lark of his song, which by turns he gives over and takes up again all day long, and this goes on, the sonnet says, through all time, without ever losing its first freshness, being a thing both new and old. *Repair* means the same thing, *renewal, resumption.* The skein and coil are the lark's song, which from his height gives the impression (not to me only) of something falling to the earth and not vertically quite but tricklingly or wavingly, something as a skein of silk ribbed by having been tightly wound on a narrow card or a notched holder or as fishingtackle or twine unwinding from a reel or winch:* the laps or folds are the notes or short measures and bars of them. The same is called a score in the musical sense of score and this score is 'writ upon a liquid sky trembling to welcome it', only not horizontally. The lark in wild glee races the reel round, paying or dealing out and down the turns of the skein or coil right to the earth floor, the ground, where it lies in a heap, as it were, or rather is all wound off on to another winch, reel, bobbin, or spool in Fancy's eye by the moment the bird touches earth and so is ready for a fresh unwinding at the next flight. There is, you see, plenty meant; but the saying of it smells, I fear, of the lamp, of salad oil, and, what is nastier, in one line somewhat of Robert Browning. I felt even at the time that in the endless labour of recasting those lines I had lost the freshness I wanted and which indeed the subject demands. 'As a dare-gale skylark' is better in that respect. The peerage would be well earned.—*Crisp* means almost *crisped*, namely with notes.

Believe me your affectionate friend

GERARD HOPKINS S.J.

* or as pearls strung on a horsehair.

Nov. 27 1882.

164

XCIV

Stonyhurst, Blackburn. Dec. 1 1882.

DEAREST BRIDGES,—You shall have Π. Π. back soon. I do not feel as if I could make any criticism of value, my mind not being fresh.

I still do not like *domeless*.[1] It is not archaeologically right, though I believe the so-called Tomb or Treasury of Atreus has a rude dome; neither does it convey much image to my mind. And I cannot see but the fourth line is poor and halting. It must be meant to express by its rhythm the act of alighting briskly, but most readers will miss this and will only find it halt, as I do even with that in view.

I agree with you that English compounds do not seem real single words or properly unified till by some change in form or spelling or slur in pronunciation their construction is disguised. This seems in English a point craved for and insisted on, that words shall be single and specific marks for things, whether self-significant or not; and it is noticeable how unmeaning our topographical names are or soon become, while those in Celtic languages are so transparent—not that their unmeaningness is any virtue, rather a vice; still it shews the tendency. But your instances are not fair: if icebergs had been common in British seas a name would have been found for them either not compounded at all[2] or if compound as good as *iceberg* is or better and certainly a great deal better than *icelump*, which is caricature. *Thimble* is singler than *thumbstall* (I do not believe it comes from that but from *thumb-le*), but it is a meaner word. The absurdity of 'finger hut' is not in its being a compound but in its impropriety, in the particular trope employed. *Fingerhood* or indeed *fingerstall* seem to me to be well enough. *Potato* is certainly one of the ugliest and most laughable words in the language and cannot well be used in verse, whereas *earthapple* is stately: *potato* has one virtue only, the being specific.

---

[1] See p. 159, n. 2.　　　　　[2] For 'at all', MS. has 'or at'.

If one is to bandy plays upon names Burns might mean Scalds and Barnes Granaries of Plenty. I have a cousin by the by called Barne or Barnes.

The very worst compound ever I heard in English was Tyndal's word *clangtint* = *klangfarbe* in German = *timbre* in French for the quality of musical instruments.

Your affectionate friend

GERARD M. HOPKINS S.J.

XCV

Stonyhurst, Blackburn. Dec. 7 1882.

DEAREST BRIDGES,—Briefly: your letter is dated the 4th, it has *two* Newbury postmarks of the 5th, a Blackburn one of the 6th, and I got it this morning. I posted $\Pi.\Pi.$ and a letter on the 4th and you, I hope, got them on the 5th: let me know that the book is not lost. It is absurd that a letter posted at latest on Tuesday shd. not reach me till Thursday and . . but not to pursue my thought, let me, if you have not already done so, hear that all is right.

Did you see the transit yesterday? With a smoked glass you could, if it was fine: here it snowed all day.

Do I understand you to say that since you have been at Yattendon some one you know has drowned himself?

Yours G. M. H.

It wd. be strange if τέχνη and τύχη[1] together did not bring some fine results out of any lot of caleidoscopic elements; still to me a pure language seems a finer thing than a mixed one— *till the mixture becomes imperceptible.*

XCVI

Stonyhurst, Blackburn. Dec. 20 1882.

DEAREST BRIDGES,—You misunderstood about those four opening lines: I did not want them replaced by others but only in some places reworded. I have told you of my objection to

[1] Passim in Aristotle, Plato: 'art (or science)' and 'chance (or luck)'.

domeless. If there were some reason for it why do you not tell me? A court I suppose to be any large room or space of a building upon the ground floor and imperfectly closed. About the being on the ground floor I do not feel quite sure, about the being imperfectly closed—above or around—I do. Courts can seldom be domed in any case, so that it is needless to tell us that those on Olympus are domeless. No: better to say the kamptuliconless courts or Minton's-encaustic-tileless courts or vulcanisèd-india-rubberless courts. This would strike a keynote at once and bespeak attention. And if the critics said those things did not belong to the period you would have (as you have now with *domeless*) the overwhelming answer, that you never said they did but the contrary, and that Prometheus, who was at once a prophet and as a mechanician more than equal to Edison and the Jablochkoff candle and the Moc-main Patent Lever Truss with self-adjusting duplex gear and attachments, meant to say that emphatically they had *not* got those improvements on Olympus and he did not intend that they should. But if you cannot see your way to this 'frank' treatment and are inclined to think that fault might be found with *domeless*, then remember that that fault is found *in your first line*.

I seem to be in a griggish mood; it must be because holidays have begun. *Your* last letter was depressed, but I do not want you to be depressed but to bring out your beautiful work as soon as possible. However to return to those four first lines. I wanted no account of the journey through the air, but that, since the fourth line was meant to be descriptive and to suit the word to the action, it should suit the word to the action better—the action of alighting on earth. That was all. For as things now are it is to me like a man dragging a lame leg after him. Could it not end somehow with a double ending like 'gladly alighting'. I have a line in *St. Winefred*, on a like occasion (this is a six-footer of course) 'shall fling their crutches from them, on heels of air departing'.[1]

[1] *Poems*, 58, p. 79. The printed line is:
Their crutches shall cast from them, on heels of air departing.

167

I am at present in a state of weakness, I do not well know why.

Believe me your affectionate friend

GERARD HOPKINS S.J.

XCVII

Stonyhurst College, Blackburn. Jan. 4 1883.

DEAREST BRIDGES,—Since our holidays began I have been in a wretched state of weakness and weariness, I can't tell why, always drowzy and incapable of reading or thinking to any effect. And this must be why I was, before that, able to do so little on your *Prometheus*.

I think the sonnet a fine work,[1] but should like the phrasing to be more exquisite in lines 2, 4, and perhaps elsewhere. Still it has to me an unspontaneous artificial air. I cannot consider the goblet and 'golden foil' a success. It is out of keeping with sons of toil and the unadornment of their brides. It is obscure too: it means, I suppose, that the goblet is of gold and that this gold sets off and is set off by the colour of the wine. This much resemblance there is, that as the goblet draws or swallows up and sort-of-drinks the liquid and the liquid at the same time swallows up and sort-of-drinks the material of the goblet so the body absorbs sleep and sleep the body. But the images of gold and crimson are out of keeping: brilliancy is only in the way. You were, you say, driven to it: I protest, and with indignation, at your saying I was driven to the same image. With more truth might it be said that my sonnet might have been written expressly for the image's sake.[2] But the image is not the same as

---

[1] The reference seems to be to an early version of Sonnet 62 in the Daniel Edition (1889 and 1890) of *The Growth of Love*. From the printed version 'goblet' and 'golden foil' disappeared, and two of G. M. H.'s rhymes, 'despoil' and 'turmoil', were introduced.

[2] *God's Grandeur, Poems,* 7:

> The world is charged with the grandeur of God.
> It will flame out, like shining from shook foil;
> It gathers to a greatness, like the ooze of oil
> Crushed.

yours and I do not mean by foil set-off at all; I mean foil in its sense of leaf or tinsel, and no other word whatever will give the effect I want. Shaken goldfoil gives off broad glares like sheet lightning and also, and this is true of nothing else, owing to its zigzag dints and creasings and network of small many cornered facets, a sort of fork lightning too. Moreover as it is the first rhyme, presumably it engendered the others and not they it. This reminds me that I hold you to be wrong about 'vulgar', that is obvious or necessary, rhymes. It follows from your principle that if a word has only one rhyme in the language it cannot be used in selfrespecting poetry at all. The truth seems to me that a problem is set to all, how to use that same pair (or triplet or any set) of rhymes, which are invariable, to the finest and most natural effect. It is nothing that the reader can say / He had to say it, there *was* no other rhyme: you answer/shew me what better I could have said if there had been a million. Hereby, I may tell you, hangs a very profound question treated by Duns Scotus, who shews that freedom is compatible with necessity. And besides, common sense tells you that though if you say A_1 you cannot help saying A_2 yet you can help saying A_1+A_2 at all; you could have said B_1+B_2 or C_1+C_2 etc. And is not music a sort of rhyming on seven rhymes and does that make it vulgar? The variety is more, but the principle the same. Come, you are as much cast in this matter as Lawes was in the Belt case—though I am grievously afraid there was a miscarriage of justice in that trial; not that I like to side against a judge's sentence.[1]

Jan. 5—Hall Caine's 'Disquisition' on Rossetti's picture of

[1] The libel case of Belt *v.* Lawes ended on 27 Dec. 1882 in a verdict for the plantiff, with £5,000 damages. The libel complained of stated that certain busts and pieces of sculpture attributed to Mr. Belt, and claimed by him, were executed by other persons in his employ. The application for a new trial was refused (though Lord Chief Justice Coleridge, besides considering the damages excessive, thought there had been a gross miscarriage of justice) but the damages were reduced to £500. In March 1884, however, the Court of Appeal confirmed the verdict of the jury, and restored the original damages. For an interesting account of this case see Chapter III of Sir Charles Oman's *Things I Have Seen,* 1933.

Dante's Dream bought by the city of Liverpool reached me this morning, I suppose from the author.[1] Noel Paton[2] is quoted as saying, with goodnatured gush, that it may be ranked with the Madonna di San Sisto. Now, you know, it may *not*, and I am considering whether I shall tell Hall Caine so.

To return to your sonnet, could you not find another rhyme? there is *spoil, despoil, turmoil*, not to speak of *coil, boil, parboil*, and Hoyle on whist—the very sight of which dreary jugglery brings on yawns with me.

You speak of writing the sonnet in prose first. I read the other day that Virgil wrote the Aeneid in prose. Do you often do so? Is it a good plan? If it is I will try it; it may help on my flagging and almost spent powers. Years ago one of ours, a pupil of mine, was to write some English verses for me, to be recited: he had a real vein. He said he had no thoughts, but that if I would furnish some he would versify them. I did so and the effect was very surprising to me to find my own thoughts, with no variation to speak of, expressed in good verses quite unlike mine.

The sonnet on Purcell means this: 1–4. I hope Purcell is not damned for being a Protestant, because I love his genius. 5–8. And that not so much for gifts he shares, even though it shd. be in higher measure, with other musicians as for his own individuality. 9–14. So that while he is aiming only at impressing me his hearer with the meaning in hand I am looking out meanwhile for his specific, his individual markings and mottlings, 'the sakes of him'. It is as when a bird thinking only of soaring spreads its wings: a beholder may happen then to have his attention drawn by the act to the plumage displayed.— In particular, the first lines mean: May Purcell, O may he have died a good death and that soul which I love so much and which breathes or stirs so unmistakeably in his works have parted from

---

[1] Hall Caine, according to his *Recollections*, was largely responsible for the sale of this picture to Liverpool.

[2] Joseph Noël Paton (1821–1901): at this time engaged on mediocre religious paintings.

the body and passed away, centuries since though I frame the wish, in peace with God! so that the heavy condemnation under which he outwardly or nominally lay for being out of the true Church may in consequence of his good intentions have been reversed. 'Low lays him' is merely 'lays him low', that is / strikes him heavily, weighs upon him. (I daresay this will strike you as more professional than you had anticipated.) It is somewhat dismaying to find I am so unintelligible though, especially in one of my very best pieces. 'Listed', by the by, is 'enlisted'. 'Sakes' is hazardous: about that point I was more bent on saying my say than on being understood in it. The 'moonmarks' belong to the image only of course, not to the application; I mean not detailedly: I was thinking of a bird's quill feathers. One thing disquiets me: *I meant* 'fair fall' *to mean fair (fortune be) fall*;[1] it has since struck me that perhaps 'fair' is an adjective proper and in the predicate and can only be used in cases like 'fair fall the day', that is, *may the day fall, turn out, fair.* My line will yield a sense that way indeed, but I never meant it so. Do you know any passage decisive on this?

Would that I had Purcell's music here.

Did you see Vernon Lee's paper in the December *Contemp.*?[2] I don't like it. She professes herself a disciple of a Mr. Edmund Gurney, who by way of reaction against the gush of programmes ('sturdy old tone-poet'—'inimitable drollery of the semi demi-

---

[1] The sonnet opens:

    Have fair fallen, O fair, fair have fallen, so dear
    To me, so arch-especial a spirit as heaves in Henry Purcell.

[2] Pp. 840–58. *Impersonality and Evolution in Music*: an article that has for its text Edmund Gurney's *The Power of Sound*. As G. M. H.'s criticism is in no sense quotation, a few of Vernon Lee's sentences are perhaps in place here: '. . . the really artistic portion of music, the portion which artistically pleases or displeases, the form, is purely abstract, ideal, unconnected with reality and life, and governed by its own inherent necessities. . . . music is . . . the most formal and ideal of all arts, unique in the fact that the form it creates resembles and signifies nothing beyond itself. . . .' She goes on to ask: 'How does this art of music live and develop, what determines the pattern to be one rather than another, upon what depend the peculiarity, the character, the whole perceptible nature of any given piece of music? . . . this musical form is not invented by any particular man, but is evolved. . . .'

171

quavers in the dominant minor' and so on) says that we enjoy music because our apish ancestors serenaded their Juliet-apes of the period in rudimentary recitatives and our emotions are the survival—that sexual business will in short be found by roking[1] the pot. This is to swing from pap to poison. Would that I had my materials ready to talk sense.

Yours affectionately

GERARD HOPKINS S.J.

Jan. 5 1883.

Is it not too much for two lines running to have the rhythm reversed in the 4th foot? as your 13 and 14. Perhaps not. Twelfth night.

XCVIII

Stonyhurst College, Blackburn. Jan. 28 1883.

DEAREST BRIDGES,—Lang may have spoken in print about vulgar rhymes, but I referred to something you said by word of mouth, as I understood you, to the same effect at Roehampton when we were talking over a chorus of Π. Π. and I had wanted you to avail yourself of some rhyme like *measure* and *pleasure*. But it is no matter now.

It turned out not to be Hall Caine himself who sent me the pamphlet. I mildly remonstrated with him against Noel Paton's matching *Dante's Dream* with the Sistine Madonna. However in his answer Hall Caine said he agreed with me. He lives in London now. There is a great deal of nonsense about that set, often it sickens one (though Rossetti himself I think had little of it); but still I disapprove of damfooling people. I think it is wrong, narrows the mind, and like a 'parvifying glass' makes us see things smaller than the natural size. And I do not like your calling Matthew Arnold Mr. Kidglove Cocksure. I have more reason than you for disagreeing with him[2] and thinking him very wrong, but nevertheless I am sure he is a rare genius and a great critic.

[1] Possibly a slip for 'rocking'; but see *O.E.D.* under 'roke'.
[2] Perhaps a reference to the conjecture on p. 134.

You do not seem quite to have understood my question about *Fair fall*, but whether you understood it or not at any rate you have answered it and set me at rest. The quotation from L.L.L. is decisive.[1] 'Fair befall your mask' must have the same construction as 'Fair fall the face beneath it'. Now 'fair befall' certainly means 'Fair fortune, all that is fair, nothing but what is fair / befall' and 'fair' is there a substantive and governs the verb. So therefore it is and does in 'Fair fall', which is what I wanted. (*Fair* is of course a substantive in *My fair* and Shakespeare says 'And every fair from fair sometimes declines'.)[2] This being so I am unwilling to alter that line, for if it will only stand, and it will, it pleases me much.

You should have been more explicit about the origin of music.

I try to get a bit of strumming every day now. Somebody left with me a volume of Bach's Fugues and, though it is like beginning at the end, as an exercise in *dead reading* I think it is very good for me and perhaps some day I shall find that I can read music pretty easily. If you like to be so good as to send me what you offer, some pieces of Purcell, it will be, as the Irish say when they beg, 'the biggest charty you ever did in your life'. I will send them back and even soon, if you wish.

Believe me your affectionate friend

GERARD HOPKINS S.J.

Jan. 29.

XCIX

Stonyhurst College, Blackburn. Feb. 3 1883.

DEAREST BRIDGES,—I cd. not venture to ask that our library should subscribe half a sovereign for an *édition de luxe* of a new book by an almost unknown author; still less could I expect, nor shd. I like, you to present me, that is our library, with a copy.[3] Here then is a downright deadlock and there is nothing

[1] Now fair befall your mask!—fair fall the face it covers! (*Love's Labour's Lost*, Act II, sc. 1, l. 124.)   [2] Sonnet 18, l. 7.
[3] Promethevs the Firegiver / Printed at the Private Press of / H. Daniel / Fellow of Worcester College / Oxford / 1883. 100 copies were printed.

for it but for me to wait for the second edition and then, like Brewer[1] in the *Mutual Friend*, 'see how things look'.

Many thanks for the anthems. I remember now that I heard the first at Magdalen. Did you remark that the first 9 notes of the Hallelujah are, with a slight change, the beginning of *Cease your funning*?

This is a terrible business about my sonnet 'Have fair fallen', for I find that I still 'make myself misunderstood'. *Have* is not a plural at all, far from it. It is the singular imperative (or optative if you like) of the past, a thing possible and actual both in logic and grammar, but naturally a rare one. As in the second person we say 'Have done' or in making appointments 'Have had your dinner beforehand', so one can say in the third person not only 'Fair fall' of what is present or future but also 'Have fair fallen' of what is past. The same thought (which plays a great part in my own mind and action) is more clearly expressed in the last stanza but one of the *Eurydice*, where you remarked it.

I quite understand what you mean[2] about gentlemen and 'damfools'; it is a very striking thing and I could say much on the subject. I shall not say that much, but I say this: if a gentleman feels that to be what we call a gentleman is a thing essentially higher than without being a gentleman to be ever so great an artist or thinker or if, to put it another way, an artist or thinker feels that were he to become in those ways ever so great he wd. still essentially be lower than a gentleman that was no artist and no thinker—and yet to be a gentleman is but on the brim of morals and rather a thing of manners than of morals properly—then how much more must art and philosophy and manners and breeding and everything else in the world be below the least degree of true virtue. This is that chastity of mind which seems to lie at the very heart and be the parent of all other good, the seeing at once what is best, the holding to that, and the not allowing anything else whatever to be even

---

[1] Brewer, with Boots, is part of the table-chorus to the Veneerings.
[2] Written above 'say', cancelled. See p. 177.

heard pleading to the contrary. Christ's life and character are such as appeal to all the world's admiration, but there is one insight St. Paul gives us of it which is very secret and seems to me more touching and constraining than everything else is:[1] This mind he says, was in Christ Jesus—he means as man: being in the form of God—that is, finding, as in the first instant of his incarnation he did, his human nature informed by the godhead —he thought it nevertheless no snatching-matter for him to be equal with God, but annihilated himself, taking the form of servant; that is, he could not but see what he was, God, but he would see it as if he did not see it, and be it as if he were not and instead of snatching at once at what all the time was his, or was himself, he emptied or exhausted himself so far as that was possible, of godhead and behaved only as God's slave, as his creature, as man, which also he was, and then being in the guise of man humbled himself to death, the death of the cross. It is this holding of himself back, and not snatching at the truest and highest good, the good that was his right, nay his possession from a past eternity in his other nature, his own being and self, which seems to me the root of all his holiness and the imitation of this the root of all moral good in other men. I agree then, and vehemently,[2] that a gentleman, if there is such a thing on earth, is in the position to despise the poet, were he Dante or Shakspere, and the painter, were he Angelo or Apelles, for anything in him that shewed him *not* to be a gentleman. He is in the position to do it, I say, but if he is a gentleman perhaps this is what he will not do. Which leads me to another remark.

The quality of a gentleman is so very fine a thing that it seems to me one should not be at all hasty in concluding that one possesses it. People assume that they have it, take it quite for granted, and claim the acknowledgment from others: now I should say that this also is 'no snatching-matter'. And the more a man feels what it means and is—and to feel this is certainly some part of it—the more backward he will be to think he can have realised in himself anything so perfect. It

[1] Philippians ii. 5–11.   [2] 'With you', cancelled.

175

is true, there is nothing like the truth and 'the good that does itself not know scarce is';[1] so the perfect gentleman will know that he is the perfect gentleman. But few can be in the position to know this and, being imperfect gentlemen,[2] it will perhaps be a point of their gentlemanliness, for a gentleman is modest, to feel that they are not perfect gentlemen.

By the by if the English race had done nothing else, yet if they left the world the notion of a gentleman, they would have done a great service to mankind.

As a fact poets and men of art are, I am sorry to say, by no means necessarily or commonly gentlemen. For gentlemen do not pander to lust or other basenesses nor, as you say, give themselves airs and affectations nor do other things to be found in modern[3] works. And this adds a charm to everything Canon Dixon writes, that you feel he is a gentleman and thinks like one. But now I have prosed my prose and long enough.

Believe me your affectionate friend

GERARD M. HOPKINS S.J.

Feb. 10 1883.

I am rueful and remorseful about P. F. But what else could come of handmade Dutch paper? I regret that Daniel made his offer. And I hope the 2nd edition will be this one's Jacob.

C

St. Wilfrid's, Preston (home tomorrow).
Easter Monday [26 March] 1883.

DEAREST BRIDGES,—To remove fatal false impressions your last (from Pangbourn) should have been answered at once, but that could not well be. It was too bad of you to think I was writing to tell you you were no gentleman; that you should be saying, like Mrs. Malaprop, whom I saw amusingly played lately, '*Me*, that means me, Captain Absolute'. It is true, remarks of universal application must apply even to present company and one cannot well help remembering that they do; I cannot

[1] Patmore, *Victories of Love* (1863), *The Wedding Sermon*, ll. 1–2.
[2] MS. 'gentleman'.   [3] Written above 'their', cancelled.

say 'all must die' and politely except my hearers and myself; but beyond this I did not aim at you. No, if I had wanted a conspicuous instance of a blackguard I should have taken myself, as I was going to do and to tell a good story too thereanent, but refrained because I thought it might look as if I wanted to draw a faint protest from you and because humility is such a very sensitive thing the least touch smutches it and well meant attempts to keep it from jolting, like the Ark when the cattle shook it, do more harm than good; but all the same I shd. have been sadly sincere and sadly truthful.

Further the only reason why I struck out *say* to write *mean* was because *say* came just before that.

And indeed how many many times must you have misunderstood me not in my sonnets only but in moral, social, personal matters! It must be so, I see now. But it would embitter life if we knew of the misunderstandings put upon us; it would mine at least.

About the artist and the gentleman I have said my say.

The interpretation of St. Paul Phil. ii 5 sqq. was, as it stands, my own. At least I thought so, but I see that some modern Catholic commentators, as Beelen (who published a N.T. grammar) and Bp. MacEvilly, give it or nearly so. Older commentators led mainly by St. Austin take ἁρπαγμόν and *rapinam* for *robbery*, that is / Christ being God thought it no sin to be what he was *and yet* humbled himself etc; but this requires a strong adversative particle in the Greek, wh. there is not. I got the sense of ἁρπαγμόν from Jowett or some modern critic: it in reality adds force to St. Austin's interpretation, which otherwise I was following. St. John Chrysostom seems to have come still nearer the sense I gave.

Human nature in me seems to feel .   .   .   . joy

.   .   .   .

.   .   .   .[1]

---

[1] Of four lines beginning this side of the leaf, the first is left, with two words of the second, and the rest has been scratched out with a knife, no doubt by R. B.

I have had a late very pleasant letter from him. He says you are not altogether recovered; that one night you seemed quite ill, though recovered next morning. Still if I were you I shd. not dwell on it.

The weather in these parts continues winterly, atrociously so.

I have completed one sonnet,[1] since I came north one — and three triolets, which have been published, but they have the taint of jest and dare not meet your eye.[2] The sonnet is a companion to 'I remember a house' (in which write 'build this world of Wales' for 'make'): perhaps I may enclose it. I am always jaded, I cannot tell why, and my vein shews no signs of ever flowing again.

Believe me your affectionate friend

GERARD M. HOPKINS S.J.

March 27.

CI

Stonyhurst, April 19 1883.

I am writing with a glass tube pen homemade and home-brewed ink.

DEAREST BRIDGES,—I wish you would write; it makes me disconsolate punctually every morning to get no letter.

I want to know if you know any one who knows music, counterpoint, *thoroughly*, or, what comes to the same thing, if you know Stainer[3] thoroughly, enough to ask him a favour. For I shall shortly have finished an exercise in the second species in two parts on 'Pray, Goody, please to moderate',[4] pretty elaborate, and I want to know on authority if it is correct and if not where.[5] It has taken much time and I shall never write anything so long again by way of exercise. It is rather, not very, pretty.

---

[1] *Ribblesdale* ('Stonyhurst, 1882'). *Poems*, 35: companion to *In the Valley of the Elwy, Poems*, 16.

[2] See later, p. 190.

[3] Sir John Stainer (1840–1901), the well-known musician, Professor of Music in the University of Oxford, 1889–99.

[4] See p. 76, n. 3.   [5] See p. 181.

I shall of course be glad to see Nero. Is there then to be a Second Part?[1] You forgot that I had read the triolet in MS. It is witty in the last[2] century but one sense of that word. I do not see that the anagrams in it are of any importance.

No more now.

Your affectionate friend

GERARD M. HOPKINS S.J.

CII

Stonyhurst College, Blackburn. May 11 1883.

DEAREST BRIDGES,—Here then is this blessed thing, which has cost more trouble than it is worth.[3] Try it yourself. Sometimes when I play it at my own pace and with my own expression I think it very good in parts and at other times and when somebody else plays it it seems to me a meaningless maundering and a wandering in a wilderness.

I think from what you say it had better not go to Stainer, though as he was my contemporary and I knew him by sight I feel drawn to him.

We hang up polyglot poems in honour of the Blessed Virgin this month. I am on one in English in three-foot couplets.[4] I do not suppose I shall find it either convenient or desirable to send you a copy. It is partly a compromise with popular taste, and it is too true that the highest subjects are not those on which it is easy to reach one's highest.

The cold half kills me.

Your affectionate friend

GERARD HOPKINS S.J.

Though the favour will be, directly speaking, to you I shall be very grateful to your friend.[5] What I want is that he should

---

[1] *Nero* was published in 1884: the second part in 1894.

[2] MS. 'lent'.   [3] The exercise in counterpoint.

[4] *Mary Mother of Divine Grace Compared to the Air we Breathe.* 'Stonyhurst, May '83.' *Poems*, 37. See R. B.'s note.

[5] It is possible only to guess who this was: the name, when it occurs later, is deleted by R. B.

mark any mistakes he may find and make any remarks he may think proper, on the margin or elsewhere. Whitsunday. I have sealed it up, but you may put onto it that the bass sounds better an octave lower or doubled.

Your letter has come, on which I have to remark—

Some of my rhymes I regret, but they are past changing, grubs in amber: there are only a few of these;

Others are unassailable;

Some others again there are which *malignity may munch at* but the Muses love. To this class belongs what you quote. You will grant that there are things in verse which may be read right or wrong, which depend for their effect upon pronunciation. For instance here if I had rhymed *drew her* to *to her* I should have meant it to be read *tó her* and not *to hér*, though in itself the latter is just as possible. You will also grant that in *drew her*, rightly read, the *h* is evanescent. Good. Now then *endured* may be read with little or with well marked circumflex—*endūred* something like *en-dew-ered*. And[1]

CIII

Stonyhurst College, Blackburn. May 18 1883.

(fine day, with a solar halo; holiday; our boys to have a match)

DEAREST BRIDGES,—Fine bass! I should think so. But did you never hear *Pray Goody* before? I am glad I have introduced it to you. (I think it far better to take fine things like that to practise on than the maundering exercises in books.) And it is but one out of a host of such masculine and (what some one called) earnest melodies, little known here and abroad I suppose totally unknown. It is simple truth that no German since Mozart has been capable of anything of the sort. The Germans are great and I believe unsurpassable in expressing mood and feeling, but for the bone, frame, and *charpente* of music they cannot come up to this kind of thing.

---

[1] Most unfortunately the rest of this postscript is missing.

On the contrary anything that Simcox[1] says is important. But for rhymes like those search the scriptures, thumb the poets, and you will find they readily allow monosyllables and dissyllables like *higher* and *fire* to rhyme.* It is true it is not very consistent of me to appeal to them when I profess to follow a more excellent way; still when I am told so and so is indefensible I must shew that it is defensible. Authority justifies it and the pronunciation can be so adjusted as to satisfy the ear. What is serious, you seem to think I took the objection overseriously. And now I think I am going out by woods and waters alone.

Yours   GERARD.

* You will say a monosyllable cannot rhyme to a monosyllable and a disyllable both at once, in the same stanza, that is. But if it can ever, then one of the two is accommodated to the other; and if one can be so can two or if one to one then one to two. Do you see the reasoning?[2]

CIV

Stonyhurst College, Blackburn. May 29 1883.

DEAREST BRIDGES,—I am very grateful and greatly indebted to your friend ——.[3] His judgment and notes are also reassuring, for the composition is in fact my second exercise and no more, in the species my first ('tis true I took trouble over it) and the objections he makes are to things Dr. Bridge's[4] book had warned me against either not properly or not at all. Here indeed is a difficulty: I do not know if there are or where I can find examples (and the examples of the great masters are the

---

[1] George Augustus Simcox, writer of verse (*Prometheus Unbound: A Tragedy*, 1867; *Poems and Romances*, 1869), editor of classical texts and author of a History of Latin Literature from Ennius to Boethius. He reviewed books for *The Academy*.

[2] This footnote is written in pale blue pencil.

[3] Name deleted by R. B.

[4] Either *Counterpoint* (1877) or *Double Counterpoint and Canon* (1877) by John Frederick Bridge.

soul of education) of existing counterpoint—if such a thing does exist; not short exercises in books (and of these I have only seen Dr. B's). Thus ——[1] speaks of 'figures repeated two or three times': now I, bless us all, put these in for beauties, especially in a passage he marks as monotonous (and so it is if I ought to have kept changing). Clearly they are against the spirit of the kind of composition; though according to that of others, as fugue. How then am I to advance without models? Somewhere models must be. And if he could tell me where, I should be glad. I hesitate over your offer to get him to write: it might entangle him in more than he meant and he will be in this busy world busy. Of course I should like it in itself.

I took to counterpoint not for itself but as the solid foundation of harmony. But I soon began to suspect it was only an invention of theorists and a would-be or fancy-music, for what is written in it? Not even the preludes to Bach's fugues. There are two-part preludes which seem as if they ought to be in the second or third species and are not, the rules are in smithereens: then WHAT IS in true counterpoint?

I meant to be as conservative as ——[1] could be and my accidentals I always intended not to be chromatic but fragments of related keys, I did not always know what.

I have exhibited a poem, which I hope to send you when I can copy it, but it is longish for copying. Yours

GERARD.

CV

Stonyhurst. June 28 1883.

DEAREST BRIDGES,—I send Purcell herewith and my thanks and regret for having kept the piece so long. It shd. have gone yesterday, I swear it should, but as I was just going to pack it I was despatched to take a party of people over the college, which lasted till post time was past. Before . . .[2]

---

[1] Name deleted by R. B.
[2] A fragment: the bottom of the leaf is torn off.

CVI

Stonyhurst, Blackburn. July 26 1883.

DEAREST BRIDGES,—What I enclose is I dare say quite too long; if so . . . .

. . . .[1]

Our year begins with autumn and the appointments for this college will be made public on the 1st of next month. It seems likely that I shall be removed; where I have no notion. But I have long been Fortune's football and am blowing up the bladder of resolution big and buxom for another kick of her foot. I shall be sorry to leave Stonyhurst; but go or stay, there is no likelihood of my ever doing anything to last. And I do not know how it is, I have no disease, but I am always tired, always jaded, though work is not heavy, and the impulse to do anything fails me or has in it no continuance.

Weather has been very wet and cold and has made me ill a little.

Believe me your affectionate friend

GERARD.

CVII

Stonyhurst, Blackburn. Aug. 5 1883.

DEAREST BRIDGES,—Though you are long and deeply in my debt, yet having things to tell you I write again.

The holidays are come and from the height of buzz and bustle we have been suddenly steeped in the dankness of ditchwater. I have leave of absence and on Thursday probably am going

---

[1] Almost half the first leaf of this letter was cut off by R. B.; the blanks, therefore, are unavoidable. The matter of the letter can, however, to some degree be recovered. Mrs. Waterhouse was compiling a Book of Prayers (finished in 1884), and it was suggested that G. M. H. should contribute. This he did: but the Prayer he sent (evidently with some diffidence) was held to be out of keeping with the undoctrinal tone of the rest of the book, and was not included. R. B. pasted it into A, and indexed it as 'a prayer written for protestants'. It is printed as Appendix I. For further remarks by G. M. H., see Letter CX.

to Hampstead and presently to Holland for a few days with my people: to explain how this comes about I must go back.

You may have met my cousin Magdalen. She lived with her widowed mother Mrs. Marsland Hopkins and her elder sister and brother at Oxford in Holywell Street. There she became engaged to Archibald Commeline then an undergraduate of Magdalen. I used to meet him there, but remember him indistinctly: he is a great friend of Sir Gore Ouseley's.[1] She was married to him on the 7th of last June from my father's house. Of course my sisters were to be among the bridesmaids, but Grace was not so and this was the reason.

When my people were abroad last year they met at Montreux on (I think) the Lake of Geneva a young man Henry Weber son to a doctor at Sensburg in East Prussia. He was attracted by Grace's playing and, the weather keeping them in, was constantly at her piano: when they parted, though they had known each other for less than a fortnight, they were both deeply in love. In spite of his frail health, his uncertain prospects, and the obvious reasons against such a match my father and mother could not refuse to let it be an engagement. After some illusory rallies, just when Grace and he had persuaded themselves that he was to recover and all would be well, suddenly at the last, he died. The news reached Grace on the very eve of Magdalen's wedding. It was an overwhelming blow. Magdalen wished the wedding to be put off, but that was neither possible nor desirable; but a gloom was cast over the day and Grace kept her room. She then set her heart on seeing her lover's grave. An escort was found for her as far as Berlin and at the station nearest Sensburg Mrs. Weber met her. Now she is with them and they treat her like one of themselves. Mrs. Weber wd. seem by all accounts to be a very sweet person. I have had a letter from Grace from Sensburg. My father and mother are going to fetch her home and that is how I am to go to Holland. As at present arranged I am to go to Hampstead on Thursday.

The first of this month was our Speechday or 'Great Academy'

[1] See p. 199.

to which guests come. Among them was Coventry Patmore: he came two days before and stayed till the day after and the Rector put him into my hands, so that I saw a good deal of him. But as your friend ——[1] knows him well I suppose I need not describe him, and moreover you affect an absence of interest in him. On my mentioning you he expressed at once his admiration of your poetry but knew it only from revie[ws] and had tried without suc[ce]ss to get it from his booksell[er] or publisher and I could not properly direct him about it. I wish you would let me know in what form it now is obtainable: the titles I mean, for I have had the books but they are not here, I think. I told him of *Prometheus*: will there be any spare copies buyable? I took him all my MS of Dixon, of whom he had never heard, and made an enthusiastic convert of him. Before bringing out this autumn the next edition of his own poems, which, he says, is likely to be the last in his lifetime, he is going to send them to me for suggestions:[2] I do not know but it was bragging to mention this; however now there it is, all blubbering in wet ink.

I suppose it will be more than a fortn[ig]ht before I am at Stonyhurst again. My appointment is renewed.

Believe me your affectionate friend

GERARD HOPKINS S.J.

Aug. 6 1883.

Tell me about Mr. ——.[1]

CVIII

The Holy Name, Oxford Road, Manchester. Aug. 10 1883.

DEAREST BRIDGES,—I cannot be at Hampstead on Monday the 13th now nor till Wednesday or Thursday. A sudden need brought me here and keeps me. I am sorry you tore up that

[1] Name cut out by R. B.
[2] The correspondence between G. M. H. and Patmore, I hope to publish later. Included in it is G. M. H.'s detailed criticism of Patmore's poems, which the latter treated with the greatest respect.

letter: why not have let me have the pennyworth? Patmore lives at Hastings: I shd. think that address enough but shall come to hear more. Yours

GERARD HOPKINS.

CIX (Postcard)

St. Giles's, Oxford. Sept. 11 1883.

It is a dreadful disappointment, but it was to be. The train at Reading did certainly seem earlier than there was any need, but I got into it without suspicion: I was whirled past Pangbourn, and by the time you were there, if you went, was almost at Oxford. The worst of it is I do not even see how another opportunity is ever to occur. G. M. H. To Stonyhurst tomorrow.

CX

Stonyhurst, Blackburn. Oct. 24 1883.

DEAREST BRIDGES,—Thank you first for very kindly copying out the poem on the Blessed Virgin and then for your letter.

You always do misunderstand me on matters like that prayer for Mrs. Waterhouse. I was not thinking of you and her, not, I mean, as using the prayers in that book or of your opinions as mirrored in them, but of the buyers of the book and the public it was meant for; which public I suppose you and Mrs. W. to know the mind and need of better than I do and therefore to be right in admitting one thing and excluding another: now in that public I regret, and surely I may, that it can no longer be trusted to bear, to stomach, the clear expression of or the taking for granted even very elementary Christian doctrines. I did not realise this well enough, did not realise that distinct Christianity damages the sale and so the usefulness of a well meant book; but now that I do what ought I to be but sorry?

But by the way you say something I want to remark on: 'Even such a doctrine as the Incarnation may be believed by people like yourself', as a mystery, till it is formulated, but as soon as it is it seems dragged down to the world of pros and cons, and '*as*

186

its mystery goes, so does its hold on their minds'. Italics the present writer's. You do not mean by mystery what a Catholic does. You mean an interesting uncertainty: the uncertainty ceasing interest ceases also. This happens in some things; to you in religion. But a Catholic by mystery means an in- comprehensible certainty: without certainty, without formula- tion there is no interest (of course a doctrine is valuable for other things than its interest, its interestingness, but I am speaking now of that); the clearer the formulation the greater the interest. At bottom the source of interest is the same in both cases, in your mind and in ours; it is the unknown, the reserve of truth beyond what the mind reaches and still feels to be behind. But the interest a Catholic feels is, if I may say so, of a far finer kind than yours. Yours turns out to be a curiosity only; curiosity satisfied, the trick found out (to be a little profane), the answer heard, it vanishes at once. But you know there are some solutions to, say, chess problems so beautifully ingenious, some resolutions of suspensions so lovely in music that even the feeling of interest is keenest when they are known and over, and for some time survives the discovery. How must it then be when the very answer is the most tantalising statement of the problem and the truth you are to rest in the most pointed putting of the difficulty! For if the Trinity, as Francis Newman[1] somewhere says, is to be explained by grammar and by tropes, why then he could furnish explanations for himself; but then where wd. be the mystery? the true mystery, the incompre- hensible one. At that pass one should point blank believe or disbelieve: he disbelieved; his brother, at the same pass, believed. There are three persons, each God and each the same, the one, the only God: to some people this is a 'dogma', a word they almost chew, that is an equation in theology, the dull algebra of schoolmen; to others it is news of their dearest friend or friends, leaving them all their lives balancing whether

[1] Francis William Newman (1805–97), younger brother of the cardinal. He had resigned his fellowship at Balliol for reasons of conscience in 1830, and was Professor of Latin at University College, London, 1846–63.

they have three heavenly friends or one—not that they have any doubt on the subject, but that their knowledge leaves their minds swinging; poised, but on the quiver. And this might be the ecstasy of interest, one would think. So too of the Incarnation, a mystery less incomprehensible, it is true: to you it comes to: Christ is in some sense God, in some sense he is not God—and your interest is in the uncertainty; to the Catholic it is: Christ is in every sense God and in every sense man, and the interest is in the locked and inseparable combination, or rather it is in the person in whom the combination has its place. Therefore we speak of the events of Christ's life as the mystery of the Nativity, the mystery of the Crucifixion and so on of a host; the mystery being always the same, that the child in the manger is God, the culprit on the gallows God, and so on. Otherwise birth and death are not mysteries, nor is it any great mystery that a just man should be crucified, but that God should fascinates—with the interest of awe, of pity, of shame, of every harrowing feeling. But I have said enough.

Oct. 25—Austin Dobson's triolet I knew well by quotation: I dare say it is the best the Rondeliers have done. The stupid fellow, to change it! Makes me think the worse of him. But yours may be carried, I think, a step farther: the fine subtlety of 'Said my ear to my eye' is not broad enough for a skit.[1] I should put it into his own mouth and entitle it[2]

.　.　.　.　.　.　.　.　.　.

The expectations I raised in Mr. Patmore about Mano were my own and got from you: I had not then seen it. Afterwards however, when I had, I wrote to him that if he got it he wd. not be disappointed; whereas he is. I have not got it by me

---

[1] Mrs. Bridges knows nothing of this. Austin Dobson's triolet is 'I intended an Ode, And it turned to a Sonnet' ('Urceus Exit,' *Collected Poems*, 1923, p. 324), which in *Proverbs in Porcelain* (1877), and there only, was altered so that ll. 2 and 8 ran, 'And it turned into Triolets', and l. 6, 'With a bunch of fresh violets'.

[2] Here follows a considerable hiatus. Only a third of the next leaf remains, and one side has on it only the beginnings of lines and cannot be understood. The cut was evidently made intentionally by R. B.

now and will not at present say more of it than this, that crowded as it is with beauties of the noblest sort, the deepest pathos and tragedy, besides a few touches of humour, finely conceived character, interest, romance, landscape, imagery, and unflagging music, still I am much of Mr. Patmore's mind: it either has not or else I have hitherto missed finding a leading thought to thread the beauties on—or almost worse, that I see one but it breaks and is unsatisfactory, namely that Mano is a kind of Adam and falls and also a kind of Second Adam and is crucified. I will write more hereafter.

I had not meant Mr. Patmore to know I wrote poetry, but since it has come naturally and unavoidably about there is no more to be said and you may therefore send me your book and I will point it and make a few corrections. You were right to leave out the marks: they were not consistent for one thing and are always offensive. Still there must be some. Either I must invent a notation applied throughout as in music or else I must only mark where the reader is likely to mistake, and for the present this is what I shall do.

I have a great deal more I could say, but must conclude. I am your affectionate friend

GERARD HOPKINS S.J.

I may presently but will not just yet avail myself of your kind offer of the loose Purcells.

I have yet heard nothing particular about Grace. She will settle down and be happy: she is too simple-minded and too sweetnatured to let herself be soured or enfeebled by a grief. She may even come to care for someone else, though no doubt she does not believe she ever could.

CXI

University College, 85 & 86, Stephens Green, Dublin.
March 7 1884

MY DEAREST BRIDGES,—Remark the above address: it is a new departure or a new arrival and at all events a new abode. I dare say you know nothing of it, but the fact is that, though unworthy of and unfit for the post, I have been elected Fellow of the Royal University of Ireland in the department of classics.[1] I have a salary of £400 a year, but when I first contemplated the six examinations I have yearly to conduct, five of them running, and to the Matriculation there came up last year 750 candidates, I thought that Stephen's Green (the biggest square in Europe) paved with gold would not pay for it. It is an honour and an opening and has many bright sides, but at present it has also some dark ones and this in particular that I am not at all strong, not strong enough for the requirements, and do not see at all how I am to become so. But to talk of weather or health and especially to complain of them is poor work.

The house we are in, the College, is a sort of ruin and for purposes of study very nearly naked. And I have more money to buy books than room to put them in.

I have been warmly welcomed and most kindly treated. But Dublin itself is a joyless place and I think in my heart as smoky as London is: I had fancied it quite different. The Phoenix Park is fine, but inconveniently far off. There are a few fine buildings.

It is only a few days since I sent the MS book to Mr. Patmore (and in packing I mislaid, I hope not lost, your copy of the poem 'Wild air, world-mothering air', so that I had to send that unfinished): he acknowledged it this morning.

I enclose a poem of Tennyson's which you may not have seen.[2] It has something in it like your Spring Odes and also some expressions like my sonnet on Spring.

I shall also enclose, if I can find, two triolets I wrote for the Stonyhurst Magazine;[3] for the third was not good, and they spoilt what point it had by changing the title. These two under correction I like, but have fears that you will suspend them from

[1] For some account of the Royal University and University College see NOTE Q.

[2] A newspaper cutting of *Early Spring* (*Tiresias and other Poems*, 1885; *Works*, 1909, p. 573).

[3] See NOTE R.

a hooked nose: if you do, still I should maintain they were as good as yours beginning 'All women born'.[1]
Believe me your affectionate friend
GERARD HOPKINS S.J.

There was an Irish row over my election.[2]

CXII

University College, 85 & 86, Stephens Green, Dublin.
March 25 1884

DEAREST BRIDGES,—Kindly forward the enclosed,[3] for I fear that a former letter, addressed to Hayton, may have miscarried (which however were such perdition as nothing else could match); kindly also be damned to you for not writing and believe me affectionately yours
GERARD M. HOPKINS.

CXIII

Clongowes-Wood College, Naas. April 16 [1884] (back at University College, Stephen's Green tomorrow)

DEAREST BRIDGES,—There could be no difficulty about the corrections, I could deal with that well enough, but I cannot spare much time; therefore I should not undertake detailed criticism. But send the plays, both or one, nevertheless.[4]

I wish, I wish I could get on with my play. Perhaps seeing yours may encourage me.

Mr. Patmore did not on the whole like my poems, was

---

[1] First printed in *Poems*, 1873.

[2] There were two candidates for the classical Chair. Dr. Walsh, President of Maynooth, strongly supported Fr. Reffé, Prefect of Studies at Blackrock; Fr. Delany, the President of University College, had the support of the Senate of the Royal University in opposing this proposition on the principle that 'unless the Catholic teaching was concentrated in a single institution [University College] there would be no chance of having a real University College'. Dr. Walsh's proposal was therefore rejected by twenty-three votes to three, and G. M. H. was appointed. The incident caused 'bitter controversy'. (*A Page of Irish History: Story of University College, Dublin, 1883–1909*, 1930.)

[3] Evidently a letter to R. W. Dixon, who had left Hayton near Carlisle, having been presented to the living of Warkworth in December, 1883.

[4] *Nero* and *The Return of Ulysses*.

unconverted to them. He expressed high admiration for some, naming the one 'Wild air, world-mothering air',* but of the rest it seems he could not make anything.

Canon Dixon sends me from Warkworth a little volume of Daniel's printing.[1] I like the get-up better than *Prometheus*. It seems there is even some advantage in publishing in this way; at least he says so, but it would be tedious to explain how, AND WHAT DOES ANYTHING AT ALL MATTER?

I cannot however hope that you will publish the two other plays this way: I do think you ought to come before the public in the usual manner. I want also to see P. F. republished.

The East wind is worse than in England.

I am in a great weakness. I cannot spend more time writing now, but am your affectionate friend

GERARD M. HOPKINS S.J.

The *Century* is an interesting serial. There is in it a saddening account of a young American poet called Sidney Lanier,[2] who had good notions about poetical form, scansion etc, and died young, in struggling circumstances. The samples of his own were something like E. A. Poe, something like Whitman, and shewed, I thought, some genius, but not of a high order; but there was little to judge from. I remark that when American poets introduce native trees, flowers, birds etc into their verse the effect to us is of a 'ciphering' note on an organ.

Stephen's Green. April 19.

* of which unluckily I had copied only a third.

CXIV

University College, 85 & 86, Stephens Green, Dublin.
April 30 1884

DEAREST BRIDGES,—The secret out: I too am engaged[3] on examination papers and must therefore be very brief.

First I am not the least surprised, not that I suspected anything but that nothing about marriage surprises me ever.

[1] *Odes and Eclogues*, 1884.   [2] See NOTE S.   [3] Here the page turns.

Next I am glad: I say every one should marry, and do not see why you did not, years ago, except that

Thirdly you were waiting for Miss Waterhouse to turn up,* which having happened and being to complete your happiness I am very glad of it and feel sure she must be both good and charming. For I have reasons not altogether a priori for judging she is both. Of course I wish you both great joy and am your (the both of yiz) affectionate friend

GERARD M. HOPKINS S.J.

I am, I believe, recovering from a deep fit of nervous prostration (I suppose I ought to call it): I did not know but I was dying.

* indeed to be born.

CXV

Furbough House, near Galway. July 18 1884.

DEAREST BRIDGES,—I must let you have a line now, I see, and write more hereafter. I ought to have answered you before, but indeed I hardly thought you were in earnest in proposing I should be your best man, pleasant and honourable as the position would be. But to show no other reasons why not, at the time you name I should be about beginning my examination work and it would be altogether impossible for me to be out of Ireland. However you do not want for friends better fitted to do the work than I.

I am here on holiday. I have been through Connemara, the fine scenery of which is less known than it should be. Yesterday I went to see the cliffs of Moher on the coast of Clare, which to describe would be long and difficult. In returning across the Bay we were in some considerable danger of our lives. Furbough House stands amidst beautiful woods, an Eden in a wilderness of rocks and treeless waste. The whole neighbourhood is most singular.

The weakness I am suffering from—it is that only, nervous weakness (or perhaps I ought not to say nervous at all, for I am not in any unusual way nervous in the common understanding of the word)—continues and I see no ground for thinking I can, for a long time to come,[1] get notably better of it, but I may reasonably hope that this pleasant holiday may set me up a little for a while. Your enquiries are very kind: there is no reason to be disquieted about me, though weakness is a very painful trial in itself. If I could have regular hard exercise it would be better for me.

The reason of course why I like men to marry is that a single life is a difficult, not altogether a natural life; to make it easily manageable special provision, such as we have, is needed, and most people cannot have this.

I shall begin my annual eight days' retreat in a few days and then return to Dublin.

Coventry Patmore has kept your MS book[2] a long time, as though it were to give himself the opportunity of repentance for not admiring all the poems, and indeed appears to look on his condition as one of guilt and near to reprobation—which is very odd of him. And I believe it will be of no avail and that like Esau and Antiochus[3] he will not get the grace and is in a fair way to die in his sins.

I find that 2557 is divisible by nothing till you reach 20, beyond which I have not tried: what then can the length of the stanza be? And what is the subject of the poem?[4]

Believe me your affectionate friend

GERARD M. HOPKINS S.J.

Write University *College*, Stephen's Green: the number is unnecessary.

CXVI

University College, 85 & 86, Stephen's Green, Dublin.
Aug. 3 1884

DEAREST BRIDGES,—I am extremely glad to hear from both of you that you and Mr. Patmore were so well pleased with one another.

---

[1] Comma misplaced at 'time'.   [2] The MS. book of G. M. H.'s poems.
[3] For Antiochus, 'a wicked root', see *Maccabees*.
[4] A reference to *Eros and Psyche*.

You did not, I hope, let him hear my remark about the MS book.

That book could be the greatest boon to me, if you are so good as to offer it—a godsend and might lead to my doing more. And if you were to complete 'Wild air', that would be the *comble*. The former copy you made of it I must have, but it got mislaid in moving to Ireland.

Did you see there was in the book a 'curtal-sonnet'[1] you had not had?

I enclose something very beautiful and almost unique.[2] I an hoping myself to publish a new and critical edition of St. Patrick's 'Confession', a work worthy to rank (except for length) with St. Austin's Confessions and the Imitation and more like St. Paul and the Catholic Epistles than anything else I know, unless perhaps St. Clement of Rome.

I am the better and fresher for my holiday: I do not know how long this improvement will last but say with St. Patrick as enclosed 'Salvation is the Lord's'.

Believe me your affectionate friend

GERARD M. HOPKINS S.J.

CXVII

University College, 85 & 86, Stephen's Green, Dublin.
Aug. 21 1884

DEAREST BRIDGES,—I must let you have a line to acknowledge, with many thanks, the receipt of the MS book and two or three very kind letters. I guessed whose was the elegant and legible hand on two of the addresses. As for the piece of a new garment, I came to the conclusion it was put in to bigout the enclosure. I also concluded that that new garment was a pair of

---

[1] *Pied Beauty*, 'St. Beuno's, Tremeirchion. Summer '77', *Poems*, 13.
[2] St. Patrick's Hymn, or 'Breastplate'—'a corslet of faith for the protection of body and soul against devils and men and vices.' For Old Irish text and translation see *Thesaurus Palaeohibernicus*, ed. Stokes and Strachan, vol. ii, pp. 354–8.

195

wedding trousers. Circumstances may drive me to use my piece as a penwiper.

It is so near your wedding that I do not know I ought to write of anything else. I could not ask to be present at it; and indeed, much as I desire to see you and your wife and her mother and Yattendon itself, perhaps that would not be so good a day for this after all as some other. Only unhappily I do not see when that other is to be. However it is a fine buoyant saying, Non omnium rerum sol occidit.

I had an interesting letter from Mr. Patmore all in praise of you.

Several things in your letters call for reply, but not now. If you do not like 'I yield, you do come sometimes,'[1] (though I cannot myself feel the weakness you complain of it in it, and it has the advantage of being plain) will 'I yield, you foot me sometimes' do? 'Own my heart' is merely 'my own heart', transposed for rhythm's sake and then *tamquam exquisitius*, as Hermann would say. 'Reave' is for rob, plunder, carry off.

I find that in correcting 'Margaret' I wrote '*world* of wan-wood' by mistake for 'worlds', as the sense requires.

Our society cannot be blamed for not valuing what it never knew of. The following are all the people I have let see my poems (not counting occasional pieces): some of them however, as you did, have shewn them to others. (1) The editor and sub-editor of our *Month* had the *Deutschland* and later the *Eurydice* offered them—(2) my father and mother and two sisters saw these, one or both of them, and I have sent them a few things besides in letters—(3) You—(4) Canon Dixon—(5) Mr. Patmore—(6) Something got out about the *Deutschland* and Fr. Cyprian Splaine, now of Stonyhurst, wrote to me to send it him and perhaps other poems of mine: I did so and he shewed it to others. They perhaps read it, but he afterwards acknowledged to me that in my handwriting he found it unreadable; I do not think he meant illegible—(7) On the other hand Fr. Francis Bacon, a fellownovice of mine, and an admirer

---

[1] *Peace, Poems*, 22, l. 4. This reading is kept.

of my sermons saw all and expressed a strong admiration for them which was certainly sincere. They are therefore, one may say, unknown. It always seems to me that poetry is unprofessional, but that is what I have said to myself, not others to me. No doubt if I kept producing I should have to ask myself what I meant to do with it all; but I have long been at a standstill, and so the things lie. It would be less tedious talking than writing: now at all events I must stop.

I must tell you a humorous touch of Irish Malvolio or Bully Bottom, so distinctively Irish that I cannot rank it: it amuses me in bed. A Tipperary lad, one of our people, lately from his noviceship, was at the wicket and another bowling to him. He thought there was no one within hearing, but from behind the wicket he was overheard after a good stroke to cry out 'Arrah, sweet myself!'

I must write once more against the 3rd.

Believe me always your affectionate friend

GERARD M. HOPKINS S.J.

Aug. 24 1884.

CXVIII

University College, 85 & 86, Stephen's Green, Dublin.
Sept. 2 1884

MY DEAREST BRIDGES AND MY DEAR MRS. BRIDGES,—This is to wish you the happiest of days tomorrow[1] and all the blessings of heaven on that and all the days of your wedded life. I did not consider the mails; the consequence is that these wishes must, like the old shoe, be sent *after* you; but there is no harm in that if when they overtake you they ever after attend you. More than this there is no need to write now.

I am affectionately yours both

GERARD MANLEY HOPKINS S.J.

[1] On 3 September 1884, R. B. married M. Monica Waterhouse, daughter of Alfred Waterhouse the architect, of Yattendon Court.

CXIX (Postcard)

University College, Stephen's Green, Dublin. Sept. 30 1884

I am in the very thick of examination work and in danger of permanently injuring my eyes. I shall have no time at all till past the middle of next month and not much then, for I have to begin lecturing and cannot now prepare. I wd. then try to read N.,[1] but you see how things stand—it wd. not be a very satisfactory recension. Send nothing just now—i.e. not till October is past the full.

Your friend may do as she likes,[2] but I disavow those things. I believe I shd. not disavow but retouch 'Elected silence' and St. Dorothy.[3]

G. M. H.

CXX

University College, Stephen's Green, Dublin. Nov. 11 1884

DEAREST BRIDGES,—My heavy examination work is now some while over and I have begun to lecture: it is time therefore that I shd. write; indeed I have done so once, but the letter did not please and this is its recast.

I was very glad you gave me some word of your married life; I wish it had been more. I have a kind of spooniness and delight over married people, especially if they say 'my wife', 'my husband', or shew the wedding ring.

I shall read *Eros and Psyche*[4] with the greatest joy; so let civilisation execute its daily eggtrick over the book with the usual adroitness as far as the south side of Stephen's Green.

Mr. Tom Arnold (but I dreamt I told you this before) asked me to write a short notice of Canon Dixon for a new edition of his handbook of English literature.[5] I did it, but whether it was

---

[1] *Nero.*   [2] Evidently as to copying his early poems.

[3] *Poems,* 3 and 1.

[4] This poem was printed at the Chiswick Press, and published in 1885.

[5] This long footnote will be found in the 'fifth edition, revised', 1885, of *A Manual of English Literature Historical and Critical.* It is printed in Vol. ii, NOTE K. For Thomas Arnold see NOTE T.

time enough (for he was in the press) and short enough (for he was under pressure) I have not heard.

I have some musical matters to speak of. Stainer has written a capital Treatise on Harmony which has earned him the heart-felt thanks of people as ignorant as myself[1] (I cannot say his Novello-Primer of the same earned them) and of others, I believe, not ignorant at all. For instance Sir Robert Stewart,[2] learned musician of this city, much given to Purcell, Handel, and Bach, says it is the most scientific treatment he has seen. Though his theory is not final, it is a great step forward and has quite a daylight, a *grand jour*, of sense. I am sure Stainer must be very nice to know and meet.

I have a great light on the matter of harmony myself, new, I need not say (framed on the model of Mr. Pecksniff's 'pagan, I regret to say'); true, I hope.

You saw and liked some music of mine to Mr. Patmore's *Crocus*.[3] The harmony came in the end to be very elaborate and difficult. I sent it through my cousin to Sir Frederick Gore Ousely[4] for censure and that censure I am awaiting.

Before leaving Stonyhurst I began some music, Gregorian, in the natural scale of A, to Collins' *Ode to Evening*. Quickened by the heavenly beauty of that poem I groped in my soul's very viscera for the tune and thrummed the sweetest and most secret catgut of the mind. What came out was very strange and wild

---

[1] The third edition of Stainer's *Theory of Harmony* was published in 1876.

[2] Sir Robert Prescott Stewart (1825–94): appointed organist of Trinity College, Dublin, in 1844; Professor of Music in the University of Dublin in 1861; and Conductor of the Dublin Philharmonic Society in 1873. He was known also as a composer, but as an organist his reputation was highest. See NOTE U for some remarks on four letters from him to G. M. H.

[3] *The Year*, of which the first lines are:

> The crocus, while the days are dark,
> Unfolds its saffron sheen;

(*Poems*, 1906, p. 428).

[4] The Rev. Sir Frederick Arthur Gore Ouseley (1825–89), from 1855 till his death Professor of Music at Oxford. He was known also as a composer, edited the church music of Orlando Gibbons, and published treatises on *Harmony, Counterpoint and Fugue, Form and General Composition*.

and (I thought) very good. Here I began to harmonise it, and the effect of harmony well in keeping upon that strange mode (which, though it is, as far as notes go, the same as the descending minor, has a character of which the word minor gives you little notion) was so delightful that it seems to me (and I think you would find the same) as near a new world of musical enjoyment as in this old world we could hope to be. To the novelty of effect the rhythm and a continued suspense natural to the mode and easy to carry further contribute too. It is meant for a solo and a double choir singing in unison, the organ or a string band bearing all the harmony. It is in three movements, something like a glee, the third returning to the first.

If this letter is dull the writer was so and wearifully tired. So goodnight, and goodnight to Mrs. Bridges or (what is more beautiful) to your wife:

I am your affectionate friend

GERARD M. HOPKINS S.J.

Nov. 12—You asked me some time since if I would write you a short paper on English scanning. I should like to do this if you still want it, but all that we Jesuits publish (even anonymously) must be seen by censors and this is a barrier which I do not know how anything of mine on a large scale would ever pass. In this particular case no doubt there would be no difficulty.

CXXI (Postcard)

University College, Stephen's Green, Dublin. Nov. 25 '84

P. F. came safe, and many thanks.[1] The form is in my eyes rather convenient than handsome. Some things struck me on reading aloud which I will mention hereafter. I have lent it to Mr. Tom Arnold. The notice of C. D. will appear, with some omissions, needful but to be regretted, because they were calculated to whet the reader's appetite, send him for more.

G. M. H.

---

[1] A new edition of *Prometheus the Firegiver* was published in this year by Bell: it was printed at the Chiswick Press.

CXXII (Postcard)

University College, Stephen's Green, Dublin. Dec. 17 '84

I have been some days annotating as desired, either gilding or else refining gold.*

I want to know in what *Athenaeum*, for I missed it and must see it, there was, as I am told, a review of P. F.[1]

The book my notice (almost entire) of C. D. is in is Thos. Arnold's Handbk. of English Literature, a wellknown work.

G. M. H.

* I shall not be long.

CXXIII

University College, Stephen's Green, Dublin.
New Year's day 1885

DEAREST BRIDGES,—I wish you and your wife a very happy new year.

I believe it would have been better for me to have gone to Hampstead as they wanted me, since it seems I need a change; at all events I am jaded. It would have been the world of pleasant to have seen you.

What a pleasure must that music have been! 'Then what charm company' etc. Now talking of music I must tell you I have a great matter on hand. It is music to the Battle of the Baltic, the tune made long ago and now I am harmonising it. My first attempt in harmony was the Crocus. I got it sent to Sir Frederick Gore Ouseley a good time ago and he has not returned it. The reason must be that finding it will not do he

---

[1] This review, of the edition published by Bell, did not appear till 24 January 1885. It is a tepid piece of work, beginning, 'If this were a translation it would be a good one,' and is more concerned with a discussion of the plot's parable than with poetic merit, though a 'fine' passage is quoted, and acknowledgement is made that 'Mr. Bridges's use of the Promethean myth is subtle and suggestive'. G. M. H. evidently refers to the enthusiastic review of nearly two columns by J. W. Mackail in the issue of the *Academy* for 22 Nov. 1884. The critic finds 'the welcome fulfilment of a remarkable promise. . . . *Prometheus the Firegiver* comes nearer, perhaps, to the Greek spirit and tone than any English play that has been written since Milton.'

cannot make up his mind to tell me so. Indeed the second and third verses were a kind of wilderness of unintelligible chords, but the first seemed to me very good. However this new thing will be intelligible,[1] and in a few days I am going to send you the first two—or two first—verses (I hold it is all the same) and then I want you, please, to get ——[2] as before to pass judgment on them—this one time more, as children go on. There is a bold thing in it: in the second verse a long ground bass, a chime of fourteen notes, repeated ten times running, with the treble moving freely above it. It is to illustrate 'It was ten of April morn by the chime'. If ——[2] should approve it I am made, musically, and Sir Frederick may wallow and choke in his own Oozeley Gore. Then I have in the background Collins' Ode to Evening I mentioned to you before, which is a new departure and more like volcanic sunsets or sunrises in the musical hemisphere than anythin ye can conçave.

One word on Psyche and volcanic sunsets. The description of the one over the Cretan Sea[3] so closely agrees with an account I wrote in *Nature*, even to details which were local only, that it is very extraordinary: you did not see my letter, did you?[4] Swinburn[e], perhaps you know, has also tried his hand—without success.[5] Either in fact he does not see nature at all or else he overlays the landscape with such phantasmata, secondary images, and what not of a delirium-tremendous imagination that the result is a kind of bloody broth: you know what I mean. At any rate there is no picture.

There is one stanza about Psyche's sister falling like a stone.[6]

[1] See Appendix III, 4.   [2] Name cancelled by R. B.

[3] *Eros and Psyche* (*P.W.*, vol. i), March, stanzas 24–6. R. B.'s note says that this description 'is a portrait of the phenomena which followed the great eruption of Krakatoa'. There is also a reference to 'the sunsets of five years ago' in *The Growth of Love*, 67.

[4] A letter of 21 December 1883, published in the issue of 3 January 1884. This, with two other letters contributed by G. M. H. to *Nature*, is printed as Appendix II.

[5] Perhaps *Evening on the Broads* (*Studies in Song*, 1880) is in question.

[6] *Eros and Psyche*, August, stanza 27.

In suggestion it is one of the most brilliant in the poem but in execution very imperfect, and therefore I have been freer there than anywhere else.

I do not want to say more of Psyche now.

I shall be proud to send you the fragments, unhappily no more, of my St. Winefred. And I shd. independently be glad of your judgment of them.

I do not believe you will succeed in producing a 12 syll. or 6 foot line which shall not, as you say, be an Alexandrine. There is, according to my experience, an insuperable tendency to the Alexandrine, so far, I mean, as this, that there is a break after the 3rd foot, cutting the line into equal halves. This is the first feature of the measure and will assert itself. It has some advantages, but it makes it monotonous; and to vary the division, the phrasing, successfully, and for long, is a most difficult matter. Common blank verse on the other hand is in this respect selfacting, for 2 ft.$+$3 or 3 ft.$+$2 or $2\frac{1}{2}+2\frac{1}{2}$, one of which divisions almost every line you can without thinking make is sure to have, are all good and even without attention they will vary one another; whereas the equal division of the Alexandrine is first poor and then nearly invariable. Nevertheless I have grappled with this; how far successfully you will judge.

In such a case, the invention of a new vehicle, nothing wiser certainly can be done than to concert action as you propose to do: it is the best substitute for a past experience and a tradition.— But it is strange that you should select for comedy what I from its pathos chose for tragedy.[1]

I have found that this metre is smooth, natural, and easy to work in broken dialogue, so much so that it produces nearly the effect of 5 foot blank verse; but in continuous passages it is a very different thing. In passionate passages I employ sprung rhythm in it with good effect.

I am going, I am glad to say, for change to Clongowes Wood

---

[1] G. M. H. for *St. Winefred's Well* and R. B. for *The Feast of Bacchus, A Comedy in the Latin Manner* (1889). See R. B.'s Note I on this play for his account of the metre used.

College, near Naas, tomorrow. I shall take Psyche with me and also try to copy out and send you the passages from *St. Winefred*. I wish it might act as a stimulus to go on with it. At times I have been very much pleased with some things in them.

You will perhaps say that besides the Alexandrine, which is a dimeter, there might be a trimeter, like the Greek. But the trimeter arises by taking the stresses of the odd feet stronger than those of the even and so coupling the feet in pairs of stronger and weaker. With quantity this subordination and coupling is easy, but in English it is hard and cannot be continuously done. Mr. Patmore has pointed out the smooth musical effect of it where it occurs, though better instances might, I believe, be quoted than the one he gives.[1] The impression of the Greek trimeter as a whole is very closely given by our 5 ft. blank verse, though the metres are different. I do not think that taking a 6 foot line would bring us any nearer the Greek trimeter than we are now, rather the reverse; probably you think the same.

I hear that in a nocturn of Field's[2] there is a chime as a ground bass. However I presume the treble is written to the bass; mine is not.

If ——[3] will not do Stainer must: one of the two you must get for me. It is but a short little thing, two verses.

Believe me your affectionate friend

GERARD HOPKINS S.J.

CXXIV

University College, Stephen's Green, Dublin. Feb. 6 1885.

DEAREST BRIDGES,—I have much to write to you, but one thing presses and I have no time for more. I beg you will very carefully attend to what I say.

[1] See *Prefatory Study on English Metrical Law*, pp. 49–50, *Amelia, Tamerton Church-Tower, etc.*, 1878, or the *Essay on English Metrical Law*, pp. 245–6, vol. ii, *Poems*, Sixth Collective Edition, 1897.
[2] John Field of Dublin (1782–1837), pianist and composer. A small group of his Nocturnes is important not only for intrinsic merit, but historically because Chopin was influenced by them.
[3] Name cancelled by R. B.

204

Some years, say five, ago there came out a tragedy, its name I do not remember but its subject was Nero's history.[1] Poppaea was in it. I read a review of it, in which was quoted a scene between Nero and Poppaea. She suggests to him the murder of Agrippina and the suggestion is of the shape 'Pray, gentlemen, do not nail his ears to the pump'. In it were the words 'No crimes, I beg, no crimes'.[2]

About this much I am certain. I was struck by the words, have often thought of them, and I believe have quoted them.

The following I am not quite sure about. When you told me of your designing a tragedy of Nero (it was by word of mouth, not letter) and said it was wonderful the story had not been made use of or more use of before (though you knew better than I did that there was one or more plays called Britannicus), I told you of the play spoken of above, and I think, I am not certain but it is likely in itself, that I quoted to you the words 'No crimes' etc.

It would be well if you could get to see that play, but in any case you will see how highly likely it is that I have here traced the history of the words 'No crimes' in your play both to their source and up their channel.

Now since I am certain about that other play and since it may very easily happen that its author or a friend or a reviewer may recall those words in it I earnestly hope it is not too late for you to strike them out of yours. Not only they are not original but an echo, but it would be almost impossible for you to give any explanation of their appearance, even the true one,

---

[1] Presumably *Nero: A Tragedy*. By Richard Comfort (Philadelphia), of which *The Academy* (6 November 1880) says: 'The art of writing unreadable tragedies in tolerably polished verse has spread to America.'

[2] Here R. B. has written the following interlinear note:

I never saw the book nor have seen it: but I remembered G M H quoting the expression, & it seemed to me as if P. had really said it. So when I wrote the play I took it as if I had found it in Tacitus. R B

Also I was experimenting without any expectation of producing what might be worth publishing. When it came to publishing I saw (as here warned) that the only person who could possibly suffer by the theft was myself—& as I was quite indifferent about that I let the words stand.

which would not be lame and laughable. I read them first to-day and I act[1] at once.

You are peculiarly liable to these echos. For instance in Octavia's second line in the *rosatio* you have 'unblamed'[2] in the same place and cadence and with the same 'affective' effect as Milton in 'Hail, holy light'.[3] Another point is not an echo exactly but a commonplace, only one to which unhappily *pereant qui bona nostra* applies: you make Nero say of his mother's attempted drowning what Macbeth or Lady Macbeth more tersely says of Duncan—'The attempt and not the deed Confounds us.' Playwrights however cannot escape this: where particular cases are pointed out they may be modified. The echos are a disease of education, literature is full of them; but they remain a disease, an evil. The above case will open your eyes. I can write no more:

I have other faults and a world of praise to find.

GERARD.

CXXV

University College, Stephen's Green, Dublin. Feb. 8 1885

DEAREST BRIDGES,—I daresay I shall be able to send you your book[4] in a day or two now. I am in the last Measure.* The first Measure is perhaps the least satisfactory and it is only at the 5th or 6th that I have begun to revise carefully.

I admire the equable beauty of the work and the quaintness and freshness of the pictures. The story you have not elevated but confined yourself to making it please. Eros is little more than a winged Masher, but Psyche is a success, a sweet little 'body', rather than 'soul'. The dramatic side of the poem is very good, the characters say all the right things, and so on. I should

* I resumed the work this morning after a long break.

[1] Written above 'strike', cancelled.
[2] *Nero*, Act IV, sc. 3, ll. 1–2:
       Hang there, sweet roses, while your blooms are wet,
       Hang there and weep unblamed; . . .
[3] *Paradise Lost*, Book III, l. 1.   [4] *Eros and Psyche.*

think it would be widely and lastingly admired. On particular points I do not further dwell.

I am now ready to send my piece of music, the two first verses of the *Battle of the Baltic*, set of course for the piano, for what else can I do? but really meant for an orchestra—if I cd. orchestrate. But this is indeed to fly before I can walk, as a severe musician told me (but I did not care) of something else. Any lights ——[1] gives me, any remarks he makes I shall be very grateful indeed for. I hope of course he will not find the thing 'impossible', not the first verse surely, which even on the piano sounds a success; but the ground bass in the second needs a body of easily distinguishable instruments to bring it out. My hope is that, however complicated the harmony, the whole wd. be quite intelligible with a choir (the bigger the better) and an orchestra. My poor Crocus went to Sir Frederick Gore Ouseley and has not been heard of since, I fear is hopelessly lost.

Remember me very kindly to Mrs. Bridges and believe me your affectionate friend

GERARD M. HOPKINS S.J.

The critical remarks above will strike you perhaps as faint praise, but take it for said that the beauties of the poem are extreme: the seagull under water[2] alone is immortal and so are lots of things, pretty well everything that amounts to a feature.

Try my music yourself, at all events the first verse, and say what you think.

[3] [Composed, as here, for the piano, for which instrument it is unfitted, because the parts and particularly the ground bass in the second verse cannot properly be distinguished; but I can do no otherwise. I am sensible that the rhythms of the second verse are very confusing and see now how bars 1, 2 might be made more intelligible, but nevertheless prefer to send it off

---

[1] Name deleted by R. B.

[2] *Eros and Psyche*, September, stanzas 5–7.

[3] This leaf was placed by R. B. at the end of CXXXV, but it seems more probable that it belongs here, and accompanied G. M. H.'s setting of the *Battle of the Baltic*.

as it is and correct afterwards. There shd. be a great body of voices and the ground bass shd. be done by bells or something of the sort. The triplets shd. be taken as made with notes of the same length as the couplets, that is the quaver is the same in both and no shorter in the triplet than in the couplet.]

CXXVI

University College, Stephen's Green, Dublin. March 24 1885

DEAREST BRIDGES,—You will have been expecting to hear from me about *Nero*, but now I cannot say much on that if I am to answer you at once. I am in a low way of health, indeed I always am, but especially now in Lent; not that I fast, but the restriction of diet makes a difference to me. The delightful old French Father who teaches Logic here (in which subject he reads, in 5 or 6 languages, everything published in Europe this century, pretty nearly) will have it that I am dying—of anaemia. I am not, except at the rate that we all are; still I could do (indeed how gladly I could)—as they say—with more life.

I do not remember the place about Hora.[1] I am sure I did not mean what you think. Rather it was some infelicity in feeling, some want of point, I think.

Nero is a great work, it appears to me, breathing a true dramatic life. As an acting play I fancy there would be found defects in it. There is plenty of story and action and you writing it and a reader reading it might overlook something and think that was enough. But for an acting play not only must there be the requisite stir of action but that action must be seen.[2] It is to the reader much the same to read a scene of Agrippina's murder with the stage directions or to read a description of it by one of the characters. There is a difference in perspective as in painting between the foreground and the background, but when all is done they are on the same level of canvas. On

---

[1] *Eros and Psyche*, September, stanza 8.

[2] R.B.'s note to this play begins: This play was not intended for the stage, as the rest of my plays are.

the stage itself it is otherwise. Agrippina's death is the climax of the story; it shd. then be the climax of the stage business. You wd. then lose the noble line about the indivisible point of time,[1] but if you have two thoroughbreds you cannot ride both at once: one must be in the stable. You will say on the Gk. stage the climax is told by mouth of messenger. But first this is really a defect, a shrinking from the crowning tragic effect; next as the scene is mostly unchanged it is readily accepted by the audience as being natural and necessary, for how else are they to know of it? But with us if the scene may be changed why not change it?

Further—the play is a History, like Henry IV etc etc. History plays are the dramatising of a string of events which did at all events really take place and so much unity is not looked for in them as in other tragedies. But the history shd. be well known. There is interesting dramatising of many historical points in your play, but some of these look 'off' or outside the play and are nevertheless not very well known, e.g. Poppaea's two Caesars, Lucan's suspension, Pallas' dismissal. It is true you make them bear, but it seems they shd. bear harder. So that I fancy the business or action is both scattered and ravelled. If everybody knew the history minutely they wd. say: So the events were scattered and these were the ravellings of circumstance, but now being but ill informed they want you to unravel and to gather up. It strikes me that these two kinds of action and of drama thence arising are like two kinds of tracery, which have, I dare say, names; the one in which the tracery seems like so much of a pattern cut out bodily by the hood of the arch from an infinite pattern; the other in which it is sprung from the hood or arch itself and wd. fall to pieces without it. It is like tapestry and a picture, like a pageant and a scene. And I call the one kind of composition *end-hung* and the other

---

[1] In the lines that follow Agrippina's speech to her assassins (Act v, sc. 2, ll. 3199–201):

> None answered, and awhile
> Was such delay as makes the indivisible
> And smallest point of time various and broad.

centre-hung and say that your play is not centre-hung enough. Now you see.

Blamed bad pens.

There are inimitable touches, such as 'The sleek extortionate Pallas! Do you defend the despicable Pallas?'[1] and Burrus's 'I never blamed your supper'[2] and Agrippina turning with 'Polla is killed' cum sqq.[3]

Every scene is good, every soliloquy beautiful to individuation. (By the by the Irish, among whom I live, have no conception of this quality: their ambition is to say a thing as everybody says it, only louder.) And therefore your avowal of plagiarism is the more shameless and your disavowal of originality the more affected;[4] but I say no more of this, especially as it is useless to dwell hard on the point of honour; if it does not prick at the first push it was blunt beforehand.

Flaws remarked—Accerronea should, I suppose, be Acerronia. Chalcocondyles seems an anachronism: were compounds so cumbrous found in Gk. at that date? There were others, forgotten.

The timing Petronius' words with Britannicus' poisoning is a very fine piece of workmanship, but I have some doubts about it on the stage[5]—whether $\tau\grave{o}$ $\tau\rho\alpha\gamma\iota\kappa\acute{o}\nu$ or $\tau\grave{o}$ $\pi\alpha\theta\eta\tau\iota\kappa\acute{o}\nu$[6] is clearly struck: it might pass as some touch of a ghastly quaintness. Experience would shew.*

'This much were all' is hard. I can give it a sense indeed, but one expects 'This all were much'.

* This scene wd. need good byplay, careful concerting. But there is no depth of stupidity and gape a race could not fall to on the stage that in real life gapes on while Gladstone negotiates his surrenders of the empire.

---

[1] Act II, sc. 4, ll. 938–9.   [2] Act IV, sc. 4, l. 2215.

[3] Act V, sc. 1, ll. 2810 sqq.

[4] This refers to remarks in R. B.'s letter: there was no author's note to the original edition of *Nero*.

[5] Act III, sc. 5, ll. 1579–1650.

[6] Aristotle's *Poetics*, passim: 'the tragic' or 'the pathetic'.

No more, as I believe I maunder.

To go back and correct myself and you—*Do* and *did* are not the weak present and perfect. Weak perfects are like *leaped, dreamed,* strong like *leapt, dreamt*; or in different instances *loved, hated* are weak, *rode, thought* strong. You meant that *do* and *did* were morally weak. But this is no discovery of yours; it is as old as Pope: 'Then expletives their feeble aid do join And ten dull words oft creep in one low line'.[1] And no doubt they do for the most part, but not in the present sentence, have a weak effect—which wd. nevertheless have been better if I had said/ They have for the most part. But Wordsworth revived them, using them with great delicacy of effect. I did not notice that you had not used them, nor indeed do I remember using them in my suggestions myself, but have no doubt you are correct about both points; nevertheless I might well suppose you had, for they quite belong to that half archaic style you there employ.

Now then about *Ulysses*. I will do what I can, but cannot promise much, in my unsatisfactory condition, weak in body and harassed in mind.

I am going to send you in a few days from *St. Winefred* (1) the first lines of the first scene, a dozen lines of dialogue or less; (2) the villain's soliloquy after the murder, 71 lines, a very great effort; (3) a dozen lines or less, beginning another soliloquy. I shall be glad of your comments. The metrical work is laborious, yet it seems to me a success. The unities will be much closer than in modern plays.

——[2] has not written, but I am getting on with the *Ode to Evening*. It seems to me like a new art, the effect is so unlike anything I ever heard. The air is plain chant where plain chant most departs from modern music; on the other hand the harmonies are a kind of advance on advanced modern music. The combination of the two things is most singular, but it is also most solemn, and I cannot but hope that I have something

---

[1] *An Essay on Criticism*, ll. 346–7: 'dull' and 'low' should be reversed.
[2] Name deleted by R. B.

very good in hand. It is so very unlike everything else that I am independent of and do not hold myself in abeyance to the judgments of musicians here; for in fact they know no more than I do what right I have to employ such and such chords and such and such progressions.

Believe me your affectionate friend

GERARD M. HOPKINS S.J.

Lady Day 1885.

CXXVII

University College, Stephen's Green, Dublin. April 1 1885

DEAREST BRIDGES,—*Ulysses* is safe, but I will not write of it now. I am afraid I cannot be of much service. Holidays are begun, but I am not in the frame of body or mind to avail myself of them for work, as I should wish.

I return your Alexandrines and enclose my own. Please return these, remarking what may strike you. Metrically they will save my commenting on yours. I daresay our theory is much the same. I hold that each half line is by nature a dimeter, two bars or four feet, of which commonly one foot is silent or lost at the pause. You will find it sometimes employed in full. The third sample is patchwork: I once thought well of the pieces, I do not know that I do now. But A and B please me well enough.[1] I do not like 'recĕnt enough'.[2]

You will see that as the feeling rises the rhythm becomes freer and more sprung: I think I have written nothing stronger than some of those lines. In the passage following Caradoc is to die impenitent, struck by the finger of God.

Your self quotation 'mortal overthrow' is from the sonnet 'In all things beautiful', last line:

Unshaken by man's mortal overthrow.[3]

I remember it, for the book is not here. It must be left in the sonnet and should therefore, I think, be changed in *Psyche*.

---

[1] The three fragments of *St. Winefred's Well*. See R. B.'s note to *Poems*, 58.
[2] Not found in the printed fragments.
[3] *P.W.*, *G. of L.*, 31: the final version has 'unsullied' for 'unshaken'.

Do and *did* 'weak' present and perfect—It is a question of usage of words. The usage I follow is, I suppose, taken from the German, but now it is established, and that is enough. I object myself to calling *do come*, *did come* tenses at all: *do, did* are tenses (of *do*); *come* is a tense (if you like) of another mood of another verb. Two tenses and two moods and two verbs do not make a tense nor a mood nor a verb. It is the same confusion to call *of him* the genitive case: it is a preposition and an accusative case. These things are obvious, but scarcely anybody sees them.

You do not seem quite to have followed my meaning about the supper. The scene was ghastly of course. I feared that your scene was not ghastly enough. The stress was on 'quaintness', that the ghastly or the tragic was carried off in a quaint coincidence instead of being driven home. But you may be right and on the stage perhaps that treatment might be the most effective.[1]

I am thankful to ——[2] and did not want him hurried, as it is plain from the *Athenaeum* itself how busy he must be kept: however that is done now. His remarks are to be sure not in my circumstances encouraging, but they are instructive and if I could manage it I should attend Sir Robert Stewart's or somebody else's course, as he advises; only that I seem more in the way to compose my own requiem, like Mozart, but in plain chant, than any other musical exercise. Still there is something I do not understand. My piece puzzled you. Why? ——[2] found it so plain, far too plain. (By the by, he does not speak of nor mark any mistake: that is the main thing, to be correct; if I am that, that is the great point gained.) As for not modulating, that was deliberate: I look on modulation as a corruption, the undoing of the diatonic style. What they call the key of the dominant, viz. one in which the fourth of the tonic is sharpened, I say is not the key of the dominant (which is in another mode than the key of the tonic and has no leading note) but the key of the tonic misplaced and transposed. I believe that

---

[1] *Nero*, Act III, sc. 5.   [2] Name deleted by R. B.

——[1] and I would give diametrically opposite names to the same things: what he calls variety I call sameness, because modulation reduces all the rich diatonic keyboard with its six or seven authentic, not to speak of plagal, modes, to one dead level of major; where he finds tameness I find variety, specific quality (not of key, which is not specific, but) of mode. Here however, I must allow, is the hitch. For if I am right in theory, in practice I am bound to give that variety by my own methods. I find a difficulty in doing so and I am obliged to resort to devices of counterpoint (would I knew more of them!). Still I do hear plenty of variety which pleases me in that piece, and I hoped others would: it seems not; there is the mischief. To me plain chant melody has an infinite expressiveness and dramatic richness. The putting in or leaving out of a single note in an 'alphabetic' passage changes the emotional meaning: all we admirers of plain chant feel this, the rest of the world (and I expect this includes ——[1]) do not; and it is the old story, Fieri non potest ut idem sentiant qui aquam et qui vinum bibunt; we are sober, they intoxicated with rich harmonies cannot taste our fine differences. When I hear one of Chopin's fragmentary airs struggling and tossing on a surf of accompaniment what does it matter whether one or even half a dozen notes are left out of it? its being and meaning lies outside itself in the harmonies; *they* give the tonality, modality, feeling, and all. But I could write reams on this matter, which time does not allow my further running on about. When the *Ode to Evening* is done or well advanced I will send you that; study it yourself till you see my meaning (it is slow and easy to play); it is a test too: if you do not like it it is because there is something you have not seen and I see. That at least is my mind, and if the whole world agreed to condemn it or see nothing in it I should only tell them to take a generation and come to me again. But as it is I am well contented with ——[1] judgment of the other thing and thankful to him for it; if I were otherwise than I am it would brisk me up and set me to work, but in that coffin of

[1] Name deleted by R. B.

weakness and dejection in which I live, without even the hope of change, I do not know that I can make or, making, could keep up the exertion of learning better.

By the by, the mark ⌐‾‾‾⌐ in the verses means a sort of spondee, two long syllables equally accented or nearly so, though nominally one of the two has the stress. This is my difficulty, what marks to use and when to use them: they are so much needed and yet so objectionable. About punctuation my mind is clear: I can give a rule for everything I write myself and even for other people, though they might not always agree with me perhaps.

Believe me your affectionate friend

GERARD M. HOPKINS S.J.

Holy Thursday '85.

You once objected to the word *fleeced*, which you will find in sample B:[1] I mean the velvetiness of roseleaves, flesh, and other things, *duvet*.

I had almost forgotten to say that Michael Field is the author of *Callirrhoe, Fair Rosamund,* and other plays one or all published very lately and much praised by the critics.[2] He is a dramatist: nought which concerns the drama concerns not him, he thinks. It might indeed do him good to know that you had never heard of him, but I hope you will not let him make up a trio of enemies (*spretae injuria formae* you know) with Marzials and Hall Caine. The last has just written a novel said to be very good indeed.[3] M. F. may perhaps be Irish: Field is a common, Michael a very common Irish name. Do be wise.

---

[1]   its rose, time's one rich rose, my hand
    By her bloom, fast by her fresh, her fleecèd bloom,
    Hideous dashed down, . ..

[2] Michael Field is the name under which Katharine Bradley (1848–1914) and her niece Edith Cooper (1862–1913) wrote numerous verse dramas and lyrics which enjoyed some reputation and still find admirers. The first volume of these ladies, containing *Callirrhoë* and *Fair Rosamond,* belongs to 1884.   [3] *The Shadow of a Crime.*

CXXVIII (Postcard)

University College, Stephen's Green.

May 4 '85—I return your book,[1] almost, I am sorry to say as if I had not read it. I could do no better. 'Providentiae nostrae incertae et non est in homine via ejus.' I will write when I can.

G. M. H.

CXXIX

University College, Stephen's Green, Dublin. May 17 1885

DEAREST BRIDGES,—I must write something, though not so much as I have to say. The long delay was due to work, worry, and languishment of body and mind—which must be and will be; and indeed to diagnose my own case (for every man by forty is his own physician or a fool, they say; and yet again he who is his own physician has a fool for his patient—a form of epigram, by the bye, which, if you examine it, has a bad flaw), well then to judge of my case, I think that my fits of sadness, though they do not affect my judgment, resemble madness. Change is the only relief, and that I can seldom get.[2]

I saw that *Ulysses* was a fine play, the action and interest well centred, the characters finely drawn and especially Penelope, the dialogue throughout good; nevertheless, perhaps from my mood of mind, I could not take to it, did not like it, beyond a dry admiration. Not however to remain in a bare Doctor Felldom on the matter, I did find one fault in it which seems indeed to me to be the worst fault a thing can have, unreality. I hope other people will think otherwise, but the introduction in earnest of Athene gave me a distaste I could not recover

[1] Presumably *Ulysses*.

[2] How serious was the question of health may be seen from remarks about G. M. H. (presumably by Fr. Darlington) in *A Page of Irish History*: 'His career was in some respects not unlike that of Mr. Curtis [a Jesuit mathematician and colleague who suffered from epilepsy], for, though he was not subject to actual attacks, he suffered more or less continuously from nervous depression, and like Curtis, he died at a comparatively early age, having been more learned than practical.' For the whole of these reminiscences, as far as they affect G. M. H., see NOTE V.

216

from. With *Prometheus* it was not the same. Three kinds of departure from truth I understand and agree to in a play—first in a History those changes and conventions without which, as in other works of art, the facts could not be presented at all; secondly a plot of fiction: though the facts never actually happened they are a picture of life and a sample of the sort of facts that do—those also subject to their own changes and conventions; lastly an allegory, where things that neither do nor could be mask and mean something that is. To this last class *Prometheus*, as I take it, belongs; moreover it was modelled on the Greek and scarcely meant for acting. But *Ulysses* is to act; and in earnest, not allegorically, you bring in a goddess among the characters: it revolts me. Then, not unnaturally, as it seemed to me, her speech is the worst in the play: being an unreality she must talk unreal. Believe me, the Greek gods are a totally unworkable material; the merest frigidity, which must chill and kill every living work of art they are brought into. Even if we put aside the hideous and, taken as they stand, unspeakable stories told of them, which stories nevertheless are as authentic as their names and personalities—both are equally imaginary; if you do not like that, both equally symbolical—, putting these out of sight and looking only at their respectable side, they are poor ignoble conceptions ennobled bodily only (as if they had bodies) by the artists, but once in motion and action worthless—not gentlemen or ladies, cowards, loungers, without majesty, without awe, antiquity, foresight, character; old bucks, young bucks, and Biddy Buckskins. What did Athene do after leaving Ulysses? Lounged back to Olympus to afternoon nectar. Nothing can be made of it. May 21, 1885. The background of distance and darkness and doom which a tragedy should always have is shut out by an Olympian drop-scene; the characters from men become puppets, their bloodshed becomes a leakage of bran. (This, upon my word, is to ply the lash and to be unpardonable.) I see the nobility of the rest, but this one touch to my eye spoils all; it looks to me like fine relief all daubed and creamed over with heavy whitewash.

I do not wonder at those ladies reading *Nero* through at a sitting. It *is* very interesting and I feel quite the same. You offered to send me a correcter copy: I shd. be glad if you now would.

I must add there was another fault I had to find with *Ulysses* and it was to the same effect and same defect, of unreality; I mean the archaism of the language, which was to my mind overdone. I hold that by archaism a thing is sicklied o'er as by blight. Some little flavours, but much spoils, and always for the same reason—it destroys earnest: we do not speak that way; therefore if a man speaks that way he is not serious, he is at something else than the seeming matter in hand, *non hoc agit, aliud agit.* I believe you agree with me in principle: if so I think that your practice in that play is beyond what your principle allows. But slight changes would satisfy me. The example of Shakspere (by a 'corrupt following', for it is an absurd fallacy—like a child having to repeat the substance of something it has been told and saying *you* and *I* wherever the speaker said *you* and *I*, whereas it should say *I* where he said *you* and so on) has done ever so much harm by his very genius, for poets reproduce the diction which in him was modern and in them is obsolete. But you know all this.

How did Michael Field in the end go off?[1]

It is too bad that I shd. so abuse *Ulysses* after your encouragement of *St. Winefred.* But how cd. you think such a thing of me as that I shd. in cold blood write 'fragments of a dramatic poem'?—I of all men in the world. To me a completed fragment, above all of a play, is the same unreality as a prepared impromptu. No, but we compose fragmentarily and what I had here and there done I finished up and sent as samples to see if I cd. be encouraged to go on—and I was encouraged; that is by your last, for before I thought you thought they wd. not do. There is a point with me in matters of any size when

---

[1] *Works and Days* (ed. by T. and D. C. Sturge Moore, 1933), the first selection from the Journal of Michael Field, contains one direct reference (p. 128) to R. B. That is feline.

I must absolutely have encouragement as much as crops rain; afterwards I am independent. However I am in my ordinary circumstances unable, with whatever encouragement, to go on with *Winefred* or anything else. I have after long silence written two sonnets, which I am touching: if ever anything was written in blood one of these was.[1]

Of two metrical criticisms you made on the fragments one I did not well understand, the other was a misunderstanding on your part.

About the music I shd. like to write at some length. But for the present I only say first, how could you think I shd. be offended at your criticism or remarks or wanted you to express yourself so modestly? May 28, 1885. Next I am much obliged for the quotations from Purcell, but could not get my household musician to play the one in open score nor have had time or opportunity of running after professionals, besides that for myself I have kept away some time now from the piano. Thirdly the bass solo you give me to shew the variety Purcell could command by the modern system—well of that beautiful passage I have to say that it illustrates the wellknown variety of the minor as we now understand it, a variety for which Purcell particularly prized it, but that that variety I did not need the illustrating of and, ahem, I can send you an illustration of my own which as it seems to me is happy in that way—made long ago. Then of course I admire and surely I could produce—it requires no more knowledge than I have already got for at least the simpler effects and in fact modulation even to remote keys and so on is not difficult to do; it may be to explain—could produce and have produced modulations, but in the two first verses of the *Battle of the Baltic* (which has some eleven) I wanted to see what could be done (and for how long I could go on) without them. ——[2] of course thought they cd. not be done without even for that length and I do not dispute the judgment; I scarcely had myself heard my second verse—for that is the great difficulty,

---

[1] R. B. suggests in a note that this is *Carrion Comfort* (*Poems*, 40); but neither sonnet can be identified with certainty.   [2] Name deleted by R. B.

in reality my only, and I fear my insuperable, one, that I cannot play. But nevertheless Palestrina and the old madrigal writers and others did produce masterpieces—and Hullah[1] says actually final in their kind, that is which you cannot develope by modern science; you can only change the school and kind—without modulations, but employing the modes; without even the authentic cadence: I wish I cd. study them. Then 'do I mean to rival Purcell and Mozart?' No. Even given the genius, a musician must be that and nothing else, as music now is; at least so it has been with all the great musicians. But I did aim at two things not in themselves unattainable, if to me far easier things were not now unattainable. But of these, if ever, hereafter.

Believe me your affectionate friend

GERARD M. HOPKINS S.J.

May 29 1885.

CXXX

University College, St. Stephen's Green, Dublin. Sept. 1 1885.

DEAREST BRIDGES,—I have just returned from an absurd adventure, which when I resigned myself to it I could not help enjoying. A hairbrained fellow took me down to Kingstown and on board his yacht and, whereas I meant to return to town by six that evening, would not let me go either that night or this morning till past midday. I was afraid it would be compromising, but it was fun while it lasted.

I have been in England. I was with my people first at Hampstead, then at Midhurst in Sussex in a lovely landscape: they are there yet. And from there I went to Hastings to Mr. Patmore's for a few days. I managed to see several old friends and to make new ones, amongst which Mr. W. H. Cummings the tenor singer and composer, who wrote the Life of Purcell: he shewed me some of his Purcell treasures and others and is going to send me several things. I liked him very much but the

---

[1] John Pyke Hullah (1812–84): see *Grove's Dictionary* for an account of his activities, and a list of his publications.

time of my being with him was cut short. I did not attempt to see you: I did not know that visitors wd. at that time be very welcome and it wd. have been difficult to me in any case to come. I am very sorry to hear of Mrs. Bridges' disappointment: somehow I had feared that would happen.

I shall shortly have some sonnets to send you, five or more. Four[1] of these came like inspirations unbidden and against my will. And in the life I lead now, which is one of a continually jaded and harassed mind, if in any leisure I try to do anything I make no way—nor with my work, alas! but so it must be.[2]

Mr. Patmore lent me Barnes' poems[3]—3 volumes, not all, for indeed he is prolific. I hold your contemptuous opinion an unhappy mistake: he is a perfect artist and of a most spontaneous inspiration; it is as if Dorset life and Dorset landscape had taken flesh and tongue in the man. I feel the defect or limitation or whatever we are to call it that offended you: he lacks fire; but who is perfect all round? If one defect is fatal what writer could we read?

An old question of yours I have hitherto neglected to answer, am I thinking of writing on metre? I suppose thinking too much and doing too little. I do greatly desire to treat that subject; might perhaps get something together this year; but I can scarcely believe that on that or on anything else anything of mine will ever see the light—of publicity nor even of day. For it is widely true, the fine pleasure is not to do a thing but to feel that you could and the mortification that goes to the heart is to feel it is the power that fails you: qui occidere nolunt

[1] Written above 'Three', cancelled.

[2] See R. B.'s note, Poems, pp. 116–17. The four that 'came like inspirations unbidden and against my will' must be chosen, I take it, from Poems 40, 41, 44, 45, 46, 47; and 38 and 39, dated August of this year, must be added to the list of possibilities for the others.

[3] For Patmore on William Barnes see Principle in Art, &c. (1889), where is reprinted an article contributed to the Fortnightly Review of November 1886; and Courage in Politics and other Essays (1921), pp. 118–26, where will be found two reviews contributed to the St. James's Gazette on 9 October 1886 and 19 December 1887. See also the North British Review for November 1859, and Macmillan's Magazine for June 1862.

Posse volunt; it is the refusal of a thing that we like to have. So with me, if I could but get on, if I could but produce work I should not mind its being buried, silenced, and going no further; but it kills me to be time's eunuch and never to beget.[1] After all I do not despair, things might change, anything may be; only there is no great appearance of it. Now because I have had a holiday though not strong I have some buoyancy; soon I am afraid I shall be ground down to a state like this last spring's and summer's, when my spirits were so crushed that madness seemed to be making approaches—and nobody was to blame, except myself partly for not managing myself better and contriving a change.

Believe me, with kind wishes to Mrs. Bridges, your affectionate friend

GERARD M. HOPKINS S.J.

Sept. 8 '85.

This day 15 years ago I took my first vows.

I hope Mrs. Molesworth is well. Where is she now?

Is your brother John going to bring out a second volume?[2]

If I had not reread your letter I shd. have left it unanswered. The expression 'The Mass is good' is, I feel sure, never used in these islands. But the meaning in the circumstances is pretty plain and must be just what you take it to be. To satisfy the obligation of hearing mass on Sundays and the 'Festivals of Obligation' one must be present from at least the Offertory to the Priest's Communion. The question is well threshed out: for laxer and for stricter opinions see the Moral Theologians passim; whose name is Legion, but St. Alphonsus Liguori will do for all (Treatise *de Praeceptis Ecclesiae* or *De Decem Praeceptis Decalogi*). However the phrase would not easily be understood by your readers or hearers. I hope to see those plays. Are the choral

---

[1] Cf. *Poems*, 50 (autograph copy dated March 17, 1889):
         birds build—but not I build; no, but strain,
     Time's eunuch, and not breed one work that wakes.

[2] His other works of verse are *In a Village, Poems* (1898), and *The Lost Parson and other Poems* (1902).

parts written strictly to the music? I never saw good poetry made to music unless that music itself had first been made to words.

CXXXI

University College, St. Stephen's Green, Dublin. Dec. 14 '85

DEAREST BRIDGES,—The first of the Catholic periodicals is the *Dublin Review*, but I am altogether unknown to them and I think nothing whatever would be gained by my forwarding them the book.[1] Our magazine is the *Month*: I know the editor of course and can and will recommend the book and though I do not want to have it to review (because, to speak the truth, it would take time, and that I can ill afford; that is the only reason; otherwise I shd. enjoy it), yet I believe he will at once ask me to do so. There is also the *Tablet* and to that I am unknown too and they do not like Jesuits, but I have always maintained the *Tablet* is a very good well conducted gentlemanly paper, unequal in ability, but some of its articles are very good and able; so that I think you shd. send them the book and Catholic households, finding a book of poetry decent and spoken highly of (if it should), will be glad to get it. No people are so nice as the English Catholic gentry. (As for the Irish Catholic gentry, by what I see, the country is going shortly to be made too hot to hold them: a persecution of them, it is no less, headed by two Archbishops has begun. Only that those two Archbishops will, I expect, shortly have a crow to pick with the Holy See. By the by Leo XIII. has written a really beautiful letter to the English bishops, the most liberally worded in dealing with those outside the Church that ever Pope, I shd. fancy, yet penned.)

Alas! has 'the gifted Hopkins' appeared in C.D.'s. 'abrupt note'?[2]—too plainly the son and literary executor of Lang's

---

[1] Presumably *Eros and Psyche.*

[2] An acknowledgement by Canon Dixon of help received in writing his account of the Jesuit Mission in Ireland. The footnote ends: 'For my knowledge of this and for other information I am indebted to my gifted friend the Reverend Gerard Hopkins, S.J.' See vol. ii, p. 129.

Gifted Hopkins (the American) who 'died of the consequences of his own jocosity'. C. D. shd. remember: 'surtout point de zèle'. It cannot help me, it may (if remarked, must) harm me. Praise of the unknown brings about the frame of mind with which one reads for the first time of the effects of Mother Seigel's Soothing Syrup, which lately burst (or oozed) upon the universe.

Yr. affectionate friend

GERARD.

Not a word to C. D.

CXXXII

St. Aloysius' Church, St. Giles's, Oxford. May 4 '86

MY DEAR BRIDGES,—Thursday May 6 is the day I must come.

You say I am to come to Hampstead Norris. So let it be, but the earliest train I cd. come by gets there at 10.57, that is, nearly 11, whereas if I went to Pangbourn I cd. be there at 10.11 and possibly by 9.7. But this last and first would involve going without breakfast; and though the later train (10.11) is 46 minutes earlier than the one to Hampstead Norris, yet I suppose the difference is more than made up for in the drive.* Even so . . . but perhaps it is the horse you are thinking of or there is some other point to be considered. However it may be, to Hampstead Norris at 10.57 I go,—unless, which perhaps posts make impossible, I hear from you to the contrary.

I must be back here at night.

Yours ever

GERARD HOPKINS.

* This will not do either, for it is incredible that either place shd. be so distant from you as to make a difference of 46 minutes and more in driving.

And I must wait at Didcot 50 minutes for that local train, O dear O dear. But you wd. have it so.

CXXXIII

University College, St. Stephen's Green, Dublin. June 1 '86

DEAREST BRIDGES,—I ought to have written 'hot foot' on my return from Yattendon, when the memory was quite fresh. It is however and will continue fragrant. That was a delightful day.

Mrs. Bridges was not as fancy painted her (indeed fancy painted her very faintly, in watered sepia), but by no means the worse for that.

I was improved by my holiday. My anxiety mostly disappeared, though there is more reason than ever for it now, for I am terribly behindhand and cannot make up. But no more of that—nor now of anything further. (A lie: look on.)

By the bye the Paravicinis gave me Richard Crawley's *Venus and Psyche*,[1] which I had long wanted to see. Did not like it. He is a true poet, but this poem is no success or at least it does not please. It is in the metre and manner markedly of *Don Juan*, mocking and discursive about modern life and so on. The verse very flowing and, where he took any pains, finely phrased. It is not serious; the scenes are scarcely realised; the story treated as a theme for trying style on. There is not the slightest symbolism.

This leads me to say that a kind of touchstone of the highest or most living art is seriousness; not gravity but the being in earnest with your subject—reality. It seems to me that some of the greatest and most famous works are not taken in earnest enough, are farce (where you ask the spectator to grant you something not only conventional but monstrous). I have this feeling about *Faust* and even about the Divine Comedy, whereas *Paradise Lost* is most seriously taken. It is the weakness of the whole Roman literature.

---

[1] *Venus and Psyche, with other Poems*, 1871. The title poem runs to three cantos, 164 pages in all. G. M. H.'s criticism is just. The tone of the poem, reminiscent from a distance of Byron's in *Don Juan*, would naturally offend him.

Give my best love to Mrs. Bridges and Mrs. Molesworth and believe me your affectionate friend

GERARD HOPKINS S.J.

I shd. add that Crawley is loose and makes his looseness much worse by quoting his original in the notes. And amazing to say, he is so when addressing *his sister*.

CXXXIV

11 Church Street, Tremadoc, North Wales. Oct. 2 1886.

DEAREST BRIDGES,—Your letter, you see, written from South Wales reaches me in Gwynedd after making a long elbow at Dublin. A delightful holiday comes to an end to-day, but I am going to take duty at Pwllheli tomorrow and start for Holyhead in the evening.

I will back Tremadoc for beauty against Fishguard. There are no myrtles, at least I have seen none, but right over the village (clean, modern, solidly built, spacious, and somewhat picturesque) rises a cliff of massive selfhewn rock, all overrun with a riot of vegetation which the rainy climate seems to breathe here. Tremadoc is said to take its name from some Mr. Madox and is in the parish of Ynys Cynhaiarn. Portmadoc half a mile off is still more modern: my landlord remembers when there were only three houses there. It is rising, but fashion has not found it. Bretons come here in jerseys, earrings, and wooden shoes to sell vegetables, and Portmadoc and all N. Wales seem to live upon slate, to get which they are quarrying away great mountains: nowhere I suppose in Europe is such a subjection of nature to man to be witnessed. The end is that the mountains vanish, but in the process they take a certain beauty midway between wildness and art. Mountains are all round. The feature of the coast are the great traethau or tracts of sand—seasand, links, and reclaimed land; two estuaries, at the meeting point of which Penrhyn Deudraeth (two tracts) stands, reach the sea hereabouts; they are commanded by Moelwyn and other mountains and by Criccieth and Harlech Castles. A long walk skirting one of these and discovering Snowdon and other grand mountain views leads to Pont Aberglaslyn and into the Pass which from that leads to the valley where Beddgelert is. The beauty of this Pass is extreme. The Glaslyn, a torrent of notably green water, runs through it and thereby hangs a sad tale. I made a drawing (its ruins enclosed)[1] of one fall of it over a rock, not at all so good as I could have wished, for water in motion, highly difficult at best (I need not say), needs the most sympathetic pencils, and this was done with an unsatisfactory HB and touched, not for the better, with a better at home; but however I thought well enough of it to mean to 'set' it and send it to you. I used milk in a saucer and put the saucer by the fire, where the gluey milk stuck it so fast to the earthenware that it could not be got off without grievous tearing. Still such as it now is I send it.

I am now at Pwllheli: a young Irish exciseman is my host.

How voluminous you are getting! I will do what I can with the 'Feast of Bacchus'.[2] Examination work is in my foreground, but that will not altogether hinder. I have just at present got Canon Dixon's proofs to a poem on Calypso.[3]

Some scenes of my *Winefred* have been taking shape here in Wales, always to me a mother of Muses. It is a drama of passion more than of character and not at all of manners, something in what I understand to be Marlowe's treatment (I could flog myself for being so ignorant as to say 'I understand to be'). You have seen fragments, I now definitely hope to finish it, but I cannot say when.

Also other things have got on a little, as my ode on Campion.

I think Fishguard must be a purely English name. If the place has a Welsh name it will have only one and Fiscard is no doubt the phonetic spelling of the Welsh attempt at Fishguard. It is odd how much mispronunciation lies in imaginary

[1] To reproduce this drawing in its present state would be unfair to G. M. H. See Appendix III for some remarks on him as an artist.
[2] Privately printed, Oxford, 1889.
[3] *Ulysses and Calypso*: the first of *Lyrical Poems*, 1887.

difficulties. *Sh* is a Welsh sound, but occurs always before vowels and is written *si* (e.g. *Siabod* pronounced *Shabod* and *siop* = *shop*), even between words, as Lewis Evans pronounced Le-wish Eevanss. But there was the analogy of Pyscod/Fish and the Welsh mould everything into a false Welsh form. Then you see Newport is English and Goodwic English or Norse, and is it Dinas or Pinas? Dinas is pure Welsh. Pinas wd. probably be Pinnace.

Our Welsh holiday came on me and my companion as a happy surprise. And though we had much rain we did Snowdon to admiration. We walked much. We fell upon honest people and lived cheap, too cheap, so that nearly £8 is left out of £20, and that is mismanagement; but my companion had to return before me. I had at first set my heart on Yorkshire and Fountains,[1] but to save journey money we went to Wales: why do I complain, when I have seen such lovely things and met such good people, unless that I always complain? But if you have not seen Pont Aberglaslyn in sunlight you have something to live for. But then we ought to have seen Bettws y Coed. We had money to see anything.

And I have read the *Castle of Otranto* and find it to be rubbish. Yet it was epoch-making, was it not? But some of these epoch-making books succeeded by virtue of new and interesting matter in spite of a poor form, for instance Ossian and in the main the Waverleys; of which last I hold, subject to wider reading and your better judgment, that, though they contain a mass of good reading and scattered literary excellences, yet as wholes they are scarcely to be called works of art and have been and are over-rated. They seem to be the products of a fine and gentle character, a fertile memory, and a flowing talent and to have even touches of genius in certain incidents, strokes of true invention; but in the general texture of them genius seems to me to be quite wanting. I think Robert Lewis Stevenson shows more genius in a page than Scott in a volume. Tell me what you think.

I have made a great and solid discovery about Pindar or

[1] Fountains Abbey, the magnificent Cistercian ruin about five miles from Ripon.

228

rather about the Dorian and Aeolian Measures or Rhythms and hope to publish something when I have read some more. But all my world is scaffolding.

With best love to Mrs. Bridges, believe me your affectionate friend

GERARD M. HOPKINS.

University College, Stephen's Green, Dublin. Oct. 4 1886.

Talking of counterpoint, good Sir Robert Stewart of this city has offered to correct me exercises in it if I wd. send some: I have sent one batch.

CXXXV

University College, St. Stephen's Green, Dublin. Oct. 6 1886.

DEAREST BRIDGES,—I forgot to speak of the copies of *Prometheus* and *Odes and Eclogues*[1] (but whose? for I do not remember that any publication of yours had that title). I could make, I think, good use of them: I should give one copy to Mr. Tyrrell[2] of Trinity and get *Prometheus* known among Trinity men if I could.

But in general Irishmen are no poets nor critics of poetry, though much alive to what we vaguely called poetry in nature and language and very capable of expressing it in a vague, a rhetorical way. They always mistake the matter of poetry for poetry. However education goes for much in such a case.

A consignment of 331 examination papers tonight, I [am sorry] to say, and more will come.

Yours   GERARD HOPKINS.

I no[w se]e my time will be so short that it will go hard with the Feast of Bacchus.

You are quite wrong about Barnes's poems—not to admire them ever so much more. I have two good tunes to two of them. I had one played this afternoon, but as the pianist said: Your music dates from a time before the piano was. The parts are

---

[1] By R. W. Dixon.
[2] Robert Yelverton Tyrrell (1844–1914), the well-known classical scholar, at this time Regius Professor of Greek in the University of Dublin.

independent in form and phrasing and are lost on that instrument. Two choristers, who were at hand, sang the tune, which to its fond father sounded very flowing and a string accompaniment would have set it off, I do believe. By the bye, I will send you this thing as a sample and if it does not suit the piano you will at least see what is meant. Consider it and return it. The harmonies are *not* commonplace, with leave of Mr. ———[1] and there is plenty of modulation. (I told you I am acting on Mr. ———[1] advice.)

CXXXVI

University College, Stephen's Green, Dublin. Oct. 13 1886.

DEAREST BRIDGES,—Fr. Mat Russell of ours (he is Sir Charles Russell's brother), who edits a little half-religious publication the *Irish Monthly*, wrote to me lately for an opinion of some Latin verses furnished him; and this led to two things. The first was my suddenly turning a lot of Shakspere's songs[2] into elegiacs and hendecasyllables (my Latin muse having been wholly mum for years) and sending him one copy (and the rest I believe I can and shall get published in the Trinity *Hermathena*[3] by means of Mr. Tyrrell). The other was that he proposed to me to introduce your poems to the fewish but not despicable readers of his little periodical.[4] Now this I must do, as soon as it shall become possible; but you must therefore send me (not for this purpose *Prometheus*, which I have, but) those pamphlets copies of which I think I left at Stonyhurst. It is no doubt wasteful work giving me presentation copies; but the above is my most permanent abode and the nest likely to be best feathered. Yours

GERARD M. HOPKINS S.J.

[1] Name cut out by R. B.

[2] See NOTE w for a list of the Latin and Greek versions by G. M. H. preserved in A.

[3] *Hermathena* (A Series of Papers on Literature, Science and Philosophy by Members of Trinity College, Dublin) contains nothing by G. M. H.

[4] *The Irish Monthly* contains no review of R. B.'s poetry by G. M. H., but two Latin versions by him from Shakespeare were printed in vol. xiv (1886), p. 628 and vol. xv (1887), p. 92.

By the bye, I say it deliberately and before God, I would have you and Canon Dixon and all true poets remember that fame, the being known, though in itself one of the most dangerous things to man, is nevertheless the true[1] and appointed air, element, and setting of genius and its works. What are works of art for? to educate, to be standards. Education is meant for the many, standards are for public use. To produce then is of little use unless what we produce is known, if known widely known, the wider known the better, for it is by being known it works, it influences, it does its duty, it does good. We must then try to be known, aim at it, take means to it. And this without puffing in the process or pride in the success. But still. Besides, we are Englishmen. A great work by an Englishman is like a great battle won by England.[2] It is an unfading bay tree. It will even be admired by and praised by and do good to those who hate England (as England is most perilously hated), who do not wish even to be benefited by her. It is then even a patriotic duty $\tau\hat{\eta}$ $\pi o\iota\acute{\eta}\sigma\epsilon\iota$ $\dot{\epsilon}\nu\epsilon\rho\gamma\epsilon\hat{\iota}\nu$[3] and to secure the fame and permanence of the work. Art and its fame do not really matter, spiritually they are nothing, virtue is the only good; but it is only by bringing in the infinite that to a just judgment they can be made to look infinitesimal or small or less than vastly great; and in this ordinary view of them I apply to them, and it is the true rule for dealing with them, what Christ our Lord said of virtue, Let your light shine before men that they may see your good works (say, of art) and glorify yr. Father in heaven (that is, acknowledge that they have an absolute excellence in them and are steps in a scale of infinite and inexhaustible excellence).

Let me hear that you got all my letters. One, begun I think in Wales and sent from here, was addressed to Judge Fry's at Bristol, the next to Yattendon and had (I believe it was that

---

[1] MS. 'necessary', cancelled.

[2] The same thought is expressed in a letter to Coventry Patmore.

[3] 'To be active in producing poetry.' Presumably a phrase coined by G. M. H.

one) a torn drawing in it. Well of course you must have got that one, but the one to Bristol with the long address you may not. Earlier ones are I think accounted for.

Did I ever send you St. Patrick's 'Breastplate' or prayer? I do now at all events. Read it and say if it is not one of the most remarkable compositions of man.

CXXXVII

University College, St. Stephen's Green, Dublin. Oct. 21 1886 (I was received into the Catholic Church this day 20 years hence.)

DEAREST BRIDGES,—Here follows the remainder, the Burden, of *Yellow sands*. You may copy it in, but you will say it is only a curiosity.

Ariel. Hark, hark.
Burden (*dispersedly*). Bow wow.
Ariel. The watchdogs bark.
Burden. Bow wow.
Ariel. Hark, hark. I hear
     The strain of strutting chanticleer
     Cry Cock a diddle dow.

Lascivae latrare; ita plaudere. At hoc juvat: ergo
   Nos Hecuba et Hecubae nos canes
Adlatrent. Gallus sed enim occinit, occinat: aequumst
   Cantare gallos temperi.

You will have seen that in one of the pieces were some phrases borrowed from Horace and Virgil. In original composition this is most objectionable, but in translation it is lawful, I think, and may be happy, since there it is question of matching the best of one language with the best, not the newest, of another.

These verses cannot appear in *Hermathena*, which admits no translations. Mr. Tyrrell said he liked them very much, but he did not himself approve of my Catullian rhythms. I employ them of choice, taking Catullus for my warrant only, not my standard, for metrically Catullus was very unsure. In my judgment his Atys, though (just like Tennyson's imitation) it shows the poet's genius, is metrically and even in other respects an unsuccessful experiment.

You would like Mr. Tyrrell. He is a fine scholar and an amiable man, free from every touch of pedantry.

I added two metrical schemes to my Greek verses for you.[1] They are inconsistent; that is to say, one is fuller than the other. I have made what I think is a great discovery; it is of a fundamental point; and I hope to publish something on it. It is shortly this. The Dorian rhythm, the most used of the lyric rhythms, arises from the Dorian measure or bar. The Dorian bar is originally *a march step in three-time executed in four steps to the bar.* Out of this simple combination of numbers, three and four, simple to state but a good deal more complicated than any rhythm we have, arose the structure of most of Pindar's odes and most of the choral odes in the drama. In strict rhythm every bar must have four steps. Now since four were to be taken to three-time, say three crotchets, (1) one crotchet had to be resolved, (2) only one at a time, and that (3) never the last. Hence the two legitimate figures of the Dorian bar were these: ∪ ∪ − − (the rising Ionic) and − ∪ ∪ − (the choriambus). But the following irregularities were allowed: ∪ ∪ − ∪ (the third paeon), either by prolonging the third syllable (∪ ∪ ≙ ∪) or by irrationally lengthening the last (∪ ∪ − ≬); − ∪ − − (the second epitrite), (which is not as Schmidt[2] thinks ≙ ∪ − −, for that wd. destroy the three-time, but ◡ − −), by resolving the first long into three instead of two, exactly as we employ triplets in music and write 3 over them; lastly the very irregular but important combination of these two licences − ◡ ≙ ∪ or ◡ − ≬ (the double trochee). The beautiful figure ◡ − − is the one most characteristic of the rhythm: Hephaestion calls it the Carian foot.

When the measure is more loosely used two new licences appear—syncopation, by which syllables are lengthened so that

[1] Preserved in A.
[2] See *T. L. S.*, Correspondence, 16 Feb. 1933 and next three issues.

three fill a bar and so that the last of one bar becomes the first of the next; and triple resolution, so that a bar can have five syllables. By means of syncopation the measure can be made dactylic and practically brought into common time. The strict Dorian can only be found in odes meant to be marched to.

I shd. say a word of the accentuation or stressing. Naturally the strongest place in the Dorian bar is the second crotchet, not the first, and I have so marked it in the schemes I sent, but perhaps it would be best to mark the first as strongest: it is made so, so to speak, by a correction, to redress the heaviness of the second crotchet. Pindar and all the poets continually pass from heavier feet, like $\smile$ – – or $\smile\smile$ – –, to lighter, – $\smile\smile$ –, where by the stress falling sometimes on a long or crotchet, sometimes on a short or quaver, a beautiful variety is given and the variety is further enhanced by making an imperfect Ionic follow a choriambus, thus: – $\smile\smile$ – | $\smile\smile$ –, by which a dactylic cadence is given but with the stress falling on different syllables of the dactyls. With all this the rhythm came to have an infinite flexibility, of which the Greeks seem never to have tired.

Thus you are not to mark ἔρως ἀνί|κατε μάχαν, ‖ ἔρως ὃς ἐν | κτήμασι πίπτεις, as here, but as here: ἔ|ρως ἀνίκα|τε μάχαν, ‖ ἔ|ρως ὃς ἐν κτή|μασι πίπτεις.[1] However the musicians no doubt took their own way with these things. By the bye, I will send you my plain chant notes to this: it greatly brings out the nature of the rhythm. Good night.

Oct. 22—Tufts of thyme from Bumpus's Helicon are to hand and I have sent three copies to Mr. Tyrrell and shall consider where to bestow the others.

I enclose the music to ἔρως ἀνίκατε μάχαν. Ahem, study it. You will find that it is (but not designedly) composed, though it contains octaves, in the older heptachord scale having the lower keynote on La (here E) and the higher on its seventh Sol (here D)—as we should speak. The music therefore is neither major nor minor, or is both and fluctuates between them, settling at last on the minor keynote. The two modes are

---

[1] Sophocles, *Antigone*, 781 sqq.

connected by Mi which is the fifth of La and the third of Do; and as the fifth is more important in a scale, being with us the dominant, than the third, so the minor mode predominates over the major. They are also connected by Sol, which is the upper extremity or keynote (not the octave) of the La-mode and the fifth or dominant of the Do-mode, and here again the upper keynote is more important than the fifth. This old heptachord scale is founded deeply in nature; it can never perish; and it is it which compels us to use and to find so much pleasure in the dominant seventh, in other words in a chord having for its two extreme notes the extremities of the hepta-chord scale. The octave and the heptachord scales both arise from doubled tetrachords, overlapping, conjunct or closed in the one case; free, disjunct, or open in the other. The vein I am working in is the application of this double system, the heptachord and the octave, in a new way, by founding the heptachord on La, not on Sol.

The above is not lucid nor perhaps all true. Perhaps the major and minor modes in the heptachord best communicate by means of the note between their keynotes, Ti (about which much might be said), flattened at option as in Greek and medieval music.

I have much more to answer in yr. letter, but want now to send this. I can also let you see some other settings of Greek to music as curiosities and some of them (as indeed the enclosed piece seems to me) as good in themselves.

With best love, your affectionate friend

GERARD.

CXXXVIII[1]

University College, Stephen's Green, Dublin. Oct. 28 '86.

DEAREST BRIDGES,—To't again; for though my last was long and tedious and the one before that, if I remember, a literary budget, I have not yet dealt with your last.

[1] At the end of this letter R. B. has written the following note:
'Wishing to keep this letter I have made a few notes in justification of

My examinations are over till the next attack of the plague. My lectures, to call them by that grand name, are begun: vae unum abiit et vae alterum venit. I was I cannot tell when in such health and spirits as on my return from Cadwalader and all his goats but 331 accounts of the First Punic War with trimmings, have sweated me down to nearer my lees and usual alluvial low water mudflats, groåns, despåir, aňd yearňings.

Now I have at much length remonstrated with Canon Dixon for slighting Wordsworth's Ode on the Intimations, at which he might have taken offence but on the contrary he took it with his usual sweetness;[1] and I beg you will my remonstrances with you about Barnes and Stephenson[2]; of both of whom, but especially S., you speak with a sourness which[3] tinges your judgment.

It is commonly thought of Barnes that 'local colour' is just what he excells in and this is my own opinion. A fine and remarkable instance (a case of colour proper) was quoted by the *Saturday* in the article on him which followed the news of his death.[4] But of him another time or never; no more now. (The expressions 'the supposed emotions of peasants' grates on me, but let it pass.)

I have not read *Treasure Island*.[5] When I do, as I hope to, I will bear your criticisms in mind. (By the bye, I am sorry

my criticisms, which were no doubt ill expressed—to give rise to such misrepresentation.

'The letter gives a true picture of G. M. H.'s views of English literature, & his judg^t of modern writers.

'About Louis Stevenson I may add that my chief "objection" to his works is merely a want of sympathy. I admire his art much, but he is constantly offending my feelings.'

He has also made certain interlinear comments, which are printed as footnotes in their place.

[1] This letter, with Canon Dixon's reply, will be found in vol. ii.

[2] Spelt thus.   [3] MS. 'with'.

[4] In the issue of 16 October 1886: an appreciative, well-informed, unsigned review. The quotation referred to is the first stanza of *Went Hwome* (*Poems of Rural Life* . . ., 1887, p. 362).

[5] Published in 1882. First printed as a serial in *Young Folks*, starting in the issue of 1 October 1881.

those poor boys lost the book because you found consecutive fifths somewhere. However give 'em Rider Haggard's *King Solomon's Mines*.[1] They certainly will enjoy it; anyone would; and the author is not a highflier.) Nevertheless I mean to deal with two of these criticisms now, for it is easy to do so on the face of them.

One is that a boy capable of a brave deed would be incapable of writing it down—well *that* boy. Granting this, still to make him tell it is no fault or a trifling one.[2] And the criticism, which ignores a common convention of romance or literature in general, is surely then some ἀγροικία on your part. Auto-biography in fiction is commonly held a hazardous thing and few are thought to have succeeded in it on any great scale: Thackeray in *Esmond* is I believe held for one of the exceptions. It is one of the things which 'O Lord, sir, we must connive at'. The reader is somehow to be informed of the facts. And in any case the fault is removeable without convulsing the struc-ture of the whole: like a bellglass or glass frame over cucumbers or flowers it may be taken off, cleansed, and replaced without touching them. So this criticism I look on as trifling.

The other criticism is the discovery of a fault of plot about the whereabouts of some schooner:[3] I take your word for it. One blot is no great matter, I mean not a damning matter.[4] One blot may be found in the works of very learned clerks indeed. *Measure for Measure* is a lovely piece of work, but it was a blot, as Swinburne raving was overheard for hours to say, to make Isabella marry the old Duke. *Volpone* is one of the richest and most powerful plays ever written, but a writer in a late *Academy* points out a fault of construction[5] (want of motive, I think, for

---

[1] Published in 1886.

[2] 'My objection was not to his telling, but to his narration being sometimes in a vein untrue to his character as required by his actions, the two being incompatible & bad as art. RB'

[3] 'This I gave as an instance of the author's art [wh. is not disguised] breaking down. RB'

[4] 'There are others in plenty—RB'

[5] A review, on 16 October 1886, by H. C. Beeching of J. A. Symonds's

Bonario's being at Volpone's house when Celia was brought there): it will stand that one fault. True you say that in Stevenson's book there are many such: but I do not altogether believe there are.

This sour severity blinds you to his great genius. *Jekyll and Hyde*[1] I have read. You speak of 'the gross absurdity' of the interchange.[2] Enough that it is impossible and might perhaps have been a little better masked: it must be connived at, and it gives rise to a fine situation. It is not more impossible than fairies, giants, heathen gods, and lots of things that literature teems with—and none more than yours.[3] You are certainly wrong about Hyde being overdrawn: my Hyde is worse. The trampling scene is perhaps a convention: he was thinking of something unsuitable for fiction.

I can by no means grant that the characters are not characterised, though how deep the springs of their surface action are I am not yet clear. But the superficial touches of character are admirable: how can you be so blind as not to see them? e.g. Utterson frowning, biting the end of his finger, and saying to the butler 'This is a strange tale you tell me, my man, a very strange tale'. And Dr. Lanyon: 'I used to like it, sir [life]; yes, sir, I liked it. Sometimes I think if we knew all' etc. These are worthy of Shakespeare. Have you read the *Pavilion on the Links* in the volume of *Arabian Nights* (not one of them)? The absconding banker is admirably characterised, the horror is nature itself, and the whole piece is genius from beginning to end.

In my judgment the amount of gift and genius which goes into novels in the English literature of this generation is perhaps

---

Ben Jonson. Here is quoted from the book: 'the heaviest blot upon Jonson's construction' is that 'he has suggested no adequate motive for Mosca's introduction of Bonario into Volpone's palace at the moment when Corbaccio is coming to execute his will, and Celia is being brought by her unworthy husband.'   [1] Published in 1886.

[2] 'No—of the means employed, wh. is physical & sh^d have been magical. RB'

[3] '[but does not make chemistry of]' R.B.

not much inferior to what made the Elizabethan drama, and
unhappily it is in great part wasted. How admirable are Black-
more and Hardy! Their merits are much eclipsed by the overdone reputation of the Evans—Eliot—Lewis—Cross woman
(poor creature! one ought not to speak slightingly, I know),
half real power, half imposition. Do you know the bonfire
scenes in the *Return of the Native* and still better the sword-
exercise scene in the *Madding Crowd*, breathing epic? or the wife-
sale in the *Mayor of Casterbridge* (read by chance)? But these
writers only rise to their great strokes; they do not write continuously well: now Stevenson is master of a consummate style
and each phrase is finished as in poetry. It will not do at all,
your treatment of him.   (Today is Degree-day at the R.U.
and a holiday.)

I have some odds to say still.

I enclose, or shall send soon after, music to Sappho's ode
to Aphrodite, more curious than beautiful, but very flowing
in a strange kind.[1] It seems to be in the heptachord scale.

I also send something meant quite in earnest which I do hope
you will like—music to a song of Barnes's. If you or anyone
staying with you, as Mr. ——[2], or anyone that knows the science

[1] *Sappho's Ode to Aphrodite* (barred as for Dorian Rhythm).

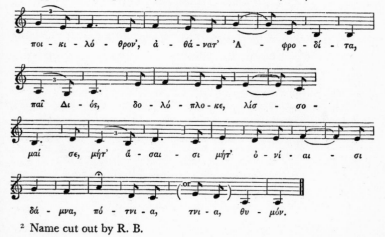

[2] Name cut out by R. B.

239

can point out any downright blunder (like consecutives) or has any contrapuntal criticisms to make on it I shall be very glad to hear and correct. It is a first draft. But I want you [to] study it, with the following points understood: (1) the parts are distinctly composed and phrased (for a first draft); it is really polyphonic, and cannot therefore be played properly on the piano: still try it there. (The middle part is in red.)

(2) The 'dry fifths' are of course intentional and necessary. For since it is the very office of the third to fix the modality (not the tonality, as they confusedly write), the omission of it may be necessary to unsettle that or to allow, as at bar 12, of another one: there the middle part softly asserts the natural minor by the, to my ear, delicious rise of a tone. (If there were four parts I cd. use the third (mi) there, but not in three.)

I am also going to send with it or soon my *Who is Sylvia?* This tune is very old, almost boyish; the setting done lately, and some faults corrected by Sir Robert Stewart (though in the end he said almost everything was wrong: perhaps he would not allow in such a composition the use of the $\frac{6}{4}$ chord, and I am ready to rewrite it and make it stricter; nevertheless you look at it and say what you think). It was to have been performed (and *Sylvia* was turned into *Erin*, for reasons) but miscarried at the last moment, the bass fighting shy of his part. These two things wd. not be at all my best, but if you shd. find anything you think well of in them it wd. be encouraging and stimulating to me. I think now it was unlucky [I] shewed ——[1] the *Battle of the Baltic*, for my purp[os]es: his criticism was just upon the piece as submitted, [bu]t the timidity in harmony would not have struck him if he had seen, I suppose, succeeding verses; but never mind that now.

I shewed my Greek verses to my colleague old Mr. Ornsby,[2] most modest and estimable of men. He praised them and wanted me to make a little volume. After some of his criticisms I altered *Tell me where* and enclose a corrected copy.

I hope I may be able some day to let you have a better water-

---

[1] Name cut out by R. B.   [2] See NOTE X.

scape from the Dargle or somewhere near Dublin. (By the bye I did soak the other in hot water, perhaps not long enough: the tenacity of the glue in milk is wonderful.)

I think I have little more to learn about the Dorian Measure now, but before writing a paper (and still more a book) on it I must have read for illustration and authority a good deal, all the poetry in it and Hephaestion and the Metricists, also the Musical writers: it is a tedious and formidable task.

Upon my word that is all, three sheets, and I am, with best love to Mrs. Bridges and Mrs. Molesworth and kind remembrances to Mrs. Waterhouse, your affectionate friend

GERARD.

I may be able to take the *Feast of Bacchus*, but not quite yet.

P.S. The ceremony is over. We gave an honorary degree to Fr. Perry S.J.[1] of Stonyhurst, the astronomer who conducts transit and eclipse expeditions to Kerguelen Island and elsewhere. We made a lady Mistress of Arts and Hearts. Ladies, girl graduates, look very nice in gowns. The Lord Lieutenant was better received than might have been expected by the (by ticket admitted) mob, considering that a harebrained pupil of mine (he got the Gulf) was there to lead the hissing.

I am going to send this tonight and pack the music tomorrow. Keep the music as long as you like, but return it. Even get opinions, competent and incompetent; if it can in any [way] be performed so that opinions can be formed.

I shall shortly be writing a review of you, and juicèd dispassionate.[2]

CXXXIX (Postcard)

University College, Stephen's Green, Dublin. Oct. 29 '86.

I send these two pieces. Of *Who is Sylvia?* observe that it is not as I wish it done, for the accompaniment to the second

---

[1] Stephen Joseph Perry, S.J. (1833–89), who observed several transits and solar eclipses, and caught dysentery while photographing the eclipsed sun of 22 December 1889, in a French convict settlement off Guiana.

[2] If this review were written, it was not published.

verse should be quite different from that to the first, but as it was necessary to simplify it for that performance which miscarried. But since the true version wd. need recopying I send this one just as it went to the nonperformers.

G. M. H.

CXL

In all things beautiful, I cannot see[1]

(first draught)

Nempe ea formosa est: adeo omne quod aut facit aut fit
   Cynthia continuo fomes amoris adest.
Stat, sedet, incedit: quantumst modo pulchra quod instat,
   Haec modo res! sequitur pulchrior illa tamen.
Nec mora nec modus est: nam quod mihi saepe negavi.
   Suavius illam unquam posse placere placet.
Quid? tacet. At taceat. Jam vera fatebor:[2] ut illud,
   Ut vincit vestros, musa, tacere choros!
Si quis in ulla volet perpellere verba silentem
   Vexet marmoreos improbus ille deos.
Hunc in Olympiaca post tot fore saecla sereno
   Intempestivum non pudet aede Jovi.

[Here follow the first three lines of the sextet, which I do not correctly remember: please send me them.]

Postremo si qua jam de re disputat, his et
   Ipsa velit Virtus dicere et ipsa Fides;
Aurea non alio sunt saecula more locuta;
   Astraeam his usam vocibus esse reor.

They are not satisfactory, I feel.

I want you to tell me about Gosse. I am concerned about him. You know of course of the attack made on him in the current *Quarterly* and I hope he will be able to make a good

---

[1] *Growth of Love*, Daniel Press Edition (1889), 32: final form, *P.W.*, vol. i. 31.   [2] MS. 'fabebor'.

defence in the main, but I have not yet seen the article myself.[1]

GERARD HOPKINS.

University College, Dublin. Oct. 31 1886.

You need not in writing join issue about Stevenson any more: instead of that you can read a book or two more of his and ripen a while.

In the above the line ' 'Tis joy the folding of her robe [?] to view' does not appear. I can expand it into a couplet, but you know I have always felt that to be the weak line in a masterpiece and have wished for something like

> 'tis joy to watch her folds fall where they do,
> and all that comes is past expectancy.[2]

And here I take the opportunity of renewing my protest against the first line of *Prometheus*. Nothing can reconcile me to 'domeless'. You yourself never offered any defence or explanation of it. It has two independent faults, either of which would condemn it: courts are uncovered spaces in their nature; all then are roofless, *a fortiori* domeless; so that the word is without point. And next domes were not used by the Greeks, the keepings of whose art and architecture you are to keep to: so then again of course the buildings of Olympus, let alone the courts, are domeless. And there remains an infelicity still. For

---

[1] A prolonged bludgeoning of Gosse's lapses from scholarship, an unsigned article by Churton Collins entitled *English Literature at the Universities* which runs to forty pages and pulverizes *From Shakespeare to Pope: An Inquiry into the Causes and Phenomena of the Rise of Classical Poetry in England*, 1885, the book form of the Clark lectures Gosse had delivered at Cambridge. Its violence produced a reaction: irony would have been a better weapon. See also *Our Literary Guides* in *Ephemera Critica, or Plain Truths about Current Literature*, by John Churton Collins, 1901.

[2] These lines have been in question before, they ran originally:

> 'Tis joy the foldings of her dress to view,
> And all she doth is past expectancy.

The final form is:

> 'Tis joy to watch the folds fall as they do,
> And all that comes is past expectancy.

when anything, as a court, is uncovered and roofless strictly speaking, a dome is just the one kind of roof it may still be said to have and especially in a clear sky and on a mountain, namely the spherical vault or dome of heaven. What *can* you say?

P.S. And I may even add that *domeless* is a heavy sink-rhythm word there. You want a lifting word—*aerial*.[1]

CXLI

University College, St. Stephen's Green, Dublin. Nov. 26 1886

DEAREST BRIDGES,—Act promptly on the following, though promptitude, I am aware, withers on Berkshire soil.

Miss Taylor of 1 Sandford Parade, Ranelagh, Dublin, last year took her degree of Bachelor of Music at the Royal University: her diploma piece, a Magnificat, was then performed and sounded learned and melodious. I was introduced to her and call on her; she lends me Blow[2] and I lend her Purcell. She is a nice unassuming girl. She is now going to take her Doctor's degree and consulted me on the subject matter of the diploma work. On consideration I saw I cd. kill two birds, a dove and an eagle, with one stone. I have advised the *Elegy on one whom grief for the loss of her beloved killed*. I added what could interest her, and she warmly welcomed the proposal. (Objections on your part, if any, are now too late and will be 'taken as read'.) I want you to send her the text; if necessary, even copied in MS: it is not too much to ask, the circumstances considered. You will appear to full orchestral accompaniment.

I have been disposing of Bridges' works as I thought best. I have a *Prometheus* and a *Nero* left and am minded to bestow them on Professor Dowden.[3]

I have improved the Latin of 'In all things beautiful'. I

---

[1] See p. 159: finally 'ætherial' was used.

[2] John Blow (1649–1708), the eminent composer of church music, overshadowed by his pupil Purcell.

[3] Edward Dowden had been Professor of English Literature in the University of Dublin (Trinity College, Dublin) since 1867.

asked you to send me three missing lines and you have not done so.

My marketing of your books brought in admiration everywhere; but publicity, fame, notoriety, and an American sale are wanted. I enclose the gentle poetess Miss Tynan's second letter.[1]

I have at last completed but not quite finished the longest sonnet ever made and no doubt the longest making.[2] It is in 8-foot lines and essays effects almost musical. Otherwise I am recovering from the effects of my Welsh holiday and returning to helplessness. Your affectionate friend

GERARD HOPKINS.

Sputters of poetry by Michael Field appear now in every week's *Academy*, vastly clever, pointed, and flowing, but serving in the end to shew Coventry Patmore was right in his opinion[3] of women's poetry.

CXLII (Postcard)

University College, Stephen's Green, Dublin. Nov. 28 '86.

Did you get from Mr. Cummings the Prospectus of the Purcell Society? And do you belong?

Books all disposed of thus: (1) Mr. Tyrrell all; (2) Miss Tynan all; (3) a young Mr. Gregg, sometime my pupil, *E. and P.*; (4) Prof. Dowden the other two.

G. M. H.

CXLIII

University College, St. Stephen's Green, Dublin. Dec. 11 1886

DEAREST BRIDGES,—Miss Taylor is full of gratitude to you for the book and of admiration at you for the poems. 'She is dread-

---

[1] A letter of 6 November 1886 from Katharine Tynan to G. M. H. thanks him for giving her three books by Mr. Bridges instead of one, and proceeds: 'I wonder how you and Mr. Yeats finished the discussion on finish or non-finish.'   [2] *Poems*, 32 (undated in A).

[3] These views can best be gathered from the essay called *Mrs. Meynell* (*Fortnightly Review*, Dec. 1892; reprinted in *Religio Poetae, etc.*, 1893; and in *Principle in Art, etc.*, 1907).

fully afraid though that she will not be able to write anything that will do the Elegy the barest justice.' Thereupon she does me the honour of asking my advice on the allotment of the numbers. Having lights I communicated them, they agreed with her own, and the work is now in hand. In the course of examining the poem for this purpose I was more than ever convinced of its extreme and classical beauty. I think however the line 'The pale indifferent ghosts wander and catch' etc[1] has a somewhat modern and vulgar *prétiosité* in the rhythm etc. It irks me to think that my own lines are faulty in this way and, if one, almost all, I am afraid. We agreed to leave out the second verse. There is no doubt that it is a splendid subject.

I mean to enclose my long sonnet, the longest, I still say, ever made;[2] longest by its own proper length, namely by the length of its lines; for anything can be made long by eking, by tacking, by trains, tails, and flounces. I shd. be glad however if you wd. explain what a *coda* is and how employed. Perhaps I shall enclose other sonnets. Of this long sonnet above all remember what applies to all my verse, that it is, as living art should be, made for performance and that its performance is not reading with the eye but loud, leisurely, poetical (not rhetorical) recitation, with long rests, long dwells on the rhyme and other marked syllables, and so on. This sonnet shd. be almost sung: it is most carefully timed in *tempo rubato*.

In sending the music to Wooldridge there was of course no harm done, but it is not worth his while (and so, with other things, I am telling him; but please card me his initials, for otherwise I cannot address the letter; or else I shall enclose it): *Who is Sylvia?* is tuneful (I hope) only, not experimental (at least as I sent it) and, what is more, not strict nor correct. The other piece is experimental, but it is slight.

My book on the Dorian Measure is going on, but may easily either wreck (by external difficulties, examinations and other ones) or founder (of its own). For in fact it needs mathe-

---

[1] The last stanza of the *Elegy* (*P.W.*, vol. ii, book i, 14).
[2] Presumably *Poems*, 32.

matics, but how can I make them up? Yet I hope, I do hope, to get out something: my purpose is, in explaining the Dorian Measure, to bring in the most fundamental principles of art, to write almost a philosophy of art and illustrate that by the Dorian Measure. If I shd. be able to publish one edition I cd. in a second edition or in a second volume add much more. I propose to print the Greek in Roman type, so that no scholarship shall be required, only study (which must be close) of the book, for it will be thoroughgoing.

Why shd. you leave Yattendon? Do not leave it. Listen to what the wise say. Σπάρτην ἔλαχες, ταύτην κόσμει.[1] And Ακεμπις says *Imaginatio locorum et mutatio fefellit multos.*

I am sorry for poor Lang, if his dejection is so deep as you describe (only that, since you speak of me, I may say that I must conceal myself or it, which it seems he does neither of). But I cannot think the political danger so great. In the meantime he writes very amusing verses in the *Saturday*, if those are his;[2] but we know people can joke in the deepest gloom. I sometimes think Lang may be the writer too of some articles dealing with Ireland. If so I wish he could find it in him to speak more gently and with more sympathy, as they call it, I mean the other-man's-point-of-viewishness. The *Saturday* does sneer, and a sneer drives the Irish to madness. (They continually do it with all their might themselves and do not even know they are doing it, do not understand what you have to complain of and so on.)

I am your affectionate friend

GERARD M. HOPKINS S.J.

Mr. Tyrrell expresses his deep admiration of your muse, his conversion, so to speak. So too young Mr. Gregg. So too Miss Tynan. But perhaps these two are 'fry'. But Mr. Dowden

---

[1] Euripides, fragment 722 (Nauck). The correct reading is κείνην for ταύτην, but the proverb is usually found with the Doric form ταύταν, which is how Cicero quotes it (*ad Att.* 4. 6. 2). The Latin translation is also often found: Spartam nactus es; hanc orna.

[2] Humorous verses, political in bent, not tasting of Lang.

I have not heard from. I told him not to acknowledge the books, but I also told him to read them and I by no means told him when he had read them not to write to you and thank you.[1]

I send tonight only one sonnet.

CXLIV

Monasterevan, Co. Kildare, Jan. 2 1887.

DEAREST BRIDGES,—It was (but first I wish you all a very happy new year) quite right to tell me what Wooldridge thought— that is what I wanted to know—and to use it as a dissuasive, if you liked; but not as a discouragement (yr. own word): discouragement is not what my complaint, in my opinion, needs. Our institute provides us means of discouragement, and on me at all events they have had all the effect that could be expected or wished and rather more. However Wooldridge and I are now in correspondence: he writes a very fine thoughtful letter. He has lately had from me a prodigious treatise of remarks and enquiries about the false fifth. Do you know what and where the false fifth is? If not, 'blush and retire'.

I am staying (till tomorrow morning, alas) with kind people at a nice place. I have had a bright light, and begun a poem in Gray's elegy metre, severe, no experiments.[2] I am pleased with it and hope you will be and also Mrs. Waterhouse, for I want

---

[1] The matter did not end here. Dowden's article, *The Poetry of Robert Bridges* (*Fortnightly Review*, July 1894), begins thus: 'Father Gerard Hopkins, an English priest of the Society of Jesus, died young, and one of his good deeds remains to the present time unrecorded. We were strangers to each other, and might have been friends. I took for granted that he belonged to the other camp in Irish politics. . . . Father Hopkins was a lover of literature, and himself a poet. Perhaps he did in many quarters missionary work on behalf of the poetry of his favourite, Robert Bridges. He certainly left, a good many years since, at my door two volumes by Mr. Bridges, and with them a note begging that I would make no acknowledgement of the gift. I did not acknowledge it then; but, with sorrow for a fine spirit lost, I acknowledge it now.'

[2] The fragment (*Poems*, 54), *On the Portrait of Two Beautiful Young People, A Brother and Sister*.

her to see it. I therefore enclose what there is of it and write no more now, but am your affectionate friend

GERARD M. HOPKINS S.J.

CXLV

University College, St. Stephen's Green, Dublin. Jan. 5 1887

DEAREST BRIDGES,—If you will more curiously consider you will see it was not exactly the word I complained of. I quoted the word.

In any case I must get to know something of counterpoint. It is the most scientific part of the science of one of the only two arts that have any science to speak of, music and architecture. And theoretically I have real lights upon it. Unhappily I can never have much literary knowledge, knowledge got from the texts of great masters.

The false fifth is not the imperfect fifth (though that is sometimes called so, but musical terminology is full of confusion): it is a fifth less than the true (which has the ratio $\frac{3}{2}$) by the interval called Didymus' comma. The difference is not so small as might be thought and has sufficed, I am inclined to believe, twice over to work a slow but complete revolution in music, first between the Periclean and the Augustan ages, next between the early Middle Ages and the Renaissance or the present time. It occurs in our diatonic scale on truly tuned instruments between Re and La, in the scale of C between D and A. Its incorrectness appears to me to make the First Mode, what Wooldridge, Rockstro[1] etc, call the Dorian, now inadmissable (if that is how the word should be spelt). I am your affectionate friend

GERARD HOPKINS.

---

[1] William Smith Rockstro (1823–95), an important influence in the musical life of his day as teacher and writer, and an instigator of the study of modal music. He wrote well-known text-books on harmony (1881) and counterpoint (1882), and was the 'first authority of his time in England' on ancient music. He became a Roman Catholic in 1876.

CXLVI

University College, St. Stephen's Green, Dublin. Feb. 17 '87

DEAREST BRIDGES,—I am joyed to see your hand again and delighted to hear your praise of the Canon's book.[1] I too have thought there is in him a vein of truly matchless beauty: it is not always the whole texture but a thread in it and sometimes the whole web is of that. But till you spoke I had almost despaired of my judgment and quite of publishing it. The pathetic imagination of *Sky that rollest ever*[2] seems to me to have nothing like it but some of Coleridge in our literature.

Mrs. Waterhouse has not written: it never indeed entered my head that she would, the piece being a fragment too. But I wanted to pay her a compliment and conceived she would like this particular poem. It is in a commoner and smoother style than I mostly write in, but that is no harm: I am sure I have gone far enough in oddities and running rhymes (as even in some late sonnets you have not seen) into the next line. I sent a later and longer version to C. D., who much admired and urged me to write lots of it. It should run to about twice the present length and when complete I daresay you will like it. I am amused and pleased at Maurice W.[3] expounding it: it is not at all what I wanted to happen, but after all if I send verse to Mrs. Waterhouse I cannot suppose no one else in the house will see it.

Tomorrow morning I shall have been three years in Ireland, three hard wearying wasting wasted years. (I met the blooming Miss Tynan again this afternoon. She told me that when she first saw me she took me for 20 and some friend of hers for 15; but it won't do: they should see my heart and vitals, all shaggy with the whitest hair.) In those I have done God's will (in the

---

[1] R. W. Dixon's *Lyrical Poems*, 1887. Dedicated to the Reverend Gerard Hopkins by the Author.

[2] The first line of the last Song in *Lyrical Poems*: reprinted in *Selected Poems*, pp. 143–4, with the title *Wayward Water*.

[3] Maurice Waterhouse. See *P.W.*, vol. ii, book v. 11.

main) and many many examination papers. I am in a position which makes it befitting and almost a duty to write anything (bearing on classical study) which I may feel that I could treat well and advance learning by: there is such a subject; I do try to write at it; but I see that I cannot get on, that I shall be even less able hereafter than now. And of course if I cannot do what even my appliances make best and easiest, far less can I anything else. Still I could throw myself cheerfully into my day's work? I cannot, I am in a prostration. Wales set me up for a while, but the effect is now past. But out of Ireland I shd. be no better, rather worse probably. I only need one thing—a working health, a working strength: with that, any employment is tolerable or pleasant, enough for human nature; without it, things are liable to go very hardly with it.

Now come on Mrs. Gaskell. What ails poor Mrs. Gaskell? One book of hers I have read through, *Wives and Daughters*: if that is not a good book I do not know what a good book is. Perhaps you are so barbarous as not to admire Thomas Hardy— as you do not Stevenson; both, I must maintain, men of pure and direct genius.

Have you followed the course of late Homeric criticism? The pendulum is swinging heavily towards the old view of a whole original Iliad. In the track of the recent dialectic investigations I have made out, I think, a small but (as a style-test) important point; but my induction is not yet complete.

I will bear in mind to send for the *Feast of Bacchus* at an early opportunity, if (but that is not certain) one should occur.

I am almost afraid I have offended, not offended but not pleased, Mr. Patmore by a late letter: I hope it is not so bad. I hope you will enjoy yourselves there: let me see, do you know Mrs. Patmore? If you do you cannot help liking her. With best love to Mrs. Bridges I am your affectionate friend

GERARD.

Yesterday Archbishop Walsh[1] had a letter in the *Freeman*

---

[1] William J. Walsh (1841–1921) had been appointed Archbishop of Dublin in 1885, despite protests by the English Government. He had been

enclosing a subscription to the defence of Dillon and the other traversers on trial for preaching the Plan of Campaign and saying that the jury was packed and a fair trial impossible. The latter was his contribution to the cause of concord and civil order. Today Archbp. Croke[1] has one proposing to pay no taxes. One archbishop backs robbery, the other rebellion; the people in good faith believe and will follow them. You will see, it is the beginning of the end: Home Rule or separation is near. Let them come: anything is better than the attempt to rule a people who own no principle of civil obedience at all, not only to the existing government but to none at all. I shd. be glad to see Ireland happy, even though it involved the fall of England, if that could come about without shame and guilt. But Ireland will not be happy: a people without a principle of allegiance cannot be; moreover this movement has throughout been promoted by crime. Something like what happened in the last century between '82 and 1800 will happen in this: now as then one class has passed off its class-interests as the interests of the nation and so got itself upheld by the support of the nation; now as then it will legislate in its own interest and the rest will languish; distress will bring on some fresh convulsion; beyond that I cannot guess.

The ship I am sailing in may perhaps go down in the approaching gale: if so I shall probably be cast up on the English coast.

After all I have written above my trouble is not the not being able to write a book; it is the not being fit for my work and the struggling vainly to make myself fitter.

Feb. 18 1887.

---

president of Maynooth College. In 1881 he supported Gladstone's Land Bill, and in 1883 had challenged public attention with 'The Queen's Colleges and the Royal University of Ireland'. He identified himself with nationalist activities.

   [1] Thomas William Croke (1824–1902), made Archbishop of Cashel in 1874; remembered for his active interest in political affairs and his strong support of the Home Rule movement.

CXLVII

University College, St. Stephen's Green, Dublin.   March 29 '87

DEAR BRIDGES,—I found your letter on coming back to town last night from Monasterevan, quite too late for return of post. However for the curiosity of the thing I answer your queries.

The irises of the present writer's eyes are small and dull, of a greenish brown; hazel I suppose; slightly darker at the outer rims.

His hair (see enclosed sample, carriage paid) is lightish brown, but not equable nor the same in all lights; being quite fair near the roots and upon the temples, elsewhere darker (the very short bits are from the temple next the ear, the longer snip from the forehead), and shewing quite fair in the sun and even a little tawny. It has a gloss. On the temples it sometimes appears to me white. I have a few white hairs, but not there.

It is a very pleasant and flattering thought that Wooldridge is painting my portrait,[1] but is it (and was yours) wholly from memory? I am of late become much wrinkled round the eyes and generally haggard-looking, and if my counterfeit present-ment is to be I shd. be glad it were of my youth.

And if Wooldridge is still with you tell him not to trouble to answer that letter at all nor to make the enquiries, which I have made elsewhere (besides which I feel pretty sure the matter never struck Rockstro nor perhaps anyone else and that I have the key to the history of modern music in what my enquiry points to, viz. that modern harmony could not arise till the old system and its tuning was got rid of and that it was goodness, not dulness, of ear which delayed its growth). Presently I hope to write to him again, not lengthily, and may enclose something.

I shd. have felt better for the delicious bog air of Monastere-van were it not that I had a sleepless night of it last night.

The young lady of my Elegy[2] was tossed in the earthquake.

---

[1] This is in the possession of Mrs. Bridges: it was done from a photograph, and was meant to be finished from life.

[2] *Poems*, 54, seems to be meant.

She and her mother ran down lightly clad and spent the next day under an umbrella (against sun, not rain). She was greatly terrified and begged and prayed her father to fetch her home, which I fancy he has not yet done.

I am yours affectionately

GERARD M. HOPKINS S.J.

If I can manage to read the Feast of Bacchus it must be in the ensuing Easter holidays. You shall hear in a day or two.

CXLVIII

University College, Stephen's Green, Dublin. Mayday 1887.

DEAREST BRIDGES,—Perhaps if you sent yr. Bacchus now I could make some suggestions. It is true I am beginning my sets of papers, but it will be not so easy later, and later still might be too late. But perhaps now is too late. The truth is I ought to have written for it before going down to Enniscorthy on Easter Monday: I had then till Saturday down in the country.

You too spoke of answering some letter of mine 'and that soon'. I do not remember what needed answering, but the words themselves are such as lead the prudent reader to prepare for the worst. He sees that you are getting leave for more delay. A promise is a kind of fulfilment; it is interest on capital; it is a light meal in the afternoon, that 'spoils dinner' and leads to that being put off two hours longer.

A beautiful Sappho has broken on Dublin, Miss Romola Tynte: she gives dramatic recitals. Oscar Wylde designed her very becoming costume and she herself, I suppose, her equally becoming name. The Muse of History in reply to correspondents calls her Mary Potter.

I have written a good deal of my book on the Dorian Measure or on Rhythm in general. Indeed it is on almost everything elementary and is much of it physics and metaphysics. It is full of new words, without which there can be no new science. Would it were done: but I hope it will have been done once for all.

With best love to Mrs. Bridges and Mrs. Molesworth AND FOR THE MATTER OF THAT (Mr. Parnell's words) Mrs. Waterhouse, I am your affectionate friend

GERARD.

Or rather to Mrs. Waterhouse kind regards.

CXLIX[1]

University College, St. Stephen's Green, Dublin.   July 30 1887

The drama ought to grow up with its audience; but now the audience is, so to say, jaded and senile and an excellence it knows of already cannot move it.   Where a real novelty is presented to it, like Gilbert's and Sullivan's operas, which are a genuine creation of a type, it responds.   However I cannot write more now and I have not the proper knowledge of the subject.

I have been reading the Choephoroi carefully and believe I have restored the text and sense almost completely in the corrupted choral odes.   Much has been done in this way by dint of successive effort; the recovery, from the 'pie' of the MSS, of for instance the last antistrophe of the last ode is a beautiful thing to see and almost certain; but both in this and the others much mere pie remains and it seems to me I have recovered nearly all.   Perhaps I might get a paper on it into the *Classical Review* or *Hermathena*:[2] otherwise they must wait to be put into a book; but when will that book or any book of mine be?

[3] he always presents his $\theta\epsilon\alpha\tau\alpha i$[4] with new types ($i\delta\epsilon\alpha s$) or ideas, $\kappa\alpha i$ $\pi\alpha\sigma\alpha s$ $\delta\epsilon\xi\iota\alpha s$, all new hits.

---

[1] R. B. evidently wished to destroy the first leaf of this letter, and of it kept only the address and date.   There is, therefore, a considerable hiatus between the date and what has perforce become the beginning.

[2] There is no contribution by G. M. H. in either review.

[3] The passage from 'he' to 'hits' was evidently meant as footnote or part of a footnote to a statement in the lost part of the letter.   Perhaps Aristophanes is in question.

[4] Written above 'hearers', cancelled.

Though I have written a good deal of my book on Metre. But it is a great pity for Aeschylus' choruses to remain misunderstood, for it is his own interpretation of the play and his own moral to the story.

What a noble genius Aeschylus had! Besides the swell and pomp of words for which he is famous there is in him a touching consideration and manly tenderness; also an earnestness of spirit and would-be piety by which the man makes himself felt through the playwright. This is not so with Sophocles, who is only the learned and sympathetic dramatist; and much less Euripides.

On Irish politics I had something to say, but there is little time. 'It only needs the will,' you say: it is an unwise word. It is true, it (that is, to govern Ireland) does 'only need the will'; but Douglas Jerrold's[1] joke is in place, about Wordsworth (or whoever it was) that could write plays as good as Shakespeare's 'if he had the mind', and 'only needed the mind'. It is a just reproach to any man not to do what lies in his own power and he could do if he would: to such a man you may well say that the task in question only needs the will. But where a decision does *not* depend on us and we cannot even influence it, then it is only wisdom to recognize the facts—the will or want of will in those, not us, who have control of the question; and that is the case now. The will of the nation is divided and distracted. Its judgment is uninformed and misinformed, divided and distracted, and its action must be corresponding to its knowledge. It has always been the fault of the mass of Englishman[2] to know and care nothing about Ireland, to let be what would there (which, as it happened, was persecution, avarice, and oppression): and now, as fast as these people wake up and hear what wrong England has done (and has long ceased doing) to Ireland, they, like that woman in Mark Twain, 'burst into tears and

---

[1] Charles Lamb to Manning, 26 Feb. 1808: 'He [Wordsworth] says he does not see much difficulty in writing like Shakspeare, if he had a mind to try it. It is clear then nothing is wanted but the mind.' (*Letters of Charles and Mary Lamb*, ed. E. V. Lucas, vol. i, p. 384.)

[2] Thus in MS.

rushing upstairs send a pink silk parasol and a box of hairpins to the seat of war'. If you in your limited but appreciable sphere of influence can bring people to a just mind and a proper resolution about Ireland (as you did, you told me, take part in your local elections) do so: you will then be contributing to that will which 'only is wanting'; but do not reproach me, who on this matter have perhaps both more knowledge and more will than most men. If however you think you could do but little and are unwilling even to do that (for I suppose while you are writing plays you cannot be canvassing electors), then recognise with me that with an unwavering will, or at least a flood of passion, on one, the Irish, side and a wavering one or indifference on the other, the English, and the Grand Old Mischief-maker loose,[1] like the Devil, for a little while and meddling and marring all the fiercer for his hurry, Home Rule is in fact likely to come and even, in spite of the crime, slander, and folly with which its advance is attended, may perhaps in itself be a measure of a sort of equity and, considering that worse might be, of a kind of prudence.

I am not a judge of the best way to publish. Though double columns are generally and with reason objected to yet I thought *Nero* looked and read well with them.[2] (I am convinced it is one of the finest plays ever written.) I have not seen Miss Taylor for long: I half fear she has given up the Elegy.

I know scarcely anything of American literature and if I knew much I could not now write about it.

I hope soon to write to Canon Dixon. Give him my best love I am happy to think of your being together.

I daresay I shall be at Haslemere within the week. Court's Hill Lodge is the name of the house and is probably now not necessary.

Monsignor Persico[3] is going about. His coming will certainly

[1] W. E. Gladstone.

[2] Between 1885 and 1894, eight plays by R. B. (issued separately but with continuous pagination) were printed, all, except *The Feast of Bacchus*, in double columns.

[3] Ignatius Persico (1823–96) was in March 1887 promoted to the titular

do good. I should like to talk to him, perhaps may. I have met him at a great dinner.

Your affectionate friend

GERARD.

Aug. 1 1887. 'Getting old'—you should never say it. But I was fortythree on the 28th of last month and already half a week has gone.

CL

Court's Hill Lodge, Haslemere. Aug. 11 1887

DEAREST BRIDGES,—If you will come here, which will be delight-ful, we cannot, I am sorry to say, give you a bed, for the house will be full, but you can lodge either at the Railway inn almost next door or[1] at Mrs. Bush's at the Gables, which is perhaps preferable, and we will find what is possible and best (for Hasle-mere is sought after and full of visitors). In the meantime I am studying your essay, truly an admirable piece of work.[2] I think however that if space allows some things should be expanded. I am making considerable notes (not of course on your paper or vellum). I have also found some oversights. The observation about l is new to me. No more now. Yours

GERARD.

CLI

Court's Hill Lodge, Haslemere. Aug. 25 1887.

DEAREST BRIDGES,—First I want to thank you, Mrs. Bridges, Mrs. Molesworth, Miss Plow, Mrs. Waterhouse, Mr. Beeching,[3]

---

archbishopric of Tamiatha and sent as Apostolic delegate to Ireland to report upon the relations of the clergy with the political movement. But before his final report had been delivered the Holy See condemned the Plan of Campaign.   [1] MS. 'at'.

[2] The MS. form of the essay, 'On the Elements of Milton's Blank Verse in *Paradise Lost*', contributed (pp. 19–37) to the edition of *Paradise Lost*, Book I, edited by the Rev. H. C. Beeching, and published by the Clarendon Press in 1887. This essay grew eventually into the well-known *Milton's Prosody*.

[3] Henry Charles Beeching was Rector of Yattendon from 1885 to 1900. He married R. B.'s niece, Mary Plow, daughter of Harriett Louisa Bridges and Anthony John Plow.

and everybody concerned for the delightful visit (would it could have been longer) I paid to Yattendon.

Then I have to say that I must have left Miss Tynan behind:[1] did I not? If so please send her to Dublin and if you found anything complimentary to remark it would be of service to me.

I must write to Mrs. Waterhouse about her little book.[2] It is charmingly written and we have all read it with great interest, but are divided as to whether it describes a fancy or a fact. I say a fact; but then ought not the place to be made known, that it may save more men?

I enclose for greater clearness on a slip what I suppose the paraphrase of 'Fallen cherub, to be weak' is.[3]

I cannot but hope that in your metrical Paper you will somewhere distinctly state the principle of Equivalence and that it was quite unrecognised in Milton's and still more in Shakespeare's time. All, but especially young students, need to [be] made clearly to understand what metrical Equivalence is, that it is in use in English now, and that it was not then—and that it was Milton's artifices, as you explain them, that helped to introduce it. Now not to say this, when the context cries for it, is . . is . . I can find nothing to call it but blasted nonsense. It is like the tedious and distracting keeping-up of mystification in a comedy; which brings me happily to the *Feast of Bacchus*.

The Menandrian period[4] appears to me the dullest and narrowest world that one could choose to lay an action in, a jaded and faded civilisation; moreover I have a craving for more brilliancy, more picturesque, more local colour: however you austerely set these things aside and I am to take the

---

[1] Probably the book of verses called *Shamrocks*, published in 1887. Her first book, *Louise de la Vallière, and other Poems*, was published in 1885.

[2] *The Brotherhood of Rest*: it described an imaginary place.

[3]   Fall'n Cherube, to be weak is miserable
       Doing or Suffering: . . .
                Paradise Lost, I, ll. 157 sqq.

[4] R. B.'s note says: 'This attempt to give Menander to the english stage is based upon his "Heautontimorumenos" as we know it through Terence.'

play for what it is. In its kind then, which has for me no attraction, and in its metre, which has to me no beauty, I think it a masterpiece. The language is a strong and chaste English; it is, I suppose, for us much what the French admire in *Télemaque* and in Racine's plays. The dialogue is everywhere nature, than which more cannot be said: I like no touch better, though there are plenty, than Menedemus's saying that Antiphila drinks and Clinia's 'Oh, father!' and what follows.[1] I daresay the metre will serve its purpose,[2] which is, I suppose, to give a slight form and pressure to the language and a corresponding degree of idealisation, and it may work well on the stage: in itself I do not admire it. The only particular fault I find is that there are many lines in which the pause in the middle, without which, as it seems to me, it is merely prose rhythm and not verse at all, is wanting. I may add that the continual determination to be smooth and lucid in style gives upon the whole a sort of childish effect. I have only read it once through and therefore add no more now. I do not however think that I shall have much more to say. I could not recommend you to write more Menandrian plays. The going to a book of astrology for gibberish, as if one sent to the Azores for hay or salt or brown paper, is a strange freak.[3]

I am going away tomorrow and expect to be in Dublin by Saturday or Sunday.

I hope Mrs. Bridges is better and, with the kindest remembrances, remain your affectionate friend

GERARD HOPKINS.

CLII

The Mourne Hotel, Rostrevor, Co. Down. On my way back
to Dublin Eve of Michaelmas '87

DEAREST BRIDGES,—I will see what I can do for you while my eggs are boiling (hard by express instructions). This, let me

---

[1] *The Feast of Bacchus*, Act v, ll. 1380 sqq.
[2] See R. B.'s Note I to this play for an account of the metre used.
[3] A reference to the pseudo-Persian spoken in the play.

tell you[,] is a beautiful spot; but to business. Where is the *Feast of Bacchus*? In my box, which will go to Dublin by goods train from Dromore, from a house once Bishop Percy's,[1] and grounds and groves by him very tastily planted then and haunted now. The book is there and I hope safe; the sense of it, with judgment thereupon, is in my head. My judgment is in substance the same as at the first reading, but my feeling is changed: I *enjoy* it more. It is 'an excellent piece of work: would 'twere done'—on the stage. In its own kind I believe it could not be bettered. I have made no notes and offer no verbal criticisms but one, that to repeat a question as Chremes somewhere does, *If I have been to town?* = *Si je suis allé à la ville?* appears to me not English: there is, unless I mistake, no such idiom.[2] The rhythm wd. I believe have an excellent effect in performance. I will not now say it has no beauty of itself: as verse it has to my ear none; but as a form, as a simple rhythm given to diction, and making such diction intermediate between verse and prose it is elegant. The value of the play is, like Terence's, as a study of human nature and in that it is firstrate; in *vis comica*, in fun, like Terence too, it is not strong: still there is enough to make me laugh aloud sometimes. This is, I believe, all I have to say and shall say on this subject and I will send the book from Dublin. Yes, I may add that, so far as I can see, nothing is gained by those amorphous lines without a middle pause (like 4+4+4): however it does not matter much (for I look on the rhythm as a rule, not as a law; as a convention, not as a nature) and I do not say they should be changed.

My broken holidays are coming to an end (now holidays and work, like sleep and waking, are dead opposite and both lose sadly by combination and enlacement) and I do not feel well: however I am in pretty good spirits. I read at Dromore another

---

[1] Thomas Percy (1729–1811) was Bishop of Dromore from 1782 till his death.

[2] *The Feast of Bacchus*, Act IV, l. 1071:
Pamphilius. Have you not found them, father? *Chremes.* If I have found them?

261

excellent romance, *Christie Johnstone* by Charles Reade: it chanced to be in the room. It seems to have been written in 1850;[1] contains some nonsense but more sense; enough wit, too much rollick; a somewhat slipshod brilliancy; an overboisterous manliness; but a true mastery of the proper gifts of a romancer and especially of the natural-unforseen, which there should be in all good romance. The abundance of genius in English romance in this age appears to me comparable with its abundance in drama in the Elizabethan: but here I am afraid I speak to deaf ears. It would be worth while reading all that Charles Reade has written. Was he a Scotchman?[2] this story is Scotch.

With other things I have not got on, but I have been touching up some old sonnets you have never seen and have within a few days done the whole of one, I hope, very good one and most of another; the one finished is a direct picture of a ploughman, without afterthought.[3] But when you read it let me know if there is anything like it in Walt Whitman, as perhaps there may be, and I should be sorry for that. I am your affectionate friend

GERARD.

The eyes are almost out of my head. Also I am at a fugue, of which I have great hopes—vocal of course.

CLIII

University College, St. Stephen's Green, Dublin. Oct. 11 1887

DEAR BRIDGES,—I will now return you *Bacchus*, with only one more remark, that so famous a text as *Homo sum* deserves a more studied rendering. I am not at all contented with yours. It seems to me it should be something like: I am a man, and one that thinks he has everything to do with what has anything to do with man. I mean, it seems to me that *having to do with is* what has to be expressed. Otherwise there is the proverb *What*

---

[1] Published in 1853.   [2] Born in Oxfordshire and educated at Oxford.
[3] *Harry Ploughman, Poems*, 43. In the facsimile (from A: see the note in *Poems*) the small hand is R. B.'s.

is everybody's business is nobody's business (the contrary of which Chremes holds) and it might be utilised.

I will enclose the sonnet on Harry Ploughman, in which burden-lines (they might be recited by a chorus) are freely used: there is in this very heavily loaded sprung rhythm a call for their employment. The rhythm of this sonnet, which is altogether for recital, not for perusal (as by nature verse should be) is very highly studied. From much considering it I can no longer gather any impression of it: perhaps it will strike you as intolerably violent and artificial.

I am your affectionate friend

GERARD HOPKINS.

CLIV

University College, St. Stephen's Green, Dublin.   Nov. 2 1887

MY DEAR BRIDGES,—You owe me a letter, but as I might wait longer and still want I write myself and ask you two things. I enclose a song turned up from a drawer to-day (if I ever gave you a copy before send this one back), which try, and try if you can like it, as I do greatly; but I am biassed: if you approve of it I shall be gladder than if it were mine.

Next please tell me how correctly to make codas to sonnets; with the most approved order of rhymes and so on. And do not say that I know and that I can find for myself and that there is one in Milton (that one is not enough), but do what I ask you. And soon: a sonnet is hot on the anvil and wants the coda.[1] It is the only time I have felt forced to exceed the beaten bounds. I hope Mrs. Bridges is well and that nothing in the way of ill health has kept you from writing. I do not know whether I told you at the time, but, for fear it should never have been said, I may write now that when I was last at Yattendon I had the impression I had never in my life met a sweeter lady than

---

[1] *Tom's Garland, Poems,* 42, has two codas, but the copy in A is dated 'Dromore, Sept. '87'. Yet this sonnet seems more likely to be in question than *Poems,* 48.

Mrs. Bridges. You may wear a diamond on your finger and yet never have seen it in a side light, so I tell you.

I hope soon to enter a batch of sonnets in my book and when I do that I can send you copies. They are the thin gleanings of a long weary while, but singly good.

I am your affectionate friend

GERARD M. HOPKINS.

CLV

University College, St. Stephen's Green, Dublin. Nov. 6 1887

DEAREST BRIDGES,—I must write at once, to save you the trouble of copying that music: I reproduced it by a jelly-process at Stonyhurst on purpose and only wanted the copy back in case you had one already. I do not remember anything about the harmony: it is the tune I think so good, and this I revived my memory of before I sent it you. I cannot at all make out the meaning of 'If your sister has learnt harmony I can't understand what the moderns mean'. Grace did learn harmony, but girls are apt not to study things thoroughly and perhaps she has not kept it up as she should. I remember years ago that the organist at Liverpool found fault with a hymn of hers, in four parts, very regular, for hidden fifths in the inner parts. But he was an ignoramus: I did not know then but I know now that hidden fifths must be and are freely used in the inner parts and are only faintly kept out of the outer ones. And see what became of him: he got drunk at the organ (I have now twice had this experience: it is distressing, alarming, agitating, but above all delicately comic; it brings together the bestial and the angelic elements in such a quaint entanglement as nothing else can; for musicians never play such clever descants as under those circumstances and in an instant everybody is thrilled with the insight of the situation) and was dismissed. He was a clever young fellow and thoroughly understood the properties of narrow-necked tubes.

I am thankful to you for the account of the Coda, over which you gave yourself even unnecessary trouble. You say the subject is treated in many books. That was just it. I had not got those books and the readiest source of information was you. It seems they are formed on an invariable plan and that Milton's sonnet gives an example. Of course one example was enough if there is but one type; but you should have said so.

I want Harry Ploughman to be a vivid figure before the mind's eye; if he is not that the sonnet fails. The difficulties are of syntax no doubt. Dividing a compound word by a clause sandwiched into it was a desperate deed, I feel, and I do not feel that it was an unquestionable success. But which is the line you do not understand? I do myself think, I may say, that it would be an immense advance in notation (so to call it) in writing as the record of speech, to distinguish the subject, verb, object, and in general to express the construction to the eye; as is done already partly in punctuation by everybody, partly in capitals by the Germans, more fully in accentuation by the Hebrews. And I daresay it will come. But it would, I think, not do for me: it seems a confession of unintelligibility. And yet I don't know. At all events there is a difference. My meaning surely *ought* to appear of itself; but in a language like English, and in an age of it like the present, written words are really matter open and indifferent to the receiving of different and alternative verse-forms, some of which the reader cannot possibly be sure are meant unless they are marked for him. Besides metrical marks are for the performer and such marks are proper in every art. Though indeed one might say syntactical marks are for the performer too. But however that reminds me that one thing I am now resolved on, it is to prefix short prose *arguments* to some of my pieces. These too will expose me to carping, but I do not mind. Epic and drama and ballad and many, most, things should be at once intelligible; but everything need not and cannot be. Plainly if it is possible to express a sub[t]le and recondite thought on a subtle and recondite subject in a subtle and recondite way and with great felicity and perfection, in the end, something must be sacrificed, with so trying a task, in the process, and this may be the being at once, nay perhaps even the being without explanation at all, intelligible. Neither, in the same light, does it seem to be to me a real objection (though this one I hope not to lay myself open to) that the argument should be even longer than the piece; for the merit of the work may lie for one thing in its terseness. It is like a mate which may be given, one way only, in three moves; otherwise, various ways, in many.

There is some kind of instinct in these things. I wanted the coda for a sonnet which is in some sort 'nello stilo satirico o bernesco'. It has a kind of rollic at all events. The coda is an immense resource to have. This sonnet, I hope, very shortly.

In glancing over the Paper[1] I am much pleased with the additions and final treatment. (I remark various faults of punctuation.) I shall nudge the professors of English about this book and paper. Just now something catches my eye, p. viii.— 'a pronunciation *eale*'.[2] Better write *eel*: that is a word. Now *eale* is not strictly 'a pronunciation' but is the actual printed word of the passage in Shakspere about the 'dram of eale', to which if you use this form you should certainly refer. Otherwise why that fantastic spelling? I am afraid it is however too late.

Mr. Tyrrell (a devout convert) sets you to Trinity men to turn 'into the original Greek'.* More, more by token! The wreck of me that remains to study anything is studying Aeschylus, chiefly the lyrics, for a book (or set of Papers in the *Classical Review* perhaps) thereon. He has made a number of happy conjectures, though I say it that know him too well, and yesterday a very happy one, *Seven against Thebes* 424–434, which redispose thus:[3] ET. θεοὺς ἀτίζων . . Ζηνὶ κυμαίνοντ᾽ ἔπη (428– 430.). |Ζεὺς δ᾽ οὐκ ἀπειλεῖ (for Καπανεὺς δ᾽ ἀπειλεῖ), δρᾶν παρεσκευασμένος (427.). |καὶ τῷδε κέρδει (viz. the having heaven on our side) κέρδος ἄλλο τίκτεται (viz. that his boastful words will prove to the

     * I do not mean literally that he says that.

[1] On Milton's prosody.   [2] Not in the first printed version.

[3] This conjecture is, I am told, brilliant but unnecessary, since the text as it stands is 'clear, logical, and Aeschylean'. But perhaps opinions may differ. The usual numbering of the lines discussed by G. M. H. is 437–47.

enemy an omen of his defeat). | $\tau\hat{\omega}\nu$ $\tau o\iota$ $\mu a\tau a\acute{\iota}\omega\nu$ . . $\kappa a\tau\acute{\eta}\gamma o\rho o\varsigma$ (424–426.) | $\dot{a}\nu\grave{\eta}\rho$ δ' $\dot{\epsilon}\pi$' $a\dot{v}\tau\hat{\omega}$ (contrasted with $Z\epsilon\acute{v}\varsigma$ above), $\kappa\epsilon\grave{\iota}$ $\sigma\tau\acute{o}\mu a\rho\gamma\acute{o}\varsigma$ $\dot{\epsilon}\sigma\tau$' $\ddot{a}\gamma a\nu$ etc (434 sqq.). The source of all the confusion was reading ZEYC | NEYC, and then supplying KAΠA and of course striking out $o\dot{v}\kappa$. But see how Aeschylus has borrowed your 'And him Zeus stayed not to deride'. Misplacing of lines in Aeschylus is almost certain.

Your affectionate friend

GERARD M. HOPKINS S.J.

No, I do not ask 'enthusiastic praise'. But is it not the case that the day when you could give enthusiastic praise to anything is passing or past? As for modern novels I will only say one thing now. It is in modern novels that wordpainting most abounds and now the fashion is to be so very subtle and advanced as to despise wordpainting and to say that old masters were not wordpainters. Just so. Wordpainting is, in the verbal arts, the great success of our day. Every age in art has its secret and its success, where even second rate men are masters. Second rate, third rate men are fine designers in Japan; second rate men were masters of painting in Raphael's time; second rate men were masters of sculpture in Phidias' time; second rate men of oratory in Cicero's; and so of many things. These successes are due to steady practice, to the continued action of a school: one man cannot compass them. And wordpainting is in our age a real mastery and the second rate men of this age often beat at it the first rate of past ages. And this I shall not be bullied out of.

For my case I shd. also remark that we turned up a difference of taste and judgment, if you remember, about Dryden.[1] I can scarcely think of you not admiring Dryden without, I may say, exasperation. And my style tends always more towards Dryden. What is there in Dryden? Much, but above all this: he is the most masculine of our poets; his style and his rhythms lay the strongest stress of all our literature on the naked thew and

[1] For R. B.'s views on Dryden see his *Collected Essays*, V, p. 123, note, and X, especially pp. 274 and 279.

sinew of the English language, the praise that with certain qualifications one would give in Greek to Demosthenes, to be the greatest master of bare Greek. I am driven to the blackguard device of a palimpsest envelope.

CLVI

University College, St. Stephen's Green, Dublin. Dec. 21 1887

DEAREST BRIDGES,—I am (humbly I mean was) truly delighted to hear of your daughter's birth, though I have left the news so long unacknowledged, and hope the little nymph and her mother are doing better and better. I mean to be of no length now;

.   .   .   .

.   .   .   .[1]

Touching Aeschylus, if you wish to translate *Prometheus* do so and the choruses with the rest: I cannot undertake them. It would not be much to my purpose: I do not care for a verse translation, but textual criticism, interpretation, and a prose paraphrase.

At Christmas if you write address Miss Cassidy, Monasterevan, Co. Kildare.

Please give my very best wishes to Mrs. Bridges and believe me your affectionate friend

GERARD HOPKINS.

What is she called?[2]

CLVII

University College, St. Stephen's Green, Dublin. Jan. 12 1888

MY DEAR BRIDGES,—I am glad that you will be back at pastoral Yattendon, but do not understand why you should be unhappy in London. Unless indeed one thing explains it, the new enemies you have made (for so of course you meant to write; but what you have written is 'new ones', that is 'friends', which

---

[1] Here a passage, which in print fills 17 lines, is omitted. It deals with a family matter in a heavily facetious tone, and concludes, A TRUCE TO THIS BUFFOONERY. Though relatively unimportant, it should be restored later.

[2] Elizabeth.

word occurs just before). I am sorry, I must say, for the tussle with Patmore.[1] The cynical remark about forgetting that people believed in their own theories does not please me. As far as I am concerned in that matter, the additions that I wanted you to make to the essay were for the essay's sake, to make it historically and logically complete; and the reader's, to put him in possession of all the necessary facts or principles—not to leave him in the dark, in that 'superior' style; mystify him—a thing I cannot abide. However the essay is, I believe, pretty nearly complete within its limits and is first rate work. I do not, so far as I remember, really think that Coventry Patmore's doctrines needed mentioning at any rate there:[2] they are mostly of wider scope and would be introduced best into a paper on English versification as a whole or on versification simply.

Yes, I shall be very glad of some copies of it. I lent my one to a young man who teaches English for the Royal University curriculum and in Mr. Tom Arnold's absence takes his class: now he can keep it. He said he wanted it in order 'to come at Saintsbury'; I warrant it is not for rhyme or rhythm he wants to come at Saintsbury, though he may stalk him behind them: no, Saintsbury writes in the *Saturday* the great enemy and writes antiIrish verse and jokes in it too. Hinc illae lacrimae. Never make an enemy, except for duty's sake; try not, even then.

My remark about my brother Everard[3] and English art was

---

[1] Mrs. Bridges finds no records of this, though she has searched some contemporary letters.

[2] Coventry Patmore's *Essay on English Metrical Law* was first printed in the *North British Review* of Aug. 1857 as *English Metrical Critics*. There is no mention of his doctrine in the first printed form of R. B.'s essay.

[3] Everard Hopkins (1860–1928) was educated at Charterhouse, and the Slade School of Art, Gower Street, where he worked under Legros, and held the Slade Scholarship for the whole three years of his studentship. Afterwards he worked regularly in black-and-white for many papers, including the *Woman's World* (under the editorship of Oscar Wilde), the *Illustrated London News*, *Atalanta*, and *Life*. He did the chief cartoon for the short-lived *John Bull*, and for many years was a regular contributor to *Punch*, for which paper, *c.* 1904, he did the third political cartoon which was started as a new feature. Apart from this work, he did a great deal in water-colour and pastel, and exhibited regularly in London.

not to be taken with such great seriousness. It is true people who constantly illustrate the Paper, like Tenniel and the rest in *Punch*, having a vogue and being seen by millions, must exercise an influence for good or bad; but my brother has no such position. However painting, drawing, pictorial art of some sort is his profession, and as you know him I thought you were aware of that.

At Monasterevan I tried to get some outstanding and accumulated sonnets ready for hanging on the line, that is in my book of MS, the one you wrote most of, and so for sending to you. All however are not ready yet, but they will soon be. I could send one tonight if time served, but if possible I should like to despatch this letter. It is now years that I have had no inspiration of longer jet than makes a sonnet, except only in that fortnight in Wales: it is what, far more than direct want of time, I find most against poetry and production in the life I lead. Unhappily I cannot produce anything at all, not only the luxuries like poetry, but the duties almost of my position, its natural outcome—like scientific works. I am now writing a quasi-philosophical paper on the Greek Negatives: but when shall I finish it? or if finished will it pass the censors? or if it does will the *Classical Review* or any magazine take it? All impulse fails me: I can give myself no sufficient reason for going on. Nothing comes: I am a eunuch—but it is for the kingdom of heaven's sake.

Did you see Wooldridge in town? No doubt. And how is he getting on? painting, music, and all. I am sure he is right in the advice he gave me, to be very contrapuntal, to learn that well. I want to do so if I can; it is the only way. I have fooled at it too much. I have found a thing that, if I had my counterpoint well at my fingers' ends, wd. be most valuable: it is that the tunes I make are very apt to fall into fugues and canons, the second strain being easy counterpoint to the first or to its fugal answer. E.g. my Crocus, which you once expressed an admiration for, makes a canon with itself at the octave two bars off and, as far as I have found, at one bar off too. This is a splendid opening for choral treatment. And I have a fine fugue on hand to 'Orpheus with his lute'; but I shall not hurry with it, but keep the counterpoint correct. There seems to be, I may remark, no book that bridges the gap between double counterpoint and fugue. For instance, I have Ouseley on both and Higgs on Fugue and neither breathes a word on so simple a point as this, that the answer in Bach and Handel enters, that is that the counterpoint begins, freely on an unprepared discord. But this is contrary to the elements of counterpoint proper. What I ought to do, or somebody else rather to have done, is to tabulate Bach's practice and principles.

We are suffering from the region-fog, as it seems to be. I have been a little ill and am still a little pulled down; however I am in good spirits. Term has begun.

There was more to say, I forget what. It seems this will not go tonight. Did you go to see Jem Smith[1] and his mates?

There, I have copied one—*Tom's Garland*. It has many resemblances to *Harry Ploughman*, a fault in me the sonneteer, but not a fault that can be traced home to either of the sonnets. They were conceived at the same time: that is how it is. But I have too much tendency to do it, I find. 'There is authority for it'—not the lady of the strachey,[2] but Aeschylus: he is always forgetting he said a thing before. Indeed he never did, but tried to say it two or three times—something rich and profound but not by him distinctly apprehended; so he goes at it again and again like a canary trying to learn the Bluebells of Scotland. To bed, to bed: my eyes are almost bleeding.

With best wishes to Mrs. Bridges, I am your affectionate friend

GERARD M. HOPKINS.

By saying you are going to register your little daughter as an Elizabeth I take you to signify that you reserve her for Mr. Beeching to christen at Yattendon.[3]

---

[1] Presumably the well-known pugilist.

[2] Malvolio soliloquizing: 'There is example for't: the lady of the Strachy married the yeoman of the wardrobe.' *Twelfth Night*, Act II, sc. 5.

[3] She was christened at Yattendon on 29 Jan. 1888 by the rector, the Rev. H. C. Beeching, and Dr. Sanday was her godfather by proxy.

Jan. 13 1888. What, by the bye, is that new departure in yr. poetry which 'it was high time' you made?—Talking of this, Hall Caine, that poor Deiphobus of yours, said in some review lately that whether a good book shall be a hit and live, or no, appears to him, from literary history, to be as purely a matter of chance as anything he knows of. And if, as I suppose, he is speaking with consideration, what he says sounds to me sense and I daresay he is right.

CLVIII (Postcard)

Jan. 18 1888. Univ. Coll., Stephen's Green, Dublin.

My young friend wants to know if Mr. Beeching's book, *Paradise Lost* Bk. the First, in the Clarendon Press, is out yet.

I have the first vol. of your Malory: I think I had better send it back, as I seldom read it. Indeed if I often read it I shd. have done it by this time and have sent it back.

G. M. H.

CLIX

University College, St. Stephen's Green, Dublin.   Feb. 10 1888

DEAREST BRIDGES,—Know that the copy of your Paper[1] never came, so that I have none at all, and you said I might have several: I am content with one and please send one; if two, I can do better still.

I laughed outright and often, but very sardonically, to think you and the Canon could not construe my last sonnet; that he had to write to you for a crib. It is plain I must go no farther on this road: if you and he cannot understand me who will? Yet, declaimed, the strange constructions would be dramatic and effective. Must I interpret it? It means then that, as St. Paul and Plato and Hobbes and everybody says, the common-wealth or well ordered human society is like one man; a body with many members and each its function; some higher, some lower, but all honourable, from the honour which belongs to

[1] On Milton's prosody.

272

the whole. The head is the sovereign, who has no superior but God and from heaven receives his or her authority: we must then imagine this head as bare (see St. Paul much on this) and covered, so to say, only with the sun and stars, of which the crown is a symbol, which is an ornament but not a covering; it has an enormous hat or skull cap, the vault of heaven. The foot is the daylabourer, and this is armed with hobnail boots, because it has to wear and be worn by the ground; which again is symbolical; for it is navvies or daylabourers who, on the great scale or in gangs and millions, mainly trench, tunnel, blast, and in others ways disfigure, 'mammock' the earth and, on a small scale, singly, and superficially stamp it with their footprints. And the 'garlands' of nails they wear are therefore the visible badge of the place they fill, the lowest in the common-wealth. But this place still shares the common honour, and if it wants one advantage, glory or public fame, makes up for it by another, ease of mind, absence of care; and these things are symbolized by the gold and the iron garlands. (O, once explained, how clear it all is!) Therefore the scene of the poem is laid at evening, when they are giving over work and one after another pile their picks, with which they earn their living, and swing off home, knocking sparks out of mother earth not now by labour and of choice but by the mere footing, being strongshod and making no hardship of hardness, taking all easy. And so to supper and bed. Here comes a violent but effective hyperbaton or suspension, in which the action of the mind mimics that of the labourer—surveys his lot, low but free from care; then by a sudden strong act throws it over the shoulder or tosses it away as a light matter. The witnessing of which lightheartedness makes me indignant with the fools of Radical Levellers. But presently I remember that this is all very well for those who are in, however low in, the Common-wealth and share in any way the Common weal; but that the curse of our times is that many do not share it, that they are outcasts from it and have neither security nor splendour; that they share care with the high and obscurity with the low, but wealth or comfort with neither. And this state of things, I say, is the origin of Loafers, Tramps, Cornerboys, Roughs, Socialists and other pests of society. And I think that it is a very pregnant sonnet and in point of execution very highly wrought. Too much so, I am afraid.

I have more, not so hard and done before, but I am not prepared . . .[1]

On referring to yr. letter I see you speak of modern music, not music of this century. It is, I suppose, as you say. I hope your rheumatism is abated, is gone: why not gone? But I have a poor, very charming friend on his back with spinal disease: when he complains of rheumatic pains his doctor rubs his hands with joy and says nothing cd. be better.

CLX (Postcard)

EVEN NOW I'VE NOT GOT THAT PAPER WHEN ARE

[Postmark, Dublin 7 March 1888.]

CLXI

University College, St. Stephen's Green, Dublin. May 25 1888

BRIDGES, have at you. Not a low, not a crow, not a bark, not a bray from either of us has crossed the Channel this long while. I am presently going gently to crow, but first I want you to send *Nero* (and anything else you like, but I recommend that) to Judge O'Hagan,[2] Glenaveena, Howth, Co. Dublin, and, if you can spare one, a copy of the paper on Milton's verse; else I shall have to give him one of mine and, what is worse, to get leave to do so. He is an interesting and able man, but old fashioned in notions of poetry, especially rhythm; he thought, without a suspicion, that Shakespeare's verse was often very

[1] The end of the letter is missing: what follows is a postscript written at the head of the first leaf.
[2] At whose country house G. M. H. occasionally stayed for a few days.

274

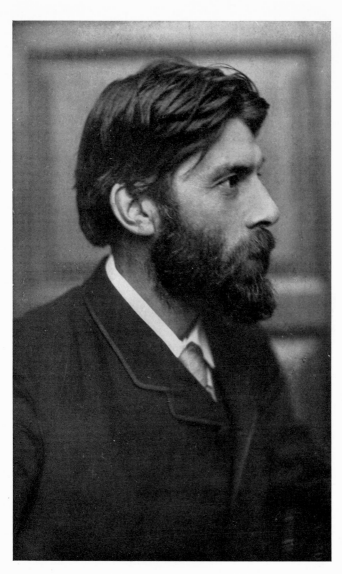

Robert Bridges
1888

rough, had never heard of the doctrine of equivalence, and so on. (And there it is, I understand these things so much better than you: we should explain things, plainly state them, clear them up, explain them; explanation—except personal—is always pure good; without explanation people go on misunderstanding; being once explained they thenceforward understand things; therefore always explain: but I have the passion for explanation and you have not.)

Whenever I read the abovementioned *Nero* I am more struck by its mastery and perfect nature (for instance Burrus's saying 'Well, well' to Seneca's pretended ignorance of his drift is a trifling but admirable touch); but in my opinion, though not archaic compared with Swinburne, Morris, and so on, it is sicklied o'er a little with an Elizabethan diction, and this is its defect.

Canon Dixon says your *Achilles*[1] is very beautiful. He also says you 'hate' his *Eudocia*.[2] I have not seen it yet, but I have the *Saturday's* disagreeable review.[3] If anything made me think the age Alexandrine (as they say), an age of decadence (a criticism that they sling about between the bursting Yes and blustering No, for want of more things to say, as also that the Academy is or is not 'above the average'—for what does it matter?— but it reminds me of my aunt's question when she went shopping with her mother as a child, 'Is goose a poultry?'—not an unreasonable question in itself and even philosophical, for strictly speaking everything either is or is not poultry, but for the purposes of criticism not enough) well, it would be to see how secondrate poetry (and what I mean is, not poetry at all) gets itself put about for great poetry, and that too when there are plenty of real, however faulty, poets living. I am thinking of people like Alfred Austin and Edwin Arnold and Austin Dobson and Lewis Morris, who have merits of course I know,

---

[1] *Achilles in Scyros*, A Drama in a Mixed Manner; published by Bumpus in 1890.

[2] *The Story of Eudocia and her Brothers*; published by H. Daniel in 1888.

[3] In the issue of 12 May 1888. See NOTE Y.

but . . . you can finish up and I know you will think harder than anything I am likely to write. I must copy it for you, more by token: Mr. Skeat has written, out of pure gall (*facit indignatio versum*), a downright good villanelle in mockery of villanelle-writing.[1] If I were Russian censor of the press it would be my joy to force rondeliers to print this piece on the titlepage of each new volume of roundels. There is one of that crew[2] has written (did I tell you before?) the very worst line I ever remember to have read in English. It is from a villanelle in

---

[1] This villanelle accompanies the letter, and is here printed from G. M. H.'s copy, with his comment below:

Villanelle.

How to compose a *villanelle*, which is said to require 'an elaborate amount of care in production, which those who read only would hardly suspect existed'.

> It's all a trick, quite easy when you know it,
> As easy as reciting ABC;
> You need not be an atom of a poet.
>
> If you've a grain of wit, and want to show it,
> Writing a *villanelle*—take this from me—
> It's all a trick, quite easy when you know it.
>
> You start a pair of rimes, and then you 'go it'
> With rapid-running pen and fancy free;
> You need not be an atom of a poet.

                                           [turn over

> Take any thought, write round it or below it,
> Above or near it, as it liketh thee;
> It's all a trick, quite easy when you know it.
>
> Pursue your task, till, like a shrub, you grow it,
> Up to the standard size it ought to be;
> You need not be an atom of a poet.
>
> Clear it of weeds, and water it, and hoe it,
> Then watch it blossom with triumphant glee.
> It's all a trick, quite easy when you know it;
> You need not be an atom of a poet.

                            Walter W. Skeat
                          (*Academy* 19 May 1888)

This has the inspiration of annoyance, a very much more vital and spontaneous thing than the pieces it satirises have.

[2] W. E. Henley, in *Ballades and Rondeaus, etc.* (ed. J. Gleeson White, 'Canterbury Poets', 1887), p. 252.

praise of the villanelle and says it, the kickshaw in question, cannot reach the roll and swell

> *Of organs grandiose and sublime*
> (A dainty thing's the Villanelle).

An effeminate thing: I wish we were rid of them.

I wrote a paper of Readings and Renderings of Sophocles this year and sent it to the *Classical Review*. The passages commented on were strung together so as to illustrate a principle of lyrical construction: it was a critical essay. After a while the editor wrote to say they had little room for original essays, but that if I liked that two of the passages, which he named, shd. appear in the form of Notes, such as scholars send to every number, they could. To this I agreed, but that was some time ago and I see no sign of their appearing; so I am afraid the whole will come to nought.[1] However, to me, to finish a thing and that it shd. be out of hand and owe its failure to somebody else is nearly the same thing as success.

For instance I began an Epithalamion on my brother's wedding: it had some bright lines, but I could not get it done.[2] That is worse. (This wedding was last month. The honeymoon was in Paris; they wrote thence in ecstacy; but had not been home long when the bride's mother died. But perhaps an affliction endears husband and wife.)

But I have had one hit. Of this I meekly bray and mildly crow. In counterpoint. I wrote a complicated canon: it was the air to Coventry Patmore's 'The crocus while the days are dark' and I made it serve as counterpoint exercise (they say canon is the best), keeping all rules as strictly as such a composition allows. At last I sent it, the first verse rather of three, which are to make a madrigal, to Sir Robert Stewart; who gave it a very good mark (and he does not flatter), suggesting amendments however, which I have since made. It was laborious, but I now can do canon easily and hope to have the two

---

[1] These notes were not printed in the *Classical Review*.
[2] The long fragment *Epithalamion, Poems*, 72.

other verses ready soon. Success in canon beats the other successes of art: it comes like a miracle, even to the inventor. It does seem as if the canon discovered the musician and not he it. But the truth is that in a really organic tune the second or third strain or both tend to be good counterpoint (with or even without bass) to the first. And then fugue is really canon at the fifth (or twelfth). So that I see a world of canon and fugue before me. I do not say I am going there. But one madrigal in canon I will finish and then I hope one in fugue. No accompaniments; and the human voice is immortal. You said nothing would come: I hope you may have been wrong.

With kind remembrance to Mrs. Bridges, Mrs. Molesworth, and Mrs. Waterhouse, I am your affectionate friend

GERARD M. HOPKINS. May 26 1888.

I do not like the sour unspiritual tone of this letter; but if I were not like that I should not have written it and there it is, now.

CLXII

Monzie Villa, Fort William, North Britain. Aug. 18 1888

DEAREST BRIDGES,—I am much in your debt for a letter, but at this time of the year you must not be surprised at that. Six weeks of examination are lately over and I am now bringing a fortnight's holiday to an end. I have leave to prolong it, but it is not very convenient to do so and I scarcely care. It appears I want not scenery but friends. My companion[1] is not quite himself or he verges towards his duller self and so no doubt do I too, and we have met few people to be pleasant with. We are in Lochaber (and are happily pestered with no sentiment) and have been to the top of Ben Nevis and up Glencoe on the most brilliant days, but in spite of the exertions or because of them I cannot sleep (which is the very mischief) and we have got no bathing (it is close at hand but close also to the highroad) nor boating and I am feeling very old and looking very wrinkled

[1] The Rev. Robert Curtis, S.J., whose appointment—to the chair of Natural Science—was made on the same day as that of G. M. H.

and altogether. . . . Besides we have no books except the farce of the fellow reading Minchin's *Kinematics*:[1] he is doing so now and dozing and shd. be in bed; this book I leave to him entirely, you may suppose, and have bought Dana's *Two Years Before the Mast*,[2] a thoroughly good one and all true, but bristling with technicality—seamanship—which I most carefully go over and even enjoy but cannot understand: there are other things though, as a flogging, which is terrible and instructive *and it happened*—ah, that is the charm and the main point. With the other half of the same shilling I bought *The Old Curiosity Shop*; never read it before, am not going to give in to any nonsense about Little Nell (like, I believe, Lang I cannot stand Dickens's pathos; or rather I can stand it, keep a thoroughly dry eye and unwavering waistcoat), but admire Dick Swiveller and Kit and Quilp and that old couple with the pony.

But business first. Your last little letter to me I never read. I never got it. I think perhaps Mrs. Bambury did and hope there was nothing in it which shd. call a blush onto her cheek as, I will say, there was nothing in Mrs. Bridges's beautifully written note of acceptance to Mrs. Bambury to cause a pang to me except of course that it was not what the envelope purported. This note I enclose.

I greatly admired the hand in which you wrote from Seaford and hope you will continue to employ it.

I will now go to bed, the more so as I am going to preach tomorrow and put plainly to a Highland congregation of Mac-Donalds, MacIntoshes, MacKillops, and the rest what I am putting not at all so plainly to the rest of the world, or rather to you and Canon Dixon, in a sonnet in sprung rhythm with two codas.[3]

Aug. 19. That is done.—I am unfortunate in the time of my letters reaching you. The last contained mockery at the

---

[1] *Uniplanar Kinematics of Solids and Fluids*, by George Minchin Minchin, 1882.   [2] Published in 1840.

[3] *That Nature is a Heraclitean Fire and of the comfort of the Resurrection*, *Poems*, 48.

Rondeliers, of whom Lang is ringleader, is he not? and you read it seated next him on your trap in the extreme confidence of a country drive; so that, too probably, you let him know what what I said and he will never forgive me. You should be very discreet about such matters.

Canon Dixon sent me his *Eudocia*. I admired it, but found it not particularly interesting as a story. It was all over genius not remarkably well employed. I did not agree with some metrical peculiarities.

I think you were not quite correct in your paraphrase of the passage in Galatians. I will say what I think it means, but perhaps not in this letter.

I was asked to my friends at Howth to meet Aubrey de Vere.[1] However he was called away to London and when I came was gone. I was disappointed, till it was mentioned that he did not think Dryden a poet. Then, I thought and perhaps said, I have not missed much. And yet you share this opinion or something like it with him. Such are the loutish falls and hideous vagaries of the human mind.

Of Handel, by the bye. If it was only recitative of his you did not like and 'wavered in your allegiance' never mind. The recitative which arose in the Renaissance at Florence, artificially and by a sort of pedantry, was to begin with bad, and Handel's employment of it always appeared to me to be his poorest part: the thing is so spiritless and mean, with vulgar falls and floundering to and from the dominant and leading note. The only good and truly beautiful recitative is that of plain chant; which indeed culminates in that. It is a natural development of the speaking, reading, or declaiming voice, and has the richness of nature; the other is a confinement of the voice to certain prominent intervals and has the poverty of an artifice.

---

[1] Aubrey Thomas de Vere, poet and critic (1814–1902). The *Memoir* of him by Wilfrid Ward gives an excellent idea of his charm and of the friendships and interests of his long life. He was a convert to the Roman Catholic Church (received on 15 November 1851), and on Newman's invitation became first Professor of English Literature in the Catholic University of Ireland.

But Handel is Handel. I was at the Glasgow Exhibition[1] (a very fine one) and heard a piece of an organ-recital ending with a chorus by Handel: it was as if a mighty besom swept away so much dust and chaff. But when you speak of sighing for *Bellini* and Palestrina, who is that Bellini? I only know of the modern Bellini.[2]

I agree about cricket and Darwinism and that 'everything is Darwinism'. But especially a ship. However the honey-comb is not quite so plain a matter as you think. The learned, I believe, are divided on the question whether the shape of the cell is really to be called a matter of mechanics. For observe: the cell can only be symmetrical, with a true hexagonal section and so on, by the bees being stationed at equal distances, working equally, and so on; in fact there is a considerable table of *caetera paria*. But this implies something more than mechanical to begin with. Otherwise the hexagonal etc cell wd. be the type *tended to* only and seldom or never arrived at; the comb wd. be like the irregular figures of bubbles in the froth of beer or in soapsuds. Wild bees do, I believe, build something like that. But grant in the honey bee some principle of symmetry and uniformity and you have passed beyond mechanical necessity; and it is not clear that there may not be some special instinct determined to that shape of cell after all and which has at the present stage of the bee's condition, nothing to do with mechanics, but is like the specific songs of cuckoo and thrush. Now to bed or rather to pack. I will therefore conclude, though there must have been more to say. With kindest remembrances to Mrs. Bridges and Mrs. Molesworth, believe me your affectionate friend

GERARD M. HOPKINS.

[1] See *A Century of Artists* (by W. E. Henley and R. Walker), a Memorial of the Glasgow International Exhibition, 1888.

[2] There is no other well-known composer of that name. The curious collocation is perhaps explained by the fact that R. B. was at this time very fond of an Aria di Chiesa, *Pietà! Signor!*, usually attributed wrongly to Stradella. R. B. thought it should be given to Bellini. Grove says: 'the composer of that beautiful composition is generally believed to be Fétis, Niedermeyer, or Rossini'.

Send the letter that went to Mrs. Bambury. Address Dublin, though possibly I may not go there for a few days more. Do not write here.

CLXIII

University College, Stephen's Green, Dublin. Sept. 7 1888

DEAREST BRIDGES,—I believe I wrote to you last from Fort William. I went thence to Whitby, to be with my brothers, and returned here after being 3 weeks away. Since, I have been trying to set a discursive MA. Examination Paper, in a distress of mind difficult both to understand and to explain. It seems to me I can not always last like this: in mind or body or both I shall give way—and all I really need is a certain degree of relief and change; but I do not think that what I need I shall get in time to save me. This reminds me of a shocking thing that has just happened to a young man well known to some of our community. He put his eyes out. He was a medical student and probably understood how to proceed, which was nevertheless barbarously done with a stick and some wire. The eyes were found among nettles in a field. After the deed he made his way to a cottage and said 'I am blind: please let me rest for an hour'. He was taken to hospital and lay in some danger—from shock, I suppose, or inflammation—, but is recovering. He will not say what was the reason, and this and other circumstances wear the look of sanity; but it is said he was lately subject to delusions. I mention the case because it is extraordinary: suicide is common.

It is not good to be a medical man in the making. It is a fire in which clay splits. There was a young man in this house in my first year, an Englishman, manly and winning too, the sweetest mannered boy. After he left us he went astray. I tried to call on him, but after many trials, finding he shunned me, I gave up trying. I hear he has made a mess of it and is going to make a new beginning in Australia.

There are as many doctors as patients at Dublin, a'most.

Feeling the need of something I spent the afternoon in the

Phoenix Park, which is large, beautiful, and lonely. It did me good, but my eyes are very, very sore. Also there goes ten. Goodnight. Sept. 8 (it is now 20 years to a day since I began my noviceship). Well and I had a great light. I had in my mind the first verse of a patriotic song for soldiers, the words I mean: heaven knows it is needed. I hope to make some 5 verses, but 3 would do for singing: perhaps you will contribute a verse. In the Park I hit on a tune, very flowing and spirited. I enclose the present form of this, just the tune, for I cannot set a bass till I have an instrument. I believe however that you can make nothing of a bare tune; at which I am surprised.—I find I have made 4 verses, rough at present, but I send them:[1] do you like them and could you add one? I hope you may approve what I have done, for it is worth doing and yet is a task of great delicacy and hazard to write a patriotic song that shall breathe true feeling without spoon or brag. How I hate both! and yet feel myself half blundering or sinking[2] into them in several of my pieces, a thought that makes me not greatly regret their likelihood of perishing.

By the bye you misquote the same modern author in writing 'airy between towers': what is not so? it should be 'branchy between towers'.[3]

I enclose by the same hand a sonnet of some standing which Canon Dixon has had and you have not. I have also several more, done at long intervals. Also another.

You asked if you might use a thought of mine about the work (it was said of a canon in music) finding the man and not the man the work: by all means; you will execute it in chryselephantine.[4]

Can there be gout or rheumatism in the eyes? If there can I have it. I am a gouty piece now.

Gouty rhymes to Doughty. Since you speak so highly of his

[1] *Poems*, 59. In R. B.'s note to this poem the date needs correction to September, 1888.

[2] Written above 'lurching', cancelled.

[3] *Duns Scotus's Oxford, Poems*, 20, l. 1.   [4] See vol. ii, p. 24.

283

book I must try to see it: to read 1200 pages I do not promise.[1] But I have read several reviews of it, with extracts.[2] You say it is free from the taint of Victorian English. H'm. Is it free from the taint of Elizabethan English? Does it not stink of that? for the sweetest flesh turns to corruption. Is not Elizabethan English a corpse these centuries? No one admires, regrets, despairs over the death of the style, the living masculine native rhetoric of that age, more than I do; but ' 'tis gone, 'tis gone, 'tis gone'. He writes in it, I understand, because it is manly. At any rate affectation is not manly, and to write in an obsolete style is affectation. As for the extracts I saw they were not good even as that—wrong as English, for instance calling a *man* a jade; and crammed with Latin words, a fault, let do it who will.

But it is true this Victorian English is a bad business. They say 'It goes without saying' (and I wish it did) and instead of 'There is no such thing' they say a thing 'is non-existent' and *in* for *at* and *altruistic* and a lot more.

Here is the tune:[3]

This is not final of course. Perhaps the name of England is too exclusive. I am

Your affectionate friend

GERARD M. HOPKINS.

Where is the letter that went to Mrs. Bambury?

By the bye, Doughty wd. not after all be grateful to you; for this is what you say: 'Monica .. suspects that I must be drivelling and *reminds me to tell you of* a very remarkable book' etc

CLXIV

University College, Stephen's Green, Dublin. Sept. 10 1888

DEAREST BRIDGES,—Though you have a good deal of pleasing modern author to comment on I add a postscript more. You must have been surprised at his saying on his return from a

---

[1] *Travels in Arabia Deserta.* By Charles M. Doughty, Cambridge, 1888; two vols.

[2] See NOTE Z for some account of these.   [3] See facsimile opposite.

is non-existent' and is far off and altruistic and but more.

Here is the tune:

What shall I do for the land that bred me, her homes and fields that

fold-ed and fed me?, Ose un-der her ban-ner and live for her hon-our:

Chorus

Un-der her ban-ner I'll live for her hon-our, Un-der her ban-ner!

live for her hon-our.

3-weeks' holiday that he could get no relief and so on. But what he wishes to be understood is that his work, which is so harassing to his mind, was only suspended for that time (which of itself was most helpful and quite necessary) and not for the time finished and done; so that there is no end to anxiety and care, but only an interruption of it, and the effect accumulates on the whole. No doubt many people are in the same anxiety about money. Also I feel lighterhearted now. (In fact we must never mind what the modern author said.)

Are you going on with your garland of English music?[1] It might be useful to you to read three (numbered as four) Papers on the subject by A. M. Wakefield in *Murray's* for July, August, and September.[2] He puts Wilbye's two madrigals 'Stay, Corydon' and 'Sweet Honey-sucking Bees', he says, above all madrigals ever written;[3] next to those he puts Orlando Gibbons's Silver Swan and 'Oh that the learned Poets'.[4] Would that I could hear some madrigals. He says there is an English 'composer, Robert Whyte,[5] whose works are on a level with those of Palestrina, whom he preceded. . . . A good collection of his MSS. are to be found in the Christ Church library at Oxford, from whence no enterprising national feeling has ever cared to unearth them.'

There is a poem on the Armada by Lewis Morris in the same

---

[1] Mrs. Bridges thinks this refers to a collection that R. B. made of the best English Motets, Madrigals and Part-songs, of various dates, procurable in Novello's octavo edition. He had them bound in one volume, arranged according to 'schools', with a short MS. account of each musician.

[2] *Foundation Stones of English Music*: six articles, July–December 1888, written to call 'the attention of the general reader to forgotten and unappreciated music'.

[3] John Wilbye (1574–1638): these madrigals are from *The Second Set of Madrigales To 3. 4. 5 and 6. parts: apt both for Voyals and Voyces*, 1609, which contains Wilbye's most enduring work. See *English Madrigal Verse*, 1588–1632, ed. E. H. Fellowes, Nos. xvii–xviii and xxxii, for text.

[4] Orlando Gibbons (1583–1625): these madrigals are from *The First Set of Madrigals And Mottets of 5. Parts: apt for Viols And Voyces*, 1612, and are his masterpieces. See op. cit., Nos. i and ii.

[5] Robert White (*c.* 1530–74): 'next to Tye and Tallis, the most important English composer of the mid-16th century. . . . Ever since Burney's time he has taken his proper place in English histories of music, though even now [1928] but little of his music has been printed.'

magazine which contains no. 1 of these Papers.[1] It is of an amazing flatness. Though constructed on patriotic and Protestant principles St. George is invoked, 'by request' and the Spaniards are allowed to invoke (or else Morris does it for them) St. James also, 'positively for this time only'. He says it makes little difference: the victory was really due to our seamen.

'Now St. George for merry England, and St. James for Papal Spain,
Our seamen are our chiefest hope, nor shall we trust in vain.'

However he principally puts his trust in princes, at least Queen Elizabeth.

'Then came Lord Henry Seymour, with a letter from Her Grace,
And Sir Francis read the missive with grave triumph on his face'

[to let you know at once, it was to the effect to use fireships, and Drake 'saw it' and entered into the fun; gravely however],

'And he sware an oath

[let Morris be communicated with and be got to say plainly, in prose if necessary, though I believe he could get it in with verse, what the exact oath was],

that come what would, her orders should be done
Before the early rose of dawn[2] [here the poetry comes in, in spite of exhausting self restraint] proclaimed the coming sun.'

The fireships were a great success. The Spanish ships

'drift into the night,
And many are crushed, and many burn, and some are sunk outright.'

May I say that the last words have just a touch of me? But you must send for it.

Now for the passage in Galatians, which, as you say, is hard.

The epistle is written to reproach the Galatians for listening to those who wd. have them be circumcised and keep the law

[1] *Murray's Magazine*, July 1888, pp. 30–4, *The Invincible Armada, 1588*: a 'patriotic' ballad of the worst type. See *The Works of Lewis Morris*, 1890, pp. 491–4.
[2] From Tennyson: God made himself an awful rose of dawn (*Vision of Sin*).

286

of Moses and recalls them to their allegiance to the Gospel, which St. Paul had preached to them. St. Paul has occasion often to employ the following familiar images—of life or conduct as a journey made or race run, of sin as a fall, and of law and hard duty as burdens borne.

This premised, in chapter v. he says the Law was made to control passion and check sin and he enumerates the works of the flesh, that is the acts of sin which passion prompts to. The Gospel or the Spirit as he calls it, that is Christianity, is quite another thing—an inspiration to do all good, and accordingly he enumerates here too the acts of virtue it prompts and inspires.[1] People prompted by such an inspiration will do nothing but good and Christians therefore need no law (23.). Their flesh, their bad passions, have been disposed of in Christ's crucifixion; they do not live for them but for and by the Spirit, the inspirations of Christianity.

Now, says he (v 25.), if the spirit is our source of life, as we profess by being Christians, we ought to ('live up to it' or, as he puts it,) walk by it. It is no use to be vainglorious and challenge one another to races not enjoined us, seeing who can go furthest and do most, 'handicapping himself' with the old Law. The meaning of this is really envy (26.) and cowardice (vi 12.) and the desire to lead (ib. 13.).

Now (vi 1.) of course I remember that[2] the flesh, that is passion, is not physically dead: Christians[3] are tempted and do fall. But, brethren, if a brother does so fall, the spiritual ones of you, that is the unfallen, who live by the inspirations of Christianity, shd. help him to rise; kindly and humbly, remembering, every man of you, that you might do the same. Bear the weight of one another in thus uplifting one another: that weight and not the burdens of the old Law, will fill out, if it is question of that, the law of Christ.

---

[1] *Epistle to the Galatians*, v. 22–vi. 10. G. M. H. is not here addressing himself to the Rheims version (see his explanation of vi. 7).

[2] Written above 'you will say', cancelled.

[3] Written above 'people', cancelled.

Sept. 11—What follows is so much condensed that it cannot be understood without much expansion: if I am right, the sense is as follows. 3. However men may deceive themselves, of themselves they are nothing and nothing they do has any moral goodness from their doing it. It is then useless for a man to compare himself, who keeps the Mosaic law, with another, who does not, or himself, who set the example of keeping it, with another, who followed his example, to his own advantage: there is no such advantage. 4. But the work or deeds done may have a goodness or badness of their own; they may, like the works of the flesh, be bad; like those of the spirit, be good; or, like those of the now abrogated Law, be meaningless and indifferent: this point is well worth men's examining themselves on. If they once did the works of the flesh and now do those of the spirit or if they once did a little of these good works and now do a great deal, then there is a positive gain, an advantage *of themselves over themselves*, and of this may be proud, that is they may exult at it; but always within the world of their own beings. 5. Then each will be bearing his own burden, that is himself, his flesh with its trials and burdens, on the road, or in the race, of life; as he has to do. In this sense each man is to keep to himself. 6. But in another way exchange, intercourse, commerce of good with good, is quite right; if for instance the spiritual impart their greater spiritual knowledge to the unspiritual and these in return do them what service is in their power. Let them by all means do as much good work this way as they can; for 7. behind all this outward shew of Jewish ceremonies and what not which men see is God who sees the heart and cannot be[1] imposed upon. Before him it is certain all works bear their own fruit and as men sow they will reap—8. from the works of the flesh (and here St. Paul throws in the discarded works of the law; for they are not spiritual, therefore they are carnal) corruption (that is either something dreadful or at least something barren), from the works of the spirit life everlasting. 9. To these last then let us apply ourselves, never minding how things look now.

[1] 'defrauded', cancelled.

10. If we have the choice it is better, as said above (6., also 1.), to let our good works be of service to Christians.

I have written the above without looking at books, of which we are not well provided. However if you wish I will consult commentators.

I find there *is* gout or rheumatism of the eyes. It will, I hope, soon pass away from mine.

Your affectionate friend

GERARD M. HOPKINS.

I have reread your interpretation of Gal. vi 1 sqq. It partly agrees with what I give below,[1] partly disagrees; but the passage cannot be understood without the expansion I have given it. I think you will see I have made it intelligible.

You are three deep with me now.

CLXV

University College, St. Stephen's Green, Dublin. Sept. 13, 14 '88

DEAREST BRIDGES,—I am interested to hear Mr. Rockstro is staying with you. It must be through Wooldridge that you know him. I know *of* him through George Fitzpatrick, a dear young friend of mine but now not seen for 5 years.

I am very glad you like the tune and greatly honoured by Mr. Rockstro's setting an accompaniment,[2] which nevertheless can scarcely be read and as yet we have no piano in the house to try it by. I believe, in spite of what he says, that it allows of contrapuntal treatment; indeed, with some improvements I have since yesterday made, it may be accompanied in canon at the octave two bars off. Nor does it strike me as unlike modal music, but quite the contrary; so that I am surprised at that criticism. I will transpose it to F of course: all keys are the same to me and to every one who thinks that music was before

---

[1] This postscript is written at the head of the letter.
[2] This evidently refers to 'What shall I do for the land that bred me'; Mrs. Bridges has a copy, with a piano accompaniment by Rockstro, in R. B.'s hand.

instruments and angels before tortoises and cats. I should like you to tell me what are the ordinary limits to voices, that I may act accordingly.

If there is good in Doughty no doubt I shall find it out (here there seems some kind of jingling and punning, not meant, but may serve for future use) and no doubt there is good as you say so. But come, is it not affectation to write obsolete English? You know it is.

I have nothing now the matter with me but gout in the eyes, which is unpleasant and disquieting. The feeling is like soap or lemons.

I heard a goodish concert this afternoon. A Herr Slapoffski (real name) played Handel's violin Sonata in A: what a genius! what a native language music was to him; such sense, such fluency, such idiom, and such beauty!

Yours ever

GERARD M. HOPKINS.

My stars! will my song be performed? But if so why not perform my madrigal in canon? a most ambitious piece and hitherto successful but suspended for want of a piano this long while. You could not help liking it if even Sir Robert Stewart unbent to praise it (the most genial of old gentlemen, but an offhand critic of music and me).[1] I can send you the first verse to see—four parts; of course no instrumental accompaniment; the canon is exact, at the octave, 4 bars off, between treble and tenor, and runs in the first verse to 44 bars, I think.

CLXVI

University College, St. Stephen's Green, Dublin.   Sept. 25 1888

DEAREST BRIDGES,—I am sorry to hear of our differing so much in taste: I was hardly aware of it. (It is not nearly so sad as differing in religion). I feel how great the loss is of not reading, as you say; but if I did read I do not much think the effect of it would be what you seem to expect, on either my compositions or my judgments.

[1] See NOTE U.

290

I *must* read something of Greek and Latin letters and lately I sent you a sonnet, on the Heraclitean Fire, in which a great deal of early Greek philosophical thought was distilled; but the liquor of the distillation did not taste very Greek, did it? The effect of studying masterpieces is to make me admire and do otherwise. So it must be on every original artist to some degree, on me to a marked degree. Perhaps then more reading would only *refine my singularity*, which is not what you want.

(While I remember it, in the other sonnet that went with that was a false rhyme you overlooked—*thronged* instead of *swarmed*: please make the correction.)[1]

But not on my criticisms either, I suspect. Wide reading does two things—it extends knowledge and it adjusts the judgment. Now it is mostly found that a learned judgment is less singular than an unlearned one and oftener agrees with the common and popular judgment, with which it coincides as a fine balance or other measure does with the rule of thumb. But, so far as I see, where we differ in judgment, my judgments are less singular than yours; I agree more than you do with the mob and with the *communis criticorum*. Presumably I shd. agree with these still more if I read more and so differ still more from you than now. Who for instance is singular about Dryden, you or I? These considerations are very general, but so far as they go they appear to be reasonable.

To return to composition for a moment: what I want there, to be more intelligible, smoother, and less singular, is an audience. I think the fragments I wrote of *St. Winefred*, which was meant to be played, were not hard to understand. My prose I am sure is clear and even flowing. This reminds me that I have written a paper for an Irish magazine the *Lyceum*,[2] organ of this College, one may say. I was asked and I rewrote something

---

[1] *To what serves Mortal Beauty, Poems*, 38, ll. 7–8. Presumably this was a new draft, or copy. R. B. has corrected the word mentioned in G. M. H.'s own copy of 23 Aug. 1885, which is pasted into A.

[2] *The Lyceum*, a monthly educational and literary magazine and review, ran from September 1887–February 1894. I am assured that it contains no contribution from G. M. H.

I had by me and it is to appear next month. And yet I bet you it will not: my luck will not allow it. But if it does, I then bet you it is intelligible, though on an obstruse subject, Statistics and Free Will—and I mean very intelligible. (This, by the bye, is a badly made logical bed; for I can only win one wager by losing the other. But never mind.)

I send an improved version of my war-song, less open to the objections made, and am your affectionate friend

GERARD HOPKINS.

What shall I . . do for the land that bred me, Her homes and fields . . that fold - ed and fed me? Be un - der her ban-ner and live for her hon-our: Un-der her ban - ner I'll live for her hon-our.

CHORUS.

Un - der her ban - ner we live for her hon-our.

CLXVII

Univ. Coll., Stephen's Green, Dublin. Oct. 3 1888.

DEAREST BRIDGES,—In spite of matter in your last for which presently, when time allows (for I shall tomorrow begin examining), you will, I assure you, 'be handled without gloves' I ask your opinion of a sonnet[1] written to order on the occasion of the first feast since his canonisation proper of St. Alphonsus

---

[1] *Poems*, 49. The version given below differs considerably from that printed by R. B. from B. See the letter of 19 October 1888.

Rodriguez, a laybrother of our Order, who for 40 years acted as hall-porter to the College of Palma in Majorca: he was, it is believed, much favoured by God with heavenly lights and much persecuted by evil spirits. The sonnet (I say it snorting) aims at being intelligible.

[1]Honour should flash from exploit, so we say;
Strokes once that gashed the flesh, that galled the shield,
Should tongue that time now, trumpet now that field
And, on the fighter, forge his glorious day.
On Christ they do; on martyr well they may:
But, be that war within, the sword we wield
Unseen, the heroic breast not outward-steeled,
Earth hears no hurtle then from fiercest fray.
Yet God the mountain-mason, continent—
Quarrier, earthwright; who, with trickling increment,
Veins violets and tall trees makes more and more,
Could crowd career with conquest while there went
Those years on years by of world without event
That in Majorca Alfonso watched the door.

Or, against singularity, we may try this:

Yet God that mountain, and that continent,
Earth, all, builds; or, with trickling increment,
Veins violets, etc.

No, this:

Yet God that hews mountain and continent,
Earth, all; that else, with trickling increment
Veins violets etc.

And I am your affectionate friend

GERARD M. HOPKINS.

And please do not put it aside 'for further neglect' but answer smart. It has to go to Majorca.

Call in the Canon, have a consultation, sit, and send result by return—or soon.

[1] Above the first line, R. B. has written: Glory is the flame of exploit.

Tell him I lately passed Warkworth on my way from Glasgow to Whitby, but there was no stopping. I looked out at the station.

CLXVIII

Univ. Coll., Stephen's Green, Dublin. Oct. 19 '88

DEAREST BRIDGES,—You remark, I am glad to find, a 'lamb-ness' in my last letter: now in the present I shall have somewhat as schoolboys say, to 'lamb in'. But first of various matters.

My little Paper on *Statistics and Free Will* obeyed the general law and did not appear; so I win that wager, if you remember. The editor made some objections which involved recasting it: I have partly done so, and when it is all recast he will no doubt find others. But meantime I get into print in a way I would not. My father wrote a little book on Numbers, the numbers one to ten, a sketchy thing, raising points of interest in a vast, an infinite subject: the *Saturday* lately had a paper on this book, making great game of it from end to end (of it and the article), including something I had contributed to it; however I was not named.[1] Last week[2] same Review has an article 'The American Poet', a comment on Gosse, who lately said, it seems, there *is* no American poet—great poet, he means, or poet proper per-haps. It ends 'After all, the whole affair is a fluke. Great poets are the results of exquisitely rare and incalculable combinations of causes, and nobody would be to blame if there were not a great poet for another century. This country does not seem likely to have another in a hurry [take that], nor have we observed him mewing his mighty youth in France, Germany, Italy, or Spain. Perhaps he is at school in Bolivia at this moment, or he may be at Johns Hopkins University, Baltimore, and his Christian name may be "Gifted" '.[3] It is an allusion to

---

[1] A review in 1½ columns (22 September 1888) of *The Cardinal Numbers*, by Manley Hopkins (1887), a 'little tract' which is treated throughout with an air of amused superiority that aims at irony. See NOTE AA.

[2] 13 October 1888.

[3] Gosse had replied to a question from the editor of *The Forum*, 'Has America produced a Poet?'; his remarks are discussed, and the writer ends by

that same 'Gifted Hopkins' the humorist 'who died of his own jocosity' that, if you remember, was meant the time before. But if Lang wrote this paper too, then, putting together that very fact that he then did *not* mean me with the fact that Gosse (you told me) admires my muse and the one that being imprudent he may have said so and others, I do not know but I may say to myself, O my soul, perhaps This Is Fame. But I don't want it and beg you will not expose me to it; which you can easily forbear from doing now that you disapprove of my γένος as vicious, and surely you shd. not vitiate taste. And at any rate I shall never cease to deplore that unhappy letter of mine you read sitting leagues and parasangs of country lanes next to Lang that morning: how could I foresee it was so dangerous to write to a remote world's-end place like Yattendon? But indeed you have told me there is plenty of intellectual life there.

Next, music. I am glad to find it is only there we are so far apart. But the contrary is true: there we agree well enough and the rift is elsewhere. I agree to your musical strictures and almost invite your rebukes and if I do not do so heartily it is because a perfect organisation for crippling me exists and the one for 'encouragemental purposes' (modern English) is not laid down yet. I agree that for contrapuntal writing we shd. read the great masters and study the rules, both. The great masters unhappily I cannot read (unless very little), but the rules I do carefully study, and just on account of the great formality of the art of music it happens that mere adherence to them, without study of examples from the masters, produces—given faculty— results of some interest and value. (I like not that last sentence: it is too much in the manner of the magazines I read and too far entirely from Doughty and the Mighty Dead.) And my madrigal in canon, so far as it has gone, is strict and Sir Robert

suggesting names of poets of all nations, and asks whether America has produced a poet on their level. He proceeds: 'These are questions which Mr. Gosse may have the temerity to answer; we prefer to leave the reply to the American conscience.' Then follows the passage G. M. H. quotes above. The allusion that follows is not clear: it can hardly be a reference to p. 153.

Stewart (a demon for rule) says it is correct and that it might even have been freer. But, as you say, you have not seen it and now that I have no piano I cannot go on with it. This morning I gave in what I believe is the last batch of examination-work for this autumn (and if all were seen, fallen leaves of my poor life between all the leaves of it), and but for that want I might prance on ivory this very afternoon. I have had to get glasses, by the bye: just now I cannot be happy either with or without them. The oculist says my sight is very good and my eye perfectly healthy but that like Jane Nightwork I am old. And, strange to say, I have taken to drawing again. Perverse Fortune or something perverse (try me): why did I not take to it before? And now enough, for I must whet myself, strop myself, be very bitter, and will secrete and distil a good deal beforehand.

However with no more stropping than the palm of my hand and chopping at a hair, no but at the 'broth of goldish flue'[1] (how well now does the pleasing modern author come in in his own illustration and support!), I can deal with one matter, the sonnet on St. Alphonsus.[2] I am obliged for your criticisms, 'contents of which noted', indeed acted on. I have improved the sestet (in itself I do not call the first version 'cheeky', the imagery as applied to God Almighty being so familiar in the Scripture and the Fathers: however I have not kept it). But now I cannot quite understand nor so far as I understand agree with the difficulty you raise about the continents and so on. It is true continents are partly made by 'trickling increment'; but what is on the whole truest and most strikes us about them and mountains is that they are made what now we see them by trickling *de*crements, by detrition, weathering, and the like.* And at any rate whatever is markedly featured in stone or what

* By the bye, some geologists say the last end of all continents and dry land altogether is to be washed into the sea and that when all are gone 'water will be the world', as in the Flood, and will still be deep and have to spare.

[1] *Harry Ploughman, Poems*, 43, l. 1.
[2] *Poems*, 49. See R. B.'s note (the date of this letter there needs correction).

is like stone is most naturally said to be hewn, and to *shape*, itself, means in old English to hew and the Hebrew *bara* / to create, even, properly means to hew. But life and living things are not naturally said to be hewn: they grow, and their growth is by trickling increment.

I will not now interpret the thought of the sestet. It is however, so far as I can see, both exåct and pregnant.

I am altogether at a loss to see your objection to *exploit* and to *so we say*. You will allow—would, I shd. think, urge on me—that where the ὄνομα κύριον[1] has nothing flat or poor about it it is the best word to use in poetry as in prose, better I mean than[2] its paraphrase. Now *exploit* is the right word, it is κύριον, there is no other for the thing meant but *achievement*, which is not better, and it is a handsome word in itself: why then should I not say it? Surely I should. By 'regular indoors work' I understand you to mean a drawing finished at home with the eye no longer on the object, something poorly thrown in to fill up a blank the right filling of which is forgotten. But 'so we say' is just what I have to say and want to say (it was made out of doors in the Phoenix Park with my mind's eye on the first presentment of the thought): I mean 'This is what we commonly say, but we are wrong'. The line now stands 'Glory is a flame off exploit, so we say' and I think it must so stand.

I am warming myself at the flame of a little exploit of my own done last night. I could not have believed in such a success nor that life had this pleasure to bestow. Somebody had tried to take me in and I warned him I wd. take him in at our next meeting. Accordingly I wrote him a letter from 'the son of a respected livery and bait stables in Parteen [suburb of Limerick] oftentimes employed by your Honoured Father' asking for an introduction to one of the Dublin newspapers 'as Reporter, occasional paregraphs or sporting inteligence'. The sentence I think best of was one in which I said I (or he) could 'give any color which may be desired to reports of speeches or Proceedings

---

[1] Proper name for a thing; exact word: a term from Aristotle's *Poetics*.
[2] MS. 'that'.

subject to the Interests of truth which must always be the paremount consideration'. It succeeded beyond my wildest hopes and action is going to be taken. The letter is even to be printed in the *Nation* as a warning to those who are continually applying in the like strain; but before this takes place I must step in.

It is as you say about Addis.[1] But why should you be glad? Why at any rate should you burst upon me that you are glad, when you know that I cannot be glad?

It seems there is something in you interposed between what shall we say? the Christian and the man of the world which hurts, which is to me like biting on a cinder in bread. Take the simplest view of this matter: he has made shipwreck, I am afraid he must even be in straits: he cannot support himself by his learned writings; I suppose he will have to teach. But this is the least. I hope at all events he will not pretend to marry, and especially no one he has known in his priestly life. Marriage is honourable and so is the courtship that leads to marriage, but the philanderings of men vowed to God are not honourable nor the marriages they end in. I feel the same deep affection for him as ever, but the respect is gone. I would write to him if I had his address, which, I am sorry to say, is still or was lately somewhere at Sydenham; for after bidding farewell to his flock he had not the grace to go away.

This is enough for the time and I will put off the lambing to another season. With kindest remembrances to Mrs. Bridges and Mrs. Molesworth, I am your affectionate friend

GERARD M. HOPKINS.

Oct. 20 '88.

CLXIX

University College, Dublin. Feb. 23 1889

DEAREST BRIDGES,—I enclose something and shall not write much. I feel inclined to send another copy to Wooldridge and then again I do not; at any rate I send none now.

[1] See NOTE B.

The Italian tour must have been very nice and I am very glad you took Mary Plow.[1] I am sorry the monks were dirty and the extreme poverty they have been reduced to does not excuse them; but I offer the following remarks. Shaving is conventional cleanliness: if it were otherwise, the longer the beard the dirtier wd. the wearer be, 'which' (in the language of St. Thomas) 'is inconvenient.' Next your countrymen at Cambridge keep their rooms, you told me, 'dirty, yea filthy', and they are not poor. Next spitting in the North of England is very, very common with the lower classes: as I went up Brunswick Road (or any street) at Liverpool on a frosty morning it used to disgust me to see the pavement regularly starred with the spit of the workmen going to their work; and they do not turn aside, but spit straight before them as you approach, as a Frenchman remarked to me with abhorrence and I cd. only blush. And in general we cannot call ours a cleanly or a clean people: they are not at all the dirtiest and they know what cleanliness means, as they know the moral virtues, but they do not always practise it. We deceive ourselves if we think otherwise. And our whole civilisation is dirty, yea filthy, and especially in the north; for is it not dirty, yea filthy, to pollute the air as Blackburn and Widnes and St. Helen's are polluted and the water as the Thames and the Clyde and the Irwell are polluted? The ancients with their immense public baths would have thought even our cleanest towns dirty.

About singing out of tune, I am not altogether displeased to hear the Italians do it, as the Germans do. Carl Rosa in an article on English Opera (= opera by anybody you like with the words in English, translated of course; *not* opera by English composers) remarks on the good ear of English audiences and amateur performers and says that he has witnessed Germans at a concert listen undisconcerted to a singer out of tune where in

---

[1] R. B. and his wife (with Mary Plow his niece, afterwards Mrs. H. C. Beeching) spent about a month (January 1889) abroad. They went to Italy (Genoa, Pisa, Florence, Rome) by way of Arles, the Riviera, and thence by the Cornice.

England half the audience would manifest signs of distress; and to the same effect of performers.

Also a good musical shrill bell at mass is pleasing and effective enough.

'The first touch of decadence destroys all merit whatever': this is a hard saying. What, all technical merit—as chiaroscuro, anatomical knowledge, expression, feeling, colouring, drama? It is plainly not true. And, come to that, the age of Raphael and Michelangelo was in a decadence and its excellence is technical. Everything after Giotto is decadent in form, though advancing in execution. Go to.

You return home to see your country in a pretty mess—to speak jokingly of matter for tears. And the grand[1] old traitor must have come home almost or quite in the same boat with you.[2] And what boobies your countrymen are! They sit in court at the Commission[3] giggling, yea guffawing at the wretched Pigot's mess; making merry because a traitor to government and then a traitor to rebellion, both in a small way, has not succeeded[4] in injuring an enemy of their own who is a traitor to government in a great way and a danger on an imperial scale; and that after a trial which has at least shewn the greatness and the blackness of the crime lawful government and the welfare of the empire have to contend with. And this I say as if Pigot were or employed the forger of those letters. For in my judgment, unless further evidence is forthcoming, those letters are genuine. But no more of this misery. With kindest remembrances to Mrs. Bridges and Mrs. Molesworth I am your affectionate friend

GERARD M. HOPKINS.

[1] Written above 'great', cancelled.

[2] Gladstone had been resting at Naples, much concerned with Italian policy; and, on account of the difficult political situation, he had given up the thought of visiting the Dufferins at Rome.

[3] The special commission appointed to report to the House of Commons on the charges brought by *The Times* against Parnell and other Irish M.P.s. See NOTE BB.

[4] MS. 'succeeding'.

Do pray return to your Seaford hand, a thing of beauty and a joy for ever. For a little more after the manner of your last and I shall not be able to read you at all.

CLXX

Univ. Coll., Stephen's Green, Dublin. March 20 1889.

DEAREST BRIDGES,—I write you a few lines tonight for an ungracious reason, because I cannot do anything needing a greater effort.

I have been thinking what a fine subject you chose in *Achilles in Scyros*. Achilles is such a brilliant figure: Shakspere did not read Homer, otherwise he could not have been guilty of that hideous and perverse freak of a cowardly Achilles in *Troilus and Cressida*. I hope you do him justice. I should like to see the play, but I do not ask to, no; I could not read it.

Mr. Jevons sent me his pamphlet.[1] I had already seen and agreed with it. I read it again and wrote to thank him and say so. I asked him to correct two references or rather give me the correct form and the references, if he knew them, of two stories, but he did not reply.

I am both flattered and dismayed about my song. It was only a sketch, a rough-hew of a song. I have been at it since and the task I have undertaken is so extremely difficult that I have not yet succeeded in it and have to put it aside at intervals, especially as I am languishing. First it is in canon at the octave at two bars: but I think scorn of such an achievement as that. But in the next verse it has to be in canon at the third above and third below at two and four bars off respectively—or to speak more precisely, the alto begins, at the sixth above; the treble, after two bars, follows, with the original tune; and the bass— which is instrumental—after four bars, brings up the rear at the sixth below. Now this requires the tune to be capable of counter- point at the octave, or with itself unchanged, and also with two

[1] Possibly *The Development of the Athenian Democracy*, by Frank Byron Jevons, formerly of Wadham College, Oxford, a pamphlet of 38 pp., printed in 1886.

other transpositions, all exact. It is, I assure you, very baffling; but I hope to do it. It almost comes of itself; so that I am persuaded by coaxing I can make it quite. Besides this I insert a firm chant. I see that the composers of canons besides the Muses and Graces should sacrifice, like Timoleon, to Fortune.[1]

Is not *Nero* to be continued?[2] It is such a rich picture of life, indeed of our life as it would be without Christianity. Only on the other hand a Second Part would have to bring in the loathsome character of Sporus,[3] which is not desirable to put on the stage. (I read yesterday that Nero choked the oracular chasm at Delphi with carcases because the oracle rebuked him for killing his mother and did literally for some time stop the mouth of the god.)

By the bye, as you are a reader of Menander, you may like to know that Dr. Theodore Koch's *Comicorum Atticorum Fragmenta*, vol. 3 containing Menander, price 16 marks, Teubner, is now out.

I shall be delighted to have the new issue of the *Growth of Love*[4] and think it well that some pruning has been practised; for on so dark and mystical a matter one may be glutted with the best of poetry. Neither should you grudge giving me a copy that will be after my time unread. For consider: you aim at oblivion; for that you descend into Daniel's den; for that you print 24 copies (so that the College of Apostles on parting could have taken two copies only for the needs of all Scythia, suppose, all Parthia, all India, and so on). Now, as some philosopher Cicero quotes[5] said, *undique tantundem viae ad inferos est* (Anaxagoras, by George); that is you can be forgotten 'as hard' at Dublin as anywhere else, at Lampsacus as at Clazomenae: what do you want more?

I have from henceforth till the beginning of May to prepare examination-papers.

---

[1] For Timoleon see Plutarch.   [2] *Nero*, Part II, was published in 1894.
[3] He is not one of the characters.
[4] LXXIX Sonnets (Daniel, Oxford; 1889): 22 copies were printed.
[5] Cicero, *Tusc.* I. 43. 104.

I have been drawing up a Paper, not for examination, you understand, on the Argei,[1] a curious subject, interesting by dint of study; but it is not corrected or copied or indeed all written. If I can get it done I shall try to publish it.

I enclose a sonnet[2] and am your affectionate friend

GERARD M. HOPKINS.

March 21 1889.

I have a good few sonnets more you have never seen.

Monasterevan, March 24—The sonnet will, I am afraid, fade: Miss Cassidy's ink is, I must say, shocking. Observe, it must be read *adagio molto* and with great stress.[3]

CLXXI

Univ. Coll., Stephen's Green, Dublin. April 29 1889.

DEAREST BRIDGES,—I am ill to-day, but no matter for that as my spirits are good. And I want you too to 'buck up', as we used to say at school, about those jokes over which you write in so dudgeonous a spirit. I have it now down in my tablets that a man may joke and joke and be offensive; I have had several warnings lately leading me to make the entry, tho' goodness knows the joke that gave most offence was harmless enough and even kind. You I treated to the same sort of irony as I do myself; but it is true it makes all the world of difference whose hand administers. About Daniel I see I was mistaken: if he pays you more than and sells you as much as other publishers (which however is saddening to think of: how many copies is it? five and twenty?)[4] my objections do not apply. Then you ought to remember that I did try to make you known in Dublin and had some little success. (Dowden I will never

[1] Puppets made of rushes that were thrown into the Tiber from the Pons Sublicius on May 15 in a yearly ceremony.

[2] Doubtless *Poems*, 50.

[3] A note by R. B. at the end of the next (and last) letter reads: The two letters preceding this one were destroyed RB.

[4] See p. 302, footnote 4.

forgive:[1] could you not kill Mrs. Bridges? then he might take an interest in you). Nay I had great success and placed you on the pinnacle of fame; for it is the pinnacle of fame to become educational and be set for translation into Gk. iambics, as you are at Trinity: this is to be a classic; 'this', as Lord Beaconsfield said to a friend who told him he found his young daughter reading *Lothair*, 'O this is fame indeed'. And Horace and Juvenal say the same thing. And here I stop, for fear of it ripening into some kind of joke.

I believe I enclose a new sonnet. But we greatly differ in feeling about copying one's verses out: I find it repulsive, and let them lie months and years in rough copy untransferred to my book. Still I hope soon to send you my accumulation. This one is addressed to you.[2]

Swinburne has a new volume out,[3] which is reviewed in its own style: 'The rush and the rampage, the pause and the pull-up of these lustrous and lumpophorous lines'. It is all now a 'self-drawing web'; a perpetual functioning of genius without truth, feeling, or any adequate matter to be at function on. There is some heavydom, in long waterlogged lines (he has no real understanding of rhythm, and though he sometimes hits brilliantly at other times he misses badly) about the *Armada*,[4] that pitfall of the patriotic muse; and *rot* about babies,[5] a blethery bathos into which Hugo and he from opposite coasts have long driven Channel-tunnels. I am afraid I am going too far with the poor fellow. Enough now, but his babies make a Herodian of me.

My song will be a very highly wrought work and I do hope a fine one. Do you think canon wd. spoil the tune? I hope not, but the contrary. But if the worst came to the worst, I could, since a solo voice holds its own against instruments, give the canon-following to a violin. I shall hear what Sir Robert

---

[1] See p. 248, n. 1.   [2] *Poems*, 51.
[3] *Poems and Ballads*, Third Series, 1889.
[4] *The Armada, 1588–1888*: a wordy rhapsody, twenty-four pages long.
[5] *In a Garden, A Rhyme*, and *Baby-Bird*.

Stewart says about it. This is how it now stands. I tried at first to make the air such that it shd. be rigidly the same in every note and rhythm (always excepting the alterations to save the tritone) in all its shifts; but I found that impracticable and that I had reached the point where art calls for loosing, not for lacing. I now make the canon strict in each verse, but allow a change, which indeed is besides called for by the change of words, from verse to verse. Indeed the air becomes a generic form which is specified newly in each verse, with excellent effect. It is like a new art this. I allow no modulation: the result is that the tune is shifted into modes, viz. those of La, Mi, and Sol (this is the only way I can speak of them, and they have a character of their own which is neither that of modern major and minor music nor yet of the plain chant modes, so far as I can make out). The first shift is into the mode of La: this shd. be minor, but the effect is not exactly that; rather the feeling is that Do is still the keynote, but has shifted its place in the scale. This impression is helped by the harmony, for as the Third is not flattened the chords appear major. The chord at the beginning of every bar is the common chord or first inversion; the $\frac{6}{4}$ may appear in course of the bar and discords are in passing or prepared. Perhaps the harmony may be heavy, but I work according to the only rules I know. I can only get on slowly with it and must hope to be rewarded in the end. Now I must lie down.

Who is Miss Cassidy? She is an elderly lady who by often asking me down to Monasterevan and by the change and holiday her kind hospitality provides is become one of the props and struts of my existence. St. Ernin[1] founded the monastery: a singular story is told of him. Henry VIII confiscated it and it became the property of Lord Drogheda. The usual curse on abbey lands attends it and it never passes down in the direct line. The present Lord and Lady Drogheda have no issue. Outside Moore Abbey, which is a beautiful park, the country is

---

[1] O'Hanlon gives twenty-five saints bearing the name Ernan, Ernain, or Ernin.

flat, bogs and river and canals. The river is the Barrow, which the old Irish poets call the dumb Barrow. I call it the burling Barrow Brown.[1] Both descriptions are true. The country has nevertheless a charm. The two beautiful young people live within an easy drive.

With kind love to Mrs. Bridges and Mrs. Molesworth, I am your affectionate friend

GERARD.

[1] See *Poems*, 54, l. 12.

ADDITIONAL NOTES

VOLUME I

NOTE A, *page* 1. See *V. S. S. Coles: Letters, Papers, Addresses, Hymns, and Verses, with a Memoir:* edited by J. F. Briscoe, with a preface by the Right Rev. Charles Gore (the memoir by G. W. Borlase), 1930, for an account of the activities and friendships of one of the leading High Churchmen of his generation. He is perhaps best remembered for his work at Pusey House, Oxford. He was a very intimate friend of G. M. H. before the latter was received into the Roman Catholic church (when the friendship probably ceased), and they discussed religious matters in great detail. Both were then friends of Liddon.

NOTE B, *page* 2. William Addis took a 1st Class in Classical Mods. in 1863, a 1st Class in Greats in 1865, and graduated in 1866. He became a Roman Catholic in 1866, was ordained in 1872, and was parish priest of Sydenham 1878–88. In 1888 he left the Church of Rome, and in 1901 returned to the Church of England. He was Professor of Old Testament Criticism, Manchester College, Oxford, 1898–1910, curate of St. Martin and All Saints, Oxford, 1909–10; and vicar of All Saints, Knightsbridge, 1910–17. His publications deal with Church History. For a short period in 1882 he was a Fellow (in Mental and Moral Philosophy) of University College, Dublin; and, with Thomas Arnold, he compiled a Catholic Dictionary. His friendship with G. M. H. was based chiefly on common religious interests, and while at Oxford the two spent much time together. The correspondence, on both sides, seems to have been destroyed.

NOTE C, *page* 4. R. B. evidently intended to give a flagon (communion vessel) to the church at Thorndon (a parish in Suffolk, between Mendlesham and Eye) where William Henry Glover, who had married Caroline Bridges, a sister some ten years older than R. B., was rector. The present rector reported the flagon to be still in use, but without the stopper. He has, however, since found the parts of this among discarded odds and ends, and joined them.

NOTE D, *page* 18. '. . . Fancy me getting up at a quarter past six: it is however done with a melancholy punctuality nearly every morning. The boys' mass is at seven; then what they call Preparation fr. 7.45–8.30; then breakfast in Hall, so to speak; at 9.30 school till 12; dinner in Hall at 1; school fr. 2 to 3; then the boys and sometimes I go to their field which they call Bosco, for a game, just now hockey but soon football; at 6 tea in Hall; from 6.30–8.30 school. My class is the fifth but besides this my work includes two private pupils who come to me fr. 8.45 to 10 on all nights but Saturday and fr. 5 to 6 on the half-holidays Tuesday, Thursday and Saturday. With reading the class books and looking over exercises (which takes a long time) I find all my time occupied. . . . The Fifth, the head class, has only five

307

boys: thus I have seven. I feel as if they were all my children, a notion encouraged by their innocence and backwardness. . . . The masters' table appears to be the dregs of Great Britain, indeed one of us is a Dutchman but I cannot spell his name: when I say dregs I only mean that they come fr. all quarters indiscriminately and I include myself: it is sweepings, not dregs I mean. They are nice souls and one of them, a very young man, I like particularly. . . . I see I have not given you a proper notion altogether of my employment, for I have my private pupils oftener. But F. Ambrose is going to make an arrangement by which I shall get some time for private reading. . . .'

NOTE E, *page* 29. Poems / by Robert Bridges / Batchelor of Arts in the University / of Oxford / Parva seges satis est / London / Basil Montagu Pickering / 196 Piccadilly W. / 1873. The dedication to Harry Ellis Wooldridge, Esq. is from 50, Maddox Street, Hanover Square; August, 30, 1873. pp. 12, 128 (counting blanks). Light blue cloth boards: paper label: printed at the Chiswick Press. The Advertisement at the end says: 'The foregoing poems, with the exception of a few that have their proper dates affixed, were written between the summers of seventy-two and seventy-three. . . .'

NOTE F, *page* 29. 'Mr. Bridges' poems have . . . a ring and a quality of their own. It could scarcely be gathered from his book that he has ever read Mr. Tennyson or Mr. Swinburne; and he sees things as clearly, speaks as simply, feels as truly, as if the modern demand for research and subtlety had never been heard. His teachers are of an elder and simpler time. . . . With the old melody there is the old repose of healthy imagination; these lyrics are "plain, and dally with the innocence of love"; they show at once true feeling and reticence. . . . Perhaps the best poem in the book is the "Elegy on a Lady, whom grief for the death of her Betrothed killed". . . . A fancy that can be strange when it chooses, and has always a power of delicate surprise, simplicity, courtliness, feeling, music of no vulgar order,—these are Mr. Bridges' qualities. His defect is to exaggerate the antique roughness of his models. . . . We think he is unsuccessful in a few pieces which aim at being humorous. . . .'

NOTE G, *page* 32. Carmen Elegiacum / Roberti Bridges / de / Nosocomio Sti Bartolomæi / Londinensi / In quo narratur Historia Fundationis / Nosocomii: memorantur Illustrissimi / Viri qui olim ibi versati sunt. Accedunt quæ-/dam de medicis et chirurgis qui in eodem loco / Hodie officiis funguntur. Sequitur denique / aliquid περὶ πράξεως sive de ratione medendi Pa-/tricii Black, in nosocomio medici senioris, / cum amicis ejus gratissimum, tum studiosis uti-/lissimum: ad eundem ipsum / Ornatissimum Virum / Patricium Black MD. etc. / Scriptum eique dedicatum / "Si qua videbuntur casu non dicta latinè, / In qua scribebam barbara terra fuit" / Londini / Impensis Eduardi Bumpus, Holborn Bars: in cujus / officina exemplaria venundantur / 1877 /

The dedication to Patrick Black is dated from 52 Bedford Square Idibus Decembr. 1876.

Additional Notes

Note H, *page* 39.

Passing by Cripplegate, where Milton lies,
Such close proximity of noble dust
Fired me in praise of him whose knightly thrust
Pierced aping chivalry, whose sightless eyes

Saw visions, and whose kingly words and wise
Our tottering Commonwealth did first adjust,
When in his golden mouth the Muse did trust
A strain too rich for common ears to prize.

O hot political spirit! thou dost now
Quench thy desires in heaven, and thy high style
May'st match with Dante, climbed upon the brow

Of Paradise a second time. Our isle
Proud of her son forgets her loss, for thou
Shalt keep her speech honoured in Heaven awhile.

Note I, *page* 49.

When I see you my heart sings
Deep within me for deep love;
In my deep heart's dreamiest grove
Your bright image comes like Spring's,
Bringing back the murmuring dove
To the wan dim watersprings.
Would my tongue could tell the things
Love seems but an echo of
    When I see you!
Hope lies dying. Time's disproof
Strips love's roses to the stings;
But the bird that knows its wings
Bear it where it will aloof,
Sings not, Love, as my heart sings
    When I see you!

THEO. MARZIALS.

Note J, *page* 70.

When, parched with thirst, astray on sultry sand
The traveller faints, upon his closing ear
Steals a fantastic music, he may hear
The babbling fountain of his native land.

Before his eyes the vision seems to stand,
Where at its terraced brink the maids appear,
Who fill their deep urns at its waters clear,
And not refuse the help of lover's hand.

O cruel jest! he cries, as some one flings
The sparkling drops in sport or scornful ire;
O shameless, brute contempt of holy things!

309

But never of their wanton play they tire,
As, not athirst, they sit beside the springs,
While he must quench in death his lost desire.

NOTE K, *page* 80. 'The poems in the smaller type, like those similarly distinguished in the author's last series, are written by the rules of a new prosody, which may very well exist by the side of the old. It is left to the judgment of the reader: but the author hopes that these verses will be read with attention to the natural quantity and accent of the syllables,—for these are the interpretation of the rhythm,—and not with the notion that all accents in poetry are alternate with unaccented syllables, nor with the almost universal prejudice that when two or more unaccented syllables intervene between two accented syllables the former must suffer and be slurred over: a prejudice which probably arises from the common misuse of unaccented for short syllables.

The use of feet which correspond to pæons, and the frequent inversions of feet in these new rhythms, render it possible for four or five unaccented syllables to follow on each other.

The author disavows any claim to originality for the novelty: this is almost entirely due to a friend, whose poems remain, he regrets to say, in manuscript.

Christmas, 1879.'

NOTE L, *page* 90.

XIV

Regret

If I could but forget, and not recall
So well my time of pleasure and of play,
The leaves and careless ecstasy of May,
The breathing summer sloth, the scented fall:

Or waking not believe that each of all
My days was one irrevocable day,
When the sweet jeopardy of Love's delay
Last held the promise of my hope in thrall;

Oh, then were hideous duty not too hard,
And manly interest in common things
Would stir my blood, and be its own reward.

But that 'tis I who once,—'tis this that stings,—
Once dwelt within the gate that angels guard,
Where yet I'd be, had I but heavenly wings.

NOTE M, *page* 101.

When gossamer floats everywhere,
And golden apples scent the air,
And round about their ancient roots
Vast pear-trees shower their tiny fruits,
And red plums blush through yellow leaves,
And summer friends have left our eaves;

When oaks alone their brown leaves hold,
And chestnut-trees have shed their gold,
And wheat is stacked and sown again,
Then wondrous tints light up our lane.

NOTE N, *page* 117.

O my vague desires!
Ye lambent flames of the soul, her offspring fires:
That are my soul herself in pangs sublime
Rising and flying to heaven before her time:

What doth tempt you forth
To drown in the south or shiver in the frosty north?
What seek ye or find ye in your random flying,
Ever soaring aloft, soaring and dying?

Joy, the joy of flight!
They hide in the sun, they flare and dance in the night;
Gone up, gone out of sight: and ever again
Follow fresh tongues of fire, fresh pangs of pain.

Ah! they burn my soul,
The fires, devour my soul that once was whole:
She is scattered in fiery phantoms day by day,
But whither, whither? ay whither? away, away!

Could I but control
These vague desires, these leaping flames of the soul:
Could I but quench the fire: ah! could I stay
My soul that flieth, alas, and dieth away!

NOTE O, *page* 147. In 1684 Purcell composed an ode or song of welcome entitled *On the King's return to White-hall after his Summer's Progress.* The words are by Thomas Flatman:

From these serene and rapturous joys
A country life alone can give,
Exempt from tumult and from noise,
Where Kings forget the trouble of their reigns,
And are almost as happy as their humble swains,
By feeling that they live:

(*Caroline Poets*, ed. G. Saintsbury, vol. iii, pp. 377–8.)

NOTE P, *page* 154. A review of Walt Whitman's *Leaves of Grass* (Washington: London, Chatto and Windus) by George Saintsbury in the *Academy*, 10 October 1874, pp. 398–400.

The introduction expresses the hope that this new edition of *Leaves of Grass*, somewhat altered, rearranged and added to, may lead to a deeper and wider study of a poet at present not clearly understood, even by lettered Englishmen. The writer proceeds:

'It is not difficult to point out the central thesis of Walt Whitman's

Additional Notes

poetical gospel. It is briefly this: the necessity of the establishment of a universal republic, or rather brotherhood of men. And to this is closely joined another, or rather a series of others, indicating the type of man of which this universal republic is to consist, or perhaps which it is to produce. The poet's language in treating the former of these two positions is not entirely uniform; sometimes he speaks as of a federation of nations, sometimes as if mankind at large were to gravitate towards the United States, and to find in them the desired Utopia. But the constitution of the United States, at least that constitution as it ought to be, is always and uniformly represented as a sufficient and the only sufficient political means of attaining this Utopia, nay, as having to some extent already presented Utopia as a fact. Moreover, passing to the second point, the ideal man is imagined as the ideal Yankee, understanding that word of course as it is understood in America, not in Europe. He is to be a rather magnificent animal, almost entirely uncultured (this is not an unfair representation, although there are to be found certain vague panegyrics on arts, and especially on music), possessing a perfect *physique*, well nourished and clothed, affectionate towards his kind, and above all things firmly resolved to admit no superior. As is the ideal man, so is the ideal woman to be. Now it may be admitted frankly and at once, that this is neither the creed nor the man likely to prove attractive to many persons east of the Atlantic. If it be said that the creed is a vague creed, and the man a detestable man, there will be very little answer attempted. Many wonderful things will doubtless happen 'when', as the poet says, 'through these States walk a hundred millions of superb persons'; but it must be allowed that there is small prospect of any such procession. One is inclined for very many sound reasons, and after discarding all prejudices, to opine that whatever salvation may await the world may possibly come from other quarters than from America. Fortunately, however, admiration for a creed is easily separable from admiration for the utterance and expression of that creed, and Walt Whitman as a poet is not difficult to disengage from Walt Whitman as an evangelist and politician. The keyword of all his ideas and of all his writings is universality. His Utopia is one which shall be open to everybody; his ideal of man and woman one which shall be attainable by everybody; his favourite scenes, ideas, subjects, those which everybody, at least to some extent, can enjoy and appreciate. He cares not that by this limitation he may exclude thoughts and feelings, at any rate phases of thought and feeling, infinitely choicer and higher than any which he admits. To express this striving after universality he has recourse to methods both unusual and (to most readers) unwelcome. The extraordinary jumbles and strings of names, places, employments, which deface his pages, and which have encouraged the profane to liken them to auctioneers' catalogues or indexes of encyclopædias, have no other object than to express this universal sympathy, reaching to the highest and penetrating to the lowest forms of life. The exclusion of culture, philosophy, manners, is owing to this desire to admit nothing but what is open to every human being of ordinary faculty and opportunities. Moreover it is to this that we may fairly trace the prominence in Whitman's writings of the sexual

Additional Notes

passion, a prominence which has given rise, and probably will yet give rise, to much unphilosophical hubbub. This passion, as the poet has no doubt observed, is almost the only one which is peculiar to man as man, the presence of which denotes virility if not humanity, the absence of which is a sign of abnormal temperament. Hence he elevates it to almost the principal place, and treats of it in a manner somewhat shocking to those who are accustomed to speak of such subjects (we owe the word to Southey) enfarinhadamente. As a matter of fact, however, the treatment, though outspoken, is eminently 'clean', to use the poet's own word; there is not a vestige of prurient thought, not a syllable of prurient language. Yet it would be a great mistake to suppose that sexual passion occupies the chief place in Whitman's estimation. There is according to him something above it, something which in any ecstasies he fails not to realise, something which seems more intimately connected in his mind with the welfare of mankind, and the promotion of his ideal republic. This is what he calls 'robust American love'. He is never tired of repeating 'I am the poet of comrades'— Socrates himself seems renascent in this apostle of friendship. In the ears of a world (at least on this side the Atlantic) incredulous of such things, he reiterates the expressions of Plato to Aster, of Socrates respecting Charmides, and in this respect fully justifies (making allowance for altered manners) Mr. Symonds' assertion of his essentially Greek character, an assertion which most students of Whitman will heartily endorse. But we must again repeat that it is not so much in the matter as in the manner of his Evangel that the strength of Whitman lies. It is impossible not to notice his exquisite descriptive faculty, and his singular felicity in its use. Forced as he is, both by natural inclination and in the carrying out of his main idea, to take note of 'the actual earth's equalities', he has literally filled his pages with the song of birds, the hushed murmur of waves, the quiet and multiform life of the forest and the meadow. And in these descriptions he succeeds in doing what is most difficult, in giving us the actual scene or circumstance as it impressed him, and not merely the impression itself. This is what none but the greatest poets have ever save by accident done, and what Whitman does constantly and with a sure hand. 'You shall', he says at the beginning of his book:

'You shall no longer take things at second or third hand, nor look through the eyes of the dead, nor feed on the spectres in books:
'You shall not look through my eyes either, nor take things from me:
'You shall listen to all sides and filter them from yourself.'

But affluent as his descriptions are, there are two subjects on which he is especially eloquent, which seem indeed to intoxicate and inspire him the moment he approaches them. These are Death and the sea. In the latter respect he is not, indeed, peculiar, but accords with all poets of all times, and especially of this time. But in his connection of the two ideas (for the one always seems to suggest the other to him), and in his special devotion to Death, he is more singular. The combined influence of the two has produced what is certainly the most perfect specimen of his work, the 'Word out of the

4010   313   s s

Sea' (in this edition it has, we are sorry to see, lost its special title, and become the first merely of 'Sea-Shore Memories'). Unfortunately it is indivisible, and its length precludes the possibility of quotation. But there is another poem almost equally beautiful, which forms part of 'President Lincoln's Burial Hymn', and for this space may perhaps be found:

Death-Carol

Come, lovely and soothing Death,
Undulate round the world serenely arriving, arriving,
In the day, in the night, to all, to each,
Sooner or later, delicate Death.

Prais'd be the fathomless universe,
For life and joy, and for objects and knowledge curious;
And for love, sweet love. But praise! praise! praise!
For the sure-enwinding arms of cool-enfolding Death.

Dark Mother, always gliding near, with soft feet,
Have none chanted for thee a chant of fullest welcome?
Then I chant it for thee—I glorify thee above all;
I bring thee a song that when thou must indeed come, come unfalteringly.

Approach, strong Deliveress!
When it is so—when thou hast taken them, I joyously sing the dead,
Lost in the loving, floating ocean of thee,
Laved in the flood of thy bliss, O Death.

From me to thee glad serenades,
Dances for thee I propose, saluting thee—adornments and feastings for thee;
And the sights of the open landscape and the high spread sky are fitting,
And life and the fields and the huge and thoughtful night.

The night, in silence under many a star;
The ocean-shore, and the husky whispering wave whose voice I know;
And the soul turning to thee, O vast and well-veiled death,
And the body gratefully nestling close to thee.

Over the tree-tops I float thee a song!
Over the rising and sinking waves—over the myriad fields and the prairies
    wide;
Over the dense-packed cities all and the teeming wharves and ways,
I float this carol with joy, with joy to thee, O Death!'

It is easy enough to connect this cultus of Death, and the pantheism which necessarily accompanies it, with the main articles of Whitman's creed. Death is viewed as the one event of great solemnity and importance which is common to all—the one inevitable, yet not commonplace incident in every life, however commonplace; and, further, it must not be overlooked that Death is pre-eminently valuable in such a system as this, in the capacity of reconciler ready to accommodate all difficulties, to sweep away all rubbish. The cheeriest of optimists with the lowest of standards cannot pretend to

314

assert or expect that everyone will live the ideal life—but Death pays all scores and obliterates all mistakes.

There remains, however, still to be considered a point not least in importance—the vehicle which Whitman has chosen for the conveyance of these thoughts. He employs, as most people know who know anything at all about him, neither rhyme nor even regular metre; the exceptions to this rule occurring among his more recent poems are few and insignificant. A page of his work has little or no look of poetry about it; it is not, indeed, printed continuously, but it consists of versicles, often less in extent than a line, sometimes extending to many lines. Only after reading these for some time does it become apparent that, though rhyme and metre have been abandoned, rhythm has not; and, moreover, that certain figures and tricks of language occur which are generally considered more appropriate to poetry than to prose. The total effect produced is dissimilar to that of any of the various attempts which have been made to evade the shackles of metre and rhyme, while retaining the other advantages of poetical form and diction. Whitman's style differs very much from that of such efforts as Baudelaire's 'Petits Poèmes en Prose', for from these all rhythm, diction, and so forth not strictly appropriate to prose is conscientiously excluded. It is more like the polymeters of the poet's namesake Walt in Richter's 'Flegeljahre', except that these latter being limited to the expression of a single thought are not divided into separate limbs or verses. Perhaps the likeness which is presented to the mind most strongly, is that which exists between our author and the verse divisions of the English Bible, especially in the poetical books, and it is not unlikely that the latter did actually exercise some influence in moulding the poet's work. It is hard to give a fair specimen of it in the way of quotation—that already given is not representative, being too avowedly lyrical—and the rhythm is as a rule too varying, complex, and subtle to be readily seized except from a comparison of many instances. Perhaps, however, the following stanza from 'Children of Adam' may convey some idea of it:

'I have perceived that to be with those I like is enough;
To stop in company with the rest at evening is enough;
To be surrounded by beautiful, curious, breathing, laughing flesh is enough;
To pass among them, or touch any one, or rest my arm ever so lightly round
    his or her neck for a moment—what is this then?
I do not ask any more delight—I swim in it as in a sea.
There is something in staying close to men and women, and looking on them,
    and in the contact and odour of them, that pleases the soul well;
All things please the soul—but these please the soul well.'

It will be observed that the rhythm is many-centred, that it takes fresh departures as it goes on. The poet uses freely alliteration, chiasmus, antithesis, and especially the retention of the same word or words to begin and end successive lines, but none of these so freely as to render it characteristic. The result, though perhaps uncouth at first sight and hearing, is a medium of expression by no means wanting in excellence, and certainly well adapted for Whitman's purposes. Strange as it appears to a reader familiarised with the exquisite versification of modern England or France, it is by no means in disagreeable contrast therewith, being at least in its earlier forms (for in some of the later poems reminiscences of the English heroic, of Longfellow's hexameters, and even of Poe's stanzas occur) singularly fresh, light, and vigorous. Nor should the language pass unmentioned—for though of course somewhat Transatlantic in construction and vocabulary, it is not offensively American. The chief blemish in the eyes of a sensitive critic is an ugly trick of using foreign words, such as 'Libertad' for liberty, '*habitan* of the Alleghanies', 'to become *élève* of mine', 'with reference to *ensemble*', and so forth; but even this does not occur very frequently. Few books abound more in 'jewels five words long'; it is hardly possible to open a page without lighting upon some happy and memorable conceit, expression, thought, such as this of the grass:

> 'It is the handkerchief of the Lord;
> A scented gift and remembrance designedly dropt,
> Bearing the owner's name someway in the corners,
> That we may see and remark, and say Whose?'

Or this of children's love to a father:

'They did not love him by allowance, they loved him with personal love.'

Or again of the grass:

'And now it seems to me the beautiful uncut hair of graves.'

Such in matter and in manner are Walt Whitman's 'Leaves of Grass', and there only remains to be added one recommendation to their study. The book, aggressive and vain-glorious as it seems, is in reality remarkably free from vituperativeness of tone. Hardly to some 'eunuchs, consumptive and genteel persons' is strong language used, and after all it rests with every reader whether he chooses to class himself with these. Amid all the ecstatic praise of America there is no abuse of England; amid all the excitement of the poems on the War there is little personal abuse of the Secessionists. No Englishman, no one indeed whether American or Englishman, need be deterred from reading this book, a book the most unquestionable in originality, if not the most unquestioned in excellence, that the United States have yet sent us.'

NOTE Q, *page* 190. There was at first great enthusiasm for Newman's attempt to create a Roman Catholic 'Oxford' in Dublin; but it was soon clear, from various signs of trouble, that the scheme was beset by many difficulties and jealousies. With Newman's withdrawal from Dublin, and his subsequent resignation in November 1858, enthusiasm dwindled and there were thoughts of dissolving the university. Then, in April 1861, a new Rector, Dr. Bartholomew Woodlock, was appointed. A site was bought, plans were approved, foundations laid, and a great demonstration organized; but the promise of progress was illusory and the buildings never rose above their foundations. The decline continued steadily from 1865 to 1873, and probably the only reason for retaining the shadow of a university was the

Additional Notes

hope of using it to drive a bargain with the English Government, though Woodlock still advocated ambitious schemes. From 1874–8 decay continued. The members of the small staff were most of them old and ill-fitted for their task. The bulk of Roman Catholics went rather to T.C.D. or the Queen's Colleges. In 1879, therefore, it was proposed to hand over the college to the Jesuit order, but this plan did not mature. The problem remained. Move and counter-move followed, which resulted in the Conservative Government bringing in a Bill of its own dealing with the Irish university question. This in its original form merely provided for an examining university (on the model of London), but it became a more generous measure before being passed on 15 August 1879. Then followed chequered attempts to put this act establishing a Royal University into practice : these are too tortuous to be entered into here. A proposal that the university should be given over to the Jesuits was for the moment rejected in favour of a plan advocating constituent colleges in or near Dublin, and the first fruit of this, University College, opened in 1882–3 with a President and small staff. The auspices were bad, however; there were rival bodies more popular; and in October 1883 articles were signed by which the management of the College passed to the Jesuits, and Fr. Delaney almost immediately announced the names of his staff.

From then on University College had a useful if somewhat harassed history. It remained largely an examining body; the pressure of this work, indeed, increased. Moreover there was dissatisfaction because students of University College had an advantage in being prepared for examination by the examiners themselves. Eventually, by a Bill that Mr. Augustine Birrell introduced on 31 March 1908, two new universities were erected by Royal Charter in Dublin and Belfast, and the former incorporated the University College of St. Stephen's Green.

This note is chiefly based on information given in *A Page of Irish History: Story of University College, Dublin, 1883–1909*, compiled by Fathers of the Society of Jesus, 1930.

NOTE R, *page* 190. There is work by G. M. H. in three numbers of *The Stonyhurst Magazine*. In No. II, July 1881, are various versions of Dryden's Epigram on Milton ('Three poets in three distant ages born'), and number v is by G. H.

> Ævo diversi tres et regione poetae
> Hellados, Ausoniae sunt Britonumque decus.
> Ardor in hoc animi, majestas praestat in illo,
> Tertius ingenio junxit utrumque suo.
> Scilicet inventrix cedens Natura labori
> 'Quidquid erant isti' dixerat 'unus eris'.

No. IX, March, 1883, contains *A Trio of Triolets*, signed Bran. The first, presumably the one not sent to R. B., runs thus :

> No. 1.—Λέγεταί τι καινόν;
> 'No news in the *Times* to-day,'
> Each man tells his next-door neighbour.

317

He, to see if what they say,
'No news in the *Times* to-day,'
Is correct, must plough his way
Through that: after three hours' labour,
'No news in the *Times* to-day,'
Each man tells his next-door neighbour.

No. 2, which R. B. pasted in A but did not print, is best served by its present decent obscurity. No. 3 is already printed (*Poems*, 68).

No. LXXII, February, 1894, contains *Ad Mariam* (*Poems*, Appendix, 84), contributed by a correspondent.

NOTE S, *page* 192. Sidney Lanier (1846–81). It is not strange that G. M. H. should have read with sympathy the work of this American poet, whose chaotic life and thwarted aspirations make him one of the minor tragedies of letters. There are points of resemblance between him and G. M. H.: he was passionately interested in music, had an intuitive conception of it, and was for a time a professional musician. In poetry he was an idealist and lover of nature, hindered by circumstance from giving his best; and he is perhaps most widely known for *The Science of English Verse* (1880, and often reprinted), an immature but valuable work, wherein he maintains that the laws of music and poetry are identical.

NOTE T, *page* 198. Thomas Arnold (1823–1900), second son of Arnold of Rugby, father of Mrs. Humphry Ward, and the Philip Hewson of Clough's *The Bothie of Tober-na-Vuolich*, has been overshadowed by his brother Matthew. After being educated at Rugby and Oxford, he attempted, with less success than Samuel Butler, to live a pastoral life in New Zealand, and later became inspector of schools in Tasmania. After becoming a Roman Catholic he returned to England in 1856. Newman offered him a post in the new Irish university, and his election to the Professorship of English Literature was approved in October, 1857. After Newman had left Ireland, Arnold was 'definitely engaged' on 6 January 1862, as chief classical master at the Oratory School, but when he felt compelled to leave the Roman communion, he naturally resigned this post, and returned to Oxford to take pupils. The breach, however, was not lasting: he was reconciled to the Roman Catholic church in 1877, became first an examiner for the Royal University of Ireland, and in 1882 a Fellow and Professor of English Literature in University College, Dublin. His *Passages in a Wandering Life* gives an account of his religious pilgrimage. As a man he was known for his 'quixotic disinterestedness'. He has been described as 'very shy, slow of speech on account of a slight impediment, far from bright in conversation, rather, to tell the whole truth, a dull-seeming person. He was, however, tall and intellectual-looking, and carried himself with a distinguished bearing like a courtier.' Among other things, he edited the *Beowulf* and part of Wyclif's writings.

NOTE U, *page* 199. Four letters from Sir Robert Stewart to G. M. H. are extant, all, unfortunately, imperfectly dated. Possibly they belong to 1886–8. They are concerned mainly with criticism of G. M. H.'s themes or essays in counterpoint, and should be of interest to musicians for the light they throw on his methods of work. In one letter Sir Robert says : 'I mark all I dislike, you are much improv'd, I rejoice to say.' Of more general interest is one dated Saturday Evng 22/^{d} May [1886], in which the following passage occurs:

'Indeed my dear Padre I *cannot* follow you through your maze of words in your letter of last week. I saw, ere we had conversed ten minutes on our first meeting, that you are one of those special pleaders who never believe yourself wrong in any respect. You always excuse yourself for anything I object to in your writing or music so I think it a pity to disturb you in your happy dreams of perfect = [here end of line] ability—Nearly everything in your music was wrong—but you will not admit that to be the case—What does it matter? It will be all the same 100 years hence—There is one thing I do admire—your handwriting—! I wish *I* could equal *that*, it is so scholar-like!'

Another letter begins: 'Darling Padre! *I* never said anything "outrageous" to you. Don't think so, pray! but you are impatient of correction, when you have previously made up your mind on any point, and I RS being an "Expert", you seem to me to err, often times, very much. Thus you will not like to be told, that . . .': a number of objections to G. M. H.'s usage follows. [For these extracts I have used typed copies: the originals have not been in my hands.]

NOTE V, *page* 216. 'Along with the appointment of Professor Curtis came that of Professor Gerard Hopkins in 1884. His career was in some respects not unlike that of Mr. Curtis, for, though he was not subject to actual attacks, he suffered more or less continuously from nervous depression, and like Curtis, he died at a comparatively early age, having been more learned than practical. The genius of Hopkins was indeed remarkable, nor was it confined to one branch of mental excellence. As a Greek scholar, had he fully utilized his talents, he could have stood in the first rank; in fact, at Balliol College, Oxford, the celebrated master, Dr. Jowett, had declared that he never met a more promising pupil. As an English poet, his work—though not without defects—is at the present day fully recognized as manifesting real genius of a high order; it has become almost the subject of a craze—so frequently is it discussed, quoted, and possibly imitated; but this poet was also an essayist, a musician, and even had a taste for higher mathematics. As a convert to the Catholic religion he was filled with enthusiasm, but as a theologian his undoubted brilliance was dimmed by a somewhat obstinate love of Scotist doctrine, in which he traced the influence of Platonist philosophy. His idiosyncrasy got him into difficulties with his Jesuit preceptors who followed Aquinas and Aristotle. The strain of controversy added to bad health had marred his earlier years; and in Ireland, owing to his political predispositions, he found himself out of harmony with his surroundings. Some of his pupils appreciated his powers and took advantage of his scholarly teaching; but on the whole he was not happy either in the College work or in the drudgery of the examinations for which he was not well fitted. It has been alleged that he ought never to have been a

Jesuit; but his love for his Order was intense, and we are permitted to believe that, though he had many trials to endure, they were mainly due to his highly-wrought temperament. If this be so, it is probable that in other circumstances he would not have had a brighter existence, and perhaps would have been deprived of the deepest consolations of his life. But to those who knew Gerard Hopkins his career will always suggest the idea of tragedy. Is not this true of many modern poets? It is consoling that, like Francis Thompson and Lionel Johnson, even if a tragic figure, Hopkins has now at long last come into his own.'

(*A Page of Irish History: Story of University College, Dublin, 1883–1909.* Compiled by Fathers of the Society of Jesus, 1930, pp. 104–6.)

NOTE W, *page* 230. MS. Book A contains:

(*a*) Latin version of 'Come unto these yellow sands'.
(*b*) Two Greek versions of 'Tell me where is Fancy bred'.
(*c*) Latin version of 'Full fathom five'.
(*d*) Latin version of 'Tell me where is Fancy bred'.
(*e*) Greek version, with prosodic scheme, of 'Orpheus with his lute made trees'.
(*f*) Latin version of 'Orpheus with his lute made trees'. (A letter from Professor A. E. Housman to R. B., of 29 June 1921, comments on this version favourably, and on (*d*) rather adversely.)
(*g*) Latin version of 'When icicles hang by the wall'.

There are, in MS. book H, certain Latin verses.

NOTE X, *page* 240. Robert Ornsby (1820–89) took a 1st Class in Greats (Lincoln College) in 1840; became a Fellow of Trinity College, Oxford; gave up a curacy to follow Newman into the Church of Rome in 1847; and was made Professor of Classical Literature in the new Irish university. Later he became private tutor to the Duke of Norfolk; returned to his university post in 1873 at the request of the Irish bishops; and in 1882 was elected to a classical Fellowship in the Royal University. The letters Newman wrote to him (printed in Ward's *Life*) show that he shared Newman's confidence.

NOTE Y, *page* 275. A hostile and Olympian review. A good part of it criticizes adversely the author's statements in his preface dealing with the measure chosen. Its temper can best be shown by a few sentences:

'Canon Dixon, whose repeated volumes of verse show him to be an excellent scholar and a connoisseur in the niceties of verse, has followed many masters, but is not without a thin and somewhat hard vein of his own. His Muse, as he seems to be conscious, is pallid and anæmic, and he strives to smarten her up with successive costumes taken from rich old mediæval wardrobes. . . . he has striven to walk in the footsteps of Chaucer, and does contrive, on occasion, to be remarkably like Occleve, which, however, is quite another matter.' And later:

'It is needless to say that there are good things in *Eudocia*. Canon Dixon is too well equipped with learning and sympathy and feeling, and has in times past shown himself too good a metrist, to fail entirely.'

Additional Notes

NOTE Z, *page* 284. *The Athenaeum* reviewed *Travels in Arabia Deserta* on 17 March 1888, and showed complete lack of discernment and no appreciation of literary value: 'the important facts of these two volumes of minute diaries could have been condensed into one small volume. Indeed, unless a diary in countries not quite unknown is written in a brilliant style or filled with most striking facts, it is a burden to readers who have no time for idling. And it must be confessed that Mr. Doughty, although an honest writer, is far from being brilliant . . .'. There is, in fact, not even faint praise (except that given to the sketches and map) for Mr. Doughty's 'dangerous and fatiguing travels'. *The Saturday Review* (31 March 1888) fears the extraordinary merits of the book may be veiled by some features of their presentation, among which comes style—'it is written in a most miraculous style, suggesting a mixture of Mr. William Morris, Mr. George Meredith, the late Mr. Carlyle, and the living Sir Richard Burton. . . .' Two specimens are given, and here is quoted the sentence: 'it seemed the jade [*sic*] might have been, if great had been his chance, another Tiberius Senex.' Twelve hundred pages of such speech are regarded as 'something of a chokepear', but the writer proceeds to point out the 'extraordinary' merits of the book. Sir Richard F. Burton wrote the long review in *The Academy* (28 July 1888). It is peculiarly interesting as coming from a writer of his temperament. The rightness of Doughty's method of travel is seriously questioned, and certain extracts are given to show his archaic style.

NOTE AA, *page* 294. In his words *To the Reader* the author expresses his 'thanks for valuable and useful criticism' to his near relative, the Rev. G. M. Hopkins, of University College, Dublin. In his *Introductory Remarks*, after reference to Mr. Frank Galton's work on spectral or imagined numbers, he explains and illustrates these 'by quoting a letter from the relation whom I have already mentioned'. In this, G. M. H., after alluding to Galton's engraved specimens as 'very fantastic and interesting', goes on to say:

'I have such a pattern. From No. 1, which as [is] scarcely seen, to 12, the numbers rise either uprightly, or leaning a little to the right, in a gloomy light. From 12 to 20, they run to the right, rising a little, and are in a cheerful daylight. From 20 to 100, the numbers are as if far away to my right, and seem as if I must go towards them, to see them properly. They are not very bright. From 100 to 1000 the figures are in another "reach"—distant and indefinite. They appear to be returning to the left. A million is in a clear light, far off, on the left. Still farther, and behind, scattered over a sort of vague landscape, are billions, trillions, and the rest—all to the left; in blocks, not in lines. On the left of number *one* are a few minus numbers, and below it, swarms of fractions. The place where these appear is gloomy grass. Backgrounds of rooms and remembered open-air scenes appear in different parts of this picture or world.' He adds, 'It is remarkable that so many people make 12, and not 10, the turning point in their patterns'.

Later, he says that the Welsh are 'clumsy reckoners, or, rather, that they employ clumsy methods for reckoning, such as, commonly, the use of *five*, as being *half ten*, instead of using ten for counting. They often count and

Additional Notes

reckon in English; but when counting aloud, they prefer the sort of symmetry which they conceive to exist in their habitual manner, and which to them is found convenient. Instead of naming *sixteen* or *seventeen*, they say *one upon fifteen*, or *two upon fifteen*. *Eighteen* is spoken of as *two nines, nineteen* as *four on fifteen*.'

G. M. H.'s father also published: *A Handbook of Average . . . with a chapter on arbitration*, 1857 (4th ed., 1884); *Hawaii: an historical account of the Sandwich Islands*, 1862 (2nd ed., 1866); *A Manual of Marine Insurance*, 1867; and *The Port of Refuge, or advice and instructions to the Master-Mariner in situations of doubt, difficulty, and danger*, 1873 (3rd ed., 1882).

To these must be added: Spicilegium Poeticum/A Gathering of Verses by/ Manley Hopkins/(Printed for Private Circulation.)/London:/The Leadenhall Prefs, Ltd.: 50, Leadenhall Street, E.C./ pp. ix, 11–180. Frontispiece by E[verard] H[opkins] after a drawing by Tony Johannot, 1848.

The book is undated: the copy I have used bears an author's inscription dated July 1892. There is a reference (p. 58) to 'my drawing-room play "The New School of Design" '.

The verses are 'the gathering out of the growth of half a century; and express several moods and feelings experienced during the changing hours of a long life'. They are miscellaneous in character, and include a long verse tale of sentiment, epigrams and humorous pieces, songs for music, and 'poems relating to religion'. There is little in the book that, as poetry, calls for remark.

NOTE BB, *page* 300. The commission sat for the first time on 17 September 1888 to determine procedure, and on 22 October the trial began, and culminated when on 21 February 1889 *The Times*, after hesitation, called as a witness the Irish journalist Richard Pigott, who had sold to the paper the incriminating documents and letters on which the charges against Parnell and his associates were based. Pigott broke down next day under the cross-examination of Sir Charles Russell (Parnell's counsel), and on the 23rd confessed to Labouchere that the letters were forgeries. He fled from England, and to avoid arrest committed suicide in Madrid. Parnell had denied on oath the authenticity of the letters, and counsel for *The Times* therefore withdrew them from the case. On 3 February 1890, Parnell's action against *The Times* was settled by payment to him of £5,000; and on 13 February the commission reported, absolving Parnell on certain grounds and censuring him on others. Gladstone throughout was Parnell's firm supporter, but his strongly worded amendment of reparation to Parnell was defeated on 10 March.

322

PRINTED IN
GREAT BRITAIN
AT THE
UNIVERSITY PRESS
OXFORD
BY
JOHN JOHNSON
PRINTER
TO THE
UNIVERSITY